PROBLEMS
IN
ETHICS

BY

MICHAEL V. MURRAY, S.J.

Marquette University

A Holt-Dryden Book

HENRY HOLT AND COMPANY, INC.

New York

IMPRIMI POTEST
    Joseph P. Fisher, S.J.
    Provincial
NIHIL OBSTAT
    John A. Schulien, S.T.D.
    Censor librorum
IMPRIMATUR
    ✠ William E. Cousins
    Archbishop of Milwaukee
Dec. 8, 1959

Acknowledgments

Grateful acknowledgment is hereby made to the various authors and publishers who kindly granted permission to quote from the following works:

To the Macmillan Company for permission to quote from *The Case for Christianity* by C. S. Lewis, 1945.

To Burns Oates and Washbourne, Ltd., for permission to quote from A. C. Pegis, *Basic Writings of St. Thomas Aquinas,* 1945 (quotations from *The Summa Contra Gentiles,* and *The Summa Theologica* I, qq. 14, 60 and 79; I-II, qq. 6, 18, 21, 90-95, 114, are from this source).

To Benziger Brothers for permission to quote from *The Summa Theologica of St. Thomas Aquinas,* translated by Fathers of the English Province, 1947 (quotations from the Summa Theologica I-II, qq. 1, 4, 19, 24, 26, 3-47, 57, 76, 82 and 94 are from this source).

To Sheed and Ward for permission to quote from A *Companion to the Summa,* 1945, Vol. II.

To Oxford University Press, Inc. for permission to quote from *The Works of Aristotle translated into English,* ed. W. D. Ross, vol. V, *Ethica Nichomachea,* 1942.

MARIAE
QUAE QUOT DIEBUS ME ADJUVAVIT
AGAM ALIQUANTULAS GRATIAS

FOREWORD

Problems in Ethics contains nothing original. My aim is to acquaint the student with the basic principles of the moral philosophy of St. Thomas Aquinas. To accomplish this purpose I was compelled to make a choice among the several works in which St. Thomas has presented his convictions on these principles, particularly his *Commentary on the Nicomachean Ethics* of Aristotle and his *Summa Theologica*. My choice of the *Summa*, however, contained the minimum of freedom. This for several reasons. Since the *Commentary* has not been translated into English the students could have no ready reference work. Secondly, since the *Nicomachean Ethics* often expresses views which are prompted by Aristotle's non-Christian beliefs, St. Thomas' *Commentary* on this ethics does not always express his own personal and Christian views. The *Summa*, on the other hand, has not only been translated into English but also expresses St. Thomas' mature and Christian thought.

But St. Thomas' ethics can hardly be understood unless one has a knowledge of his speculative philosophy. This book, then, presupposes that the student has had some acquaintance with this philosophy. Nevertheless, I recall, where necessary, some of the principles and conclusions of the Thomistic philosophy of man and metaphysics in order to show how much St. Thomas' science of the moral act depends upon his speculative science. Besides I have attempted to relate the moral philosophy of St. Thomas to his moral theology. Believing that an adequate moral philosophy is impossible unless ethics be "subalternated" or subordinated to theology, I have, again, where needed, referred to Thomistic theology in order to supply for the deficiencies of a purely philosophical ethics.

Because of the purpose of this book there is little reference, if any, to the history of ethics. One semester spent on the study of the Thomistic principles of ethics is short enough. To attempt to introduce the opinions of other ethicians would result in either foreshortening the study of St. Thomas' principles to the point that he receives no more than an honorable mention or in mutilating the opinions of other ethicians to the extent that they become mere names attached to an absurd opinion.

Neither does the book contain material with which the "applied" or "special" ethics is concerned, and which is usually found in college textbooks on ethics. The reason, I believe, is obvious. Although the specific application of the general principles of ethics is useful and certainly deserving of consideration, yet the study of how the principles are to be applied must be pursued only after the principles themselves have been understood in their complete or full exposition. The aim of this book is such an exposition and only that. Whether this aim has been accurate and the book has hit its mark is a judgment which must be made by others. Because I have had undergraduate students in mind, I have tried to keep the language as nontechnical as possible. That I have not avoided all technical language is evident, but it is impossible to avoid technical terms of a science completely.

My debt of thanks must be paid to Father Francis C. Wade, S.J. He was the irritating goad that would not be discouraged even when I balked, refusing to go on with the work. My thanks, too, must go to Father Gerard Smith, S.J., chairman of the philosophy department of Marquette University, who was kind enough to read the manuscript and patient enough to offer countless suggestions; and to Miss Esther Diehl, who spent countless weary hours with the manuscript.

MICHAEL V. MURRAY, S.J.

CONTENTS

CHAPTER I

THE PROBLEM AND DEFINITION OF ETHICS

1. All Men Seek Happiness

Happiness is something which must be reckoned with the good things of life. One of the most obvious facts of man's consciousness is that in his deliberate activity he desires to be happy, and this fact has been expressed by different men. Plato wrote: "What human being is there who does not desire happiness? There is no one, said Cleinias, who does not." (*Euthydemus* 279) Plato's disciple Aristotle repeats the same idea in the opening words of his *Nicomachean Ethics:* "Every art and every inquiry, and similarly every action and pursuit, is thought to aim at some good; and for this reason the good has rightly been declared to be that at which all things aim." (*Nic. Ethics*, I,1,1094a) He continues: "verbally there is very general agreement that all men seek the good and both the general run of men and people of superior refinement say that it is happiness." (*ibid.* I,4,1095a,16-19) St. Augustine expresses it: "All men agree in desiring the last end, which is happiness." (*De Trin.* XIII,3)

However, although all men seek happiness, that which they seek is expressed differently by different men, and, as Aristotle writes, "the many do not give the same account as the wise." (*op. cit.*

1

I,4,1095a,20) In fact, a search for the views which men have of happiness would uncover the most various and curious notions. Any and every good that man can conceive has been proposed as happiness: wealth, power, health, the pleasures of the body, self-realization, self-perfection, the perfection of the race, self-expression, self-interest, virtue, and countless others—all have been proposed. But whatever the object may be, all are agreed in this: it is that object which will make men happy. Even the Pessimist, and it seems strange to say it, must be included in the number of those who want to be happy. After all, the Pessimist is the man who, being despondent about the ills and evils of life, despairs of ever obtaining happiness. He would like to obtain happiness, but yielding to hopelessness, he looks upon all life as a disappointment in which he should have as few desires as possible in order that he be disappointed as little as possible, and so be as happy as possible. But, as Chesterton has said, "all pessimism has a secret optimism for its object." The Pessimist is happy in his unhappiness. In every instance the desire to be happy is the dynamo that drives men on and on, to work, love, and achieve.

But it is not always easy to determine how one is to obtain real happiness even though all men desire it. For even though all men desire happiness, it does not follow that all men know and, therefore, desire that particular good in which perfect happiness is actually to be found. St. Thomas has expressed this in the following manner:

We can speak of the last end in two ways: first, considering only the aspect of last end; secondly, considering the thing in which the aspect of last end is realized. So, then, as to the aspect of last end, all agree in desiring the last end; since all desire the fulfillment of their perfection, and it is precisely this fulfillment in which the last end consists. But as to the thing in which this aspect is realized, all men are not agreed as to their last end; since some desire riches, as their consummate good; some, pleasure; others, something else. Thus to every taste the sweet is pleasant, but to some the sweetness of wine is most pleasant; to others, the sweetness of honey, or of something similar. Yet that sweet is absolutely the best of all pleasant things, in which he who has the best taste takes most pleasure. In like manner that good is most complete which the man with well-disposed affections desires for his last end. (S.T. I-II,1,7c.)

Here, then, are two facts which we must accept▮ all men seek happiness▮ different men propose different objects which will make them happy. The problem resulting from these is whether it is possible to discover that object which is actually happiness for all men. St. Thomas is of the opinion that it is possible, that the true and real object of happiness is that which the man of right desires wishes to obtain. Can we, then, demonstrate with certainty what that object is which will give perfect happiness to all men? Can we have a science of happiness?

And over and above this, there is the problem of how can man obtain this object. True, men seek happiness, but their problem, throughout life on this earth, is to select and do the kind of actions which are conducive to true happiness. Is it possible, then, to establish rules, which are universally true, by which men can determine the actions which will bring them to perfect happiness? Can we have a science of the human actions which are conducive to perfect happiness? Some say that we cannot have a science of happiness or of the human acts which lead to it. The whole problem centers about the notion of science.

2. *Ethics Is a Science*

Whenever we speak of a particular science we have in mind a definite and limited field of knowledge, a fact or a group of facts, a specific method for arriving at the truth of these facts, and a certain body of conclusions regarded as true for all persons and for all times. Scientific knowledge always includes a set of laws and principles in accordance with which particular facts are said to be explained. These laws are illustrated in the various phenomena occurring within any given scientific area, and complete mastery of the field that is being studied would enable one to see each fact in its proper relationship to all the laws or principles involved in that particular science.

In the light of these characteristics, can we say that ethics is a science, comparable to other fields of knowledge, with contents which are generally accepted as reliable and true for everyone? Are there laws or principles in the field of morals that are true for all peoples and at all times? Can we be objective in the field of ethics so that the conclusions we reach represent something more than individual opinion? These questions are fundamental for the study of ethics, and it is highly important that we provide an answer to them before we proceed to investigate and evaluate the many and varied theories of human conduct to which individuals of every age have subscribed.

Opposition to the view that ethics is a science is often based on the assumption that there is no adequate method of arriving at truth in this field of knowledge. Unlike the physical sciences in which we have the experimental method, ethics has no such procedure by which we can establish the validity of the conclusions reached. In the physical sciences it is comparatively easy to find out whether a particular judgment or proposition is true. All we need to do is conduct laboratory experiments under controlled conditions, and thus prove or disprove the proposition. But ethics has no such method. We cannot experiment in this way in ethics. Suppose I am in doubt whether it is morally permissible for me to administer a painless death to my cancer-infected brother. I certainly cannot determine the question by experiment. Moral activity cannot be described in terms of mathematical quantities nor be weighed and measured in terms of mathematical quantities nor be weighed and measured like physical or chemical entities.

The physical sciences purpose to describe phenomena as they actually exist. Hypotheses can be stated and they can be established by comparing them to the facts. If these hypotheses agree with the facts of our experience the hypotheses are true. But in ethics the truth cannot be dependent on the observation of the facts of human activity, of what actually exists. The purpose of ethics is not a description of human activity, as it has been observed in the past, nor a description of how men act in the present, nor of how they will act in the future. Ethics is concerned with the way men ought to act at all times and in all places; it is concerned with a norm according to which particular human acts are to be judged good or bad. Or we may say, and it will be discussed later in the chapter on law, that ethics is unlike the physical sciences in that it is normative and not descriptive.

Obviously, such a view that ethics is not a science is an opinion in which only the experimental sciences are sciences. Those who espouse the positivistic approach to science take this view. The Positivists are of the opinion that science is possible only when there are sensory phenomena and only when these data can be subjected to exact mathematical measurements and expressed in mathematical formulae. Because moral good and evil cannot be measured nor expressed in this way, ethics in this positivistic opinion is nothing more than a reporting of how men are acting at a particular time or in a particular culture and the right or wrong of human activity is determined by a statistical statement of the majority's manner of acting. The Positivists, moreover, deny that ethics can be a science because science, so they say, advances by prediction based upon hypotheses which are followed by controlled experimental verification, but human acts, the data of ethics, being free are not capable of such prediction.

The basis, as we have said, of the view that ethics cannot be a science is that only the experimental sciences are sciences[This opinion is opposed to the traditional philosophical definition of science as a certain knowledge of things in their causes] Implied in this definition is the fact that a science is a body of systematized knowledge, that is, a science is concerned with a definite, particular aspect of reality for which principles are discovered. This is true of an experimental science and it is also true of a philosophic science. The science of philosophy studies that aspect of reality which is being, and ethics, which is a philosophic science, is interested in that aspect of being which is the human act. Furthermore, since science deals with things in their causes, philosophy studies the ultimate causes of being, ethics the causes of human acts—that is, the ultimate purpose of human actions, the laws and principles regulating the use of means to obtain this purpose—and it demonstrates its conclusions. Because ethics completely fulfills the definition of science formulated by the philosophers it is as true a science as any experimental science.

Ethics, then, is not an experimental science, but a philosophical science. Now every science accepts some facts or group of facts of experience about which each particular science discovers and establishes general laws or principles to express and to account for these facts. Physics, for example, accepts the fact of motion; biology, that of life; mathematics, the fact of quantity. All these sciences are concerned with their particular objects or facts in order that general laws may be established about these particular objects.

Philosophy, too, is concerned with a fact or facts. It is concerned with the fact that things are in order that it may discover the ultimate laws or principles of their being. Among the facts with which it is concerned is the fact that all men seek happiness in their human activity. It is with this fact that ethics is concerned. Ethics wishes not only to discover the ultimate reason for this fact and the meaning of happiness, but also the laws by which man can obtain the happiness which he desires in his human actions.

Sciences have two main methods of approach to their subject matter. Which shall be used depends on the nature of the facts they study and on the viewpoint they adopt.

The deductive method starts with accepted axioms, postulates, and definitions, and proceeds to their application. The mathematical sciences are examples of this method. The inductive method starts with the given experience of the world and proceeds by observation, hypotheses, experiment, and classification to the formulation of general laws. The physical sciences are examples of this method.

The science of ethics uses both methods, with emphasis on the deductive. Although it does not disregard experience, it cannot be based on experience alone, which is limited to the *way things are* and cannot touch the *way actions ought to be*. Ethics begins with a definite view of the universe and of man drawn from metaphysics and the philosophy of man (postulates), from which certain moral principles follow as logical necessities. Ethics explains and develops the implications of these principles and indicates their application to the several spheres of human conduct. Clearly, then, ethics uses the deductive method. However, because ethics is a practical science dealing with the everyday problems of human conduct, and not with some abstract conception, it must always remain in contact with the facts of experience. It is necessary to emphasize this aspect of ethics. We cannot draw a fixed scheme of individual actions which all men must mechanically and necessarily perform in order to obtain happiness. We cannot give a mathematical formula for happiness as we would give one for some complicated mathematical problem. The reason is that each man is an individual. No two are alike, and it would be impossible to list all the differences between any two given individuals. Individuals differ not only in physiological characteristics such as size, weight, color of skin, physical strength, but also in mental abilities, temperament, and social qualities; individuals differ in the circumstances in which they live and in the environment in which they grow. Yet in spite of all these differences, it is possible for man using his reason correctly to come to some knowledge of the general laws or principles which should guide his actions towards happiness.

3. Definition of Ethics

Ethics may be defined as the *science of the moral rectitude of human acts as means of obtaining perfect happiness.* The word ethics comes from the Greek word *ethos* meaning *custom.* The Latin word for custom is *mos* (in the plural, *mores*). From these words we have the English words ethics and morals. Consequently, ethics is also called moral philosophy.

Etymologically, then, ethics or moral philosophy is the study of human customs. Some customs are mere conventions, such as we may read about in books of etiquette or social behavior. These are fashions which vary in different parts of the world and at different times, and we know that we can change them as we please. We are accustomed to call these manners rather than morals. But there are other customs which we know are not subject to change because they are more essential or fundamental, such as obedience to parents and civil authority, telling the truth, paying our debts, and keeping our promises. Such conduct and the laws guiding it are not merely customary but right. We judge that any deviation from such conduct is wrong. We also think that these customs are the result not of any whims but of some fixed principles of human nature. We are also habitually inclined to call these customs morals. It is with these customary actions that ethics deals.

Ethics, then, is concerned with the right and wrong in human actions. However, we must be clear about the problem of ethics. There is a difference between morals or customary actions and ethics. As far as history is able to tell us, all peoples, no matter how primitive or uncivilized we may call them, have had their own morality, their laws, which regulated their conduct in their search for happiness. We shall see, when we deal with conscience, that nature and the Author of nature have taken care to give to each individual a tendency to establish for himself a set of principles which is applicable to everyday life, without having to wait for a long and complicated education to know the detailed conclusions of science. These general laws of morals or customary actions which men follow in order to obtain happiness are called morals or customary actions. Ethics, or moral philosophy, however, is the scientific treatment of morality or customary actions. In other words, morals is a code of right and wrong of human actions which each individual establishes for himself by natural inclination; ethics is a scientific discussion of morals.

4. Philosophical Study of Morals

The history of morals, as we can see from the preceding, begins when man begins. Moreover, many men in ages past have presented many ordered treatises on morals. We need only to recall the works of the now famous Confucius, or the writings of Hammurabi, or of the Persians and Egyptians, of the Hebrew Prophets, or the words of the New Testament to realize the long history of morals. In Greece, alone in the ancient world, philosophical treatment of morals found a place. Ethics, properly so called, is first met with in Socrates (470-399 B.C.). According to the teaching of Socrates the end of all human activity is happiness and the means to obtain it is virtue. According to him, since man's actions were always directed toward what he believed to be the good, it was impossible for man to be bad deliberately. It was possible for man to be mistaken in his judgment about what is good. In fact, mistakes of judgment were bound to happen whenever man permitted reason to be influenced by emotions and physical desires. Ignorance concerning the good, which was brought about in this way, would cause man to do things which were wrong, but if man had knowledge he would never act evilly. Since the proper function of reason was to give guidance and direction to all life's activities, all the virtues are but so many kinds of prudence. Plato (427-347 B.C.), the disciple of Socrates, has an ethics similar to his master's, but more clearly stated. The highest good of man consists in the imitation of the Absolute Good. This imitation is obtained imperfectly in this life, perfectly in the next. Virtue, the means to this imitation of the Absolute, is that by which man orders his conduct according to the dictates of reason. But unlike Socrates, Plato does not consider virtue to be knowledge alone, or prudence alone, but also justice, temperance, and fortitude—which cannot be identified with prudence. By means of these four virtues the good life, or the limitation of the Absolute Good, is obtained through the harmonious functioning of the various parts of man.

The influence of Plato's thought on subsequent writings in the field of ethics can scarcely be overestimated. However, Aristotle (384-322 B.C.), Plato's most brilliant pupil, possessed a more prosaic type of temperament than his teacher and he presented a more detailed and systematic ethics so that he must be considered the real founder of ethics. Actually Aristotle wrote two, perhaps three, treatises on ethics. Unlike Plato, who began with the assumption of the existence of the Ideas, Aristotle begins with the facts of experiences. He begins with the fact that all men, like everything else, seek the good. Goodness is the development and expression of those potentialities latent in everything. The highest good of man is the ultimate goal of all human living. Every action aims at the satisfaction of some desire, but many things are desired not as ends in themselves but only because they may be used as instruments for the achievement of a goal that lies beyond. The ultimate goal pre-supposed in all these instrumental goods is what is meant by goodness itself. The discovery of the meaning of this goodness is the major task of the study of ethics. What is the ultimate good of man, what is his happiness, to which all other goods are instruments? Aristotle answers that the purpose of any class of objects is to be found not in that which it has in common with other classes of objects, but in that which constitutes its essential nature. Now that which distinguishes man from other creatures is his rational nature. Hence, man's good life is to be found in the proper use of reason. And the highest good or happiness for man consists in the highest activity of which man is capable. This is contemplation, that is, the most perfect activity of his reason. All other goods are means to this ultimate life of reason. This life of reason is to be attained through virtue. But as Aristotle does not accept personal immortality, the life of contemplation is for this present life; however, it is of fleeting duration and enjoyed by few men.

The systematic treatment of Aristotle's ethics is to be found in his *Nicomachean Ethics*. It has been more influential than any other Greek ethics. Although the most influential commentary on this treatise is *In decem Libros Ethicorum Aristotelis ad Nicomachum Expositio* (*Commentary on the Ten Books of Aristotle's Nicomachean Ethics*) written by St. Thomas Aquinas about the year 1261-1267, yet because there is no English translation, the easiest references to Thomistic ethics are to be found in the *Summa Contra Gentiles* and the *Summa Theologica*, which will be used for the basis of this present work. I have used St. Thomas as the basis of the present treatise on ethics not because I wish to force the reader or the student by the great authority of St. Thomas, but simply because I wish to express what I think is the philosophical truth of the matter. Since I think that St. Thomas has expressed it in such a brilliant manner, St. Thomas is frequently quoted verbatim for a better exposition of the problem. Authority as we know is the least or weakest of all philosophical argument. The arguments given by St. Thomas fall or stand by the reason behind them; so do the arguments I give.

5. *Actions with Which Ethics Is Concerned*

From this short survey of part of the history of ethics, it is apparent that ethics is to aid man in obtaining happiness. Men seek happiness. Ethics, therefore, deals with those actions which can lead man to happiness, or to his perfect good. Since man, as Aristotle points out, is different from all other corporeal creatures in his rational nature, the happiness or perfect good that he seeks is that which is obtained by rational acts, by acts of choice resulting from knowledge; and, consequently, only the deliberate, free actions of man are the subject matter of ethics. Or we may say that ethics establishes rules only for the deliberate, free actions of man as means to happiness. This is said for the following reasons: (1) we are happy when we possess what we want; happiness, then, is the object of knowledge and desire, or in other words, happiness is to be obtained only through deliberate and free actions; (2) happiness is the result of those actions for which we are responsible, i.e., of those actions which are deliberately and freely performed; (3) free actions alone are in our power, and concerning these actions alone can rules be prescribed, not concerning those actions which are performed necessarily, or without deliberation, or through ignorance.

As human beings, we are so constituted that a large part of our activity is not subject to our control. We act because we cannot help ourselves or because circumstances are beyond our control. The physical traits we have inherited, the innate tendencies we possess, and much of our behavior as biological organisms are outside the field of deliberation and choice. Such actions which are not performed *knowingly* and *willingly* have no ethical significance because they have not that quality which is required for moral responsibility and of themselves they do not lead to happiness. For example, a man may have a good digestive tract or good reflexes, he may take delight in them, but he is not responsible for them, since they were given to him by nature. Again, a man may have a naturally pleasing personality and by reason of it he may influence many people; he is not responsible for the personality; he is for the way he uses it. Or finally, while driving an automobile, a man may accidentally injure a child who has darted into the path of the vehicle; the man may, it is true, feel sorrow that the child has suffered, but he cannot reasonably blame himself for what has happened, and he should feel no moral responsibility for the results of his action of driving the automobile. Such actions of themselves do not contribute to man's happiness. Such actions are called *acts of man*, but *not human acts*. They are not dealt with in ethics.

There are, however, other acts which have an ethical significance, for they are conducive to happiness, because they are under the direct control of the will. Such actions fall under man's control because he knows, at least to some extent, what he is doing, and he wills, at least to some degree, to do them. These acts are called human acts, and they are the subject matter of ethics. We will make a complete analysis of these acts in Chapter III.

6. Further Considerations of the Definition of Ethics

Ethics or moral philosophy has been defined as the science of the moral rectitude of human acts. It seems necessary to clarify this definition. First of all, we know that science is a habit of the intellect by which the intellect has a certain facility to demonstrate true conclusions from first principles. In other words, a science includes a set of facts from which it draws true conclusions by the use of definite principles or laws, and does so not by a hit-or-miss method but with facility and, therefore, with regularity, so that there is an intellectual power and facility of seeing principles or laws in facts and facts in principles.

Moreover, since science is knowledge, science is of two kinds as knowledge is of two kinds: speculative and practical. Practical knowledge is for the purpose of use; it is a knowledge that the possessor may use to obtain some further good besides knowledge. The science of medicine, for example, shows the physician how to bring health to the body; the science of engineering, how to use the knowledge of stress and strain to construct bridges. Speculative knowledge, on the other hand, has for its purpose knowledge for its own sake, the truth of things. For example, metaphysics gives man a knowledge of the order of being; dogmatic theology, of divine things. Wherefore, because knowledge is divided into practical and speculative by reason of its purpose or end, science is divided into practical and speculative. In practical science the intellect has a facility in knowledge for the sake of using it for a purpose other than the knowledge itself; in speculative science the knowledge is possessed for itself alone.

But, as St. Thomas points out, a science may be speculative in one respect and practical in another, depending upon whether the principles of the science are immediately or mediately applicable and applied to the facts or the subject matter. Take for example medicine. This science not only establishes laws which are applicable to concrete situations, but it also applies them to a diseased body. We may designate it accordingly as a practico-practical science, i.e., as knowledge which is more of an art than a science, for it is concerned more with the perfection of the object than with the knowledge itself, and particularly with the knowledge of how to make man himself more perfect. Ethics, on the other hand, is pre-eminently the practical science, i.e., the practical science in the highest degree, because it is immediately and essentially concerned with the knowledge of how man ought to regulate his conduct rather than with the actual regulation of his conduct. In other words, ethics establishes rules for human conduct and in this respect it is a practical science; but it is not concerned with the immediate application of this knowledge to concrete human acts and in this respect it is a speculative science. Consequently, ethics is called a speculativo-practical science.

Some knowledge is speculative only, some is practical only, and some is partly speculative and partly practical. In proof whereof it must be observed that knowledge can be called speculative in three ways: first, in relation to the things known, which are not operable by the knower; such as the knowledge of man about natural or divine things. Secondly, as regards the manner of knowing—as, for instance, if a builder were to consider a house by defining and dividing, and considering what belongs to it in general: for this is to consider operable things in a speculative manner, and not as they are operable; for operable means the application of forms to matter, and not the resolution of the composite into its universal formal principles. Thirdly, as regards the end, for the practical intellect differs from the speculative by its end, as the Philosopher says (De Anima, III, 10,433a,14). For the practical intellect is ordered to the end of operation; whereas the end of the speculative intellect is the consideration of truth. Hence if a builder were to consider how a house can be made, but without ordering this to the end of operation, but only towards knowledge, this would be only a speculative consideration as regards the end, although it concerns an operable thing. Therefore, knowledge which is speculative by reason of the thing itself known is merely speculative. But that which is speculative either in its mode or as to its end is partly speculative and partly practical; and when it is ordained to an operative end it is strictly practical. (S.T. I,14,16c.)

In order that we make this definition of ethics more precise, let us compare it to the intellectual habits of art and prudence with which ethics is sometimes identified. First of all, ethics is not art. St. Thomas writes:

Art is nothing else but the right reason about certain works to be made. And yet the good of these depends, not on the disposition of man's appetite, but on the goodness of the work done. For a craftsman as such is commendable, not for the will with which he does a work, but for the quality of the work. Art, therefore, properly speaking, is an operative habit. And yet it has something in common with the speculative habits, since the disposition of the things considered by them is a matter of concern to the speculative habits also, although they are not concerned with the disposition of the appetite towards their objects. For as long as the geometrician demonstrates the truth, it matters not how his appetite is disposed, whether he be joyful or angry; even as neither does this matter in a craftsman, as we have observed. And so art has the nature of a virtue in the same way as the speculative habits, in so far, namely, as neither art nor a speculative habit makes a good work as regards the use of the habit, which is distinctive of a virtue that perfects the appetite, but only as regards the ability to work well. (S.T. I-II,57,3c.)

Art, therefore, is a habit of the practical intellect by which a man is able to make things according to right reason. While it is true that art presupposes and includes certain intellectual habits, such as knowledge of methods and details of procedure, it also includes mental and bodily abilities by which the knowledge of these methods and procedures can be used well. For example, an architect is an artist not only because of his knowledge and understanding of techniques and methods of erecting edifices, but particularly because of his power of mentally creating edifices, and of physically executing these mental pictures which he conceives. Neither does it matter what the intentions of the artist may be, for art has for its purpose an object or a work made according to right reason; its perfection is found not in the action of the artist but in the thing produced. Because ethics is concerned with knowledge and not with making, it is therefore not an art.

Neither is ethics prudence. St. Thomas not only distinguishes between art and prudence, but also between ethics and prudence:

Where the nature of virtue differs, there is a different kind of virtue. Now it has been stated above that some habits have the nature of virtue, through merely conferring ability for a good work; while some habits are virtues, not only through conferring ability for a good work, but also through conferring the use. But art confers merely ability for good work, since it does not regard the appetite, whereas prudence confers not only ability for a good work, but also the use, for it regards the appetite, since it presupposes the rectitude of the appetite.

The reason for this difference is that art is the right reason of things to be made, whereas prudence is the right reason of things to be done. Now making and doing differ, as is stated in Metaph. ix [Meta. VIII, 8,1050a,30], in that making is an action passing into external matter, e.g., to build, to saw, and so forth; whereas doing is an action abiding in the agent, e.g., to see, to will, and the like. Accordingly, prudence stands in the same relation to such human actions consisting in the use of powers and habits, as art does to external makings; since each is the perfect reason about things with which it is concerned. But perfection and rectitude of reason in speculative matters depend on the principles from which reason argues: just as we have said above that science depends on and supposes understanding, which is the habit of principles. Now in human acts ends are what principles are in speculative matters, as is stated in Ethics vii [Nic. Ethics VIII,8,1151a,16]. Consequently, it is requisite for prudence, which is right reason to be done, that man be well disposed with regard to ends; and this depends on the rectitude of his appetite. Therefore, for prudence there is need of moral virtue, which rectifies the appetite. On the other hand, the good things made by art is not the good of man's appetite, but the good of the artificial things themselves, and hence art does not presuppose rectitude of the appetite. The consequence is that more praise is given to a craftsman who is at fault willingly, than to one who is unwillingly; whereas it is more contrary to prudence to sin willingly than unwillingly, since rectitude of the will is essential to prudence, but not to art. Accordingly it is evident that prudence is a virtue distinct from art. (S.T. I-II,57,4c.)

From this quotation we may conclude that prudence is a habit of the practical intellect by which the possessor is able to do what is in accord with right reason. Whereas, then, prudence has for its purpose the performance of good actions, ethics has for its purpose the knowledge of good actions. The study of ethics is an attempt to find out what it means to live a good human life. This quest is purely an intellectual one and should not be confused with the effort to achieve these ends, which is prudence. The purpose of the study of ethics is not to make one good, at least immediately, but to enable one to know what goodness is. The teaching of ethics is not designed to make people live better, except of course as this result may be expected to follow from a clearer understanding of what it means to live well both as individuals and as members of society.

We mentioned that Socrates was of the opinion that bad actions are always the result of ignorance; hence, knowledge always culminates in good actions. This error has been repeated very often in the history of philosophy—and how often we hear of it in much of contemporary education theory! It is the result of identifying knowledge with virtue or science with prudence. To know is not the same as to do. One may possess a complete knowledge of ethics yet not perform good actions. If one who knew ethics were to live his life according to his knowledge, he would be not only a good ethician but also a prudent man. But the fact is that we do find ethicians who are not prudent, and many prudent men who are not ethicians.

But let us sum up what we have said about ethics as compared to art and prudence. Ethics is a speculative habit of the practical intellect by which man is *able to know* the human acts which can bring him to true happiness. Prudence, on the other hand, is a habit of the practical intellect by which man is *able to do* what is in accord with right reason in order that he may obtain true happiness. Art, finally, is a habit of the practical intellect by which man is *able to make* things according to right reason. Ethics confers the knowledge of the rectitude of human acts. Prudence confers not only the ability for good action, but also the ability to do the good actions. Art confers only the ability for making things. Consequently, even though ethics is a practical science it does not follow that from a knowledge of ethics there will be good moral actions nor actions of art.

7. *Moral Philosophy and Moral Theology*

Many writers regard ethics as any scientific treatment of the moral order and divide it into theological, or Christian Ethics, which they call Moral Theology, and philosophical, which they call Moral Philosophy. While I have no wish to enter into the question of the legitimacy of this distinction, it is necessary to point out the difference between moral theology and moral philosophy, and at the same time to say something of the need which some think ethics as a philosophy has for theology.

Since we do have moral theology and moral philosophy, the question of how they differ is a legitimate one. Both are, in fact, sciences which establish and explain principles of what man ought to do and how he ought to live to obtain true happiness. How, then, do they differ? To answer this question, let us note the distinction between theology and philosophy which St. Thomas gives.

We must bear in mind that there are two kinds of science. There are some which proceed from principles known by the natural light of the intellect, such as arithmetic and geometry and the like. There are also some which proceed from principles known by the light of a higher science; thus the science of optics proceeds from principles established by geometry, and music from principles established by arithmetic. So it is that sacred doctrine is a science because it proceeds from principles made known by the light of a higher science of God and the blessed. Hence, just as music accepts on authority the principles taught by the arithmetician, so sacred science accepts the principles revealed by God. (S.T. I,1.2c.)

Like all sciences, both philosophy and theology consist in a number of accurate facts, a number of general principles, and a certain intellectual discursive power and ease of deriving conclusions from the general principles about these facts or subject matter. But they differ in many ways. The first way in which they differ is in their subject matter. Sometimes the subject matter, or the facts, are so different that the subject matter of theology is altogether beyond the limits of philosophy. For example, the human reason by its own innate power, by progressing from principles derived from sense experience, can obtain certain truths concerning God and His nature, i.e., that He exists, that He is one, that He is infinite, etc. But it is also clear that other kinds of knowledge—i.e., that He is Three in One; that the Third Person, the Holy Spirit, enlightens the intellect and moves the will to good actions—are beyond the power of the human intellect to know if left to itself. Sometimes, too, the subject matters are the same but nevertheless they do not completely coincide, so that the truth with which theology deals is the same as that with which philosophy is concerned, but theology offers a knowledge which philosophy could never give. Thus, the end of man is God and philosophy can arrive at this conclusion, but how this end can be attained by human nature or what it means is outside the sphere of philosophical knowledge, while theology gives the answer.

A second way in which the two sciences differ is in the principles from which they reason. Theology reasons from supernatural principles which have been revealed by God and accepted by faith; philosophy reasons from principles derived from sense experience. Thus, the theologian draws his arguments from facts and principles which have been revealed by God. The philosopher, on the other hand, draws his arguments from being itself, the knowledge of which he has obtained through sense experience. A theologian in showing that God is One will appeal to Sacred Scripture: "See ye that I alone am, and there is no other God besides me." (*Deut.* 32,39) A philosopher, on the other hand, proves that there can be only one God from the nature of a plurality of beings.

A third difference lies in the way in which the philosopher and the theologian reason. In philosophy, which is concerned with the nature of created beings and which moves upward from them to God, the consideration of the creatures comes first, and that of God last. In theology, on the other hand, which is concerned with creatures in relation to God, the consideration of God comes first, and that of creatures last in so far as they are images and vestiges of God, subject to His Wisdom, Authority, Grace, etc. As St. Thomas writes:

There is a two fold wisdom: namely, worldly, which is called philosophy and which considers inferior causes, that is, caused causes, and it judges according to them; and divine, which is called theology, and which considers superior causes, that is, divine ones, and it judges according to them. The superior causes are called divine attributes, such as Wisdom, Goodness, Divine Will, and things like that. (De Potentia, I,5c)

These same differences distinguish moral theology from ethics or moral philosophy. Like ethics, moral theology deals with the moral actions of man. But whereas ethics establishes laws by the following of which man will obtain true happiness, and explains how man ought to conduct himself in order to obtain this happiness by drawing conclusions from facts and principles which human reason has acquired through sense experience, moral theology has its origin in supernaturally revealed truths. It presupposes man's elevation to the supernatural order, and it draws its conclusion of how man ought to live to obtain true happiness from the many principles of Christian revelation which are given along with this fact of supernatural elevation.

The difference between theology and philosophy having been seen, another question arises: Does philosophy depend upon theology and, more pertinent to the present subject, does ethics need theology? This is not a question the answer to which is self-evident and, moreover, there is no general agreement about the answer.

According to one group of Catholic philosophers, among whom is Maritain, ethics, as a practical science, as a science that orders the actions of man as he actually exists, is impossible unless it is subordinated to theology. These philosophers contend that if ethics is regarded as a purely philosophical science, it is an abstraction divorced from man as he actually is. The grounds for their contention are the many revealed facts about man which theology gives us but which philosophy either cannot or does not know.

Theology tells us that man is not actually in what has been termed the *state of pure nature*. Rather man is in a supernatural state wherein he is aided by supernatural graces and revealed rules of divine positive law and ordered to the Beatific Vision of God in Heaven. It tells us further that man is now saddled with the consequences of original sin. If man is actually in the supernatural order and must act under the conditions of divine grace and the difficulties resulting from original sin, an ethics, so the argument goes, which prescinds or ignores these facts is bound to be inadequate. In other words, an ethics which does not deal with man as he actually is in a supernatural state, with a human nature which has been externally weakened by original sin, is not a practical science. As a result, Maritain along with others contends that ethics as an adequate practical science is possible only if it is subordinated to theology, if it accepts principles from theology and so establishes a science of human conduct.

The dependence of one science on another is not unusual. As we know from the *Summa Theologica* (I,1,2), one science may be dependent upon another science. In fact, the principles of every particular science are borrowed from a higher science, for no science demonstrates its own principles. Mathematics does not prove that things which are equal to the same thing are equal to each other, nor does physics prove the legitimacy of induction. If each science had to prove its own principles, and the principles upon which these in their turn rested, there would be an infinity of premises which would be impossible to traverse, and the human mind could never of itself make that voyage over the sea of an unlimited number of propositions.

Since, therefore, sciences assume their own proximate first principles, which are proved by other superior sciences, there is a hierarchy of sciences. The Scholastics have always held rigidly to a hierarchy of sciences. The physics of the Middle Ages, for example, which was a kind of philosophy of nature, received its principles from metaphysics, but physics in its turn delivered its principles over to botany; arithmetic subordinated itself to metaphysics, and music and geometry subordinated themselves to arithmetic, while optics was subordinated to geometry. There was a formal subordination between what they called a subaltern and a superior science. (*De Trinitate Boetii*, 2,2, ad 5) St. Thomas very clearly teaches that to deny the dependence is to make science mere opinion or a matter of faith, and that if it limits itself to mere empirical knowledge, it would draw but dubious conclusions. (*De Veritate*, 14,9, ad 3) Consequently, although music, for example, is subordinated to the science of arithmetic, one may study and use music even though the principles of arithmetic upon which it is based are unknown. As a result, music is a science in its own right, even though it accepts its principles from another science. We must say, then, that music is subordinated to and dependent on arithmetic, and that music operates on a level of reasoning below that of arithmetic because it uses the principles of arithmetic to arrive at its conclusions. So with all other physical sciences; one science accepts principles from another science, and all accept principles from the science of metaphysics.

The conclusion to be drawn from this consideration is that if one physical science can accept principles from another science, and by using these principles advance to further conclusions and thus become another science, and this without any violence to human reason, then human reason would suffer no violence if philosophy accepted some principles from a higher science, i.e., from theology. Moreover, if philosophy did accept some principles from theology, it would of necessity be subordinated to and dependent upon theology, as one physical science, which accepts its principles from another science is subordinated to and dependent upon that science from which it accepts its principles. If, consequently, ethics accepts some principles from theology, ethics is subordinated to and dependent upon theology. But such dependence on or subordination to theology would not make ethics identical with theology, any more than music is identical with arithmetic because it accepts certain principles from arithmetic. Since ethics establishes laws and draws conclusions from a consideration of the nature of man obtained through sense experience, it is philosophy, even though it accepts certain other truths about the nature of man and his activities which reason alone cannot know.

A further conclusion to be drawn from this consideration is that if we wish to have a really practical science of ethics applicable to man as he is, so that we may know how he is to conduct himself to obtain true happiness, and if true happiness consists in something not natural but supernatural, and if the means to obtain this true supernatural happiness are not mere natural means, we must accept these facts from theology, if we cannot know them from reason. If we abstract from these facts given by theology, we shall not have a practical science, a science that applies to man as he actually exists, but an abstraction that applies to a hypothetical man, a man in the *state of pure nature.*

Not all of the Catholic philosophers wish to go along with those who contend that ethics must be subordinated to theology. There are others, like J. M. Ramirez, O.P., and Dom Odon Lottin, who contend that such a subordination of ethics would make it not philosophy but theology, for an ethics which accepts its principles from theology is not a philosophical ethics, but a moral theology, whereas ethics is philosophy both in its method and in its principles. Moreover, it is not altogether true to say that a science built upon man considered without his supernatural elevation is a pure abstraction that is applicable to a hypothetical man, a man in the state of pure nature. It can be granted, and it must, that human reason of itself can know nothing of the supernatural elevation of man, of man's weakened nature which is the result of original sin, but even though all this be granted, we can still consider man prescinding from this elevation and from the knowledge of the consequences of original sin, and what we know about this nature so prescinded is still a knowledge of man and we have a science of ethics about such a nature. Such a human nature in the state of pure nature would be an abstraction, but it would not be a hypothetical nature, for man in this state is essentially a man and his obligations, his rule of conduct, would be naturally essential. Philosophy could make a true and valid evaluation of man's obligations on this natural state. True, it would not be a complete or perfect appraisal, but it would not be false. And being true, the Catholic ethician would supplement it with what he knows from theology and thus make it a complete or adequate ethics.

We can understand the view of these philosophers better, perhaps, if we consider the ultimate end of man. Theology tells us that man's ultimate end is the Beatific Vision of God; philosophy tells us that man's end is the possession of God in knowledge and love. What philosophy tells us is true, but it is not complete, for it does not tell us how man is to obtain this end or in what this possession essentially consists. Theology does, and so gives an ultimate explanation of that for which philosophy gives an inadequate or incomplete explanation. Consequently, theology gives a better, a more perfect account of that which philosophy can account for only in an imperfect manner. But the point is that philosophy is not wrong, and, not being wrong, is a science even though it is incomplete.

The same is true of many other problems concerning man's conduct. Philosophy can, by a consideration of man's nature known through reason alone, give an account of the facts of human existence, but it is not always a complete account. To be complete it must accept the explanation given by theology. Philosophical ethics, then, does not deal with a hypothetical man, a man divorced from all circumstances of human life, but with a man divorced from the supernatural aspect of his existence. What ethics says about such a man does fall short of a complete explanation of man as he actually exists, but it is not false. Such an ethics would be, and is, so it is contended, a true practical science of human conduct.

Here, then, are the two views of Catholic writers regarding the relation of ethics to theology. One group maintains that ethics as a practical science is impossible unless it be a subordinate science of theology; the other maintains that ethics is a science in its own right, but needs theology for completion. In any case, there is admittedly, by both groups, a need for theology in addition to ethics. This need, perhaps, is a scandal to many an ethician and philosopher, for does not the very purpose of philosophy exclude faith? It does not seem to, for certainly a philosopher has need of some faith too. Faith and knowledge need to differ not so much in their objects as in the means to obtain them. *Knowledge* is an assent to something which we perceive as true by the light of reason alone. *Faith*, on the other hand, is an assent to something as true because it is said to be true by one who has authority in a particular field of truth. I know by the light of reason that two plus two are four, but I who have never been to Rome, assent to the proposition that the Quirinal is one of the seven hills, when it is made by one who is an authority in the geography of Rome. Faith is of two kinds: natural and supernatural. *Natural* faith is the assent to something as true because of the authority of the man who has said it. *Supernatural* faith is an assent to something as true because of the authority of God who has revealed it.

That even the scientist and the philosopher must have some faith seems clear, for as the scientist must accept from another science the principles of his own particular science, so the philosopher must accept some of his principles, at least in the beginning; for, if he were to attempt to prove everything at the beginning, no progress would or could be made, for no man can know everything at one and the same time, but he must accept something at the start in order that he may progress in truth.

The necessity for supernatural faith is found in the limitation of human reason itself. Sometimes man needs supernatural faith to assent to revealed truths which are necessary for him, but which of themselves exceed the power of human reason; sometimes he needs supernatural faith to assent to revealed truths which are necessary for him for, although they do not exceed human reason, they could not be known in the conditions and circumstances in which man exercises his reason. These truths can neither be proved nor disproved by reason. These truths are important because they make a difference in men's lives whether they believe in them or not. Life will have a different meaning according as we accept or reject them as true.

Let us take one example which is pertinent to the present subject. Christian revelation proposes the Beatific Vision as the end of man. This is an issue which involves a whole series of truths which affect man's conduct. We cannot brush it aside with the statement that we will make no decision concerning it. It is impossible for us to remain neutral in regard to it. To ignore it is to take a stand. Whether we choose to think about it or not, the fact is that we must act as though it exists or does not exist. We cannot avoid taking a stand of some kind in order to regulate our lives. If we are not to attain to the Beatific Vision, two alternatives might be thought concerning the end of man's life: either life is to end with the grave or life will continue beyond the grave in an eternity of successive enjoyments. If the former alternative were true—that man is to live some years on earth and then death is to be the end of all—it would be reasonable to try to get as much pleasure out of this life as possible, in which case right and wrong, good and bad, would be merely a matter of convenience, not a matter of obligation and order. If the latter were true, the next life would not be much different from the present and death would have no meaning, for if life after death is an eternity of successive enjoyments of man's abstracted knowledge of God, man will be eternally seeking the good as he is now and, consequently, this life will have no termination to its search. If, however, man is to live an eternity of perfect happiness in the possession and love of God in the Beatific Vision, then it is true that death will mean the end of all search and man will be completely at rest in the enjoyment of the Highest Good.

On purely philosophical grounds it is possible to prove that man's end is perfect happiness in the rational possession of God, but concerning what this possession means and how it is ultimately to be acquired philosophy has no answer. Theology, however, has, for it teaches that the Beatific Vision is man's end. Here, then, we have an example of the need that the philosopher has for faith. It is faith that gives completion to the philosopher's inquiry into the end of man. Philosophically we can prove that man's natural end is happiness, natural happiness, which consists in the satisfaction of those cravings which belong to and spring from man's bare nature; it is the kind of happiness man would be destined to if he were left on the purely natural plane. Mere reason cannot pass beyond this point, but reason realizes that such a happiness cannot be a termination for man's search. Christian revelation adds to this the concept of supernatural happiness, the Beatific Vision, a concept that supposes a free gift of God lifting man above his natural capacity and enabling him to attain to the Highest Good in a way that is utterly beyond the reach of human nature left to itself.

The supernatural order, then, should not be thought of as opposing, but as supposing the natural and adding to it; hence whatever is said about man in the natural order is true, though incomplete, about man in the supernatural order. The fact, then, that man actually has been raised to the supernatural plane does not invalidate any of the conclusions we reach in a purely natural study of man. Consequently, an ethics based upon a consideration of man's nature without its supernatural elevation is true even though it may be an incomplete ethics. For completion, theology with its truths about man's supernatural elevation is required. In our consideration, we will, when necessary, have recourse to theology and faith in order that we may bring our ethics to completion.

8. Ethics and Metaphysics

In addition to needing theology, as we have explained, ethics is also dependent upon metaphysics and the philosophy of man. In the system of St. Thomas it is impossible to develop a science of ethics, of the right and wrong, the good and the bad of human actions independently of metaphysics and the philosophy of man. To do so would be to imply that man and his moral activity are in isolation from the rest of the scheme of creation. This implication is not true; the study of man and the study of man's activity must be considered as part of that one great movement, as it were, in which all things outside of God play their part, which has its origin in God and is carrying itself onward and upward to God. In other words, just as God made all things with a definite purpose, so he made them of a definite nature in order that they might attain that purpose. All things, then, are to be considered in this divine scheme of things; each one is to play its part so that the scheme may be fulfilled. To know this order and scheme, then, the nature of being itself must be known. To study man's activity, or anything else for that matter, as independent of this real context of being would be to have a distorted and false view of man and all things.

All things have been endowed with a definite nature in order that they may reach a definite end. Each creature is situated in a definite relationship to every other. Because the nature of man is only one nature among the many that have been created by God, it follows that just as other things attain their purpose by being used properly, so man must use his nature properly to attain his purpose. To understand Thomistic ethics we must realize that St. Thomas looked upon the world as a rational world, a world of purpose and order. It was not a new view; St. Thomas continued the tradition of the classic Greek philosophers, but elevated it with a supernatural vision of purpose and order. To understand St. Thomas' ethics we must know the interpretation of human nature which was developed by St. Thomas, the Thomistic philosophy of being and philosophy of man. But in summary we may say that Thomistic ethics is based on the principle that man has a purpose in life, that his nature and, therefore, his activity cannot be studied independently of God and other beings to which he stands in a necessary relationship; that his nature can offer a norm of judgment for the good and bad, the right and wrong of actions.

9. *Postulates of Ethics*

Because Thomistic ethics is so closely related to his other philosophical sciences we must, to understand his ethics, accept certain principles that have been proven in other parts of St. Thomas' philosophy. These principles have been traditionally, at least from the time of Kant, called postulates. A word must be said about the word *postulate* and its historical significance.

Outside of Scholastic circles not a few writers on ethics, and I have in mind particularly William James, accept three—namely, the freedom of the will, the immortality of the soul, and the existence of God—as principles of ethics. These must be accepted, according to these philosophers, not because they can be proven, but because they are reasonable. Now, by reasonable they mean that these are valuable in the sense that if we accept them they make life better. What is meant by value in life is impossible to define and we shall not at the present time try to discover what these writers mean by value. But, be that as it may, the originator of this outlook is Immanuel Kant. The root of Kant's difficulty is his epistemology, according to which the human intellect can know only the appearances of things, the phenomena, but can never know the thing itself, the noumenon. Consequently, Kant in his *Critique of Pure Reason* (1781), which is a treatise on theoretical philosophy, concludes that it is not possible to demonstrate these three truths philosophically. Nevertheless, because of his theory of *obligation* of human actions, he recognized the need of these, so he said that human reason must demand or postulate them even though it could not prove them. Hence, in his *Critique of Practical Reason* (1788), which is a treatise on practical philosophy, Kant accepted these three propositions as true in order that he might establish a science of ethics. As a consequence of the use of the word postulate in relation to these three truths, many Scholastic writers on ethics have likewise called them postulates.

But we must note, and this is important for what we will say later on, there is a difference between the Kantian and the Scholastic sense of the term *postulate*. Both the Kantians and the Scholastics are agreed that these three propositions must be accepted or the science of ethics is impossible. However, Kant and his followers say they must be accepted even though they are not demonstrable truth, while the Scholastics and, as far as we are concerned, St. Thomas, contend that they are demonstrated in the philosophy of man and in metaphysics. In a Thomistic ethics, then, these postulates are truths which we accept and do not prove, not because they cannot be proven, but because they have been proven and, consequently, we can accept them as principles with which we begin our study of ethics. That they are necessary is clear. If God does not exist there is no Highest Good for man. God is not only man's Creator, the Source from which he comes, but also man's Last End, the Goal of all his striving. Without God as the Absolute Lawgiver and Supreme Judge there could be no moral law prescribing what we ought to do, and therefore no *ought* and no ethics. If man is not free to order his actions for an end, there is no point in trying to teach him how to do so. Unless the human will is free, a man cannot choose between right and wrong, is not responsible for what he does, and cannot direct the course of his life. All acts of a man are equally right if they are his only possible acts, for no acts can be wrong if they cannot be avoided. If man is not immoral, there is no reason for his looking for a reward or punishment in a future life, and no point in sacrificing himself in this life in order to do the good and avoid the evil. Since we see that virtue often goes unrewarded and vice unpunished in this world, why be good, especially when it is hard, if it makes no difference in the long run?

These three propositions are the postulates of Thomistic ethics. They are required, for without them we cannot understand the actions of man. They are accepted from Thomistic metaphysics and philosophy of man, for without these sciences we cannot understand man who is a part of the great field of being which is studied in Thomistic philosophy. Hence, the ethician need not try to prove them; they have been proven and he takes them over. Postulates, then, in our ethics are premises or principles which we accept as proven. They are starting points. Not only can they be proven, but they have already been proven. To prove them again would be a waste of time and energy; to prove them again would be unscientific, for if we were to prove our postulates again and again we would so limit our knowledge that progress would be impossible.

10. *The Division of Ethics*

Because the purpose of ethics is to consider how human activity is ordered to man's last end or happiness, the science of ethics is divided into two main parts. The first part is called *Theory of Ethics* or *General Ethics*. In this part the general principles universally applicable to all human activity are established. The principles and conclusions studied in this part of ethics are the universal premises which man must use to arrive at more detailed or specific conclusions about his moral activity.

The second part, *Special Ethics* or *Applied Ethics*, is a consideration of the particular good or evil acts man is to do or avoid in his free activity. A word of caution is necessary. We should remember that ethics is a science, and in ethics as in any science we cannot expect to have the certitude about individual facts or acts which we have about the principles that are applicable to the facts or acts. The principles of a science are universally true and about them we have certainty; but the further we descend into the realm of individual application of these principles, the further we draw away from the universality of principles to the details of the individual, the less certainty we have. Naturally, the closer knowledge is grouped about the first principles, the more certain it is. One can readily be certain that a tree is not an ox because of the statement's proximity to the principle of contradiction and the principle of identity. The first principles of thought are the foundation of all our intellectual constructions, and there is no certitude unless knowledge can be resolved back into the first principles. The nearer we get to first principles, the closer we get to certitude. It is not easy to see the relation, for example, between a first principle of thought and the proposition that every dream is an unfilled sex libido as the Freudians would have it. Hence, there is not the certainty about an individual fact that there is about a principle.

The same is true of the General Ethics and Special Ethics. In moral science there is not always an absolute certainty and universality, because it is difficult in many instances to see the relation between the first and fundamental principles and the remote applications of these principles to the concrete, existential order. Since the principles of ethics about which we have certainty and universality are applied to individual, free actions, we have not the same certainty about their applications that we have about the principles themselves. Nevertheless, in Special Ethics, since we prescind from the concrete, individual, detailed human acts, we have a very proximate approach to a universal application of the universal principles.

In Special Ethics, then, we apply the universal principles which we have established in General Ethics. Now, if the purpose of establishing the universal principles is that man may properly order his free actions to his true happiness, there are as many parts of Special Ethics as there are different spheres of activity in which man may order his activity to his end. Now man must direct his action in the context of three distinct orders. As an individual, man has his own problems. Another kind of action is characteristic of man as a member of a family. Finally, man must act as a member of a political society. Man occupies a well-defined position in the universe, and his moral worth stands or falls with the attitude he adopts in his everyday acts towards himself, towards his family, and towards his fellow citizens. This threefold relationship is common to every man born into the world, and independent of every other arrangement and condition he may later make. It affects the individual as such. Hence, the general principles of ethics must find application in these three different orders. Because of this fact, we divide Special Ethics into three different parts.

Man must at times order his actions to his end as an individual with his own particular problems. Although we now call this part of Special Ethics *Individual Ethics*, St. Thomas called it *monastics*, from the Greek word *monos*, meaning one. Sometimes man must act as a member of a familial group. He is naturally a member of a family; hence many of his actions are for the good of the family. St. Thomas called this part of ethics *economics*, from the Greek word *oikos*, house, and *nemein*, to manage. But we can see how disconcerting economics as applied to the family would be when in present-day terminology economics is a science dealing with the ordering of wealth. Hence, we call this part *Family* or *Domestic Ethics*. Finally, man is a citizen of a state. As a member of civil society he must perform actions which are for the good of the state. Along with St. Thomas we call this *Politics*.

Readings

Aristotle, *Nicomachean Ethics*, bk. I, c. 1-3.
Brosnahan, T. J., *Prolegomena to Ethics*, Introd., c. 1.

Cronin, Michael, *The Science of Ethics*, vol. I, c. 1.

Gilson, E., *Moral Values and the Moral Life*, pp. 1-19.

Leibell, J. F., *Readings in Ethics*. The following articles will be helpful as an introduction to the study of ethics:

"The purpose of ethics," Aristotle, pp. 1-3.

"Definition and scope of ethics," V. Cathrein, pp. 3-6.

"The necessity of ethics," Vincent McNabb, pp. 6-11.

"The golden mean in philosophy," C. S. Devas, pp. 11-13.

"Methods of ethics," Michael Cronin, pp. 13-19.

"History of ethics," V. Cathrein, pp. 19-31.

"The necessity of postulates," H. S. Spalding, pp. 35-36.

"Postulates," Timothy Brosnahan, pp. 36-39.

"Arguments in proof of the existence of God," St. Thomas, pp. 39-48.

"The teleological proof," Bernard Boedder, pp. 48-57.

"The argument from conscience," George H. Joyce, pp. 57-66.

"The common consent of mankind," T. J. Walshe, pp. 66-69.

"Why some do not believe in God," Joseph Rickaby, pp. 69-71.

"Immortality of the soul," Michael Cronin, pp. 71-88.

"Freedom of the will," Michael Maher, pp. 89-98.

"Freedom," John G. Vance, pp. 98-105.

"Determinist theories," Cardinal Mercier, pp. 106-111.

"Morality without free will," Joseph Rickaby, pp. 111-120.

"Certitude," Michael J. Ryan, pp. 120-129.

"The illative sense," Cardinal Mercier, pp. 129-152.

Maritain, J., *Science and Wisdom*, pp. 70-140; 192-220.

Pegis, A. C., "Matter, Beatitude and Liberty," *Maritain Volume of the Thomist*, pp. 265-280.

Phelan, G. B., "Theology in the Curriculum of Catholic Colleges and Universities," *Man and Secularism*, pp. 128-240.

Sidgwick, H., *History of Ethics, passim*.

St. Thomas' proofs for the postulates of Ethics are found in his *Summa Theologica*: for God's existence in I,2,3; for free will in I,83,1; for immortality in I,75,2. Some of the surrounding material should be read to make the argument clear. A. C. Pegis' *Basic Writings of St. Thomas Aquinas* is a convenient edition.

CHAPTER II

THE END OF MAN

1. *Ethics Is a Study in Teleology*

The purpose of ethics is to establish rules of human conduct in order that man may obtain true happiness. No man can be expected to knowingly seek true happiness unless he knows what it is. Once he sees what it is, he can be guided by it not only in the pursuit of his main life purpose but also in the selections of all those things which may be used as means towards that end. We must know the end of man before we can begin to establish rules of conduct for obtaining it.

As we have stated before, all men do seek happiness, but not all men are in agreement as to the meaning of happiness. As a result of this difference of opinion about the meaning of happiness men differ in their opinions about what is good and bad in human conduct. The correct rule of conduct cannot be discovered, then, as some have wished, from a study of the way in which men have lived. A history of the various customs which have been observed by different groups of men will furnish interesting material for the sociologist and the psychologist, but it will not reveal a moral standard by which these customs can be judged. A history of this kind can tell us only what customs have been observed and what standards of human conduct have been recognized. It cannot tell us whether the customs were, and are, really good.

As is clear, the reason for the difference of customs is the difference of the meanings of happiness. Consequently, just as custom does not of itself give us the norm for correct human conduct, so an inquiry into the diverse meanings which men have attached to happiness will not give us the true meaning of happiness. We cannot, therefore, discover the meaning of happiness nor the correct rule of human conduct from a gathering of opinions about happiness or about rules of conduct which different men have followed. All that such a collection would do would be to demonstrate that all men seek happiness, which we already know, and that they regulate their conduct according to their meaning of happiness, which seems to be logical. From such a study we should not find the meaning of happiness, but only opinions about the meaning of happiness, and since opinion is not science, such a study would not be of help in ethics.

Where, then, are we to find the meaning of true happiness? Since all men desire happiness, we will have to find the meaning of happiness in the nature of this desire. As we cannot say that flying is good for an airplane, nor blossoming for a flower, nor eating oats for a horse, unless we know the end or purpose of an airplane, a flower, and a horse, so we cannot determine what happiness or good for man is, unless we know what is the end or purpose of this desire which all men have for happiness. Now man is not free to seek happiness; he necessarily seeks it. To seek happiness is a necessary inclination of the will of all men, as all airplanes are made to fly and flowers to bloom. If, then, we can discover what men desire in perfect happiness, we can discover what this happiness is. St. Thomas writes concerning man's desire for happiness:

> The will tends naturally to its last end, for every man naturally wills happiness. All other desires are results from this natural desire, since whatever a man wills he wills for the sake of the end. Therefore, that love which is the love of the good that a man naturally wills as an end is his natural love, but the love which comes of this, which is of something loved for the sake of his end, is the love of choice. (S.T. I,60,2)

In every one of man's deliberate actions, the whole aggregate of which is human conduct, man seeks either complete happiness necessarily as his ultimate end, or a partial happiness as a means to his end. Or we may say that man necessarily seeks complete happiness, but he realizes that in many of the actions which he does he is obtaining only partial happiness, but such partial happiness advances him along the road to complete happiness. We can, then, from a consideration of this universal desire which all men have for happiness, conclude to the nature of true happiness. I might add that unless we are correct about this fundamental point of the meaning of true happiness, the desire for which is in all men, then our ethics, which is to establish rules for obtaining it, will be not only erroneous but dangerous.

We begin our study of ethics, then, with a consideration of the end of human conduct. To study things from a consideration of their end is a study of teleology, from the Greek word *telos*, meaning *end*. If, therefore, the science of human conduct is only possible providing we know what is true happiness (which is the purpose of human conduct), then the science of ethics is necessarily a study in teleology.

2. *The Meaning of End, Good, Final Cause*

To study what true happiness is, let us proceed by considering the following: (1) the meaning of end, good, final cause; (2) the end of all things; (3) the end of man. This consideration will be somewhat lengthy for it touches upon the subject-matter of metaphysics and natural theology, but it is necessary for an understanding of the meaning of happiness, the end of man.

THE MEANING OF END

An end is that towards which an action tends. It is that which an action does. For example, the end of the action of assimilation of food is the breaking down of the food substance and the building of it into the substance of the organism which is assimilating. Consequently, an end is that object aimed at in any effort or action; it is that towards which the agent strives, puts forth effort to attain. We can expand this notion of end by quoting from St. Thomas:

For in those things which clearly act for an end, we declare the end to be that towards which the movement or the agent tends; for when this is reached, the end is said to be reached, and to fail in this is to fail in the end intended. This may be seen in the physician who aims at health, and in a man who runs towards an appointed goal. Nor does it matter as to this, whether that which tends to an end be endowed with knowledge or not; for just as the target is the end of the archer, so it is the end of the arrow's flight. Now the movement of every agent tends to something determinate, since it is not from any force that an action proceeds, but heating proceeds from the heat, and cooling from the cold; and therefore actions are differentiated by their active principles. Actions sometimes terminate in something made, as for instance building terminates in a house, and healing in health: while sometimes it does not terminate, as for instance, in the case of understanding and sensation. And if action terminates in something made, the movement of the agent tends by that action towards the thing made; while if it does not terminate in something made, the movement of the agent tends to action itself. It follows therefore that every agent intends an end while acting, which end is sometimes the action itself, sometimes a thing made by the action. . . . Again, in all things that act for an end, that is said to be the last end beyond which the agent seeks nothing further. (C.G. III,2)

We should note that it is characteristic of an end that *it is sought for on its own account.* Thereby it differs from *pure means,* which is sought for only that a true end may be attained. A pencil, in the hand of a writer, in the act of writing, is not an end but a pure means. However, a particular thing may be sought both for its own sake and also as a means of attaining some further object. Thus a boy may seek ice cream because he likes it, and also because he wants to grow up to be a football player. Consequently, we can enumerate many different ends, and some of these can be the ends about which St. Thomas speaks in the above quotation: (1) *Proximate end* is that on account of which anything is immediately done or intended. (2) *Intermediate end* is that on account of which a proximate end is sought, and which in turn is sought for another end. (3) *Ultimate end* is that on account of which all other ends are sought. Thus a student may exert himself to acquire good grades, because he wishes to please his parents, for he knows that in pleasing his parents he is pleasing God and by this means he can obtain his ultimate happiness. In this act of the student the good grades are the proximate end of his work in school, but this is an intermediate end in relation to his other end of pleasing his parents, and both of these ends are intermediate ends in relation to his ultimate happiness.

It is possible that the ultimate end be sometimes *absolutely last* and sometimes *relatively last*.

An end is absolutely last or ultimate when it is that for the sake of which all other ends are sought within the entire range of the agent's activities and which itself is not reasonably referred to any further end because by its nature it cannot be so referred. Thus we may take the student who wants to obtain ultimate happiness. Ultimate happiness is that which he wants and there is no other end to which this can be referred.

An end is relatively last when it is that for the sake of which all other ends within a certain sphere of activity are sought, but is an intermediate end to an absolutely ultimate end. Let us take the student again. Within the sphere of education the acquisition of knowledge is the ultimate end; all his activities within this sphere are directed to this end. However, this end can be and should be referred to another, namely, to obtain ultimate happiness. A relatively last end is not the absolutely last end, but should be used for a higher end; it can claim a certain amount of a man's energies, but not all. Thus, the activities of a student should not exclude his activities as a man, which are and should be directed to his perfect happiness.

The *end of the action* and the *end of the agent* must also be distinguished. The first is that for which the agent's work or action is suited by its very nature; the other is that good which the agent selects for the purpose of his work. Thus, the end of the action of laying bricks is the laying of bricks; of the action of making watches is the putting the springs and cogs and screws together to make a watch. The end of the agent who lays bricks is to make money; that of the maker of watches, fame or money. It is conceivable, of course, that both these ends coincide, but not necessarily, and generally they do not. Thus, a bricklayer might have no other purpose in view than that he lay bricks, but most probably he would also desire to earn a living or build a house by his activity. There is a further distinction to be placed in the end of the action. The end of the action may be *exterior* to the action itself, for example, the house erected by the bricklayer; the house is something extrinsic to the action of laying bricks. Or the end of the action may be the action itself, as, for example, an act of knowing or sensing; these actions are their own ends. Consequently, we must say that the end of the agent might be something exterior to the action itself, or it might be the action itself.

These are the different kinds of ends for which an agent acts. But the question arises: Does everything which acts act for an end? The answer is yes, for if there were no determined end to be obtained by an action, there would be no reason for the action. For if all effects or ends were indifferent, or of the same attractiveness, there would be no reason why one effect should be produced rather than another. For example, if a physical body had not the determined end to fall downward but was equally determined to fall every way, there would be no reason why it fell downward. If a brute beast were equally attracted to self-preservation and self-destruction, there would be no reason why it should do one rather than the other. If doing good and doing evil were equally attractive to man, there would be no reason why he should do either. If there is an action, it is because of a determined end. St. Thomas explains this necessity by saying:

Were an agent not to act for a definite effect, all effects would be indifferent to it. Now that which is indifferent to many effects does not produce one rather than another. Therefore, from that which is indifferent to either of two effects, no effect results, unless it be determined by something to one of them. Hence it would be impossible for it to act. Therefore every agent tends to some definite effect, which is called its end. (C.G. III,2)

Not only does every agent act for an end, it also acts for an ultimate end. To explain this statement, let us take the example: a man studies in order to obtain knowledge in order to obtain power in order to obtain position in order to obtain independence in order to obtain ease. In this whole series it is the last item which is the reason for the whole series: it alone is the reason why the man acts at all; it is the only reason why the man uses or seeks any of the others. Each action terminates in a particular end, which end becomes a means to another end. If then we call the last end to be obtained the final or ultimate end, all the others, except the first, will be appropriately called intermediate ends, and the first the proximate end. But it is also clear that although the last end is the last end to be obtained, it is the first end in the mind of the man who acts, for it is because of this end that he does anything at all; it is the first to be desired and the only one which moves him to act. If, then, there were not a last end there would be no action. It is perfectly conceivable that a man want any of these ends as the last. He might want to study just to have knowledge, or he might want to study in order to have knowledge in order to have power, and so on. But no matter what is the first thing he desires, it is that thing which is the ultimate end. Consequently, if there were no ultimate or final end, there would be no action.

But having said this much, it will be necessary at once to observe that a final or ultimate end may be final only in a given series of acts, and that it may become a means at the beginning of another new series. It is, therefore, only relatively final. Thus ease, which is the final end in the series which begins with studying, might be the beginning of a whole new series of ends and means in the line of ease. Having acquired ease a man might want to be the golf champion of the world. A man may, then, have a multiplicity of relatively ultimate ends, but he also wants an end of such a nature that it will completely and permanently and perfectly satisfy him, an end which will utterly exhaust, as it were, his powers of desiring, so that beyond it he cannot desire anything further. This end is called the *absolutely* ultimate end. Such an end will be the cause of his complete or perfect happiness. Such an end all men desire.

Let us, for the sake of summary put all of this in another way.

A thing is intended either for its own sake or for the sake of something else. In the former it is an *end*, in the latter a *means*. A means always supposes an end; it is called a means precisely because it lies between the agent and the end, and its use brings the agent to the end. The same thing may be both means and end in different aspects, for it may be sought both for its own sake and for the sake of something further. This kind of thing is called an *intermediate* end, and there may be a long series of such intermediate ends, as when a man wants A in order to get B, B in order to get C, C in order to get D, etc.

That which is sought for its own sake and not for the sake of anything further is a *last* end or *ultimate* end. It closes the series of means and ends. It may be a last end only in a relative sense, closing a particular series while the whole and larger series is directed to some further end. The end which closes a series but is the means to another is called the *relatively* ultimate end; the end which closes all series is called the *absolutely* ultimate end.

Now in a series of means and ends we must distinguish the order of *intention* from the order of *execution*. The first thing that comes to mind (the order of intention) is the end, and the means are chosen with a view to accomplishing the end; but in the order of actual carrying out of the work (the order of execution) the means must be used first, and the last thing that is obtained is the end. The last end, then, is called *last* only because it is last in execution; it is always *first* in intention. St. Thomas proves this:

That which is first in the order of intention is the principle as it were moving the appetite; consequently if you remove this principle there will be nothing to move the appetite. On the other hand, the principle in execution is that wherein operation has its beginning; and if this principle be taken away no one will begin to work. Now the principle in the intention is the last end; while the principle in execution is the first of the things which are ordained to the end. Consequently on neither side is it possible to go on to infinity; since, if there were no last end, nothing would be desired nor would any action have its term nor would the intention of the agent be at rest; while, if there is no first thing among those that are ordained to the end, none would begin to work at anything and counsel would have no term but would continue indefinitely. (S.T. I-II,1,4c.)

THE MEANING OF GOOD

Not only does every agent act for an end, the end or purpose of every action is the *good*. The reason why an end can move an agent is because the end confers something that is good or suitable upon the agent. The end is that towards which an activity tends and each activity can tend only towards its own good. St. Thomas writes:

> For that every agent acts for an end clearly follows from the fact that every agent tends to something definite. Now that to which an agent tends definitely must needs be befitting to that agent, since the agent would not tend to it save because of some fittingness thereto. But that which is befitting to a thing is good for it. Therefore every agent acts for a good. (C.G. III,3)

To make this quotation clear: Everything that acts tends towards an end. Every time we use our faculties, for example, we use them to attain some end. We use our visual sense to see; seeing is the end of the faculty of sight. We use our auditory powers to hear; hearing is the end of the power of hearing. We use our will to love; loving is the end of the power of will. The reason why our powers or faculties tend towards an object is that the object can confer a perfection or a good on the power. Seeing is a perfection of the power of sight; hearing, of the power of hearing; loving, of the power of will. Therefore, *end* and *good* are identical. The same thing is both. It is the end in so far as it is the terminus of activity, i.e., that to which an action tends; it is good in so far as it is satisfying to or is suitable or benefitting to the power which acts.

Hence, in its broadest and most generic acceptation we may say that *good is that which satisfies an appetite*; evil, therefore, is that which does not satisfy an appetite. Sometimes, even in one being, a great many appetites are present, and it is even possible that these may be in partial conflict with one another, i.e., the same object will satisfy one appetite but will prevent the satisfaction of another appetite. For example, the same food that will satisfy the appetite of the palate will often hinder the attainment or preservation of that which is more desired than the pleasures of the palate, namely, our health and life. Because, then, it is not always easy to say whether an object is good or evil, it is possible to distinguish several kinds of goods.

Because we have defined good as that which satisfies an appetite we can enumerate several kinds of goods by distinguishing between the objects whose goodness is suitable or satisfactory to the appetites which desire them. We can distinguish between *perfect good* and *imperfect good*. Perfect good is that which is fitting or satisfactory in the highest degree. Such a good is the perfection of the being that desires. Thus, if a being has many appetites, the perfect good is that which completes the highest appetite. The activity of vegetation, for example, although it is the perfect good for a vegetable, could not be such for brute animals, since they have the higher appetite of sensation. In man the perfect good is that which is befitting his rational appetite. We may say, and it will be proven presently, that the perfect good of all things is God Himself. Imperfect good is that which is fitting or satisfactory in an imperfect degree. For all things, the imperfect good is anything short of God. As far as man is concerned, every good that is not God Himself is an imperfect good, for no created good can perfect or complete the being of man, but all created goods can be means to the perfect good or God.

We may distinguish between the *real* and the *apparent* good. Real good is that which is fitting and satisfactory for all the appetites of the agent taken as a unitary nature, i.e., that which is suited to the appetite most in harmony with the nature of the being that seeks it. The real good, therefore, is conformed to the principal end of the agent that seeks it; hence, this good might be the perfect good or an imperfect good in so far as it is the ultimate or some other good which leads to this ultimate good. Every good which is not the ultimate good or does not lead to it is an apparent good. Apparent good is that which is fitting or satisfactory for one or more of the appetites of the agent, but not for the agent taken as a unitary nature. We may, therefore, say that every good that is not a real good is an apparent good. Or we may say it in another way: an apparent good is a real evil. Thus, refusal to study is a good as far as one's love of laziness is concerned, but evil as far as one's intellect is concerned. So, as far as the sense of taste is concerned, it is good for a diabetic to consume quantities of sugar, but it is bad for the whole man. As a result of this distinction, too, we must say that every moral evil is an apparent good.

From these distinctions which we have made of the good, we must conclude that although the good is that which is fitting for an appetite, the good of objects is not an arbitrary relation determined solely by the enjoyment the agent experiences in the possession of an object which has been desired. The good of an object is also determined by its aptitude for perfecting the being of the agent who enjoys it. Let us see what this means with regard to the good of man.

Man sometimes acts for ends for which he knows he should not act; such ends are not real but apparent goods. Why is it true that these are apparent goods? We have said that a real good is that which perfects an agent as a unitary nature. It follows, then, that if man is to obtain the good befitting him as a human being the end for which he acts must be in accord with reason, must be approved of by reason. An action of this kind involves two factors: (1) the will itself, or the will influenced by the sense appetites, desiring the end; (2) reason approving or disapproving of the end.

Because of these two factors the relation between the human agent and the desired end may be of two kinds. If the end attained is desired by the will and sense appetite and approved of by reason it is a real good because its being is such that reason sees it as good and so it perfects human nature, and because the will can reasonably enjoy it. On the other hand, if the end attained is not approved of by reason, the will or the sense appetite may, indeed, enjoy it, but the enjoyment does not make the end good. In fact the end is bad and reason disapproves of it because it sees it as bad, and the will by enjoying it enjoys it unreasonably. Such an end, therefore, does not perfect human nature because it is evil. The point is that the enjoyment, desire, or appetite is not the only factor in determining the good of an end or object; the end or object itself must be good if it is to perfect an appetite.

Because of this bilateral relation between an appetite and its good, we can distinguish the human or moral good into the becoming and agreeable good. These are two aspects of the same good and they are simultaneously present. The *becoming* good is that which reason approves of because it sees it as perfecting man's human nature. The *agreeable good* is the enjoyment which the possession of the object of which reason has approved. Finally, a *useful good* is anything which reason approves of because it sees it as a means of perfecting man.

THE MEANING OF FINAL CAUSE

The notion of cause is intimately connected with end and good. We have seen that everything which acts, acts for an end. But the end must necessarily be good, for no agent tends to something unless it is befitting or satisfying. The end, therefore, not only is good but is also a cause of the action of desiring. By cause is meant *a principle which in some way influences the production of something.* There are four principles or cause which account for things: (1) *Efficient* cause is a principle which by its own action determines the being of a thing; it has a direct bearing on the effect without entering into the intrinsic constitution of the effect. (2) *Final* cause is that which influences the efficient cause directly by giving the efficient cause a motive or reason for acting, and through this motivating influence the final cause influences the effect. The influence of an efficient cause is exerted first and foremost on the effect; the influence of a final cause is exercised first and foremost on the intellect and will of the agent, and through them on the effect. (3) *Material* cause is that out of which a thing is made; hence, it enters into the intrinsic constitution of things. (4) *Formal* cause is that by reason of which a thing is in a definite species of being; hence, it too enters into the intrinsic nature of things. Each of these four causes has its own proper and peculiar activity, each contributing in its own special way to the production of the effect or new existent.

The final cause is the only cause in which we are interested in ethics. *A final cause is that on account of which or for the sake of which something exists or is done.* This definition means that a final cause gives reason to an agent for acting. As we have seen, everything that acts acts because it desires a good. It is clear, however, that only intelligent agents can recognize good and, hence, have reason for acting. Consequently, only intelligent agents know that the reason why they are acting is to obtain a good. If other agents without intelligence act to obtain good, and they do, it is because they are directed to the good or end by an intelligent agent. Thus, for example, orange trees do act in order to produce oranges: oranges are the end of orange trees and the production of oranges is good for them. However, orange trees in no way know that they are acting for this purpose. But this purpose is known by Him Who made orange trees and it is the reason why He made them as they are and why they act the way they do. But in man, the cause is altogether different. Man knows why he acts: he desires a certain good and it is this good that moves him to act. The end or the good is what moves him. As we have said, the end is the first in the order of intention but the last in the order of execution.

Because finality is the purpose for which a thing acts we must, therefore, know the purpose to really understand a thing and its actions. Since we do not know natures immediately, we must reason to them through their activity; since activity follows the natures of things, we arrive at a knowledge of natures from activity. But since activity is meaningless without purpose, unless we know the purpose we understand fully neither activity nor natures. If, therefore, we wish to understand the free activity of man, we must know the meaning of happiness, the purpose for which man acts. It is the same with all other things: to know them fully we must know their finality. All things work for an end, and all things are moved or move to an end in so far as the end gives a reason or motive for acting or as the end directs the things in their activity. Thus we must say that *end, good,* and *final cause* are all the same. When something is thought of as the object of desire or appetite it is called *good.* When it is thought of as the terminus of an act, that to which the action is directed, it is called an *end*. When it is considered as the reason why something is done it is called a *final cause*. Thus, for example, a man works in order to acquire money. Money is termed the good in so far as it satisfies one of his appetites or desires; it is called end in so far as it is the object to which he directs his activity or work. It is final cause in so far as it gives him a recognized motive for working. St. Thomas writes:

Things that know the end and things that do not know the end are equally directed to the end; although those which know the end are moved thereto per se, whereas those which do not know it tend thereto as directed by another, as may be seen in the archer and the arrow. Now those that know the end are always directed to a good as their end; because the will, which is the appetite of a previously known end, does not tend towards a thing except under the aspect of good, which is its object. Therefore those things also that do not know the end are directed to a good as their end. (C.G. III,16)

All things, then, are moved to action by reason of some end to which they are inclined as something good for them. Intelligent creatures are moved because they recognize the end as something good and thus have reason or motive within themselves for their activity. Irrational creatures are moved by their own natures which are the means that the Intelligent Creator of their being uses to obtain that which is good for them. In either case there is a finality or moving cause for their actions. In the case of the former it is recognized by the creature agent; in the latter it is recognized by the Intelligent Mover. St. Thomas again explains it thus:

Every agent either acts by nature or by intellect. Now there can be no doubt that those which act by intellect act for an end, since they act with an intellectual preconception of what they attain by their action, and they act through such a preconception; for this is to act by intellect. Now just as in the preconceiving intellect there exists the entire likeness of the effect that is attained by the action of the intellectual being, so in the natural agent there preexists the likeness of the natural effect, by virtue of which the action is determined to the appointed effect; for fire begets fire, and an olive produces an olive. Therefore, even as that which acts by intellect tends by its action to a definite end, so also does that which acts by nature. Therefore every agent acts for an end. (C.G. III,2)

3. The End of All Creatures

All things, as we have seen, act for an end which is good for them. This action must follow from the fact that God created all things, for unless God has an end in view, a good to be obtained, for His creatures, He would not be acting as an intelligent being.

Now everything that is produced through the will of an agent is directed to an end by that agent, because the good and the end are the proper object of the will; and therefore whatever proceeds from a will must needs be directed by Him who endowed things with the principles whereby they act. Consequently, God, Who in Himself is perfect in every way, and by His power endows all things with being, must needs be the Ruler of all, Himself ruled by none; nor is anything to be expected from His ruling, as neither is there anything that does not owe its being to Him. Therefore, as He is perfect in being and causing, so He is perfect in ruling. (C.G. III,1)

Now God is not some external force moving all things to an end. We must remember that God moves things to their peculiar ends by their natures. In other words, things move to ends in various ways and under the influence of different appetites or powers of nature. An *appetite* is a disposition, a tendency, or an inclination towards an action and through that action towards the attainment of some object or end. Appetites are of two kinds: (1) *Innate* appetite is an inclination towards an object by an interior principle without cognition. All creatures have such innate appetites for ends. We have mentioned one in regard to man: the innate appetite for perfect happiness. The plants and brute animals have innate appetites for certain actions called instincts. The elements have within themselves inclinations to perform certain activities, i.e., affinities among themselves. (2) *Elicited* appetite is an inclination towards an object which is previously known by reason or sense. Thus, brute beasts and men desire objects because they have some previous knowledge of these objects. Horses are drawn to sugar because they have received it; men have a desire for Paris because they have heard so much about it.

All things, both those which have only innate appetites and those which have elicited appetites, move towards ends under the rule of the Provident God who has created them for a purpose and directed them to that purpose through their natures and appetites. Those with innate appetites only are moved necessarily; those with sensible elicited appetites also move necessarily; but those with intellectual elicited appetites are moved freely towards their end.

It is easy to understand how natural bodies devoid of knowledge are moved and act for the sake of an end. For they tend to an end as directed thereto by an intelligent substance, in the same way as an arrow, directed by the archer, tends to the mark. Because as the arrow receives its direction to a fixed end through the impulse of the archer, so too, natural bodies receive an inclination to their natural end from their natural movers from whom they derive their forms, powers, and movements. Therefore it is also clear that every work of nature is the work of an intelligent substance, because an effect is ascribed more especially to the direction of the first mover towards the end than to the instruments which receive that direction. For this reason the operations of nature are seen to proceed to the end in an orderly manner as do the operations of a wise man. (C.G. III,24)

Whereas the irrational creatures are moved to their end by a necessary impulse of nature under the direction of God, rational creatures move to their end by reason of their own direction, which is a free direction resulting from their free will:

The effect of this ruling [of God] is seen to differ in different things, according to the difference of natures. For some things are so produced by God that, being intelligent, they bear a resemblance to Him and reflect His image. Hence not only are they directed, but they direct themselves to their appointed end by their own actions. And if in thus directing themselves they be subject to the divine ruling, they are admitted by that divine ruling to the attainment of their last end; but they are excluded therefrom if they direct themselves otherwise. (C.G. III,1)

From this analysis we can safely conclude that all things are acting for some end or purpose. It remains only to determine what that end is which they all seek. As we have said, things act only in so far as they seek an end which is good. God, therefore, is the object or end of all things. This is said for the following reason: an agent always acts or makes something for some personal reason, i.e., to advance in virtue, to obtain pleasure or wealth, etc.; hence, when God creates, He can do so only in order that creatures in some manner may be referred to His own good. Consequently, God is the end of all creatures:

Order among ends is consequent on the order among agents. For just as the supreme agent moves all second agents, so all the ends of a second agent must be directed to the end of the supreme agent, since whatever the supreme agent does, it does for its own end. Now the supreme agent is the active principle of the actions of all inferior agents, by moving all to their actions, and consequently to their ends. Hence it follows that all the ends of second agents are ordered by the first agent to its own end. Now the first agent of all things is God, as we proved in the Second Book (II,15). And His will has no other end but His own goodness, which is Himself, as we showed in the First Book (I,74). Therefore all things, whether they were made by Him immediately or by means of secondary causes, are ordered to God as their end.

The last end of every maker, as such, is himself, for what we make we use for our own sake; and if at any time a man makes a thing for the sake of something else, it is referred to his own good, whether his use, his pleasure, or his virtue. Now God is the producing cause of all things; of some immediately, of others by means of other causes, as we have explained above (III,15). Therefore He is the end of all things. (C.G. III,17)

4. *The End of Man*

From these considerations about end, good, and final cause, we must conclude that all creatures are directed to the Divine Goodness as their last end; that the end of man is to attain to the Divine Goodness not as other creatures without knowledge, but with knowledge, since man's intellect is his specific characteristic which must be satisfied. In other words, the final end of man, that which is befitting to him in his specific characteristic, is knowledge of God. God alone is able to fill up, as it were, to perfect and to satisfy wholly that power, namely, the intellect, which is the power that distinguishes man from all irrational creatures. As St. Thomas writes:

> Now, seeing that all creatures, even those that are devoid of reason, are directed to God as their last end, and that all reach this end in so far as they have some share in the likeness of Him, the intellectual creature attains to Him in a special way, namely, through its proper operation, by understanding Him. Consequently this must be the end of the intellectual creature, namely, to understand God. (C.G. III,25)

The conclusion that the end of intellectual creatures is to know God is inevitable. The whole structure of St. Thomas' thought is built upon a solid empiric foundation. Starting with the experiential fact that all things act for an end which is good, He explains this fact with the help of the first principles of thought and of the nature of being. As a metaphysician he realizes that not only must this world of created beings have an efficient cause, God, but a final cause, God, as well, and that God as the final cause must be the end and the good which all creatures are to attain according to their diverse natures and appetites. As an ethician he realizes that morality is meaningless without an end. Consequently, he considers the question of whether God, whom he has proved in metaphysics is the ultimate end of all creatures, is also the ultimate end of man in his practical and, therefore, in his moral life. The arguments which he considers strengthen him in the conviction that God is the end of man in his moral life.

We must recall that we are now speaking of the absolute ultimate end of man's moral acts both in regard to the end of the actions themselves and in regard to the intention of the moral agents. In other words, we are asking whether man in his moral actions seeks his perfect happiness in the possession of God and whether his actions not only by their very nature, but also by man's intentions are directed to this possession of God. Or we can put the question in another way. Can we establish that the ultimate end of man's moral activity is the possession of God in knowledge and love?

It is true, as we have said, that although man acknowledges that he is seeking happiness, many men refuse to accept this happiness as being the possession of God in knowledge and love. St. Thomas, then, reviews the many answers that have been given to the question of what is the ultimate end of man, but he considers them so many palpable errors. We can do no better than to repeat these traditional answers as he has done and to give his reasons for rejecting them. The diverse and strange notions about the ultimate end of man are conveniently grouped into: (1) external goods; (2) goods of the body; (3) goods of the soul.

EXTERNAL GOODS?

To consider the first goods: will any of the so-called external goods, such as honor, glory, wealth, or power, be the object which if possessed make man completely happy?

What about *honor?* Honor consists in respect shown by others. It is something passively received by man. Will honor make a man supremely happy? St. Thomas replies:

Man's ultimate end and happiness is his most perfect operation, as we have shown above. But man's honor does not consist in something done by him, but in something done to him by another who respects him. . . . Only the good can be worthy of honor, and yet it is possible even for the wicked to be honored. Therefore it is better to become worthy of honor, than to be honored. Furthermore, the highest good is the perfect good. Now the perfect good is incompatible with any evil. But that which has no evil in it cannot possibly be evil. Therefore that which is in possession of the highest good cannot be evil. Yet it is possible for an evil person to receive honor. Therefore honor is not man's supreme good. (C.G. III,28)

Since man's greatest good or happiness cannot be honor, might it be *glory?* Glory consists in being famous and the general recognition and praise of a person's good name. This is not an ultimate end and hence could not be perfect happiness:

Men seek praise and distinction through being famous, so that they may be honored by those whom their fame reaches. Therefore glory is sought for the sake of honor, and consequently if honor be not the highest good, much less glory. . . . Besides, it is better to know than to be known, because only the higher realities know, whereas the lowest are known.

Therefore man's highest good cannot be glory, which consists in a man's being known. (C.G. III,29)

Perhaps the supreme happiness of man is *wealth?* Without a doubt money and wealth have been pursued by more men as the ultimate good than any other material object, and yet any thinking man will easily realize that wealth is no more than a means to some nonmaterial good.

It is evident that wealth is not man's highest good. For wealth is not sought except for the sake of something else, because of itself it brings us no good, but only when we use it, whether for the support of the body or for some similar purpose. Now the highest good is sought for its own, and not for another's sake. . . . Besides . . . Man's highest good must consist in obtaining something better than wealth, since wealth is something directed to man's use. Therefore man's supreme good does not consist in wealth. (C.G. III,30)

The last of the external goods which has been proposed as perfect happiness for man is *power.* Will this make a man perfectly happy? St. Thomas replies:

Man is said to be good especially according as he approaches the highest good. But in respect to his having power, he is not said to be either good or evil, since not everyone who can do good deeds is good, nor is a person evil because he can do evil deeds. Therefore the highest good does not consist in being powerful. . . . Every power implies reference to something else. But the highest good is not referred to anything further. Therefore power is not man's highest good. (C.G. III,31)

All these goods are good, but they are not good enough. They cannot be perfect good, simply because they are not perfect good. While they may be the source of some happiness, they can, at the same time, be the cause of evil and are often the reason for much unhappiness, and the perfect good cannot lead to unhappiness. As St. Thomas writes:

Four general arguments may be cited to make clear that happiness is not made up of any outer good that we have mentioned. The first is that happiness as the supreme good for man can have no part with evil, and everyone knows that any of the values cited may be met with among good people, but also among the wicked. Besides, it is the way of happi-

ness that it has a self-sufficiency about it, as we read in the Ethics (I, c. 6) that once happiness is had, no good needful for man is wanting. And we may suppose a man to have got all of the aforementioned goods and yet he might be without many things that are humanly needed, such as education and health. The third reason is that happiness is wholly a good and is never a source of evil for anyone, which may not be said of the goods in question, for instance, Ecclesiastes (5,12) says that richest is something kept to the hurt of the owner, and so of the others. A last argument is that man is meant for happiness by reasons that are at work within him; he is by nature meant for it. But the goods we have passed in review hinge on the world outside man, and often on luck or fortune; so they are called goods of fortune. All this makes it clear that happiness cannot in any way lie in them. (S.T. I-II,2,4c)

As a result of our review of St. Thomas' consideration of the external goods which have been proposed by some as the object of man's perfect happiness, we can say several things about the nature of the object which will give man perfect happiness. First of all, the ultimate good must have four characteristics: (1) It must be sufficient of itself to satisfy man's desires. (2) It must be such that no evil can come from it. (3) It must be such that no evil is present in it. (4) It must be something that can satisfy man internally, in the intellect and will, because man's peculiar powers or appetites are in these. Secondly, man cannot be satisfied with a good which is external to him, such as we have reviewed. Consequently, we have made some progress in our search for what will make man completely happy. The good of man must be something internal. The probability is that perhaps some internal good can satisfy man. Since man is composed of body and soul, we will have to consider the goods that are internal to these, namely the goods of the body and of the soul.

GOODS OF THE BODY?

Let us look at the goods of the body as a possible answer to our quest for perfect happiness. The goods of the body may be carnal pleasure, health, beauty, and strength. The first difficulty about saying that these are the ultimate end of man is that we are saying that man himself is his own end, is his own ultimate good. And more, the satisfaction and preservation of man's body cannot form the ultimate good and last end, because, even if we were to grant that the preservation of the human being were the ultimate good of man, it would not follow that the last end of man consists in some bodily good. True, the human being is composed of body and soul, and though it is true that the being of the body depends on the soul, it is not true that conversely the being of the soul depends on the body. On the contrary, the body is ordered in view of the soul, as matter is ordered in view of the form. In neither case, therefore, could the last end of man be identified with some good of the corporeal order.

Could, therefore, *carnal pleasure* be the perfect good of man? Of course, we shall have to say that it cannot. Moreover, if we look at carnal pleasure, we must say that such pleasure is never an end but always a means. And as a means can never be the ultimate end, so pleasure cannot be the ultimate end of man. Let us just look at this a moment. With actions there is a concomitant pleasure, and with sense activity there is an accompanying sense or carnal pleasure. The question is: Is the sense pleasure for the activity, or the activity for the sense pleasure? The answer is obvious. No activity is defined except by its end; hence the activity is for its end. But since the pleasure accompanies the activity and is defined by it, it must be for the sake of the activity and its end, and not *vice versa*, for if the activity and its end were for the sake of the pleasure, the activity would be defined not by its end but by the pleasure, which it is not. Therefore carnal or sense pleasure cannot be the highest good of man. At most it is a byproduct of man's activity, or it is a means to obtain happiness, but it cannot constitute the essence of perfect happiness.

It has been shown that according to nature's order pleasure is for the sake of operation, and not conversely. Therefore, if an operation be not the ultimate end, the consequent pleasure can neither be the ultimate end, nor accompany the ultimate end. Now it is manifest that the operations which are followed by the pleasures mentioned above are not the last end; for they are directed to certain manifest ends; eating, for instance, to the preservation of the body, carnal intercourse, to the beget-

ting of children. Therefore the aforesaid pleasures are not the last end, nor do they accompany the last end. (C.G. III,27)

Nor, finally are *health, beauty* and *strength* the ultimate happiness of man. They are had by both the good and the bad; they are subject to fortune; they are had in common with animals.

Like arguments avail to prove that man's highest good does not consist in goods of the body, such as health, beauty, and strength. For they are common to good and evil, they are unstable, and they are not subject to the will. Besides, the soul is better than the body, which neither lives nor possesses these goods without the soul. Therefore, the soul's good such as understanding and the like is better than the body's good. . . . These goods are common to man and other animals, whereas happiness is a good proper to man. Many animals surpass man in goods of the body, for some are fleeter than he, some more sturdy, and so on. Accordingly, if man's highest good consisted in these things, man would not excel all animals, which is clearly untrue. Therefore human happiness does not consist in goods of the body. (C.G. III,32)

GOODS OF THE SOUL?

Since man's highest good cannot be found in any of these external goods or in the goods of the body, we should, perhaps, find it in the soul. If ultimate happiness is in the soul we should find it either in the soul itself or in its operations. Does the soul itself or its operations and its pleasures constitute perfect happiness? If by perfect happiness we mean not the attainment or possession or enjoyment of perfect happiness, which indeed pertain to the soul, but the object which is the source of perfect happiness, it must be said that it is none of the goods of the soul, but subsists outside of and infinitely above the soul. Happiness is something belonging to the soul, but that which constitutes happiness is something outside the soul. Let us be clear about this, for this is the crucial point of our discussion.

A distinction has to be made between *objective happiness* (Becoming Good) which is the thing that will bring man perfect happiness, and *subjective happiness* (Agreeable Good) which is the attainment and enjoyment of that thing. It is impossible that perfect happiness, that is, the thing which will make man happy, be the soul or anything connected with the soul. The soul, considered in itself, is only in potency: its knowledge and its powers of operations and its virtues are in need of being brought from potency to act. But whatever is in potency exists only in view of the act. It is, therefore, clear that the human soul exists in view of some other thing, i.e., to live, to be wise, to be good, etc., and that consequently, it is not its own last end. Again, it is evident that no good of the human soul constitutes perfect happiness, the highest good. The good which is the last end can only be a perfect good which fully satisfies the appetite. Now, the human appetite, the will, tends, as we know from the philosophy of man, to the universal good. On the other hand, it is obvious that every good inherent in the finite soul is but a finite and participated good. It is, consequently, impossible for any of these goods to constitute the supreme good of man and to become his last end. That supreme good may consist, as we know, only in a perfect good, fully satisfying the appetite, and since nothing can satisfy the human will except the universal good which is its proper object, it follows that every created and participated good is incapable of constituting the supreme good and ultimate happiness. Human happiness consists therefore in God alone, as in the first and universal good and the source of all other goods.

With this knowledge of what objective happiness consists in, we must now consider what is subjective happiness. The exact meaning flows from the fact that the term "end" may have two senses. It may mean an actual thing which is desired and which, if obtained, will give perfect happiness (Becoming Good); thus money is the end pursued by the miser. It may also mean the acquisition or possession or enjoyment of what is desired (Agreeable Good); thus the end which the miser seeks is the possession of the money. These two senses must be carefully kept apart in considering perfect happiness. We now know what it is in the first sense, namely, the Uncreated Good, God, who alone in His infinite goodness is able to satisfy the will of man perfectly. But what perfect happiness is, taken in the second sense, that is, the possession or enjoyment, is a matter which we will consider now.

As we said before, the word "end" has two meanings; first, it stands for the very thing which we seek to gain, and then for the use that is the gaining or having of this thing. If we mean by the human goal the thing itself that men want as an end, the full human goal cannot be the soul or anything belonging to it. The reason is that the soul, studied in itself, is a kind of potential thing: it is potentially wise before it is actually wise, and potentially good before it is actually good. Now the potential exists for the actual, which is its complement, hence the impossibility that anything, the nature of which is to be in potency, would be the supreme good. This rules out the soul as its own objective, and likewise any activity or habit proper to it. For the good which is the main good is a good that fulfills one's whole desire for good, but human desire or will is a desire for the universal good, whereas any good united with the soul is shared and fragmentary. So the supreme good of man is not any of these things.

If, however, we mean the attainment of the supreme good for man or the having or using of it, it is true that the human soul has something to do with the supreme good, for it is through the soul that man reaches happiness. The very thing, then, which is sought as an end, is that in which happiness consists, and which makes man happy and the attaining of this thing is called happiness; hence it must be granted that happiness is a feature of the soul. Still, that in which happiness consists is something outside the soul. (S.T. I-II,2,7c)

5. The Attainment of the Ultimate End of Man

St. Thomas has examined all the things which might be advanced as man's perfect happiness. All of them have been shown to be insufficient. He has concluded that if no created good outside or inside of man can be the object of perfect happiness, we must say that God, the Uncreated Good, is the object which alone will afford man perfect happiness. It is certain, then, that man's ultimate end, his perfect happiness, is the possession of God by knowledge and love.

But having arrived at this unavoidable conclusion, there are other questions which we can ask about man's perfect happiness.

We can speculate how this happiness is to be realized, for there are many obscurities here, which the human intellect cannot perfectly clear up. If God is the ultimate end of man, we still want to know how this conclusion can be true. There is a most serious difficulty contained in it, for there is a large disproportion between man and the object of his desire. Man is finite, God is infinite; man is capable of limited enjoyment, but God the object of man's desire is the Infinite Good; man becomes like God, not in the sense in which other creatures do in so far as they imitate a perfection of God, but in the sense that man possesses God and in possessing Him contains in some way the fullness of being.

It seems at first sight that, viewed under these aspects, perfect happiness is a created good. Doubtless the cause or object of happiness is something uncreated, but the acquisition and possession by man of his last end is necessarily human, and consequently something created. We may add that this something—i.e., this acquisition, possession, and enjoyment—is an operation, an act, because perfect happiness constitutes the highest perfection and, therefore, the highest good of man implies an act, as potency implies imperfection. Man's highest good, therefore, consists in action. Because it does we shall now try to obtain some notion of the nature of this operation by which perfect happiness is attained and the nature of this attainment. We shall investigate these questions under three headings: (1) The power by which man attains God; (2) the nature of this attainment; (3) the need of a special help from God for this attainment.

THE POWER BY WHICH MAN ATTAINS GOD

The operation by which man attains to perfect happiness belongs to the rational part of the soul, to the exclusion of every other power. For it cannot be claimed that perfect happiness could be reduced to an operation of the sensitive or vegetative powers: we have seen that the very object of perfect happiness does not consist in bodily goods, and these are the only goods which are accessible to the sensitive or vegetative operations of the soul; they are, therefore, incapable of conferring perfect happiness. Moreover, as we have said, perfect happiness is a good proper to man. Therefore, it follows that unless those powers and their activities which are proper to man are satisfied, man will not be perfectly happy. Now, man has the operations of the sensitive and vegetative powers in common with other creatures; hence, such operations are not capable of giving man his proper happiness. Man's highest powers, the intellect and will, must be the powers which man must use to obtain happiness. Our choice of what power must operate in the attainment of essential happiness lies between these two.

It appears that of the intellect and will, which are the rational powers of the soul, the intellect is the only power capable of grasping directly the object of man's perfect happiness. We must distinguish within perfect happiness what constitutes the very essence of it from the delight which is certainly always linked with it, but is in the last analysis only accidental to it. In view of this distinction, it becomes clear that perfect happiness cannot consist essentially in an act of the will. It is true that all men desire their last end and the possession of this represents the supreme happiness, but it is not the will that apprehends or possesses any end. The will desires ends when they are absent and enjoys them when they are present. But to desire an end is not to apprehend it; at most it means to move towards it. And enjoyment of an end arises in the will only when the end is attained. In other words, the will enjoys an object only on condition that it be present, but it is the intellect that makes the object present. One must not argue, according to St. Thomas, as if the object becomes present simply because the will enjoys it. The essence of perfect happiness consists, therefore, in an act of the intellect; only the enjoyment accompanying it can be considered as an act of the will. St. Thomas explains:

As it was said before, happiness comprises two things: one is the very essence of it and the other is as it were its natural companion, that is, the enjoyment which goes with it. As for that which is the very essence of happiness, I say that this cannot possibly be an act of the will. From what has preceded, it is clear that happiness is the attainment of the ultimate end, and this does not consist in an act of the will, for the will is moved by desire towards the end when this is not had and by rejoicing and being at rest when it is had. But the desire of the end, taken in itself, is not the attainment of the end; so much is plain; it is only a movement towards the end. And as for enjoyment, we would say that this comes to the will from the fact that the end is present, and not, on the contrary, that anything becomes present from the fact that the will enjoys it. There must, then, be something other than the act of the will to make the end present to the will. This is evident in the instance of sense objects. If one could get hold of money by the act of wanting it, the miser would have gold as soon as he began to desire it. The fact is, he has not got it to begin with, and he obtains it only by getting his hands on it or in some such way, and his joy over possessing it dates from that moment. The same procedure holds in the case of knowable objects: in the beginning we wish to reach some intelligible end, but we cannot do this unless it becomes present to us by an act of the intellect, and it is only then that the will finds joy and comes to rest in the end attained. Thus the very essence of perfect happiness lies in the act of the intellect. (S.T. I-II,3,4c)

THE NATURE OF MAN'S ATTAINMENT OF GOD

These arguments all presuppose the principle that if perfect happiness is attainable by a human operation, it can be attained only by the most perfect and highest operation. This same principle enables us to assert further that perfect happiness must consist in an operation of the speculative intellect rather than of the practical intellect. For the most perfect power of the intellect is that of which the object is the most perfect, namely, the essence of God. Now this essence is the object of the speculative, not of the practical intellect. The act constituting perfect happiness must, then, according to the theory of St. Thomas, be of a speculative nature, and this amounts to saying that this act must consist in contemplation. Or to put it in another way, since happiness consists essentially in an act of the intellect or in the knowledge of God, the next question is concerned with the nature of this act of the intellect by which man possesses God. Again, there is question of a choice for St. Thomas. The intellect has two functions. By the speculative intellect the truth is possessed for its own sake, for knowledge itself, and the intellect rests content in this contemplation. By the practical intellect truth is possessed in order that it may be useful to attain something else; thus art and prudence pertain to the practical intellect. From this distinction between the speculative and practical intellect it is clear what St. Thomas' choice has to be. He is speaking about the operation of the intellect by which man attains to perfect happiness, to his ultimate end. Since the practical intellect attains truth for use, its operation cannot be the essential act of perfect happiness. It must be concluded, then, that man's perfect happiness consists in an act of the speculative intellect whereby he knows God.

Accordingly, if man's ultimate happiness does not consist in external things, which are called goods of fortune, nor in goods of the body; nor in goods of the soul, as regards the sensitive part; nor as regards the intellectual part, in terms of the intellectual virtues which are concerned with actions, namely, art and prudence; it remains for us to conclude that man's ultimate happiness consists in the contemplation of truth. . . . For this operation alone is proper to man, and it is in that none of the other animals communicates. (C.G. III,37)

St. Thomas pursues the problem further. Since this speculative knowledge of God can be acquired in several ways, namely, by faith, by a confused knowledge, by demonstration, and by intuition, the further question arises: which of these four kinds of knowledge essentially constitutes man's perfect happiness? St. Thomas is relentless in his pursuit of this problem of perfect happiness for man, and I think that it would be profitable for us to follow his reasoning. But, at the same time, we should realize that St. Thomas is solving these present problems on the basis of his principles of philosophical thought. Not everyone is in complete agreement with him either in regard to his principles or in the way he solves the question of how man obtains happiness essentially. All Catholic philosophers are in perfect agreement with St. Thomas in saying that perfect happiness of man consists in the possession of God through his rational powers; but from this point on, there is no general agreement. However, we wish to pursue St. Thomas' thought with regard to how man does obtain perfect happiness, that is, God. St. Thomas is of the opinion that perfect happiness does not consist in a knowledge by faith, for perfect happiness consists essentially in the operation of the intellect, while in faith the will claims for itself the principal part, inasmuch as in faith the will must determine the intellect to give assent.

It has been shown that ultimate happiness does not consist chiefly in an act of the will. Now in knowledge by faith, the will has the leading place; for the intellect assents by faith to things proposed to it, because it so wills, and not through being constrained by the evidence of their truth. Therefore man's final happiness does not consist in this knowledge. (C.G. III,40)

Neither can perfect happiness consist in that general and confused knowledge that all men have of some supermundane being which in some way governs the movement and order of the universe. Such knowledge is so mixed with error and imperfect that it cannot equal the knowledge of the wise men of this world, much less the intellect which apprehends the supreme truth, as St. Thomas explains in the third chapter of the Third Book of his *Contra Gentiles*.

Neither is the knowledge by demonstration sufficient for perfect happiness, because happiness must be something universal and attainable by all men, whereas only a few can arrive at this knowledge by demonstration. This knowledge, moreover, is not only mixed with error and is, therefore, capable of becoming more perfect, but it also lacks the certainty required of perfect happiness. And, finally, since this knowledge is based on sense knowledge it is arrived at through many negations. Consequently, although it is a proper knowledge of God, for it does tell us that God is and is distinct from the sensible world, yet with it we are ignorant of what God is.

There is also another knowledge of God, higher than the one just mentioned, which is acquired by means of a demonstration, and which approaches nearer to a proper knowledge of Him; for by means of a demonstration many things are removed from Him, so that in consequence we understand Him as something apart from other things. For demonstration proves that God is immovable, eternal, incorporeal, utterly simple, one and the like, as we have shown in the First Book. Now we arrive at the proper knowledge of a thing not only by affirmations, but also by negations. For just as it is proper to man to be a rational animal, so it is proper to him not to be inanimate, or irrational. Yet there is this difference between these two modes of knowledge, that when we have a proper knowledge of a thing by affirmation we know what that thing is; and how it is distinguished from others; whereas when we have a proper knowledge of a thing by negations, we know that it is distinct from others, but remain ignorant of what it is. Such is the proper knowledge of God that can be obtained by demonstrations. But neither does this suffice for man's ultimate happiness. . . . For things belonging to one species attain to the end of that species, because nature achieves its purpose always or nearly always, and fails in a few instances, because of some corruption. Now happiness is the end of the human species, since all men naturally desire it. Therefore happiness is a common good that can be attained by all men, unless some obstacle occur to some whereby they be deprived of it. Few, however, attain to the possession of the afore-mentioned knowledge of God by way of demonstration, because of the obstacles to this knowledge mentioned at the beginning of this work. Therefore this knowledge is not essentially man's happiness. (C.G. III,39)

St. Thomas pursues his quest further. Some have thought that a speculative science of sensible things would constitute perfect happiness; others that a knowledge of separate substances (angels) or even of one's own soul should be enough to give man perfect happiness. St. Thomas, however, thinks that these theories are erroneous because of the very nature of the objects known in these different knowledges and of the nature of human knowledge.

To consider the speculative sciences first: In the speculative sciences, the range of our knowledge cannot extend beyond the first principles of the sciences, for the whole of every science is virtually contained in the principles whence it is deduced. But the principles of speculative knowledge are known to us only by means of sensible knowledge; the knowledge of these sciences cannot, therefore, carry our intellect beyond the point to which the knowledge of sensible things can advance it. All that is needed, therefore, is to consider whether the knowledge of the sensible could constitute the highest degree of happiness of man, i.e., his highest perfection. The answer is evidently in the negative. The higher cannot find its perfection in what is inferior to it as such. The lower cannot contribute to the perfection of the higher unless it participates, however inadequately, in a reality beyond itself and even beyond the perfection to which it contributes. For example, it is evident that the form of a stone or of any other sensible object is inferior to man. If, therefore, the form of the stone, in sensible knowledge, confers some perfection on the human intellect, it does so not inasmuch as it is simply the form of a stone, but in so far as this form participates in some reality of a higher order than the human intellect, e.g., the intelligible light or something else of this kind. Here we gather the conclusions which we have reached in the philosophy of man concerning the value and range of human knowledge. Its proper object is the sensible; the human intellect cannot, therefore, find perfect happiness and its highest perfection in the knowledge of sensible objects to which the speculative sciences are limited.

By the same token the knowledge of separate substances or of the soul cannot be perfect happiness, for in this life we know them only through abstraction from the phantasm, and therefore by means of the sensible. Such an abstractive knowledge of these spiritual substances is a knowledge through negations though proper. And even though in the next life we shall have a perfect knowledge of such beings, they are only imperfect beings which are existing because of participation in being. We shall, therefore, desire to know about the Supreme being.

THE NEED OF A SPECIAL HELP FROM GOD

All we have been saying means, of course, that the essential and true happiness is not of this world. Such happiness, St. Thomas necessarily concludes, can be found in the full view of the essence of God. In order to understand the meaning of this conclusion, it is important to keep the following two principles in mind. The first is that man is not perfectly happy as long as there is something to be desired and searched for. The second is that the perfection of a power of the soul is always measured by the nature of its object. Now the object of the intellect is the essence of a thing. The perfection of the intellect is, consequently, measured by the more or less deep knowledge of the essence of its object. If, for example, a given intellect knows the essence of a certain effect without this knowledge enabling it to know the essence of its cause, we say that this intellect knows the existence of the cause, but not its nature, the *an sit*, but not the *quid est*; in short, it could not be said that it knows the cause perfectly. A natural desire, therefore, in that intellect which knows that the effect has a cause, is to know what that cause is. This is the source of all curiosity, and of that "wonder" which Aristotle says is at the root of all inquiry. Someone seeing an eclipse of the sun judges at once that this phenomenon has a cause; but since he is ignorant of the cause, he wonders, and because he wonders he searches for it; and this search will end only when he discovers in its very essence the cause of the event.

Let us now recall what the human intellect knows of its creator in the theory of St. Thomas. We know that initially it knows no other essence but that of sensible and created objects, and that it advances from this knowledge to that of the existence of the First Cause, but without attaining to the essence of this cause in its perfection. Man, therefore, feels the natural desire to know fully and to see directly the essence of God. That which will satisfy the capacity of the speculative intellect, in other words, is the intuitive or immediate knowledge of God Himself so that God's essence is not only that which is known but also that by which it is known. This is a most serious conclusion for St. Thomas, and it requires some explanation. This brings us to the third point, namely, whether there is need of a special help from God to have this knowledge in which man has perfect happiness?

According to the opinion of St. Thomas, the human intellect first and directly knows only the essence, of sensible objects which have come to it through sense cognition. In order that the human intellect have such a knowledge it is necessary that the possible intellect be informed by the intelligible species which the agent intellect abstracts from the phantasm. Since the natural mode of knowledge is, therefore, through the abstraction of essences from sensible objects, it follows that God, because he is not a sensible object, cannot be known in his essence directly by the human intellect. If such a knowledge is to be had, and it is this in which perfect happiness consists, God must give the human intellect a special help.

Whatever exceeds the limits of a given nature, cannot be acquired by that nature except through the agency of another; and thus water does not flow upwards unless it be moved by something else. Now it is beyond the limits of any created nature to see God's substance, because it is proper to every created intellectual nature to understand according to the mode of its substance. But the divine substance cannot be understood, as we proved above. Therefore no created intellect can possibly attain to a vision of the divine substance except by the agency of God, Who surpasses all creatures. (C.G. III,52)

As a result of his speculation, St. Thomas has clearly argued himself into a definite position: Perfect happiness for man is the possession of God. No thinking man can deny this, and certainly all Christian philosophers accept this conclusion. But St. Thomas goes further and says that such possession can only mean an intuitive knowledge of God. No one can deny the validity of such a conclusion if he is willing to accept St. Thomas's reasoning. However, such a conclusion runs up against a blank wall: reason seems to demand a special help if man is to arrive at his ultimate end, but reason can see no way of getting this special help. Consequently, human reason must stop here and say to itself, a special help would certainly give an answer to the difficulty, but human reason can find no answer. As a consequence human reason seems to be right, but it cannot give the satisfying, the complete answer. We do desire the complete answer and, fortunately, theology comes to our help. This special help which God gives to the human intellect by which it may see God immediately is called the *Light of Glory* (*Lumen Gloriae*). This terminology is accepted because, speaking in an analogous manner, this special help does for the human intellect in its direct knowledge of God what the agent intellect does for the human intellect in its direct knowledge of sensible essence, or what light does for the sense of vision. Light, as we know, makes actually visible things which are only potentially visible in darkness. The agent intellect by its abstraction makes actually intelligible the essences of sensible objects which are only potentially intelligible before the action of the agent intellect. In fact, the agent intellect is frequently called a natural light by so many philosophers and the reason is easily discernible. So the *Light of Glory* makes the human intellect able to understand what it could not understand of itself. Because God is most intelligible in himself, there is no need of any help to make him more intelligible as there is need of an agent intellect to make sensible objects actually intelligible. But there is need of a special help for the human intellect whereby it may be able to know directly God who is intelligible.

To so sublime a vision the created intellect needs to be raised by some kind of outpouring of the divine goodness. For it is impossible that the proper form of anything become the form of another, unless this other bear some resemblance to the thing to which that form properly belongs. Thus light does not actualize a body which has nothing in common with the diaphanous. Now the divine essence is the proper intelligible form of the divine intellect, and is proportionate to it; for these three, understanding, means of understanding and object understood are one in God. Therefore that same essence cannot become the intelligible form of a created intellect, except because the created intellect participates in some divine likeness. Therefore this participation in a divine likeness is necessary in order that the divine substance be seen. . . . In order that the divine essence become intelligible, which is requisite in order that the divine substance be seen, the created intellect needs to be raised to that capacity by some higher disposition. . . . Now, owing to the fact that we derive our knowledge of intelligible beings from sensible things, we transfer the terms employed in sensible knowledge to our intellectual knowledge; especially those terms which pertain to the sight, which of all the senses is the highest and most spiritual, and therefore most akin to the intellect. It is for this reason that intellectual knowledge is called sight [visio]. And because bodily sight is not effected without light, those things which serve for the perfection of intellectual vision are called light; and so Aristotle compares the agent intellect to light, because the agent intellect makes things actually intelligible even as light somehow makes things to be actually visible. Accordingly, the disposition whereby the created intellect is raised to the intellectual vision of the divine substance is rightly called the light of glory; not indeed because it makes the object actually intelligible, as the agent intellect does, but because it makes the intellect able to understand actually. (C.G. III,53)

We have now reached the end of our quest of the nature of man's knowledge of God whereby man is perfectly happy. Man will never reach his last end and his highest perfection except by his union with God, the only object whose contemplation can entirely satisfy the highest powers of his soul and raise him to complete perfection. This union is effected by the Light of Glory, by which the human intellect is raised in power, whereby the divine essence is not only the object known but also the intelligible species of the human intellect. Along with this act whereby the intellect apprehends the divine substance, the will performs its act of enjoyment and rejoicing. Hence, the delight that the will finds in the possession of the vision of God follows the intellectual act of vision.

This perfect happiness transcends man and his nature, yet it seems, according to St. Thomas' speculation on the meaning of the knowledge which gives man perfect happiness, to be required in order that man may be happy. St. Thomas writes:

Since, then, it is impossible for a natural desire to be empty (and it would be, were it impossible to arrive at understanding the divine substance, for all minds desire this naturally), we must conclude that it is possible for the divine substance to be seen through the intellect. . . . It is sufficiently clear, from what has been said, what manner of vision this is. For we have proved that the divine substance cannot be seen by the intellect by means of any created species. Therefore, if God's essence is to be seen at all, it must be that the intellect sees it through the divine essence itself; so that in that vision the divine essence is both the object and the medium of vision. (C.G. III,51)

This very transcendency of the end of man implies a problem for the ethician. We have mentioned in the first chapter that ethics needs theology for completion or for an aid to clarify certain obscurities. The present problem of man's happiness and how he may obtain it is a case in point.

6. Ethics and Theology

Man's happiness must consist in the possession of God. This is a conclusion based on purely philosophical grounds. And more: according to the philosophical reasonings of St. Thomas, this happiness consists essentially in an act of the intellect, but not in merely any act of the intellect, but only in that act which will satisfy man's natural desire to know fully and to see directly the essence of God. This vision alone will give man perfect happiness, and it would certainly appear that man through reason itself can arrive at this conclusion. St. Thomas also appreciates that such a knowledge of God is not a natural knowledge, for it is not within the power of the human intellect to know the essence of God directly. Hence, if there is to be such a knowledge, God Himself must aid man to obtain it. Philosophy, however, knows nothing about such a help, whereas theology does, for it tells us that the Beatific Vision is the end of man and that it is to be obtained by the Light of Glory. Theology, then, gives completion to our philosophical quest for the end of man; it supplies the clarity to the obscurity of our philosophical speculation.

7. *Happiness for the Body*

Let us close this chapter with a word of caution. In our consideration of the end of man we have emphasized the soul and its activity; hence, there is danger of missing or forgetting the part to be enjoyed by the body in perfect happiness. The body is part of the human composite and so it seems that it too must participate in perfect happiness. Even when the soul is enjoying the Beatific Vision with its rational powers, it is not a soul that is wholly separated from the body. This union with the body is also had when man reaches his ultimate end, for "since it is natural to the soul to be united to the body, it is not possible for the perfection of the soul to exclude its natural perfection." (*S.T.* I-II,4,6) Before perfect happiness is attained, the body is as it were the servant of the soul and its instrument for such inferior operations as help man to gain perfect happiness; in perfect happiness, the soul, rewarding its servant, bestows incorruptibility upon it and permits it to share in its beatitude.

Consequently we must say that perfect disposition of the body is necessary, both antecedently and consequently, for that happiness which is in all ways perfect. . . . Antecedently, because as Augustine says "if the body be such, that the governance thereof is difficult and burdensome, like unto flesh which is corruptible and weighs down upon the soul, the mind is turned away from the vision of the highest heaven." Consequently, because from the happiness of the soul there will be an overflow onto the body, so that this too will obtain its perfection. (S.T. I-II,4,6c)

Although we have no philosophical proof of the resurrection of the body and, consequently, of the union of man's immortal soul with his corruptible body after death, still it seems befitting that such a union will take place and perfect happiness will be enjoyed by the whole man, both body and soul. This is the conclusion of St. Thomas:

Since it is natural to the soul that it be united to the body, it cannot be that the perfection of the soul would exclude its natural perfection. And so, we have to say that the perfect disposition of the body is required for the happiness which is perfect. (S.T. I-II,4,6c)

Readings

Aristotle, *Nicomachean Ethics*, book X.

Cronin, Michael, *The Science of Ethics*, I, pp. 46-88.

Farrell, W., *A Companion to the Summa*, II, pp. 1-20.

Gilson, E., *Moral Values and the Moral Life*, pp. 26-36; 37-51.

Higgins, Thomas, *Man as Man*, pp. 7-11.

Klubertanz, George, "Ethics and Theology," *The Modern Schoolman*, XXVII (1949), pp. 29-39.

Leibell, J. F., *Readings in Ethics*, pp. 35-129. The list of articles and authors which appear in these pages has been given in Readings at the end of Chapter I.

O'Connor, W. R., *The Natural Desire for God*.

——— *The Eternal Quest*.

——— "The Natural Desire for God in St. Thomas," *New Scholasticism*, XIV (1940), pp. 213-265.

Pegis, A. C., "Nature and Spirit: Some reflections on the Problem of the End of Man," *Proceedings of the American Catholic Philosophical Association*, XXIII (1949), pp. 62-79.

Rickaby, Joseph, *Aquinas Ethicus*, I, pp. 1-38.

Salmon, E., *The Good in Existential Metaphysics*.

Smith, G., "The Natural End of Man," *Proceedings of the American Catholic Philosophical Association*, XXIII (1949), pp. 47-61.

St. Thomas Aquinas, *Summa Contra Gentiles*, III, pp. 1-63.

———— *The Trinity*, trans. Sr. Rose Emmanuella Brennan, pp. 187-197.

CHAPTER III

THE MORAL ACT

1. Human Acts

Because perfect happiness is the absolutely ultimate end of man in so far as man is a rational being, only those acts which are the result of his rational nature, only those acts which are the result of knowledge and free choice, are conducive to this happiness. Now, because we have defined ethics as the practical science of the moral rectitude of human acts as means of obtaining perfect happiness, it follows that ethics is concerned with those acts which are the result of man's rational nature.

Clearly, then, we must divide the actions which man performs into two classes. Man has a complex nature. He is the agent of actions which are the same as those of minerals and brutes. *Minerals* —he is subject to the same laws of physics as stones and rocks; should he fall out of a door of an airplane which is flying above the ground he will fall to the ground like any stone or package would; his body is subject to the same chemical laws of attraction and repulsion as any other chemical substance of similar nature. *Brutes*—he experiences sensations of cold, heat, sex, reactions to external stimuli as they do. All of these are *acts of man*, that is, acts which man has in common with other creatures. These are necessary acts; of themselves, they are not under man's control, and, consequently, no rules can be set down for them. They are not voluntary acts and so they do not of themselves confer on man any perfection which is distinctly human. Indirectly, however, in so far as they are subject to the will or might influence the will, they are to be considered in the science of ethics. The consideration of these actions will be left to the chapter on the Passions. The *human acts*, however, are those which are proper to man because they proceed from the free will, that is, they are the result of deliberation of the intellect and the choice of the will.

Of actions done by man those alone are properly called human, which are proper to man as man. Now man differs from irrational animals in this, that he is master of his actions. Wherefore, those actions alone are properly called human, of which man is master. Now man is master of his actions through his reason and will; whence, too, the free-will is defined as the faculty and will of reason. Therefore those actions are properly called human which proceed from a deliberate will. And if any other actions are found in man, they can be called actions of man, but not properly human acts, since they are not proper to man as man. (S.T. I-II,1,1c)

Man, then, is capable of placing two kinds of acts: (1) A *human act* is one of which man is master. It is a deliberate act of the free will and one for which, therefore, man is morally responsible. Such an act is either good or bad. To study it in order to discover the ultimate reason why it is good or bad is the aim of the science of ethics. (2) An *act of man* is one of which he is not master, because he does not deliberately or consciously control it simply because he does not freely will it, and for which he is not morally responsible. Such acts, for example, are done in a state of distraction, in sleep, in infancy, or in reflex movements. Such acts have no ethical significance.

Since human acts are the proper acts of man and, consequently, are the acts with which the science of ethics deals, we must look a little further into their meaning. Such acts are characterized by three essential qualities: (1) *knowledge*; (2) *voluntariness*; (3) *freedom*.

KNOWLEDGE

A human act is one whose source is knowledge and free choice. The will depends upon the intellect. It desires only what has been known and presented to it by the intellect as desirable, and it chooses only what has been so presented. The intellect, then, must propose a good before the will can choose. Now this good proposed is not some general good, but a most specific or determined good which the intellect grasps as an end and thus proposes to the will. This good so grasped includes not only the object of the action which the will chooses, that is, the termination of the action, but it includes also the circumstances or the particular conditions of the object as well as the intention, that is, the reason why the action is chosen. Thus suppose I choose to kill a man in order to rob him. This would be a human act as far as knowledge is concerned if the three following factors were known to me: (1) The *object*, that is, that which terminates the action; e.g., if the person is an innocent man, the object is murder, for the fact that the man is innocent specifies the action. (2) The *end*, that is, the reason for desiring and choosing the external object; e.g., to rob him. (3) The *circumstances* are the peculiar conditions of the object, that is, the determinations of the object; e.g., the man I kill is my brother. These three elements constitute the end or object grasped by the intellect and in so far as they are grasped and in so far as they are presented to the will as good, the action which is chosen is a human act.

But not only is the intellect needed to propose the end to be attained, it must also pass judgment on the moral nature of the *means* to attain the end, as well as the suitability of the means to attain the intended end. We deliberate by reasoning about the means available, discarding the inappropriate and evaluating those which seem to be appropriate for attaining the end. The intellect must know and grasp all these elements of object, circumstances, intention and means before it presents them to the will for its choice of decision if the act which is done is to be a perfect human act.

VOLUNTARINESS

The statement that an act is a human act means not only that its source is in knowledge but also that it is caused by the will, that it is voluntary. The term voluntary is from the Latin *voluntas*, meaning will. A voluntary act is accordingly a willful act, one which proceeds from the will as from an internal principle or cause. But to proceed from will is not enough; a voluntary act must also include a knowledge of the end for the obtaining of which the will acts. Hence St. Thomas defines the voluntary:

It is of the nature of a voluntary act that its principle be within the agent, together with some knowledge of the end. (S.T. I-II,6,2)

We may, then, define a voluntary act as one *which proceeds from the will with a knowledge of an end.* But this should be clear from the nature of the will: as every will-act depends upon knowledge, so all voluntary acts presuppose a knowledge of end. Hence, a voluntary act is not purely and simply a spontaneous act which comes into being without some intention of the agent; rather, the reason why a voluntary act comes into being is the fact of knowledge of an end. Every voluntary act, true, is a spontaneous act, but not vice versa. For some actions may be called spontaneous that are performed without any knowledge of end as such, because they spring from an intrinsic principle within the agent. Such are the actions of animals, and those of our own that proceed from the sensitive appetite. In such actions we pursue our natural needs without consciousness of formal causality; we act for ends, but without being conscious of ends as such. Other actions may be called spontaneous because there is in the agent a principle not merely of action, but of action for an end. And, therefore, since their acting and their acting for an end are both from an intrinsic principle, their movements and acts are said to be voluntary.

FREEDOM

At first thought one might be inclined to identify voluntariness with freedom and to think that because an act is free it must be voluntary. This equivalence is not always the case. To be voluntary, an act must proceed from the will with a knowledge of the end. To be free, it must also proceed from the will, but without any intrinsic determination to an end. A free act, then, is one kind of voluntary act. It is a voluntary act which results from the choice among two or more alternatives, at least the alternatives of acting or not acting. In this life, with one exception, all voluntary acts are free acts, because the will-act can never be necessitated to a particular good which is its object. That one exception is man's wish or desire for perfect happiness. This desire proceeds from man's will but it is not a free act because he cannot choose otherwise.

As a result of this summary description of the human act we can now understand what we have known from experience and observation, namely, that human acts are morally imputable to agents just in so far as the agents are considered the sole moral causes, that is, in so far as these acts have their source in internal principles. The agents are considered to be such causes in proportion as they know what action they are doing and why, and freely choose to do it. An example will make these aspects of the human act clear.

Oliver Twist picks somebody's pocket. He may do this act simply because he wants to steal. He may do it because he is ordered to do so by Fagin, whose punishment he fears if he should not obey. Or, finally, Oliver may erroneously think that he recognizes his own pocketbook which he wants to recover.

Obviously, the physical act of taking from another is imputable to Oliver for in each case he performed the act of taking a pocketbook from another and he knew what he was doing and he freely chose to do it. But the moral imputability is not the same in each of the examples given. In the first case, Oliver is simply guilty of stealing. In the second case, there is some doubt as to the imputability because of the fear of an evil which may befall him. In the third instance, Oliver is clearly not guilty of stealing. Although, then, the effect is objectively the same, namely, taking something which does not belong to him, the acts cannot be imputed uniformly to Oliver. The reason for the difference lies precisely in the fact that the will is inclined to different known ends. To be voluntary the act not only must come from the intrinsic principle, the will, but it must come after knowledge of the end and circumstances surrounding the end of the act. But in every instance, Oliver has chosen freely because he had alternatives of acting or not acting.

To sum up. An act is voluntary if it proceeds from the will with knowledge of the end. An act is free if it is the result of choice. We return, then, to what we said at the beginning of this section, namely, that human acts are those which proceed from the intellect and the will which freely chooses. St. Thomas writes:

In order to make this clear, we must take note that the principle of some acts is within the agent, or in that which is moved; whereas the principle of some movements or acts is outside. For when a stone is moved upward, the principle of this movement is outside the stone; whereas, when it is moved downward, the principle of this movement is in the stone. Now of those things which are moved by an intrinsic principle, some move themselves, some not. For since every agent or thing moved acts or is moved by an end, as was stated above, those are perfectly moved by an intrinsic principle whose intrinsic principle is one not only of movement, but of movement for an end. Now in order that a thing be done for an end, some knowledge of the end is necessary. Therefore, whatever so acts or is moved by an intrinsic principle that it has some knowledge of the end, has within itself the principle of its acts, so that it not only acts, but acts for an end. On the other hand, if a thing has no knowledge of the end, even though it has an intrinsic principle of action or movement, nevertheless, the principle of acting or being moved for an end is not in that thing, but in something else, by which the principle of its action towards an end is imprinted on it. Therefore such things are not said to move themselves, but to be moved by others. But those things which have a knowledge of the end are said to move themselves because there is in them a principle by which they not only act but also act for an end. And, consequently, since both are from an intrinsic principle, i.e., that they act and that they act for an end, the movements and acts of such things are said to be voluntary; for the term voluntary signifies that their movements and acts are from their own inclinations. Hence it is said that, according to the definition of Aristotle, Gregory of Nyssa and Damascene, the voluntary is defined not only as having a principle within the agent, but also as implying knowledge. Therefore, since man especially knows the end of his work, and moves himself, in his acts especially is the voluntary to be found. (S.T. I-II,6,1c)

From this quotation we can gather that the human act is a willed act which follows the apprehension of something as desirable. Where there is strictly speaking no knowledge of an end, there is no will, and just as knowledge varies so the willed act must vary. In the preceding chapter it was shown how all creatures move or are moved to their end in different ways dependent on their natures. All things below man—the inanimate, vegetative and brute creatures—move towards their end but they in no wise recognize it. Consequently, they are moved by an Intelligence, whom we call God, who is external to them. True, their actions do spring from a source which is within them, nevertheless this source is not wholly internal, for the natures which they have and by which they act for their end have been given to them by this external Intelligence in order that he might move them to the end which he has chosen. Because they necessarily move according to their received natures, they are in no way responsible for their actions and, consequently, they cannot place moral or human acts.

Man, too, can move or be moved in this way. We have called such actions of man acts of man. But over and above such actions man can move in a purposeful manner: man can and does move because he recognizes ends or goods; and this recognition makes him responsible for his acts, because the cause is wholly within him. It also makes him responsible for his refusal to act in certain conditions. In this regard St. Thomas writes:

The word voluntary is applied to that of which we are masters. Now we are masters in respect of to act and not to act, to will and not to will. Therefore just as to act and to will are voluntary, so also are not to act and not to will.

Voluntary is what proceeds from the will. Now one thing proceeds from another in two ways. First, directly; in which sense something proceeds from another inasmuch as this other acts; for instance, heating from heat. Secondly, indirectly; in which sense something proceeds from another through this other not acting; thus the sinking of a ship is set down to the helmsman, from his having ceased to steer.—But we must take note that the cause of what follows from want of action is not always the agent not acting; but only then when the agent can and ought to act. For if the helmsman were unable to steer the ship or if the ship's helm be not entrusted to him, the sinking of the ship would not be set down to him, although it might be due to his absence from the helm.

Since, then, the will by willing and acting, is able, and sometime ought, to hinder not-willing and not-acting; this not-willing and not-acting is imputed to, as though proceeding from, the will. And thus it is that we can have the voluntary without an act; sometimes without the outward act, but with an interior act; for instance, when one wills not to act; and sometimes without even an interior act, as when one does not will to act. (S.T. I-II,6,3c)

Because a voluntary act is an act which proceeds from the will with knowledge of an end, we may distinguish between an act of *commission* and an act of *omission*. The former is done in order to obtain some end which is known by the intellect. A willed act of this kind may lead to external action or it may not, but whether it does or does not the agent is responsible for the willed act. Thus, for example, a boy may decide to lie to his parents if and when he is asked by them the time of his arrival at home the preceding night. Whether he actually lies when the parents question him or not, he has placed an act of commission, because he had willed that he would lie; he has placed a moral act.

The voluntary act of omission may be of two kinds: (1) One fails to perform an external act because he wills that this act be omitted. In these circumstances, the agent does not perform the external act, because he wills something else, but he should will this external act. Thus, a student may fail to give the proper advice to a fellow student over whom he has great influence, because he hopes that this fellow student and his wrong doing will be discovered by the authorities and be punished. (2) Or one fails to will not only the external act but also the internal in a situation in which he ought to make an act of the will. Thus, a student knowing that another student over whom he has great influence is associating with bad companions, makes no act of the will to help, but he should. In both of these instances of omission the agent is responsible for not-willing or not-acting, because he should will or act.

There is just one more distinction in the voluntary act which we must briefly touch upon. It is the distinction between the *commanded* and the *elicited* act of the will. We are conscious both of voluntary acts of the will that do not get beyond the will itself and of some that issue into movements of one or the other of the faculties under the control of the will. The former are called elicited acts of the will; the latter, commanded acts.

The elicited acts of the will follow one another in a certain order and are correlated with acts of the intellect. This correlation of will and intellect is a complex psychological process which can be studied in psychology. All we wish to do at the present is to enumerate the elicited acts of the will. They are six. Three are about the end: *wish, intention,* and *enjoyment.* Three are about the means: *choice, consent,* and the *use* of the powers to carry out the command. Although the command is an act of the intellect, and St. Thomas makes it such, still, since the command follows the will's choice and precedes the will's act of using the powers under its dominion, those acts which are performed by these powers are called commanded acts.

The act of the will is twofold: one is its immediate act, as it were, elicited by it, namely, to will; the other is an act of the will commanded by it, and put into execution by means of some other power; e.g., to walk and to speak, which are commanded by the will to be executed by means of the power of locomotion. (S.T. I-II,6,4c)

Because the will is an intrinsic principle inclined to the good known by the intellect, the will cannot will unless it wills something. Consequently the will may terminate in some object which involves no external activity, such as a man's love or hate for his fellow man. Such an act is an act, the object of which is an act of the will itself. This act of the will is called the elicited act of the will and it is wholly internal to the will itself. The will may terminate in an object which is external to the will itself; it may be the action of some other faculty which is under the command of the will, such as the freely chosen act of studying, or of singing, or of imagining some person, thing or activity. This is a commanded act of the will, and is physically distinct from the elicited act. If nothing more is sought than the exercise of that faculty, as when one goes merely to walk or swim, that action is the will's object. If the commanded act moves to some object proper to itself, as when the hand attempts to seize money or the eye to see an object, the object to be attained by the commanded faculty is also the will's object. The commanded act and the elicited act of the will, though physically distinct, constitute a voluntary unity: the commanded act is the means chosen by the will to attain its desired object. However, the truly human act is always and only the inner elicited act of the will. It alone is free, and the commanded acts are spoken of as free because they result from the will's free choice. Without the will they could not be free at all. Hence, the commanded acts derive all their intrinsic and essential good or evil from the elicited act. For example, a man resolves to commit murder. As soon as he determines to do so he is guilty, for the malice of an act is in the act of the will. If later he carries out his evil intention he may incur, in addition, the responsibility for supporting the wife and children of the murdered man.

2. *Circumstances Affecting the Voluntary Act*

Although the human act has been analyzed by considering separately the three different elements of knowledge, freedom, and voluntariness, we should not conclude that these three elements function independently of each other. We should never lose sight of the existential unity of the rational supposit we call man. "Actions belong to supposits," says St. Thomas. Not the will, not the intellect, but man acts; he acts by means of intellect and will. So, too, does he act by his body in conjunction with his intellect and will. All of these have a bearing on the moral act and should be taken into consideration when we are trying to perceive the moral act as it is. The cutting-up, the dissecting of the psychological process into distinct parts, should never make us forget the unity of the moral act.

I see a certain object; I love it; I want it; I choose what appears to me the most apt means; I proceed to get the object. I reach it; I enjoy its possession. The operations of the intellect and will in such a process are obviously successive and distinct. The morality of the act, however, is one, for this unity of the moral act is due to the intention of the will which directs and unifies all the resulting operations of intellect and will by its efficient causality. The moral act which embraces such a complicated psychological sequence has real unity. It is the unity of intention of the will to its end.

But because it is the whole man which acts and not merely the intellect and will, conditions extrinsic to these powers may affect them in their operations and so we must distinguish between a *perfect voluntary* act, which is one in which there is full knowledge and full consent of the will, and an *imperfect voluntary* act, which is one that lacks either knowledge or consent or both in some degree. It is these conditions which may affect the whole man, and which may modify his moral actions, which now have to be considered.

St. Thomas lists five modifying factors of knowledge and free choice: *violence, concupiscence, fear, ignorance, and habit.* Let us consider the five for a better understanding of the human act.

VIOLENCE

Violence is physical coercion. Violence is an extrinsic physical force applied to a nature by an extrinsic agent. Because violence causes in the subject a change which is opposed to its natural inclination, the subject does not concur in the change caused by violence. The classical example is that of a stone thrown upward. The motion is caused by an extrinsic principle and is against the natural inclination of the stone. We may, then, define violence as a movement from without tending to force the agent to act against his choice.

Violence is directly opposed to voluntariness. However, it cannot reach the will directly, for it touches only external acts and not the internal act of the will itself, in which voluntariness resides. We can continue to will the opposite, no matter how violently we are forced to do the external act. Hence, the act we are forced to do is voluntary, contrary to the will, so long as the violence is resisted. Somebody may have the physical force to make us do something but he cannot make us will it. The reason is to be found in the nature of the will itself. *First,* the will is an inclination to good. Now no good except the good in general can necessitate the will; all other known goods cannot necessitate the will. And more, since violence is a known evil it cannot move the will to act at all, for the will is inclined only to good. *Second*, the will is an intrinsic principle of action, an efficient cause of action to obtain some good which the intellect knows to be good; hence, no finite cause can immediately or directly cause the will to act.

Let us put it in another way. When we call something violent, we are referring to what is contrary to the inclination of an agent. Now the act of the will is an inclination towards a good known by the intellect. Hence, just as a thing is called natural because it follows its own, or acts according to its own, inclination of nature, so something is called voluntary because it is in accord with the inclination of the will which is so disposed because of an intellectually known good. It is, then, impossible for that which is violent to be voluntary; otherwise we would have to say the inclination of the will is towards an evil known by the intellect, which is not the inclination of the will.

As regards the commanded act of the will, then, the will can suffer violence, in so far as violence can prevent exterior members from executing the will's command. But as to the will's own proper act, violence cannot be done to the will. The reason for this is that the act of the will is nothing else than an inclination proceeding from an interior knowing principle, just as the natural appetite is an inclination proceeding from an interior principle without knowledge. Now what is compelled or violent is from an exterior principle. Consequently, it is contrary to the nature of the will's own act that it should be subject to compulsion or violence; just as it is also contrary to the nature of the natural inclination or the movement of a stone to be moved upwards. For a stone may have an upward movement from violence, but that this violent movement be from its natural inclination is impossible. In like manner, a man may be dragged by force but it is contrary to the very notion of violence that he be thus dragged of his own will. (S.T. I-II,6,4c)

Although, then, violence cannot affect the will directly, that is, the elicited act, it can affect the external, that is, the commanded act. It is difficult at times to determine how far an agent who is suffering violence is to be held responsible for the act, and this for two reasons: (1) Because an act may not be wholly due to violence, for a man may resist violence and yet to some extent cooperate with it. (2) Even when the violence is such as cannot be resisted, still the will retains its power of determining itself independently of the external force.

Because of the intimacy of violence with the voluntary act we may ask this question: Must one always resist the external act to which an aggressor is compelling us? We may answer by distinguishing between an act which is not evil in itself and one that is evil. If the action which the aggressor is forcing me to do is not evil, I do not have to offer any resistance. If, however, the action is morally evil, then, I must at least offer internal resistance, that is, I cannot will the evil action. Must I offer external resistance? Again, we must distinguish. We must offer that external resistance which is required to keep me from giving my internal consent to the evil action. Frequently, external resistance, even though it be ineffective in obtaining release from the violence, serves the purpose of showing one's lack of consent to the act to which one is being forced and in helping one to refuse internal consent to the external action.

Let us sum up what we have said about violence and the human act. The external or commanded acts of the will can be directly compelled by a force contrary to the inclination of the will. In so far as they are, they are called *involuntary* actions. But the elicited acts are always *voluntary*, since they are secure against all compulsion of this kind. And so, too, if the commanded acts are according to the will of the agent, they are called *voluntary*; but they are called such, not because they are voluntary in themselves, for since they are commanded by the will they are necessary, but by an extrinsic denomination, because they are subject to the will.

THE PASSIONS—CONCUPISCENCE

We have now seen that nothing from without can force the will to act; let us now consider whether anything within man can force the will. The great interior sources of violence are the passions.

If concupiscence were to destroy knowledge altogether, as happens with those whom concupiscence has rendered mad, it would follow that concupiscence would take away voluntariness. And yet, properly speaking, it would not make the act involuntary, because in beings bereft of reason there is neither voluntary nor involuntary. But sometimes in those actions which are done from concupiscence, knowledge is not completely destroyed because the power of knowing is not taken away entirely, but only the actual consideration in some particular act. Nevertheless, this itself is voluntary, according as by voluntary we mean that which is in the power of the will, for example, not to act or not to will, and in like manner not to consider; for the will can resist the passion. (S.T. I-II,6,7 ad 3)

Although St. Thomas does not use this terminology, we are now accustomed to speak of antecedent and consequent concupiscence and the meaning of these terms can be found in the above quotation. This terminology helps towards an understanding of the effect of concupiscence on the human act.

Antecedent concupiscence is that which is present independently of any act of the will; it arises unbidden by the will. Let us take the example of Baseball Player Tom, a man of irascible nature, who is standing at the plate ready to swing at the ball when the catcher flips the bat with his glove and Tom misses the ball. Tom flushes with anger. This anger is automatic and occurs before Tom realizes it. When sensible objects are presented to the sense appetites, these appetites are aroused instantly to feelings of anger, hatred, shame, joy, desire, etc. They arise spontaneously from the disposition of the body, from some hereditary weakness, etc.

Consequent concupiscence is present as the result of the will. Baseball Player Tom, after adverting to his rising anger, will not be reasoned with, but he deliberately fosters it, for he wishes to settle accounts with the catcher. He intentionally broods over the situation, vividly remembering what the catcher has done.

Having distinguished between these two kinds of concupiscence, we now return to the question of whether concupiscence affects the human act. The human act, we must recall, is characterized by knowledge, voluntariness and freedom of choice. If, then, concupiscence interferes with any of these elements it alters the human act. But let us see if and how this is possible.

Antecedent concupiscence may destroy both voluntariness and freedom. Concupiscence may be so strong or may arise so suddenly that it destroys all reason, and as a result the intellect can know neither good nor bad. As a consequence, the will, which is inclined only to good, is not inclined at all. Any act, then, which follows as a result of such concupiscence is neither free nor voluntary. Such acts happen with those whom concupiscence has rendered insane or mad either momentarily or permanently. For example, it is possible that the sight of one who has wronged a dear one may cause a person to be incapable of thought and, therefore, incapable of a willed act. However, this incapacity would not, properly speaking, make the actions performed by such a person involuntary—against the inclination of his will—but absolutely nonvoluntary. For in beings bereft of reason there is neither voluntariness nor involuntariness. Generally, however, concupiscence does not destroy all reason and, consequently, persons generally know what they are doing and freely choose to do what they do.

Antecedent concupiscence does not generally destroy freedom or voluntariness but rather increases the voluntariness of the act. Even though concupiscence might arise unbidden, nevertheless the agent who acts in such a state of passion usually is responsible for his act because he knows what he is doing and freely does it. We need only to consult experience to see that this is true. Let us take a common experience for an example of this situation. The death of a member of a family may influence one to promise many acts for the benefit of the soul of the deceased. It is certainly clear that the passion of sorrow arises here independently of any act of the will and this sorrow has had a direct influence on the will in its choice of choosing what it will do to help the departed soul. True, this sorrow is not free, for we are not considering one who chooses to have his relative die. But no one can say that such sorrow takes away all power of deliberation nor all inclination of the will. Nevertheless, such sorrow may make calm deliberation very difficult, for the motives to promise or not promise cannot be weighed with perfect impartiality. Consequently, the freedom of choice is limited, for the judgment is clouded by this sorrow. The will, however, is inclined more strongly towards one side than the other, for it wills to do what is most beneficial for the deceased. From this example we can conclude that deliberation is certainly limited; hence the element of knowledge is restricted by such passion, but the voluntariness of the human act performed under its influence is not decreased but increased.

Let us look at this proposition in more detail. The reason for saying that with such concupiscence the voluntariness of the human act is increased lies in the very nature of the sense appetite. The object of concupiscence is a sensible good. The desire of the will is towards the good perceived by reason. So if the will acts when concupiscence is present both the object of the will and the object of sense are in agreement and so there is greater voluntariness. Thus, the desire to be free from the physical inconvenience of sorrow will influence the will to act more readily, to be more inclined to choose those actions which are means of fleeing from the sensible evil, but at the same time the sensible evil interferes with calm deliberation because the motives for acting cannot be weighed with perfect impartiality, and the freedom of choice is impaired because of the strong inclination of the will to flee the sensible evil.

Consequent concupiscence does not lessen but increases voluntariness. It does decrease the freedom of the act, but not of the cause. Because consequent concupiscence is either deliberately aroused or fostered, it is voluntary in itself and any action which follows as a result of such concupiscence is imputed to the agent, for in willing the concupiscence the agent must necessarily will the results of such concupiscence in so far as he has knowledge of the result. Baseball Player Tom, in our example, deliberately broods over the action of the catcher. He knows that he is becoming angrier, but he continues to work himself into a rage which causes him to lose control of himself, and without knowing what he is doing, he hits the catcher with the bat. From this example, it is clear that the concupiscence, which we call rage or anger, is deliberately fostered; hence the agent is responsible for the passion. It is equally clear that he did not know what he was doing when he was striking the catcher, for he had lost control of himself. Because calm deliberation was impossible in such a state, he could not freely choose. The action of striking the catcher with the bat, therefore, was not a free act in itself; however, because Player Tom deliberately allowed himself to get into this state, he was responsible for the anger as well as for all which followed as a result of the anger in so far as he knew what would follow. The effect, then, is certainly voluntary for Tom willed it in willing the concupiscence; more, the effect which he willed is intensified by his passion which is in complete accord with his willed act.

Concupiscence does not cause involuntariness but, on the contrary, makes something to be voluntary. For a thing is said to be voluntary from the fact that the will is moved to it. Now concupiscence inclines the will to desire the object of concupiscence. Therefore the effect of concupiscence is to make something to be voluntary rather than involuntary. (S.T. I-II, 6,7c)

To sum up the influence of concupiscence on the human act: If the concupiscence is such as to destroy all power of reason, and it has arisen unbidden by the will, the act which follows from such concupiscence is not a human act; it is nonvoluntary, for it lacks both knowledge and free choice. If the *concupiscence* is *consequent* to the act of the will, it does intensify the voluntariness of the act, and may make the act involuntary in itself, but voluntary in cause; hence free in its cause, but not free in the act itself. *Antecedent concupiscence* may interfere with calm deliberation and in so far as it does, it destroys the perfection of the human act. But either kind of concupiscence, in so far as some deliberation is present, does not destroy the voluntariness of the human act, but rather adds to the intensity of the act because it adds sense attraction to the will attraction.

FEAR

Fear is an emotion arising from the apprehension of threatened evil, and prompts us to seek to avoid the evil. Because it is an emotion of the irascible appetite, fear is something arising within the agent itself because of some impending evil. In this respect fear differs from violence, which is something external to the agent and may be the cause of fear. Another way in which fear differs from violence is that fear is always concerned with an evil which is about to come to an agent, whereas violence is a present evil.

There is another way in which violence and fear differ. Violence causes an agent to perform an involuntary act; fear, however, in almost all circumstances, causes an agent to act voluntarily because the agent knowingly and freely chooses to perform the act to which he is inclined by fear. Thus St. Thomas writes:

Things done through fear and compulsion differ not only according to present and future time, but also in this, that the will does not consent, but is moved entirely counter to that which is done through compulsion; whereas what is done through fear becomes voluntary because the will is moved towards it, although not for its own sake, but because of something else, that is, in order to avoid an evil which is feared. For the conditions of a voluntary act are satisfied, if it be done because of something else voluntary; since the voluntary is not only what we will for its own sake as an end, but also what we will for the sake of something else as an end. It is clear therefore that in what is done from compulsion, the will does nothing inwardly, whereas in what is done through fear, the will does something. According as Gregory of Nyssa says, in order to exclude things done through fear, a violent action is defined not only as one whose principle is from the outside, but with the addition, in which he that suffers violence concurs not at all; for the will of him that is in fear does concur somewhat in that which he does through fear. (S.T. I-II,6,6, ad 1)

Of course, when we speak of fear being unable to destroy the voluntariness of the will, we are speaking of that fear which is antecedent to the act of the will and which does not take away the use of reason completely. Obviously, if the agent is thrown into such a panic that he loses all self-control, all power of reason, by which he can make a rational choice, his action will not be voluntary; hence there would be no ethical problem about such an action unless, of course, when after the fear has left him he does not disapprove of the act, if the act were objectively good, or approve of it, if it were objectively bad.

In most cases when fear is present, the agent retains the use of his faculties and is responsible for acting rationally. He is thus obliged depite his fear to refrain from acts which are unlawful, otherwise he is guilty of evil acts. There seems, however, to be an element of involuntariness about an act which is done as a result of fear. To explain this we must distinguish between the act considered in the abstract and the same act considered in the concrete.

It is true that if we look at an act done because of fear in the abstract, that is, apart from the particular circumstances in which it is placed, we might say that the act is involuntary, because the act does not proceed from the will but from something else which brought the fear. However, actions are always done in concrete circumstances, and when we consider the action done by reason of fear in the concrete it is always voluntary. Let us take an example. A bishop is brought before a court which is ruled by godless and militant anti-Christian leaders. The bishop is offered the alternative of denying his God or suffering torture until death. It is a question, therefore, of life or death. He chooses the latter. Now certainly no one would choose torture and death just for their own sake. The reason why the bishop is choosing a horrible death is because of the fear that the court has brought. Hence it would seem that such an action or election is completely involuntary. This is in the abstract, the action considered apart from the circumstances. But it is otherwise in the concrete. Let us look at the problem in the concrete.

Actually the bishop knows that he is faced with a terrifying dilemma: deny his faith and keep his life or affirm his faith and lose his life. He can think the situation over and conclude that there is no purpose of keeping his life if he denies his faith, for he will lose it eternally by denying his faith, so he wills to affirm his faith and to sacrifice his life although he wills it reluctantly. In this act of the will there is *absolute voluntariness*. If conditions were otherwise, he would not give up his life, but conditions are not otherwise. Hence, there is a practical situation with which he is faced, and in this situation the will chooses to do away with the lesser of two goods, his life, and to preserve the greater, his faith. Of course there is a certain amount of involuntariness here, for if conditions were different the bishop would preserve his life; hence he wishes that he did not have to give up his life; hence, too, there is a *relative involuntariness*, i.e., relative to other conditions he would not will to die, and relative to these conditions he wishes that he did not have to will the way he does. In other words, does the bishop give up his life because he wills it? We must say, yes. The circumstances are such that he does not will to keep his life. Is there reluctance? Yes, because he wishes that he did not have to give up his life. Hence, he is both voluntary and involuntary, as St. Thomas writes:

I answer that, as the Philosopher says, and likewise Gregory of Nyssa in his book, On Man, such things as are done through fear are of a mixed character, being partly voluntary and partly involuntary. For that which is done through fear, considered in itself, is not voluntary; but it becomes voluntary in this particular case, in order, namely, to avoid the evil feared. But if the matter be considered rightly, such things are voluntary rather than involuntary; for they are voluntary absolutely, but involuntary in a certain respect. For a thing is said to be absolutely according as it is in act; but according as it is only in the apprehension, it is not so absolutely, but in a certain respect. Now that which is done through fear, is in act in so far as it is done. For, since acts are concerned with singulars, and since the singular, as such, is here and now, that which is done is an act in so far as it is here and now under other individuating circumstances. Hence that which is done through fear is voluntary, inasmuch as it is here and now, that is to say, in so far as, under the circumstances, it hinders a greater evil which was feared; . . . And hence it is that what is done out of fear has the nature of what is voluntary, because its principle is within. . . . But if we consider what is done through fear, as outside this particular case, and inasmuch as it is repugnant to the will, this is merely a consideration of the mind. And consequently what is done through fear is involuntary, considered in that respect, that is to say, outside the actual circumstances of the case. (S.T. I-II,6,6c)

We must conclude, therefore, that actions done through fear are voluntary, but they are in a sense involuntary. In this respect fear differs from concupiscence with respect to the voluntary in the human act. Concupiscence is in harmony with the will, i.e., the sense appetite is attracted to a sensible good and the will is attracted to an intelligible good. The situation is different with fear. Fear is revulsion from some sensible evil, real or apparent, so that when it accompanies the will which is attracted towards the good there is a sensible aversion to the sense evil and an intellectual attraction to the rational good so that the evil of sense is accompanied by the good of reason.

He who acts from fear retains the repugnance of the will to that which he does, considered in itself. But he that acts from concupiscence, e.g., an incontinent man, does not retain his former will whereby he repudiates the object of his concupiscence; rather his will is changed so that he desires that which previously he repudiated. Accordingly, that which is done through fear is involuntary, to a certain extent, but that which is done from concupiscence is in no way involuntary. For the man who yields to concupiscence acts counter to that which he proposed before, but not counter to that which he desires now; whereas the timid man acts to that which in itself he desires now. (S.T. I-II,6,7, ad 2)

When we are considering this problem of fear we should recall that we are speaking about actions which are the result of fear, actions which are done *through* or *because* of fear, actions which are *motivated* by fear in such a way that if the fear were not present the action would not be done. One may do something *in* fear or *when* fear is present. A man may rob a bank in fear that he be apprehended, or a boy may go to a party in fear that his father may find out about it, but the reason for robbing the bank or going to the party is not fear, but avarice or pleasure. Hence, to act *with* fear is not the same as to act *from* fear. A person may act with fear and yet have such pleasure and voluntariness in the act that it would be done even if the fear were removed. An act which is done because of fear or from fear would not be done at all if the fear were not present. Thus, I give up my money to an armed bandit only because of fear of being killed.

Another fact that we should remember is that *positive law invalidates an act which is done because of fear*, not because the act which a person does from fear is not voluntary in itself, but because it is for the common good that an act so done be invalidated in certain cases. The conditions required for such invalidation depend on the particular legislation and the kind of act that is being legislated for. There is one condition, however, that is generally regarded as necessary in all cases, namely, that the fear be unjustly brought, that is, that it be brought by one who has no right to bring such fear to an agent. Thus contracts unjustly extorted through fear can be invalidated by positive law; the invalidation does not come from lack of voluntariness, but from the fact that positive law uses its authority to nullify such contracts for the common good.

IGNORANCE

Ignorance is another circumstance which may affect the human act. Ignorance is the absence of knowledge in one who has the faculty of knowledge. Hence, only rational beings are properly said to be ignorant. It is apparent just how ignorance may affect the human act, for since a human act is that which proceeds from the will with knowledge, anything which alters knowledge itself is bound to affect the human act. There are several cases of ignorance, and we will treat of them all.

If ignorance causes involuntariness it is in so far as it deprives one of knowledge, which is a necessary condition of voluntariness, as was declared above. But it is not every ignorance that deprives one of this knowledge. Accordingly, we must take note that ignorance has a three-fold relationship to the act of the will: in one way concomitantly; in another consequently; in a third way, antecedently. (S.T. I-II,6,8c)

To what degree then, does ignorance affect the voluntariness of human acts. To answer this question we must distinguish between the different kinds of ignorance.

Concomitant ignorance is ignorance which accompanies the performance of a moral action, but it is not the cause of the action. In other words, ignorance is concomitant when an action is done *in* ignorance, but not because of ignorance, and therefore would have been done even if ignorance had been replaced by knowledge. Consider this example: A man wishes to kill another man, but never has had the opportunity to do so. One day, while hunting deer, he shoots a moving object thinking it a deer and it is later discovered that he has killed the man whom he wished to murder. It is true that the hunter did not know what he was doing at the time that he did it. But it is also true that he has done wrong. Although the wrong was not planned as it happened, nevertheless, the wrong was not contrary to the wishes of the agent. He was not unwilling that this evil result should follow and he is morally responsible for the death. Since the ignorance which was present was not the cause of the action of shooting, such ignorance does not affect the voluntariness of the act. The voluntariness of the act is accounted for by other reasons.

Concomitantly, when there is ignorance of what is done, but so that even if it were known, it would be done. For then ignorance does not induce one to will this to be done, but it just happens that a thing is at the same time done and not known. Thus, in the example given, a man did indeed will to kill his foe, but killed him in ignorance, thinking to kill a stag. And ignorance of this kind, as the Philosopher states, does not cause involuntariness, since it is not the cause of anything that is repugnant to the will; but it causes nonvoluntariness, since that which is unknown cannot be actually willed. (S.T. I-II,6,8c)

Consequent ignorance (also called *vincible* or *culpable* ignorance) is ignorance which is consciously and voluntarily procured and fostered by the agent. There are two kinds of consequent ignorance: (a) The first, ignorance which is *directly willed*, i.e., the agent actually strives to remain in ignorance; he does not care to know so that he may plead ignorance as an excuse for what he wants to do. Thus, a student refuses to read notices or dodges those who might inform him about certain regulations of the school so that he may offer ignorance as an excuse for his misbehavior. This sort of ignorance is called *studied* or *affected* ignorance. (b) The second is *indirectly willed*, i.e., the agent simply neglects to learn but he does not actually wish to be ignorant. Thus one may make some effort to acquire knowledge, but not enough; one may think that he just cannot acquire knowledge, and after a little effort just gives up trying; one may know that the knowledge can be acquired, but be too lazy or careless to search for it. This ignorance is called *crass* or *gross* or *supine* ignorance, especially when there is question of a grave culpability, as when, for example, a student of medicine does not learn the use of common drugs during his medical studies and in consequence of his ignorance a human life is lost. Now, neither of these kinds of consequent ignorance makes an act involuntary, for the simple reason that the act done under their influence is due to that of which they are the effect. Or, in other words, because the ignorance is willed, the acts which the ignorance causes are willed.

What has been said is not to be interpreted as meaning that

these various kinds of consequent ignorance or vincible ignorance have the same degree of moral responsibility attached to them. The culpability of this ignorance depends on the amount of effort put forth to dispel it, and the amount of effort called for depends on the importance of the matter and the obligation of the agent to possess such knowledge. Every one, evidently, has some consequent or vincible ignorance, but since there is no moral obligation to overcome this ignorance, there is some consequent ignorance which does not have ethical value. A teacher of ethics or a lawyer does not need to know anything about nuclear energy; such merely negative ignorance is ethically valueless. But the ethical significance and the moral culpability are entirely different if the teacher of ethics teaches without knowing ethics or if the lawyer practices law without a knowledge of justice. Consequent or vincible ignorance has an ethical value only when the agent has a moral obligation to gain knowledge.

Ignorance is consequent to the act of the will, in so far as ignorance itself is voluntary; and this happens in two ways in accordance with the two aforementioned modes of the voluntary. First, because the act of the will is brought to bear on the ignorance, as when a man wills not to know, that he may have an excuse for his sin, or that he may not be withheld from sin, that is called affected ignorance.—Secondly, ignorance is said to be voluntary, when it regards that which one can and ought to know, for in this sense not to act and not to will are said to be voluntary as was stated above. And ignorance of this kind happens either when one does not actually consider what one can and ought to consider (this is called ignorance of evil choice and arises from some passion or habit), or when one does not take the trouble to acquire the knowledge which one ought to have; in which sense, ignorance of the general principles of law, which one ought to know, is voluntary, as being due to ignorance. Accordingly, if in either of these ways ignorance is voluntary, it cannot cause what is involuntary absolutely. Nevertheless it causes involuntariness in a certain respect, inasmuch as it precedes the movement of the will towards the act, which movement would not be, if there were knowledge. (S.T. I-II, 6,8c)

Antecedent ignorance is ignorance which is not willed and is possessed before an act is done and is the cause of the act in such a way that the act would not be done if ignorance were not present. For example: Many people are seeking and obtaining divorces and remarrying; many of these are ignorant of the law of God concerning divorces and remarriages; if they knew the law they would not violate the law. Hence, their actions are due to antecedent ignorance.

Ignorance is antecedent to the act of the will, when it is not voluntary, and yet is the cause of man's willing what he would not will otherwise. Thus a man may be ignorant of some circumstances of his act, which he was not bound to know, with the result that he does that which he would not do, if he knew of that circumstance. For instance, a man, after taking proper precautions, may not know that someone is coming along the road, so that he shoots an arrow and slays a passer-by. Such ignorance causes what is involuntary absolutely. (S.T. I-II,6,8c)

Let us suppose an automobile racer who has been around the race track six times and thinks that he knows the track well enough to speed up when he wishes. Coming to a turn he steps on the gas, but failing to negotiate the turn his car hurtles the wall and kills several spectators along with himself. If the auto racer has taken all due precautions, and if he thought that he could make the turn in spite of the speed, he is not morally responsible for the deaths, because the fatal action was done in ignorance and as a result of ignorance. If the racer had known, he would not have acted the way he did. His act is in no way voluntary because he did not will the evil which resulted from his act; the evil is involuntary, for he did not want it.

Antecedent ignorance is also called *invincible* or *inculpable* ignorance, which is ignorance that cannot be overcome because the requisite knowledge cannot be acquired. A person can be invincibly ignorant for one of two reasons: either he does not realize that he is ignorant, and so it does not cross his mind that there is any knowledge to be acquired; or he does realize his ignorance, but he just cannot acquire the knowledge.

It seems obvious that if a person does not know that he is ignorant but wills what his intellect presents to him as good or evil, he is responsible for what he wills even though what he wills is objectively the opposite of what he wills, for as we have said, a human act is that which is done as a result of knowledge and will. Thus we must say that if a person chooses to refuse to fight in the army because he thinks war is immoral, he is choosing a good because his intellect so enlightens his will. Such a person is ignorant but he does not realize his ignorance and he is therefore acting as he sees things.

On the other hand, a person might know that he is ignorant, but also realize that no matter how much time and energy he puts forth he cannot gain knowledge. If, as here, the knowledge cannot be gained by any means, no matter how difficult, the ignorance is *absolutely* or *physically* invincible. If the knowledge cannot be obtained by a reasonable amount of effort, such as normally prudent and good men would feel obliged to use in the circumstances, the ignorance is *practically* or *morally* invincible, even though absolutely it is vincible. Let us take an example of a baby sitter who is told by the parents of the baby that she must take a certain bottle from the medicine cabinet at a definite time of the night and give a dose of the medicine to the baby. She does take the bottle with the proper label and gives the baby a spoonful of the liquid. But the following morning the baby is dead. There is no doubt that the baby sitter could have left the house and sought out a chemist and asked him to analyze the contents of the bottle. But should we expect such extraordinary and unthought-of methods before the baby sitter gave the contents of the bottle to the baby? Of course we would not. A man may be physically able to walk a hundred miles to obtain a bit of information, but it would be unreasonable to expect this effort except in a matter of the utmost importance. Such ignorance is certainly practically invincible but absolutely vincible. Consequently, we must say that an action which results from such ignorance is involuntary.

It is not imputed as a sin to a man if he fails to know what he is unable to know. Consequently, ignorance of such things is called invincible, because it cannot be overcome by study. For this reason such ignorance, not being voluntary, since it is not in our power to be rid of it, is not a sin. Hence it is evident that no invincible ignorance is a sin. On the other hand, vincible ignorance is a sin, if it be about matter one is bound to know; but not, if it be about things one is not bound to know. (S.T. I-II,76,2c)

We may sum up all that we have been saying about ignorance with the following quotation from St. Thomas:

Ignorance differs from nescience in that nescience denotes mere absence of knowledge. Therefore whoever lacks knowledge about anything can be said to be nescient about it; in which sense Dionysius puts nescience in the angels. On the other hand, ignorance denotes privation of knowledge, i.e., lack of knowledge of those things that one has a natural aptitude to know. Some of these we are under an obligation to know, those, namely, without the knowledge of which we are unable to accomplish a due act rightly. Therefore, all men are bound in common to know what belongs to faith, and the universal precepts of law; and each individual is bound to know matters regarding his duty or state. However, there are other things which a man may have a natural aptitude to know, yet he is not bound to know them: e.g., the geometrical theorems, and contingent particulars, except in some individual case. Now it is evident that whoever neglects to have or do what he ought to have or do, commits a sin of omission. Therefore through negligence, ignorance of what one is bound to know is a sin; whereas it is not imputed as a sin to a man, if he fails to know what he is unable to know. Consequently, ignorance of such things is called invincible, not being voluntary, since it is not in our power to be rid of it, it is not a sin. Hence it is evident that no invincible ignorance is a sin. On the other hand, vincible ignorance is a sin, if it be about matters one is bound to know; but not if it be about things one is not bound to know. (S.T. I-II,76,2c)

HABITS

The last circumstance which we have to consider as a possible modifier of the voluntariness of human acts is habit. Because we will deal with virtue, which is a species of habit, in a future chapter, we are here interested only in one aspect of habit, namely, how it affects the voluntariness of the human act.

A habit, as we will see, is a somewhat permanent quality of an operative power resulting from repeated use of that power and as a result of this added quality the power is capable of operating more easily and promptly. As a result of habit the power produces its acts almost spontaneously and with little or no deliberation on the part of the agent. Now the manner in which habit modifies or affects the voluntariness depends on the manner in which it is acquired, and on the manner in which it is permitted to remain. Consequently, we may say the following about habit and its effect on the voluntary.

Some habits are freely acquired. A man may deliberately acquire the habit of driving an automobile or he may deliberately set out to become a crack pistol shot. Evidently these habits are voluntary in their cause, for the agent has foreseen the results of his habit. The acts, then, resulting from such a voluntary habit are imputable to the agent. Let us suppose, however, the case of a man who has deliberately acquired the bad habit of swearing. But then he desires to stop swearing and he makes the intention of not swearing again. If he inadvertently swears again because of the bad habit, such swearing is not imputable to him, because at the time he did not know what he was doing and it was involuntary.

We may freely acquire a habit, not because we want the habit, but because we will those acts which are habit forming. Thus a person may will to drink or to use narcotics or to smoke and know that such acts are habit forming. Obviously in willing the acts he must also will the habit.

Habits acquired involuntarily take away freedom in those acts which result from the habit. It is possible for a person to acquire a habit unintentionally either because he did not realize that he was performing the action so frequently or because he had no notion that such acts were habit forming. Thus there is the case of a boy of seven years of age who was a confirmed alcoholic. He had acquired the habit in ignorance that such drinking was habit forming. Again, there are some who have acquired the habit of using irreverently the names of God. They have learnt such expressions from their elders and it never occurred to them that such blasphemy was wrong or that a repetition of such speech would develop into a habit. In such cases the persons are not responsible for the existence of the habits or for the acts which inadvertently follow from it, so long as they are ignorant that they have the habit.

When, however, a person recognizes that he has such a habit, he must either will to retain the habit or to rid himself of it. Either the rejection or acceptance of the habit is a distinct act of the will. If the agent accepts the habit then it becomes a voluntary habit in itself and the acts which result are voluntary in cause. If he rejects the habit, the habit itself remains involuntary and the acts which result from it are involuntary just in so far as they are contrary to his desires.

We have now completed our consideration of the modifiers of the human act. St. Thomas treats of the first four in an explicit manner, but the last we have added in order that our treatment may be complete. But it is well to notice that these modifiers are applicable to what we might call normal people. There are certain neurotic or psychopathic conditions, abnormal conditions, which may either lessen or completely destroy voluntariness. Such abnormal conditions must, of course, be taken into consideration when judging the human act. However, we may say that when and if they do not interfere with knowledge, voluntariness, and freedom, they are within the realm of ethics; they are pertinent to ethics just in so far as they influence these elements of the human act.

3. *Direct and Indirect Voluntary*

We have considered the meaning of the voluntary and the conditions which are necessary for the voluntary. We also know what are the conditions and circumstances which may affect the voluntary act. We now have a means of judging every act as ethically significant. It is clear that only those acts which man consciously and deliberately elects to perform, and in the degree in which he performs them knowingly and willingly, are matters of ethics.

To perform a human act, then, requires the intention of the human agent. An intention means that the agent knows a purpose or an end which he perceives as good, either apparent or real, and that he elects to attain that end and to use the means to attain it. Clearly, then, man acts ethically when he acts to attain that which pleases him and when he wishes to act. But sometimes, necessarily attached to those acts which please man and which he wishes to do, there are consequences which do not please him and which he does not wish to attain. Thus, a captain of a submarine wishes to torpedo an armed merchant ship filled with cargo for the enemy, but at the same time he does not wish to kill the several hundred innocent women and children who are on the merchant ship. It is not always easy to decide the course of action one ought to follow in this and similar cases, for it is not always easy to say whether in willing the act we are always held accountable for all the consequences, and particularly, whether, if the consequences are bad, as in the above example, we are bound to refrain from performing an act to which these evil consequences are attached.

To study such cases is of vast importance to the ethician. In fact their importance can scarcely be exaggerated. Most cases of practical difficulty to decide between right and wrong, arise out of them. To understand such cases we shall have to distinguish between *direct* and *indirect* voluntary.

Here two points should be observed: First, a thing may be voluntary either in itself, as when the will tends towards it directly, or in the cause when the will tends towards that cause and not towards the effect (as in the case with one who wilfully gets drunk, for in that case he is considered to do voluntarily whatever he does through being drunk). Secondly, we must observe that a thing is said to be voluntary directly or indirectly: directly, if the will tends towards it; indirectly, if the will could have prevented it, but does not. (S.T. I-II,77,7c)

A *direct voluntary* act, then, may be defined as an act which terminates in an object which is willed as an end or as a means to an end. Thus a man kills a bird in order to eat it. He directly wills the killing of the bird as a means to an end, and he directly wishes the eating of the bird as an end. If an agent wills the end he must will the means to the end. If a man wills to get drunk, then he must will the actions which are done in the state of intoxication when he foresees they will happen.

An *indirect voluntary* act is an act which terminates in an object which is not willed as an end or as a means to an end, but which is foreseen in some way as attached to an end or means which is directly willed. Thus, the captain of the submarine wills the sinking of the merchant ship and he wills the firing of the torpedoes. At the same time he wills the killing of the women and children. But all of these effects are not willed in the same way. The sinking of the ship and the torpedoing are willed *directly*, for that is what the captain directs his actions to directly; the killing of the women and children are willed *indirectly*, for this effect is connected with the sinking of the ship but the captain does not wish it, nor is it the reason why he torpedoes the merchant ship.

The distinction between direct and indirect voluntary is most important, and we should clearly distinguish between the two. As a rule it is a simple matter to judge whether an act is directly voluntary, i.e., when we want the good effect or the evil effect. It is not, however, so easy to judge about the indirect voluntary, and whether we are responsible for the effects of the action, and whether we should refrain from doing actions which have a desired direct and an undesired indirect result.

The first question, namely, whether in willing an action which has a consequence which we do want, we necessarily will the consequences we do not want, is easily disposed of. If a human agent knows that attached to his act there are certain consequences, be they good or bad, then whether he likes these consequences or not, he is the voluntary cause of them and so he wills them, for in willing the action from which these consequences come, he must will the consequences even though they displease him. Such an act is called an act which is voluntary in cause, that is, the effect or a necessary concomitant of something which is directly willed. When we do an act we do the whole act, just as when we buy an automobile we buy the whole auto. So a man is said to will and be the cause of consequences which, taken in themselves, he would not wish to procure, just as in buying the automobile we really will to own the whole automobile though there may be some features about the automobile which may displease us, and even though we have no pleasure in owning some parts of it. The will, therefore, is the cause of the consequences which we do not wish, and if we have a knowledge that these consequences will follow from our act we are rightly held responsible for them.

But a serious difficulty arises. Granting that the agent is responsible for these consequences which he does not wish, is he obliged not to perform the action if the consequences which he does not want are evil? Now although we have not treated of everything which enters into the solution of this question, still this problem falls so naturally into the consideration of the voluntary act that we must treat of it at this time.

In discussing an action which has a twofold effect, one good and the other bad, we must understand that we are not considering the act in its individual circumstances of time, place, person, and intention, because in such circumstances every act is either morally good or bad. We are considering the act in the abstract, that is, apart from these circumstances, and in the abstract an act may be good, bad, or indifferent, morally. Thus, the act of reverencing God is morally good in itself; the act of blaspheming God is morally evil in itself; the acts of walking, writing, or speaking are morally indifferent. Indifferent acts are neither directed to a good or to a bad end in themselves. The goodness or badness of these acts is determined by the intention of the agent. Thus, walking to obtain exercise or legitimate pleasure is good walking; walking to commit burglary is bad walking.

Bad acts are of two kinds: (1) *Actions that are evil as regards the very substance of the act.* Such actions under all circumstances, if knowingly and willingly performed, are evil. The morality of such actions is absolute, for they are bad by their very nature and, consequently, they do not depend on particular conditions or intentions for their evil. Thus, hatred for God or murder or lying are bad in themselves and no circumstances imaginable could make these acts other than evil. (2) *Actions that are evil because of the lack of the right to perform them in the one acting.* In these acts the substance of the act is indifferent, but since the one performing the act has no right to perform it, the act is evil. Thus, to take the property of another may be either good or evil. It is evil if the one taking another's property has no right to do so because the owner is rationally unwilling that one take his property. This is the usual case. In some cases, however, taking another's property is not evil, as when a destitute, starving man takes from another's superfluous goods what he needs to survive.

With these distinctions, the question is restated: Do we have to refrain from actions from which there are two effects? To answer this question we must distinguish. (1) If both effects are good, then we can always act; this is clear. (2) It is also clear that if both effects are bad, we can never act, for the obvious reason that we must necessarily wish at least one of the bad effects, and in so wishing we do wrong. It is likewise true that if the means are bad we can never place the act even though the end may be good, for since the voluntary is necessarily related to the means as well as to the end, in electing the means, which are bad, we elect that which is evil. (3) If one effect is good and the other is bad, and this is the main difficulty, we can act under certain conditions. Even though we know that certain evil effects will follow along with the good effect we can act if the four following conditions are fulfilled:

(a) *The act is of itself good or indifferent.* If the act itself is evil, evidently it is forbidden, for there could be no morally good effects.

(b) *The good effect is equally proximate.* That is, the good effect is as immediately and directly the result of the act as the evil effect. In other words, the good effect cannot be the consequence of the evil effect. If the evil effect is the cause of the good effect, then the evil effect is *directly intended*, at least as a means to the good effect. But to directly intend evil is always wrong, for we are always bound to avoid directly what is morally bad, and to direct the will to an evil means is not to avoid moral evil.

(c) *The bad effect must be merely permitted.* The evil effect must not be desired in itself, but the good effect must be directly intended. For if the bad effect is desired in itself, evil is desired directly, and it is never morally permissible to will or desire evil directly. One can never do good, wishing at the same time to do evil. Thus, a doctor cannot give a patient morphine if he knows that it will be habit forming.

(d) *There must be a proportionate grave reason for permitting the foreseen evil effect to happen.* There must be a sufficient cause for permitting the evil effect. A sufficient reason is always required for the doing of an act from which an evil effect follows. And since the good effect is our excuse in the present case, the present condition amounts to saying that between the good and the evil effect there must be a proportion. No one could for the sake of a small good do an act from which a very great evil results. Thus, one cannot place his life in danger just to save his dog, but he could to save another person's life.

If these four conditions are fulfilled, an act, which in itself is either good or indifferent, is morally permissible, in spite of the evil consequences to which it leads. But if even one of these conditions be unfulfilled, then the act is forbidden. Following these rules we shall be able to compute when an act may morally be performed, which, though good or indifferent in itself, involves consequences that are evil. But of the two questions proposed, the first, namely, how far the effects of our actions may be regarded as voluntary, is the more important for our present purposes, for we are at present attempting to give a general account of what acts are voluntary and human and, therefore, are subject to ethical rules.

Readings

Aristotle, *Nicomachean Ethics*, bk. III, cc. 1-5.
Bourke, Vernon J., *St. Thomas and the Greek Moralists*, pp. 15-21.
Cronin, Michael, *The Science of Ethics*, I, pp. 28-46.
Farrell, W., *A Companion to the Summa*, II, cc. 2, 5-7.
Gilson, E., *Moral Values and the Moral Life*, pp. 52-60.
Klubertanz, George, "The Unity of Human Activity," *The Modern Schoolman*, XXVII (1950), pp. 75-103.
Leibell, J. F., *Readings in Ethics*. The following articles are useful for a study of the moral act:

"The norm of morality," Thomas Slater, pp. 155-156.
"The norm of moral rectitude," V. Cathrein, pp. 156-162.
"Human acts," Walter H. Hill, pp. 162-165.

"Hindrances to accountability," Michael Cronin, pp. 191-193.
"The passions," Arthur Devine, pp. 207-212.

Pegis, A. C., "Necessity and Liberty," *New Scholasticism*, XV (1941), pp. 18-45.
Phelan, G. B., "Person and Liberty," *New Scholasticism*, XV (1941), pp. 53-68.
Plato, *Laws*, bk. IX.
Rickaby, Joseph, *Aquinas Ethicus*, I, pp. 232-244.
Smith, G., "Intelligence and Liberty," *New Scholasticism*, XV (1941), pp. 1-17.
St. Thomas, *Summa Theologica*, I-II, qq. 6, 7, 11-17.

CHAPTER IV

THE PASSIONS

1. *The Need to Consider the Passions*

We have decided that ethics is concerned with human acts, which are acts that result from the recognition of a purpose and the means to the purpose, and from the choice of this end and this means. Man, therefore, acts ethically when he performs acts which are proper to man. We have also described the nature of these acts of the will. But lest there be a distorted view of the nature of the acts which man performs, we should recall that man is something more than an intellect and a will; man is also an animal and, although he acts strictly as a rational being when he acts freely, nevertheless, such acts are always in conjunction with his animal nature, for man always acts as a man. Now, because ethics is the science which treats of the moral acts of man, it must include in its field of inquiry the acts performed by the whole man who is both rational and animal, if it is to be a complete science of the human act. The passions of the human composite are precisely those aspects of the human act which must be the subject of scientific study if we are to have an exact knowledge of man's moral conduct.

It is not an easy task to describe the passions. Although almost everybody admits the fact of the passions, the different attitudes towards them as well as the investigations of them have served to confuse the general notion of the passions. From the beginning the Stoics and Epicureans were at odds over the meaning of the passions. The norm of goodness of the Epicureans was the natural impulses as expressed in sensuous feelings and desires, and so they gave precedence to the emotional side, wholly, or almost wholly, denying the rational side of man. The Stoics, on the contrary, held that man's emotional nature should be absolutely divorced from reason, and that the rational side of his nature should be wholly independent of emotion. For the Epicureans reason was the servant of the emotions; for the Stoics the emotions were rebels against reason and as such should be rooted out. An antithesis of this kind necessarily resulted in exaggeration which has historically persevered: On the one hand we have those who in a puritanical attitude have outlawed all the passions from the moral life, refusing them any legitimate function in the motivation, direction or control of conduct. On the other hand we have the attitude, and it is certainly modern, which identifies passion with all that is best in man: thus all of man's troubles, be they personal, economical, social, domestic or religious, are said to spring from the fact that man has not given his passions full play.

In much modern psychological literature the term *passion* generally signifies a strong uncontrolled emotion. By emotion is understood a complex feeling of a vivid kind following upon sensations or perceptions in which appetitive consciousness predominates. An emotion is called passion, when it becomes so strong that other appetites or sensuous movements are rendered passive by it, or when from habitual indulgence, it has produced a deep-seated inclination, or when it is the expression of a vehement tendency of temperament combined with a defective power of self-control. Understood in any of these senses its common characteristic is that in its presence the reflective and deliberate use of reason is practically arrested, or impeded.

2. The Meaning of the Passions

The Thomistic sense of the term keeps closer to the original meaning of the word. In a generic sense passion is a condition of being acted on by something distinct from the faculty or nature affected. More precisely it applies to faculties receptive of physiological change, and consequently is peculiar to faculties of man's animal nature, which as they are localized in corporeal organs are susceptible of physical qualifications. We may put it in another way. We know from the philosophy of man that there are cognitive aspects of consciousness. Sensation, perception, imagery, instinct, and memory all represent knowledge processes whereby the mind becomes possessed of a certain object. The term of activity, in each of these processes, is an object of which the mind has made itself the owner; the object becomes part of the subject in such a way that the object is part of the conscious data of the subject. But there is another group of functions, also mental or conscious in character, which may be said to be the reverse of the cognitive process, inasmuch as they project our consciousness towards an object as it is in itself, rather than as it exists in the mind. The term of activity in these processes is an object of which mind becomes a part; the subject becomes united to the object in such a way that the subject takes on the characteristics of the object. This sort of act is called in Thomistic terminology an *appetition* or *desire*. It is a process of what in modern terminology is called the mechanism of desire as contrasted with that of knowledge; and since desire is the result of cognition or knowledge, the desire must therefore stand in causal relationship to knowledge. The distinction between the two is clear in the theory of St. Thomas, as, for example, when he states:

For the act of the apprehensive power is not so properly called a movement as the act of the appetite; since the operation of the apprehensive power is completed in the very fact that the thing apprehended is in the one that apprehends, while the operation of the appetitive power is completed in the fact that he who desires is borne towards the desirable thing. (S.T. I,81,1c)

But appetite or desire may exist on a sensory or an intellectual level. In the former case it gives rise to feelings and emotions; in the latter to acts of the will. For the present we are interested in the fact of sensory appetite. Such an appetite is the product of a psychological power, since it includes the object of consciousness on the one side, and nervous activities on the other. All of us are familiar with what is meant by feeling. It is present in every act of our conscious life. St. Thomas clearly recognizes its presence. Any conscious act tends to produce feelings of pleasure or dissatisfaction. When the conscious act produces an effect which is not opposed to the inclinations of the agent, there is an experience of pleasantness; but as soon as a psychological operation meets with an impediment we feel dissatisfaction. Pleasant feelings are like signposts in consciousness pointing to conditions which are biologically as well as sensibly favorable to the organism; unpleasant feelings, on the other hand, are indications of unfavorable conditions such as overtaxed energies, injury, or distress. St. Thomas recognizes that such feelings are for the sensory or biological good of the individual to the extent of saying that the vigorous, healthy, and normal exercise of every growing power results in feelings that are satisfying and gratifying; whereas excessive activity or excessive restraint produces feelings of dissatisfaction.

Operations are pleasant, in so far as they are proportionate and connatural to the agent. Now, since human power is finite, operation is proportionate thereto according to a certain measure. Wherefore if it exceeds that measure, it will be no longer proportionate or pleasant, but, on the contrary, painful and irksome. And in this sense, leisure and play and other things pertaining to repose, are pleasant, inasmuch as they banish sadness which results from labor. (S.T. I-II,32,1, ad 3)

Such feelings of pleasure or dissatisfaction are connected with the sensible powers undergoing or being modified by a stimulation which either agrees or conflicts with the inclinations of the sense appetite. Consequently, we may define a feeling as *a consciously pleasant or unpleasant movement of the sense appetite.*

When such a feeling is characterized by notable physiological changes—glandular secretion, respiration, pulse beat, etc., we call it an emotion or passion. The changes are regarded by St. Thomas as parts of the passions. For him passions are *movements of the sensory appetites, following upon conscious recognition of some stimulus, and characterized by definite modifications in the normal activities of the body.* In an emotion or passion there are several psychological factors: (1) There is the *cognitive* aspect of passion, since it always originates in some kind of knowledge. It may be memories, images, perceptions, or apprehensions which are the origins of the stimulus that is consciously recognized; and it is essential to passion that the stimulus be in the cognitive consciousness before it can produce a passion. Thus a person, a gesture, a word, must first be recognized as something that is agreeable, pleasant or complimentary or beautiful to the spectator before it can arouse his love. (2) Then there is the *affective* phase of passion, which takes the form of an impulse or tendency or desire to project consciousness outward and attach itself, by a positive or negative attitude, to some external object or situation. Thus, for example, in love consciousness tends towards an approach or union with the object; in hate, towards a flight from the object. This phase of the passion is the essential constituent, and is always characterized by a feeling of pleasure or dissatisfaction. (3) There are *organic changes* which always follow the perception. These include the discharge of nervous energies and various reactions in the physiological system. Such reactions in the agent are the result of passive modifications caused by the stimulus which determines the organism to responses of an attractive or repulsive character.

So far we have explained the psychophysical element of passions. We might approach the same phenomena of our conscious life from the viewpoint of metaphysics, on which the solution of the problem of passions really hinges. To suffer a passion is, as we have seen, to feel or to receive something: something happens to our sensory appetite or desire, which consists in determining it in a definite way because an object or situation has been recognized. Now God, who is pure act, cannot receive anything and, consequently cannot experience passions. Leaving God we come to angels, who are not pure act, but who have different degrees of potentiality; there is, therefore, something which they have not but could receive. But such reception on the part of pure spirits is not properly called passion, but rather acts of the intellect and will.

Leaving the angels we come to man, where we find a greater degree of potentiality. We know that the human intellect has no innate ideas but that it must receive its knowledge from without. Man's faculty of knowledge must receive its knowledge from without. His faculty of knowledge must receive something from the object in order to know. His faculty of desiring is still more dependent, for it depends first on the idea which is caused by the object and then it depends on the object itself. Because the rational desires of man are not about things except by way of ideas which he gets from the things themselves, the rational desires of man are more passive than the intellect. Here again, we do not apply to the reception of intellectual knowledge and rational desire the terms passion or emotion, but rather call them acts of the intellect and will. But when we descend to the sense desires of man, we discover even greater passivity in them than in the rational desires, for the rational desires are based on what the reason apprehends as good, while the sense desires depend upon what is good for the soul as united to the body. Such desires, in other words, are immediately dependent upon objects of sense which directly affect the body and, therefore, change the passivity of matter into act; and through the body the soul is united to the object. Consequently, in sense desire there is found the greatest potentiality, for these desires, while they depend upon objects and the perception of objects, depend far more upon the perception of objects known as good by the soul, not as a rational good, but rather as a good of the sense. Such desires are called passions. Hence a passion is a modification of something received accidentally in the soul because of its union with the body. Because of this union the object as a sensible good calls up a response of attraction or repulsion that begins in the body and rises to the soul.

Before leaving this inquiry into the meaning of passion or emotion let us restate the whole in somewhat simpler terms. The soul is made up of intellect, will, and sensible appetite, among other constituents. The first two are rational, and the third is irrational: the third is the seat of the passions. In a disembodied spirit, or an angel, there are no senses, no sensible appetites, no passions. The angel, the departed soul, can love and hate, fear and desire, rejoice and grieve, but in the pure spirit these are not passions; they are acts of intellect and will alone. So man often loves and hates, and does other acts that are synonymous with corresponding passions, and yet there is no passion, though this experience is very exceptional. The man is working with his calm reason; his irrational soul is not stirred. To an author, when he is in the humor for it, it is a delight to write, but it is not a passionate delight. The will finds satisfaction in the act; the irrational soul is not affected by it. Or a penitent is sorry for his sins; he sincerely regrets them before God; his will is heartily turned away from them, and wishes that those sins had never been; at the same time he sheds no tears, his features are unmoved, not a sigh does he utter; and yet he is truly sorry. It is important to bear these facts in mind: else we shall be continually mistaking for passion what are pure acts of will, or vice versa, misled by the identity or name.

But on the other hand, passions are organic affections aroused by sensible goods or evils. We are all, for example, born with the five senses, yet each one of us is affected differently by the objects of these senses. We all like to hear things, but some of us are affected differently by the same sound. The sound of thunder or the sight of lightning will cause some to shudder, and perhaps to grow faint and pale. Some will control themselves at an athletic event or contest; others will lose control of themselves—when the team they favor scores, a bloom spreads over their faces, while a defeat of their favorite will also be apparent in their faces. We could multiply such examples. But the main point is to see that the passions are concerned with the irrational part of the soul, that part which affects the organic parts of the human composite—as the blush of shame. The characteristic mark of a passion is the sensible working on the body. Hence passions are characterized by a transformation of the normal conditions of the body and its organs in such a way that these changes appear in an external manner.

Hence, passions are common to man and brute, but impossible to an angel or a disembodied spirit. Nevertheless the names of various passions are often used analogically to denote affections of the will that are entirely, or at least chiefly, due to intellectual cognition, as when we are said to love science, to hate ignorance, to desire honor, to enjoy a joke, to admire virtue, to detest vice. These are mental states that arise from and pertain to the rational portion of the soul. But owing to the substantial union of the body and soul, such mental states will affect the body sensibly so that passions will be present. Such operations of the intellect and will, i.e., love of knowledge, laughter, shame, etc., are not concerned with the good or evil of sense, while the passions are. But though the sense appetite is distinguished from the will or rational appetite, yet they are not two wholly unrelated powers, since the one man is both will and sense appetite and rarely operates with the one power without the other being brought into play. There is a concomitance of the intellect and phantasm, so that an intellectual operation will move the phantasm and that so strongly that the body is notably moved. In like manner, what attracts the sensitive appetite will attract the *affective* will, though on reflection the *elective* will may reject it. On the other hand, a strong affection and election of the will cannot be present without the sensitive appetite being moved, and that so strongly that there is a notable movement in the body.

3. *The Main Divisions of the Passions*

Evidently all passions are not the same. But how are we to tell one from another and how are we to classify them? There have been different classifications given by, for instance, Francis Suarez in his *De Actibus Humanis,* Tractatus IV, Disputatio I; by Descartes in the *Treatise on the Passions,* Article 51 sqq.: by Spinoza in his *Ethics,* which closely follows Descartes; by Martineau, *Types of Ethical Theories,* Part II, Book I, Chapters V to VII; by Maher in his *Psychology,* Chapter XX. But no classification has been so successful or thoroughgoing as that of St. Thomas. Here we find an arrangement which is based on solid empirical observation, and which explains more satisfactorily the relation of the passions to human activity.

As we have said, passions properly so called are movements of the sense appetite, which are attended by a notable modification of the body. Such movements are the results of sense perceptions of objects which are attractive or repulsive to the desires or inclinations of the sense powers. Now the object presented by sense cognition may be agreeable to the body because it either brings pleasure or relieves pain, when the absence of the former or the presence of the latter is a discomfort to the animal nature, and there is in consequence of the cognition a sense movement towards the object; or the object may be disagreeable to the body, and there is a movement away from the object which is not accompanied by great effort or inconvenience. The power by which such movements are caused is called the *concupiscible* appetite. The passions relating to this power are called concupiscible. Or the object presented by sense cognition may be a sensible good, the attaining of which is beset with difficulties and results in strong effort; or a sensible evil, the escape from which requires difficulty and effort. The power in which this movement resides is called the *irascible* appetite; the passions relative to it, the irascible.

The sensitive appetite is one generic power, and is called sensuality; but it is divided into two powers, which are species of the sensitive appetite— the irascible and the concupiscible. In order to make this clear, we must observe that in natural corruptible things there is needed an inclination not only to the acquisition of what is suitable and to the avoiding of what is harmful, but also to resistance against corruptive and contrary forces which are a hindrance to the acquisition of what is suitable, and are productive of harm. For example, fire has a natural inclination, not only to rise from a lower place, which is unsuitable to it, towards a higher place, which is suitable, but also to resist whatever destroys or hinders its action. Therefore, since the sensitive appetite is an inclination following sensitive apprehension (just as natural appetite is an inclination following the natural form), there must needs be in the sensitive part two appetitive powers:—one, through which the soul is inclined absolutely to seek what is suitable, according to the senses, and to fly from what is hurtful, and this is called concupiscible; and another whereby an animal resists the attacks that hinder what is suitable, and inflict harm, and this is called irascible. Whence we say that its object is something arduous, because its tendency is to overcome and rise above obstacles. (S.T. I,81,2c)

Under the heading of these two species of passion we can place many subdivisions. But before outlining the different kinds of passions, some observations are to be made. First, the concupiscible and irascible appetites cannot be reduced to one principle, because at times these appetites are in conflict with each other as, for example, when man performs unpleasant tasks, against the inclination of his concupiscible appetite, in order that, following the irascible appetite, he may overcome difficulties to obtain a moral good. A man putting forth strenuous efforts to overcome the enticements of the flesh is such an instance. Now an appetite cannot be opposed to itself. Consequently, we must say that these two appetites cannot be reduced to one. Secondly, the same appetite that is attracted by a sensible good is repelled by the contrary evil. The power that desires the pleasant abhors the unpleasant. Thirdly, the irascible appetite arises out of the concupiscible. Before a man can make a strong effort to obtain a good or to avoid an evil, he must desire the good and hate the evil.

Let us now proceed to the kinds of passions. The classification has a twofold basis, one of which holds for the two species of appetites. This basis is the good and evil of the sense object. The other basis holds for the irascible appetite alone. This basis is the insuperable or superable difficulty of obtaining the good or avoiding the evil.

Accordingly there is a twofold contrariety in the passions of the soul: one, according to the contrariety of objects, i.e., of good and evil; the other, according to approach and withdrawal in respect of the same term. In the concupiscible passions the former contrariety alone is to be found; viz., that which is based on the objects: whereas in the irascible passions, we find both forms of contrariety. The reason of this is that the object of the concupiscible faculty, as stated above, is sensible good or evil considered absolutely. Now good, as such, cannot be a term from which, but only a term to which, since nothing shuns good as such; on the contrary, all things desire it. In like manner, nothing desires evil, as such; but all things shun it: wherefore evil cannot have the aspect of a term to which, but only of a term from which. Accordingly every concupiscible passion in respect of good, tends to it, as love, desire, joy; while every concupiscible passion in respect to evil, tends from it, as hatred, avoidance or dis-

like, and sorrow. Wherefore, in the concupiscible passions, there can be no contrariety of approach and withdrawal in respect of the same object.

On the other hand, the object of the irascible appetite is sensible good or evil, considered not absolutely, but under the aspect of difficulty or arduousness. Now the good which is difficult or arduous, considered as good, is of such a nature as to produce in us a tendency to it, which tendency pertains to the passion of hope; whereas, considered as arduous or difficult, it makes us turn from it; and this pertains to the passion of despair. In like manner the arduous evil, considered as an evil, has the aspect of something to be shunned; and this belongs to the passion of fear: but it also contains a reason for tending to it, as attempting something arduous, whereby to escape being subject to evil; and this tendency is called courage. Consequently, in the irascible passions we find contrariety in respect of good and evil, as between hope and fear: and also contrariety according to approach and withdrawal in respect of the same term, as between courage and fear. (S.T. I-II,23,2c)

All the passions, therefore, proceed radically from sensible love or sensible desire of the good which is to be possessed either by approaching a sensible good object or by fleeing from an object that is perceived as an evil. But as the modes of moving towards the good or fleeing the evil are various we have the classification of the passions. The *concupiscible* passions are those affections or modifications of the sensible appetite which are inclined to sensible objects as simply good or evil, that is, as good or evil which are immediate, or easy to obtain or avoid. The stages of the movements towards the good or away from the evil are three: (1) An initial responsive stage by which the appetite has simply a feeling of like or dislike for the object: an inclination to an object apprehended as good; an aversion to an object cognized as evil. (2) A progressive stage, by which it reaches out for the object or shrinks away from it: an inclination to embrace an object because apprehended as good but not yet possessed; an inclination to flee from an object not yet possessed and cognized as evil. (3) A quiescent stage in which it possesses the good it reached out for or endures the evil it could not escape: and an inclination to an object possessed and apprehended as good; an inclination to flee from an object possessed and apprehended as evil. Hence we have three passions in the movement of the concupiscible appetite towards good: *love, desire, delight;* and three in the movement of the same away from evil: *hate, aversion, sadness.*

In classifying the *irascible* passions we must bear in mind that their object is not good or evil as such, but good that is hard to get and evil that is hard to shun. The irascible appetite, therefore, is faced with a twofold contrariety in its object, namely, that between good and evil, and that between the surmountable or insurmountable difficulties of obtaining the good or avoiding the evil. Consequently, the movement of this appetite, unlike that of the concupiscible appetite which is simply turned towards the good and away from the evil, may be a movement towards or away from the same object, according as sense perception exhibits either the good that appeals or the difficulty that repulses. First, with regard to the good: if the difficulty seems surmountable, the passion aroused is an optimism of obtaining the good, or *hope;* if it is apprehended as a good which is impossible to get because of the difficulties involved, the passion aroused is a feeling of despondency, of the uselessness of effort, of *despair.* Secondly, with regard to the evil: this may be either an evil that is anticipated or expected, or an evil that is present and experienced. If the evil that seems to threaten one seems at the same time to be unavoidable, the passion aroused is that of *fear;* if, on the contrary, it is apprehended as a danger that can be overcome, the passion of *daring* is aroused. If, finally, the evil is present and one actually is experiencing the evil, there arises the passion of *anger.*

In this classification, we note that every passion has its contrariety, except that of anger. Anger is not a simple passion but springs from the concurrence of many, as St. Thomas shows and as we will later discuss. It presupposes hate of a harm inflicted, desire and hope of reparation or reprisal on the cause of it. If we wish to look for a contrary to it, we shall find that it is a freedom from the evil which is either the presence of a good, and then there is joy, or the absence of a good, and then there is sadness. Both of these are passions of the concupiscible appetite. There is, therefore, no contrary to anger, and the only way to escape from it is to calm oneself. If we make allowance for this exception it will be possible to draw up a classification of the passions according to pairs. The following diagram is such a classification.

THE PASSIONS OF MAN

Appetite	Object	Passions	Movement of Sense Appetite
Concupiscible	Good	Love	Sensible like of object
		Desire	Sensible approach to object
		Delight	Sensible possession of object
	Evil	Hate	Sensible dislike of object
		Aversion	Sensible retreat from object
		Sadness	Sensible possession of object
Irascible	Arduous Good	Hope	Sensible approach to object which is attainable
		Despair	Sensible approach to object which is unattainable
	Arduous Evil	Daring	Sensible approach to an evil which is an obstacle to a desired good
		Fear	Sensible retreat from an evil which is an obstacle to a desired good
		Anger	Sensible possession

From this diagram we see the following: Good objects generate in the concupiscible appetite a certain inclination in respect to the good. Such an inclination pertains to the passion of *love*, to which *hatred* is opposed in respect to the evil. Again, if the good is loved, but not yet possessed, it arouses in the appetite an impulse to acquire it. This pertains to the passion of *desire*, to which *aversion* is opposed in respect to the evil. Finally, when the good is possessed, it causes the appetite to rest, as it were, in the satisfaction of attainment. This pertains to the passion of *joy*, to which *sadness* is opposed in respect to the evil.

In respect to the irascible passions, the good not yet possessed arouses *hope* and *despair*, and in respect to the evil not yet avoided, we have *courage* and *fear*. As for the difficult good already possessed there is no passion in the irascible appetite, because such a good no longer has the aspect of difficulty. But with regard to the difficult evil which actually inflicts itself on the appetite, there is another kind of movement in the sense appetite, which is the passion of *anger*.

With this classification of the eleven passions, to which all other passions or emotions can be reduced, let us now consider them in some detail.

4. The Passion of Love

Quite evidently at the very root of the activity of the passions is love. For, if the passions are movements of the sense appetites, only a good, which is the end of all activity, can be the cause of sense movement. It is love which is first aroused by an object that is pleasant or good. It is love that is the source of the movement whereby the agent is directed towards a desired end in order that it may possess and enjoy it.

As a matter of fact, by extending the term a little, we can say that love is the cause of all movement in so far as an object, under the aspect of good, calls forth a response (and this is love) to a movement towards the object (and this is desire) in order that rest may be found in the object (and this is joy). Such a movement, as has been pointed out by Aristotle, is a circular movement: the object known as good moves the knowing subject towards itself and in it the subject will find rest. The movement stops in that whence the movement began. Now by this extension of the term to all circular movement we can distinguish three kinds of love. In love's most essential meaning—the first response of an appetite to an object known as good to the appetite or nature involved—we can distinguish the response of inorganic elements to each other, of animals to food and of men to good. The difference which distinguishes the first from the other two is that the knowledge followed is not the knowledge of the chemical or inorganic element itself, but of its Maker. The hydrogen element loves the oxygen element in the sense that while the oxygen is good for the hydrogen and the hydrogen responds to this goodness, it does not know that oxygen is good; it merely follows a blind drive of nature. Both animals and men, however, have knowledge and it is their individual knowledge which leads on their particular appetites.

Of course all three are to be found in man: there is the response, for example of his weight to the pull of gravity; of his ears to the melody of a light opera; of his rational appetite or will to the appeal of the beauty of a virtuous life. It is these last two in which we are principally interested at the present. In these the principal elements are the recognition of a good and the movement towards that good, one of which is a passive, and the other an active element.

Passion is the effect of the agent on the patient. Now a natural agent produces a twofold effect on the patient: for in the first place it gives it the form; and secondly it gives it the movement that results from the form. Thus the generator gives the generated body both weight and the movement resulting from weight: so that weight, from being the principle of movement to the place, which is connatural to that body by reason of its weight, can, in a way, be called natural love. In the same way the appetible object gives the appetite, first, a certain adaptation to itself, which consists in complacency in that object; and from this follows movement towards the appetible object. For the appetitive movement is circular, as stated in De Anima iii. 10 [Aristotle, De Anima, Bk. III,10,433b,24]; because the appetible object moves the appetite, introducing itself, as it were, into its intention; while the appetite moves towards the realization of the appetible object, so that the movement ends where it began. Accordingly, the first change wrought in the appetite by the appetible object is called love, and is nothing else than complacency in that object; and from this complacency results a movement towards that same object, and this movement is desire; and lastly, there is rest which is joy. Since, therefore, love consists in a change wrought in the appetite by appetible object, it is evident that love is a passion: properly so called, according as it is in the concupiscible faculty; in a wider and extended sense, according as it is in the will. (S.T. I-II,26,2)

Love, therefore, is an attraction to good as known. But there are two degrees of love, and the difference between them and their moral value is important. We have no difficulty in recognizing the difference between these two loves. The first type is what has been called *selfish love*. It must be understood that this word "selfish" is not used in a derogatory sense. Rather it is descriptive of that love which is attracted to objects because such objects offer some good to it. Such love seeks to own objects, to assimilate objects to itself, to use objects for its own good. Selfish love really has no regard for the substantial nature or personality of the object or person loved except that it belong to or is good for the one loving. All animal love, or the love of passion, is selfish love, or as is usually said, a *concupiscible* love.

In contrast to selfish love is what has been called *love of benevolence*. It is the love that includes the love of friendship and the love of God. Unlike the other love, this love does not seek to own objects, to use objects for itself; rather it sees in the object another self so that it has great respect for the individuality or personality of the object loved. It springs from an impulse or affection, a tenderness whereby love wills nothing but the good of the beloved. As a consequence of such love there is an intimate union in which mutual accord in the affections of the appetites and in the movements of the minds express themselves in similarity of desire and activity.

Rational love, as we so well know from experience, may be of either kind. We may love a man because he is virtuous in order that we may advance in virtue; or because virtue is that which God desires to seek in man. Now neither of these loves is the love of passion, or the product of passion, yet they are either concupiscible or benevolent love. They are not the passion of love because admiration of this kind is the part of spiritual or rational love; whereas sense attraction belongs to the love of passion.

If this is the nature of love, what causes it? There are just three causes of love, causes that are not mutually exclusive but rather so related that one is the condition for and is included in the other. They are similarity, goodness, and knowledge. We have said that an attraction of the lover for the loved is the origin of love. If this attraction is merely possessed by the senses, the love resulting is sensitive love, the love of passion; whereas the contemplation of goodness or beauty is the beginning of spiritual or rational love. Yet, though apprehension of the good by the intellect is necessary in order that love be spiritual, yet love is not measured by the knowledge we have of the object. Rather love is measured by the intensity of the attraction of the lover for the object loved, by the degree of complacency in the lover for the beloved.

The element of goodness is no less fundamental, for goodness is the one and only object that attracts any movement of the appetite. Be it a real or an apparent good, only good can be the object of love. It is not nearly so true that love is blind as it is that love has keener sight to see the good of persons and objects which to less penetrating eyes seem but evil and ugly.

Love, finally, is caused by similarity. We often hear the expression that opposites attract. This is far from the truth. The attraction is similarity. If we see in another the good that we ourselves possess, we are attracted to the good of the other as towards ourselves; in fact the other is another self. We desire for the other what we desire for ourselves just because the other is another self. It is from this kind of similarity that love of benevolence, either of friendship or of the love of God, arises.

The cause of the love of concupiscence, however, is not a similarity that lover and the object of his love actually possess; rather it is a similarity that the love is potentially able, desires, to possess. For that reason the love of concupiscence has utility for its purpose; it is attracted towards a good in order that it might possess it for its own purposes. He who loves with a love of concupiscence is hopeful that he can possess the known good. Hence the love of passion is a love of concupiscence: the sense knowledge of a known good moves the agent to possess, to own, the object.

Likeness, properly speaking, is a cause of love. But it must be observed that likeness between things is twofold. One kind of likeness arises from each thing having the same quality actually: for example, two things possessing the quality of whiteness are said to be alike. Another kind of likeness arises from one thing having potentially and by way of inclination, a quality which the other has actually: thus we may say that a heavy body existing outside its proper place is like another heavy body that exists in its proper place: or again, according as potentiality bears a resemblance to its act; since act is contained, in a manner, in the potentiality itself.

Accordingly the first kind of likeness causes love of friendship or wellwishing. For the very fact that the two men are alike, having, as it were, one form, makes them to be, in a manner, one in that form: thus two men are one thing in the species of humanity, and two white men are one thing in whiteness. Hence the affections of one tend to the other, as being one with him; and he wishes good to him as to himself. But the second kind of likeness causes love of concupiscence, or friendship founded on usefulness or pleasure: because whatever is in potentiality, as such, has the desire for its act; and it takes pleasure in its realization, if it be a sentient and cognitive being. (S.T. I-II,27,3c)

From these outlines of the causes of love, it is really remarkable how love shows us what we are. The objects of our love are so many reflections, mirrors as it were, giving us back accurate pictures of what we are or what we want to be. This is why the ancient philosophers could so truly say that a man is what he loves, and why it is so true to say "tell me who your friends are, and I'll tell you what you are," for whether the object be very far below and utterly unworthy of man, or very high, even infinitely above him, where his love is there is a statement of what man is. It is still more overwhelming, if we look into the effects of love.

It is altogether impossible to discuss the effects of love in this section. In fact we will never know them completely and appreciate them adequately until we reach our end. But we can touch upon them briefly. There is first of all the effect of union. In the love of concupiscence it is a union that is real, for the lover desires to bring about a real union with the object which he needs for himself. In the love of benevolence, the union is no longer real and material, but it is nevertheless an immediate union for it is love itself that is the union. And the object loved is only another self. This union is a union approaching as closely to identity as is possible without the destruction of either the lover or the loved so that there is a mutual sympathy, understanding, and mutual sharing in the good that each possesses.

How close this union is can be further clarified by looking at the second effect of love, inherence or indwelling. The very word inherence indicates that the bond of loves makes the beloved and the lover very nearly essential parts one of the other. The person or thing loved is never out of the mind of the lover; the mind of the lover is like a home where the thing or person loved moves about with complete familiarity, leaving an impression on every thought, image, memory, desire, so that once the object of love has passed out of the life of the lover, his mind is left lonely, desolate, empty. But let St. Thomas express it:

This effect of mutual indwelling may be understood as referring both to the apprehensive power and to the appetitive power. Because, as to the apprehensive power, the beloved is said to be in the lover, inasmuch as the beloved abides in the apprehension of the lover, according to Phil. 1, 7, For that I have you in my heart: while the lover is said to be in the beloved, according to apprehension, inasmuch as the lover is not satisfied with a superficial apprehension of the beloved, but strives to gain an intimate knowledge of everything pertaining to the beloved, so as to penetrate into his very soul. Thus it is written concerning the Holy Ghost, Who is God's love, that He searcheth all things, yea the deep things of God (I Cor. 2,10).

As to the appetitive power, the object loved is said to be in the lover, inasmuch as it is in his affections, by a kind of complacency: causing him either to take pleasure in it, or in its good, when present; or, in the absence of the object loved, by his longing, to tend towards it with the love of concupiscence, or towards the good that he wills to the beloved, with the love of friendship: not indeed from any extrinsic cause (as when we desire one thing on account of another, or wish good to another on account of something else), but because the complacency in the beloved is rooted in the lover's heart. For this reason we speak of love as being intimate; and of the bowels of charity. On the other hand, the lover is the beloved, by the love of concupiscence and by the love of friendship, but not in the same way. For the love of concupiscence is not satisfied with any external or superficial possession or enjoyment of the beloved; but seeks to possess the beloved perfectly, by penetrating into his heart, as it were. Whereas, in the love of friendship, the lover is in the beloved, inasmuch as he reckons what is good or evil to his friend, as being so to himself; and his friend's will as his own, so that it seems as though he felt the good or suffered the evil in the person of his friend. . . . Consequently in so far as he reckons what affects his friend as affecting himself, the lover seems to be in the beloved, as though he were become one with him: but in so far as, on the other hand, he wills and acts for his friend's sake as for his own sake, looking on his friend as identified with himself, thus the beloved is in the lover. (S.T. I-II,28,2c)

All the other effects of love follow from these two. From the union of the lover with the beloved follows ecstasy, because the lover when he truly loves is carried out of himself, and surely if our minds and hearts are buried in another we are carried out of ourselves. From this union follows zeal, for he who loves is moved against all that hinders his gaining the object of his love or against that which hinders the beloved from gaining all that he desires. And the intensity of our zeal for the beloved is the exact measure of the intensity of our love.

The discussion of love has been quite long. But it has served a purpose. St. Thomas puts it very simply: "love is the cause of all things the lover does." We can make this statement absolutely universal and say that love is the cause of everything that anyone does, and in saying so we come into contact with the First Cause of all action and of all being, God. He creates because He loves. And the very being and movement of things are caused by the act by which God loves Himself. It is because God loves Himself as the First Good that all other movements tend toward God, and so are movements of love. Love, then, in man is the cause of all movements and, since we are concerned with the passions at the present time, the cause of all passions. If we understand what love is, we will be able to understand what the other passions are.

5. *The Passion of Hate*

Love, then, is necessarily first among the passions. Since a passion of the soul implies first of all a movement of an appetite towards a sensible object which has called forth a response, the first movement of any passion must be found in love. We see the truth of this in the passion of hate which stands in opposition to love. Point for point hate is contrary to love. Just as there is a concupiscible love, or a sense attraction for a sensible good, so there is a sense hatred, or a sense repulsion from a sensible evil; just as there are spiritual loves of concupiscence and benevolence for the rational good, so there are spiritual hates for the rational evil. As the object of love, therefore, is good, that of hate is evil.

Since the natural appetite is the result of apprehension (though this apprehension is not in the same subject as the natural appetite), it seems

*that what applies to the inclination of the natural appetite, applies also
to the animal appetite, which does result from an apprehension in the
same subject, as stated above. Now with regard to the natural appetite,
it is evident, that just as each thing is naturally attuned and adapted to
that which is suitable to it, wherein consists natural love; so has it a
natural dissonance from that which opposes and destroys it; and this is
natural hatred. So, therefore, in the animal appetite, or in the intellectual
appetite, love is a certain harmony of the appetite with that which is
apprehended as suitable; while hatred is dissonance of the appetite from
that which is apprehended as repugnant and hurtful. Now, just as whatever is suitable, as such, bears the aspect of good; so whatever is repugnant, as such, bears the aspect of evil. And therefore, just as good is the
object of love, so evil is the object of hatred. (S.T. I-II,29,1c)*

And since we must define an appetite by its object, the good towards which the appetite is inclined, we must say that love is the
cause of hate, for we must love an object before we can hate its contrary. In other words, unless there are goods, or goals, towards which
appetites are inclined, there are no loves. If there are no loves,
there are no hates, for there is nothing from which we would turn
away.

Because love is the cause of hate, love is always stronger than
hate, for an effect can never be stronger than its cause. Yet at times
hate seems to be stronger than love. The reason is that hate is more
keenly felt than love. The sensible perception of a good is more in
accord with, more natural for, the sense appetite, than the sensible
perception of an evil. Thus, for example, the hate felt at the presence of pain or suffering appears to be greater than the love experienced in the presence of pleasure. Actually, however, the hate is
not greater than the love, for the only reason why we hate pain is because we love pleasure, and since pleasure is more habitual, more
natural, more in accord with the natural appetites, we do not experience love as keenly as we experience the hate in time of suffering since the latter is something out of the ordinary, something not
natural, something dissatisfying for the appetite. For the same reason we experience a keener love when the object of love is absent
than when it is present. It is also true that hate appears to be
stronger than love because a comparison is made between a hate and

a love which are not mutually corresponding. Thus, we say that we hate ice cream more than we love pie. Actually this is a false comparison; our hatred of ice cream is not greater than our love for no ice cream, which is perceived to be a good. There is no hate unless there is a love, and because love is an attraction to a good which is the end of all movement, hate can be only a turning away from an evil which would hinder the gaining of the good. Because, then, an appetite is concerned with ends, and hate with means, love must be stonger than hate, since movement towards an end is always stronger than towards the means.

So, too, as love has good for its object, nothing that is good in itself can be the object of hate. No one, therefore, can hate himself except accidentally, that is, in so far as he is deceived about his own nature or is attracted towards the apparent good and so hates the real good. Neither is it possible to hate the truth, for it is convertible with the good which all must desire, but accidentally one may hate a particular good, being under the mistaken impression that it is false and, therefore, evil.

6. The Passion of Desire

Desire is midway between love and pleasure or joy. We are attracted to good, and this is love; we take pleasure in the good that we possess, but if the good to which we are attracted is not possessed, we have desire. As a consequence, if we look at our desires we have a most infallible indication of what we love and what will give us pleasure.

And if we look at our desires, we will find that they are of two kinds. There is the sensible desire—and this is the passion—for sensible goods and it always carries with it the organic changes that are peculiar to all passions; there is also the desire in the intellectual appetite or will. The first belongs to our animal nature, because we desire such things as nourishment, drink, rest, exercise, and sex as do the brutes. These desires reach out for the goods to which the natural appetites are naturally inclined, and there are as many desires as there are appetites. Such desires, in a word, are as natural as the appetites themselves. The objects of these appetites and, consequently, of these desires are characterized by quantity, not by quality. That is to say, the good is sought for in a certain amount sufficient to supply the natural want, but this or that particular good is not sought. A hungry man, for example, as a hungry animal desires food; he is not particularly interested whether it be caviar or bread and butter. And at the sight of such good, there will be the physical reaction which we call passion.

But in man other desires may be and are directed to objects which we think good or desirable, not because they are necessary but because our apprehension presents them as desirable. If a thirsty man, therefore, demands champagne but not water, or a hungry man wants filet mignon but not roast beef, there is an intellectual desire, a desire for something beyond that which his nature demands. Similarly it is possible to desire wisdom and other spiritual goods which are proper to man and his rational desires.

Desire is the craving for pleasurable good. Now a thing is pleasurable in two ways. First, because it is suitable to the nature of the animal; for example, food, drink, and the like; and desire of such pleasurable things is said to be natural. Secondly, a thing is pleasurable because it is apprehended as suitable to the animal: as when one apprehends something as good and suitable, and, consequently, takes pleasure in it: and desire of such pleasurable things is said to be not natural, and is more wont to be called cupidity.

Accordingly desires of the first kind, or natural desires, are common to man and other animals: because to both there is something suitable and pleasurable according to nature: and in these all men agree; wherefore the Philosopher [Aristotle, Nic. Ethics III,11,1118b] calls them common and necessary. But desires of the second kind are proper to men, to whom it is proper to devise something as good and suitable, beyond that which nature requires. Hence the Philosopher [Rhet. I,11,1370a,18] says that the former desires are irrational, but the latter, rational. And because different men reason differently, therefore the latter are also called [Ethics, III,11,1118b,14] peculiar and acquired, i.e., in addition to those that are natural. (S.T. I-II,30,3)

From this it follows that natural desires are finite and limited, for the animal appetites are restricted to that which satisfies even though at different times we can desire different foods and drink, etc., since pleasure is an indefinite object. But the rational desire of man is in all senses infinite, since such a desire is subject to reason, and reason never stops this side of the infinite.

7. *The Passion of Aversion*

Opposed to desire is aversion. Just as desire follows love, so aversion follows hate. If the appetites are attracted to a good we wish to possess the good; if the appetites are turned away from an evil, we wish to flee from the same evil. Aversion is not precisely fear, though it is often confused with fear. Aversion is rather a passion that has an absent evil for its object. The evil is not present to us, but there is the possibility that it will come to us. It is an evil that is neither difficult to overcome nor imminent—these qualities belong to fear. Aversion is not caused by an evil object of which we are afraid, nor from which there is the danger that it will overcome us; we simply do not like the evil in aversion. Thus, we might feel aversion to a detailed account of an operation by a surgeon, or we might experience aversion to a murder which the newspapers have outlined in all its details. Evils of this kind are not present to us, yet we just do not like them and because of our dislike we experience an organic change.

8. *The Passion of Delight*

We all know the passion of delight, the sensible thrill, the feeling of well-being, the lightness of head and heart of which we are conscious when we have what we want. We might say that delight is the culmination of love and desire: we are joyful when we possess that to which we are attracted and which we desire. The passion of delight is so extensive a subject that it is impossible to discuss it fully in this section. All we wish to do is to touch upon the main characteristics of this passion.

We might point out, first of all, that delight like all passions is a movement of the sensible part of the soul. It consists in a pleasure which starts in the sense appetite when the sensible good suitable to a nature is consciously possessed.

Two things are requisite for pleasure; namely, the attainment of the suitable good, and knowledge of this attainment. Now each of these consists in a kind of operation: because actual knowledge is an operation; and the attainment of the suitable good is by means of an operation. Moreover, the proper operation itself is suitable good. Wherefore every pleasure must needs be the result of some operation. (S.T. I-II,32,1c)

Delight like desire may be either physical or spiritual. In fact, delight differs from joy precisely by reason of the difference between physical and rational pleasure. (S.T. I-II,31,3) If the good, the possession of which is the source of pleasure, is a sensible good, then we have delight, which is a passion. But if the good is a rational good, we have joy. So the animals, because they lack reason, and men, because they have sense appetites, have delight or pleasure; but man can experience joy and can turn pleasure into joy. Considered in themselves the spiritual joys are greater than the delights which the senses experience, for the spiritual joys deal with greater good, and our union with these goods is much more intimate, perfect, and enduring. The contrast between the joy which we experience when solving a mathematical problem and the pleasure of a cigarette shows us there is no comparison between the values of the two.

Yet the pleasures of sense are more keenly felt than those of the intellect, for several reasons. One is that sensible pleasures always effect organic changes, making the pleasure more vivid and therefore better known in intensity; another, that sense pleasure counteracts sorrow, while spiritual joys have no corresponding sorrow, except the sorrow of the loss, which again is experienced in the sense appetite.

If therefore we compare intellectual pleasures with sensible pleasures, according as we delight in the very actions, for instance in sensitive and in intellectual knowledge; without doubt intellectual pleasures are much greater than sensible pleasures. For man takes much more delight in knowing something, by understanding it, than in knowing something by perceiving it with his sense. Because intellectual knowledge is more perfect; and because it is better known, since the intellect reflects on its own act more than sense does. Moreover intellectual knowledge is more beloved: for there is no one who would not forfeit his bodily sight rather than his intellectual vision, as beasts or fools are deprived thereof, as Augustine says in De Civitate Dei. (De Trin. xiv,4)

If, however, intellectual spiritual pleasures be compared with sensible bodily pleasures, then, in themselves and absolutely speaking, spiritual pleasures are greater. And this appears from the consideration of the three things needed for pleasure, viz., the good which is brought into conjunction, that to which it is conjoined, and the conjunction itself. For spiritual good is both greater and more beloved than bodily good: a sign whereof is that men abstain from even the greatest bodily pleasures, rather than suffer loss of honor which is an intellectual good. Likewise the intellectual faculty is much more noble and more knowing than the sense faculty. Also the conjunction is more intimate, more perfect and more firm. More intimate, because the senses stop at the outward accidents of a thing, whereas the intellect penetrates to the essence; for the objects of the intellect is what a thing is. More perfect, because the conjunction of the sensible to the sense implies movement, which is an imperfect act: wherefore sensible pleasures are not perceived all at once, but some part of them is passing away, while some part is looked forward to as yet to be realized, as is manifest in pleasures of the table and in sexual pleasures: whereas intelligible things are without movement: hence pleasures of this kind are realized all at once. More firm, because the objects of bodily pleasure are corruptible, and seen pass away; whereas spiritual goods are incorruptible.

On the other hand, in relation to us, bodily pleasures are more vehement, for three reasons. First, because sensible things are more known to us, than intelligible things. Secondly, because sensible pleasures, through being passions of the sensitive appetite, are accompanied by some alteration in the body; whereas this does not occur in spiritual pleasures, save by reason of a certain reaction of the superior appetite on the lower. Thirdly, because bodily pleasures are sought as remedies for bodily defects or troubles, whence various griefs arise. Wherefore bodily pleasures, by reason of their succeeding griefs of this kind are felt the more, and conse-

quently are welcomed more than spiritual pleasures, which have no con-
trary griefs, as we shall state farther on (q.xxxv,5). (S.T. I-II,31,5c)

There are many causes of delight and joy flowing from love. But whatever we may indicate as the cause, it is essentially a union which is the effect of love. The conscious possession of a good that is suitable for us, the union of ourselves with the good whether that good be the good of memory or hope, of actual possession or possessed by a friend, is the reason for delight and joy. Inevitably the effect of pleasure and joy is an enlargement of the soul which is manifested by one's inclination to take in all the good of which one is aware. Such an expansiveness is easily seen in the pleasure afforded by some sensible enjoyment such as a good meal. The same is true in the spiritual order, for with the possession of the good there comes to a man the consciousness that he has added to his perfection and the resulting desire to be kind and considerate and good to others.

9. *The Passion of Sorrow*

As the union of love joins good to us and gives us pleasure and joy, so the union effected between ourselves and evil causes sorrow. Sorrow is not the same as pain, neither is sadness of soul the same as sorrow of body. The former is something which the intellectual appetite suffers; the latter belongs to the sense appetite, and is therefore, a passion. Both, however, originate from love, but indirectly through hate. Just as all movements of the appetites towards the good begin with love which originates with the soul being attracted to the good, so hate, which has its origin in love, is the cause of sorrow and pain.

Pleasure and pain can arise from a twofold apprehension, namely, from the apprehension of an exterior sense; and from the interior apprehension of the intellect or of the imagination. Now the interior apprehension extends to more objects than the exterior apprehension: because whatever things come under the exterior apprehension, come under the interior, but not conversely. Consequently that pleasure alone which is caused by an interior apprehension is called joy; and in like manner that pain alone which is caused by an interior apprehension is called sorrow. And just as that pleasure which is caused by an exterior apprehension, is called pleasure but not joy; so too that pain which is caused by an exterior apprehension, is called pain indeed but not sorrow. Accordingly sorrow is a species of pain, as joy is a species of pleasure. (S.T. I-II,35,2c)

Because sorrow implies not only an evil that is present, but also the perception of the evil, it is not too difficult to see that sorrow, interior sorrow, is much greater than exterior sorrow or pain. We often undergo exterior pain, which affects us through our bodies, in order to attain to some higher good desired by our will. And if we look over the sorrow and pains of life, we will discover that few can actually make a claim to spiritual or interior sorrow. Almost all of our sorrows are physical, opposed to the passion of pleasure, to sense pleasure. In the domain of spiritual joy there is real difficulty finding an opposite to joy, except sorrow for sin. Certainly there is no sorrow opposed to such intellectual joy as contemplation and knowledge bring (unless we have recourse to sensible nature, which might experience a fatigue of body as an accompaniment of such intellectual joy, but there is not a sorrow that is opposed to this intellectual joy). But by far sorrow is a passion, a sensible reaction to the exterior pain which comes to us.

The effects of the passion of sorrow are many. St. Augustine calls this passion a kind of sickness. (*The City of God*, XIV,7,8) Because it has its origin in a present evil, this passion can bring many other evils to man: it can weaken our power of command; wear down our power of resistance; interfere with our power of apprehension and even at times cause melancholy and insanity. The remedy for sorrow is pleasure, tears, sleep, but above all, the contemplation of truth, which seems to be far fetched, but is actually the surest and best means to dispel sorrow.

The greatest of all pleasures consists in the contemplation of truth. Now every pleasure assuages pain as stated above: hence the contemplation of truth assuages pain or sorrow, and the more so, the more perfectly one is a lover of wisdom. And therefore in the midst of tribulations men rejoice in the contemplation of Divine things and of future Happiness, according to James *1,2:* My brethren, count it all joy, when you shall fall into divers temptations: and, what is more, even in the midst of bodily tortures this joy is found; as the martyr Tibertius, when he was walking barefoot on the burning coals, said: Methinks, I walk on roses, in the name of Jesus Christ. (S.T. *I-II,38,4c*)

10. *The Passion of Hope*

In the last six sections we have gone through the concupiscible passions, those which, as we have pointed out, have for their objects either good which is not difficult to obtain or evil from which it is not difficult to flee. We have seen that love is the basic passion, the foundation of all action, the source from which springs every other activity. There were six of these passions. We must now consider the irascible passions, those which are concerned with good and evil as difficult to get or avoid. There are five of these passions, and the lack of balance comes from the fact that anger has no opposite. No one doubts that hope is a passion, but it is so easily confused with desire that some might hesitate to put it into the class of irascible passions. Yet it is not the same as desire; rather it presupposes desire and it is through desire that hope, like all the passions, is joined to the first of all passions, which is love. Thus there is an intimate connection between the concupiscible and the irascible passions. Because love is so fundamental, all hope or despair, all courage or fear, all anger take their rise from love and its consequent desire. Without the concupiscible passions there would be no necessity for the irascible passions.

Hope is not mere desire or movement towards an object that is apprehended as good. Hope, rather, is a movement towards a known good—and in this it presupposes desire—which is apprehended as difficult to obtain, yet possible. Hope, therefore, is a passion that deals with the difficult but in the confidence that victory can be had. It meets the difficulties that arise in its movement towards the good. Thus we may desire to graduate with the highest honors; but if we are sure that we are not capable of mastering several of the subjects, we will have not hope but desire, pure and simple. But if we know of the difficulties involved but still feel sure that we can, though with difficulty, overcome them, hope is the guiding motion of our pursuit of these honors.

The species of a passion is taken from the object. Now, in the object of hope, we may note four conditions. First, that it is something good; since, properly speaking, hope regards only the good; in this respect, hope differs from fear, which regards evil. Secondly, that it is future; for hope does not regard that which is present and already possessed: in this respect, hope differs from joy which regards a present good. Thirdly, that it must be something arduous and difficult to obtain, for we do not speak of any one hoping for trifles, which are in one's power to have at any time: in this respect, hope differs from desire or cupidity, which regards the future good absolutely: wherefore it belongs to the concupiscible, while hope belongs to the irascible faculty. Fourthly, that this difficult thing is something possible to obtain; for one does not hope for that which one cannot get at all: and, in this respect, hope differs from despair. It is therefore evident that hope differs from desire, as the irascible passions differ from the concupiscible. For this reason, moreover, hope presupposes desire: just as all the irascible passions presuppose the passions of the concupiscible faculty. (S.T. I-II,40,1c)

Because hope deals with the future, it would seem strange to say that there is hope in the animals. The animals never overcome the limits of space and time, of the present and the past, the concrete and the particular. Only the spiritual can rise above these limits and see into the future. Yet animals hope, and in this fact we see the essential nature of the passion of hope, namely, that it deals with the sensible appetite; we also see in this fact the uniformity, the metaphysical unity of the universe wherein appetites move all things which move. St. Thomas (S.T. I-II,40,3) insists there is a kind of hope in the animals, but a hope which follows from a knowledge that is not in the animals but in God. It is a kind of natural instinct—placed in animal nature by God, which will send the dog racing over the fields to catch a squirrel, but prompt him to stop when the squirrel has climbed a tree—to overcome difficulties when there is a prospect of attaining the object, but to leave off when this prospect vanishes.

11. *The Passion of Despair*

Set over against hope is the passion of despair: as hope is concerned with a good that is difficult to obtain, despair is concerned with a good which is impossible to obtain. But only thus far does their opposition or contrast go. In order to see why this limitation holds, let us recall that we can look upon all the passions, except pleasure and sorrow, as movements to or away from some end or goal, for passions are nothing more than activities of the sense appetites to obtain some good or avoid some evil.

But there is a difference between the concupiscible and the irascible passions. The concupiscible passions can be divided into pairs of opposites because they seek different goals: some seek the good; others avoid the evil. The irascible passions are grouped in pairs, but they are not movements in the same direction even though they have the same object: some go towards the object; others away from the same object. Hope and despair deal with the same difficult good, the one moving towards it, the other away from it. Hope is confident that the difficulties can be overcome and so moves towards the difficult good, but despair, in view of the insuperable difficulties, turns away from the good to which the agent was first attracted.

There are several causes of hope as well as of despair: knowledge and experience, youth and age. The most hopeful people in the world, according to St. Thomas, are the young people and the drunkards, for youth and wine are quite apt to paint the world in rosy hue. But hope and despair are also fostered by experience, for both knowledge and action make men sure of what they can do and cannot do; but, as St. Thomas points out, since it is not doing but thinking that causes us despair, experience gives us two motives for hope and one for despair.

The object of hope is a future good, difficult but possible to obtain. Consequently a thing may be a cause of hope, either because it makes something possible to a man; or because it makes him think something possible. In the first way hope is caused by everything that increases a man's power; e.g., riches, strength, and, among others, experience: since by experience man acquires the faculty of doing something easily, and the re-

sult of this is hope. Wherefore Vegetius says (De Re Millit. i): No one fears to do that which he is sure of having learnt well.

In the second way, hope is caused by everything that makes man think that he can obtain something: and thus both teaching and persuasion may be a cause of hope. And then again experience is a cause of hope, in so far as it makes him reckon something as possible, which before his experience he looked upon as impossible. However, in this way, experience can cause a lack of hope: because just as it makes a man think possible what he had previously thought impossible, so, conversely, experience makes a man consider as impossible that which hitherto he had thought possible. Accordingly experience causes hope in two ways, despair in one way: and for this reason we may say rather that it causes hope. (S.T. I-II,40,5c)

12. *The Passion of Fear*

Unlike hope and despair, which are movements about a good, fear and courage deal with evil. Fear is a passion that is the opposite of hope: a known evil which is hard to face, and which we feel we cannot bear if it does come, though we have some hope of escaping it. It is a passion which we might call a passion of defeat, but not the same as sorrow because it is concerned with a future evil rather than a present evil. Fear is dread that we experience because we apprehend a danger, an evil, which we do not like: the evil is not present to us and we hope to avoid it.

Fear regards a future evil which surpasses the power of him that fears, so that it is irresistible. Now man's evil, like his good, may be considered either in his action or in external things. In his action he has a twofold evil to fear. First, there is the toil that burdens his nature: and hence arises laziness, as when a man shrinks from work for fear of too much toil. Secondly, there is the disgrace which damages him in the opinion of others. And thus, if disgrace is feared in a deed that is yet to be done, there is shamefacedness: if, however, it be in a deed already done, there is shame.

On the other hand, the evil that consists in external things may surpass man's faculty of resistance in three ways. First by reason of its magnitude; when, that is to say, a man considers some great evil the outcome of which he is unable to gauge: and then there is amazement. Secondly, by reason of its being unwonted; because, to wit, some unwonted evil arises before us, and on that account is great in our estimation: and then there is stupor, which is caused by the representation of something unwonted. Thirdly, by reason of its being unforeseen; because, to wit, it cannot be foreseen: thus future misfortunes are feared, and fear of this kind is called anxiety. (S.T. I-II,41,4c)

The cause of fear is something that exceeds our power to repel and is external to ourselves. In general there are two causes of fear. The first is love of some object, because something is feared that is about to deprive one of that which he loves. Another cause of fear is the recognition that we do not possess the power to overcome the evil that is on the point of hindering us from obtaining what we love. We often hear the expression that we should fear sin. But really there is no reason to fear sin. After all, sin is wholly within our power; no one can trick us into it, we do not fall into it by accident. We might quite reasonably be afraid of the occasions of sin, because they do not depend upon us; but sin does. But we can be afraid of fear, for the objects which are the causes of fear are not completely under our control. The phantasms of terror, for example, which are caused by our sensible nature, are beyond our control. Thus we may fear that we will be threatened by the necessity of fearing.

Because fear is dread of evil, it leads to a desire to flee from the evil. But more than this. Physically fear causes depression, lowering of vitality, derangement of the digestive organs, and the inability of action. If a fear is great the imagination is excited, impressions are exaggerated, the power of judgment and reasoning is disordered, and control of attention is impaired. All this we know from our own experience.

13. *The Passion of Daring*

Fear is the passion of defeat, for fear is victory over the man who is frightened. Whereas fear gives up hope of conquering the evil and flies from the evil, daring or boldness is confident of victory over the evil and is the passion most contrary to fear. Like fear, daring has evil as its proper object, but the movements of the two passions are contrary: fear moves away from the evil; daring advances towards the evil hopeful that it will be overcome.

Just as the cause of fear is love for some object, so the cause of daring is love. But in the matter of fear connected with the good there is an evil, and so great is the evil that we despair of obtaining the good; in fact, in fear by fleeing from the evil we flee from the good which we hoped for. In daring, however, joined to the good there is an evil, but so great is the good and so great our hope of attaining it that we approach the evil with confidence, feeling that we can overcome it. Hence, daring has its origin in love through hope: because we hope to overcome the evil, we love the good which is present with the evil.

To appreciate the meaning of daring as a passion we ought to distinguish it from courage, which belongs to the rational appetite of man and is a virtue. Since the passion of daring depends upon sense knowledge it is aroused immediately at the perception of an evil to be overcome in the pursuit of a good; it rushes into danger without realizing the difficulties to be met, and consequently, it is easily discouraged. Thus a young boy rushes into a fight with a stronger boy because the stronger boy has said the object of affections of the younger boy is not pretty. But the younger boy rushes into a danger which he has not properly evaluated; he will also give up and run when the stronger boy has struck him with a fist that is directed to his eye. The daring was buoyed up by hope, but it was a hope that had no strong foundation in reality. The rational emotion of courage, on the other hand, depends upon reason. It is slower to movement; in fact, at the beginning there may be all the external manifestations of the passion of fear, such as trembling and organic disturbance. Sometimes in courage there is a misjudgment of the danger involved, but there is nothing that is not foreseen, except when the danger is actually less than was expected. Courage is not surprised or discouraged at difficulties, for it foresees them; it is not dejected because of defeat, because it expects it. It does not withdraw from evils or difficulties because it is based on hope that they are to be overcome. Courage is the virtue of a strong man, who fully realizing the danger, knowing all the difficulties and defects, still goes into the danger. We have the perfection of courage in the saints, who evaluating the evils of sin, the enemies of God, the defects and defeats and even death, plunge into all these dangers confident in the almighty power of God.

Daring, being a movement of the sensitive appetite, follows an apprehension of the sensitive faculty. But the sensitive faculty cannot make comparisons, nor can it inquire into circumstances; its judgment is instantaneous. Now it happens sometimes that it is impossible for a man to take note in an instant of all the difficulties of a certain situation: hence there arises the movement of daring to face the danger; so that when he comes to experience the danger, he feels the difficulty to be greater than he expected, and so gives way.

On the other hand, reason discusses all the difficulties of a situation. Consequently men of fortitude who face danger according to the judgment of reason, at first seem slack, because they face the danger not from passion but with due deliberation. Yet when they are in the midst of danger, they experience nothing unforeseen, but sometimes the difficulty turns out to be less than they anticipated; wherefore they are more persevering. Moreover, it may be because they face the danger on account of the good of virtue which is the abiding object of their will, however great the danger may prove: whereas men of daring face the danger on account of a mere thought giving rise to hope and banishing fear. (S.T. I-II,45,4c)

14. *The Passion of Anger*

The last of the passions is anger. It is also the strangest. Its strangeness is apparent for many reasons. We have said that it has no opposite; but, apparently making up for this deficiency, it unites in itself many other passions. More than this. All the other passions are divided from each other into opposites because of the contrariety of motions or movements, but anger has within itself the two movements. Like all the irascible passions, it has its roots in love, but unlike all the others, it arises from the union of many passions: in anger there must be, over and above love, sorrow that an injury has been done us and hope of revenge. Unlike all the other passions, it has a double goal, a goal of evil and a goal of good: it seeks revenge as a good to be desired, hoped for, and thoroughly enjoyed; it rushes aggressively at the injury done as at an evil to be remedied by demanding satisfaction.

When a man is angry, he wishes to be avenged on someone. Hence the movement of anger has a twofold tendency: viz., to vengeance itself, which it desires and hopes for as being a good, wherefore it takes pleasure in it; and to the person on whom it seeks vengeance, as to something contrary and hurtful, which bears the character of evil.

We must, however, observe a twofold difference in this respect, between anger on the one side and hatred and love on the other. The first difference is that anger always regards two objects: whereas love and hatred sometimes regard but one object, as when a man is said to love wine or something of the kind, or to hate it. The second difference is, that both the objects of love are good: since the lover wishes good to someone, as to something agreeable to himself: while both the objects of hatred bear the character of evil: for the man who hates wishes evil to someone, as to something disagreeable to him. Whereas anger regards one object under the aspect of good, viz., vengeance, which it desires to have; and the other object under the aspect of evil, viz., the noxious person, on whom it seeks to be avenged. Consequently it is a passion somewhat made up of contrary passions. (S.T. I-II,46,2c)

Anger differs from hate in many ways. Hate is a continuous affection against evil, something deep set; anger is an intense, impetuous, sharp passion that comes to a crisis quickly. Hate wishes evil to another because it is evil, anger because it is just. Anger wishes evil to come to its object in the sight of all men and with the full recognition of the sufferer as to why it has come; hate is satisfied even with a secret suffering, and, providing the evil be sufficient, it does not matter whether the sufferer be conscious of the reason why it has come. Thus an angry man may wish to see him who has injured him brought to a public confession; but one who hates desires to see him or what he hates even destroyed. The man in anger feels grief but not the man who hates. At a certain point anger stops and is appeased when full satisfaction is made, but not so hate. Thus hate is without limits, insatiable, it wishes not the evil of punishment but evil as such; anger is over when sufficient punishment is meted out. Consequently, we may say hate is directed to evil, but anger is directed to both good and evil.

The cause of anger is always an unjust act directed against him who is angry. This injury may be physical or nonphysical, real or imaginary. In other words, the real root of anger is another's contempt for us. Whoever is angry is angry at being despised, flouted to his face, and set at nought, either in his own person or in the person of one whom he venerates and loves, or in that cause that lies close to his heart. But the contempt that is the cause of anger must be a conscious contempt. We are never angry with those who unconsciously injure us. Moreover, anger is never aroused by an injury brought by those whom we consider of less importance than ourselves. A man who is sure of his own preeminence, his own ability, who has no doubt of himself, is not seriously bothered by whispers, jealousy, or the activity of rivals. It is the small man, the man who is not sure of himself and of his powers, who is angered. Again, if we suffer, but think that we deserve to suffer, we are not angry. But if we have suffered a wrong which has been done coolly and deliberately, then we are angry, because the slight is most considerable.

All the causes of anger are reduced to slight. For slight is of three kinds, viz., contempt, despiteful treatment, i.e., hindering one from doing one's will, and insolence: and all motives of anger are reduced to these three. Two reasons may be assigned for this. First, because anger seeks another's hurt as being a means of just vengeance: wherefore it seeks vengeance in so far as it seems just. Now just vengeance is taken only for that which is done unjustly; hence that which provokes anger is always something considered in the light of an injustice. Wherefore the Philosopher says (Rhet. ii,3) that men are not angry, if they think they have wronged some one and are suffering justly on that account; because there is no anger at what is just. Now injury is done to another in three ways: namely, through ignorance, through passion, and through choice, on purpose, or from deliberate malice, as stated in Ethics, v,8 [Nic. Ethics V,8,1135b,20-25]. Wherefore we are most of all angry with those who, in our opinion, have hurt us on purpose. For if we think that someone has done us an injury through passion or through ignorance, either we are not angry with them at all, or very much less: since to do anything through ignorance, or through passion takes away from the notion of injury, and to a certain extent calls for mercy and forgiveness. Those, on the other hand, who do an injury on purpose, seem to sin from contempt; wherefore we are angry with them most of all. Hence the Philosopher says (Rhet. ii,3) that we are either not angry at all, or not very angry with those who have acted through anger, because they do not seem to have acted slightingly. (S.T. I-II,47-2c)

The effects of anger are first of all something pleasant: we feel delight that evil has come to him who has injured us. We even feel satisfied in the hope that justice will be brought to him who has done us harm. This feeling, however, is on condition that the evil does not go beyond the bounds of reason. In this connection it must be noticed that of all the passions, anger is a human passion: anger always demands an evil proportionate to the injury done. There is no such comparison between the evil and the good in other passions. Consequently what we call anger in the animals is often sheer fright or hate. The further effects of anger are grave physical trouble such as inability to speak, fixation of the eyes, flushing of the face. The mental effects of anger are the inability to judge and reason.

15. *The Passions Are Natural*

There are two questions left relative to the passions. The first is: Are they good or bad in themselves? Are the passions, in other words, natural? And if they are natural, whence have they the quality of moral goodness or evil which is attributed to them? To this question or these questions we must say that in themselves the passions are neither good nor bad. All men have them, because they are the natural result of sense objects affecting the sense powers. Moreover, since the animals also have passions there can be no question of morality if the passions alone are considered. Morality, as we know, enters in when an act is willed and, consequently, morality is a quality of the passions when the passions are the object of the will. Sometimes the passions are aroused independently of

and antecedently to any act of the will. In so far as they are, there is
no morality in the passions. Sometimes, however, they are the result
of willing. Thus, a man may be sensibly attracted to a good; a good
that is sensibly attractive arouses the passion of concupiscence; such
a concupiscible love may be wrong because the will has chosen it
even when the intellect has shown it to be an evil. The intellect
and will can rule a passion, can convert one passion to another.
Thus, what is an object of the passion of hate can become, by reason and will, an object of love, and vice versa. So all the passions of
man become morally good or evil when they are integrated with the
rational powers of man. This seems to be the point of controversy
between the Stoics and the Aristotelians:

*On this question the opinion of the Stoics differed from that of the Peri-
patetics: for the Stoics held that all passions are evil, while the Peripatetics
maintained that moderate passions are good. This difference, although it
appears great in words, is nevertheless, in reality, none at all, or but little,
if we consider the intent of either school. For the Stoics did not discern
between sense and intellect; and consequently neither between the intellectual and sensitive appetite. Hence they did not discriminate the passions of the soul from the movements of the will, in so far as the passions
of the soul are in the sensitive appetite, while the simple movements of
the will are in the intellectual appetite: but every rational movement of
the appetitive part they called will, while they called passion, a movement
that exceeds the limits of reason. Wherefore Cicero, following their opinion (De Tusc. Quaest. iii,4), calls all passions diseases of the soul: whence
he argues that those who are diseased are unsound; and those who are unsound are wanting in sense. Hence we speak of those who are wanting in
sense of being unsound.*

*On the other hand, the Peripatetics give the name of passions to all
the movements of the sensitive appetite. Wherefore they esteem them
good, when they are controlled by reason; and evil when they are not controlled by reason. Hence it is evident that Cicero was wrong in disapproving (ibid.) of the Peripatetic theory of a mean in the passions, when he
said that every evil, though moderate, should be shunned; for, just as a
body, though it be moderately ailing, is not sound; so, this mean in the
diseases or passions of the soul, is not sound. For passions are not called
diseases or disturbances of the soul, save when they are not controlled by
reason. (S.T. I-II,24,2c)*

Because the passions can be under the control of reason, it is fitting that they should be obedient to reason, for, since man is composed of not only his rational nature but also of his sensitive nature, the goodness of man's acts is increased if not only the rational but also the sensitive appetites are moved to good. Moreover, if the passions are under the control of reason, the acts of the rational appetite are more intense and easier to perform so that the control of the sense appetites is a growth in the moral virtues of fortitude and temperance which would increase the virtues of prudence and justice.

16. The Passions Are a Cause of Conflict

The last question relative to the passions is: Why is there a conflict between the rational and sensitive appetites, if the passions are natural? St. Paul in his epistle to the Galatians has noticed this deformity in man: "The impulses of nature and the impulses of the spirit are at war with one another; either is clean contrary to the other." (*Gal.* 5,17) This same twisted condition of the spirit and the flesh has been noticed by many philosophers. We ourselves notice in our personal lives that our senses are not always in harmony with our better judgment, that there is a lack of obedience of the sense appetites to reason; hence there is often a struggle to be reasonable in thought and in action.

On philosophical grounds there is no explanation why this condition of contrariety of appetites should exist in the unity of the human person. If body and soul, reason and sense constitute a unity of being, why this distortion? We have to go outside of philosophy for an explanation. Theology will tell us that original sin is the reason for it. From the account of Adam and Eve as given in the book of Genesis, we know that all the children of our first parents are born with a nature that is at war within itself as a result of original sin. Revelation tells us that Adam and Eve before their sin were in a state of preternatural peace and harmony in which they possessed gifts that were something more than mere human nature, and in a state of supernatural grace in which they longed for things that were not within the reach of their human nature. These gifts and graces were lost after the Fall. The privation of these gifts and graces has wounded, left its mark on human nature. That wound we experience in several ways. In one way by the conscious fact of the struggle between sense appetites and reasonable acts. In another way by the sense of loss we experience in our longing for the Beatific Vision which is unattainable by our own natural powers.

Everything takes its species from its form, and we have said above that the species of original sin is taken from its cause. Consequently, the formal element of original sin must be considered in respect of the cause of original sin. But contraries have contrary causes. Therefore, the cause of original sin must be considered with respect to the cause of original justice, which is opposed to it. Now the whole order of original justice consisted in man's will being subject to God. This subjection, first and chiefly, was in the will, whose function it is to move all the other parts to the end. Hence, when the will was turned away from God, all the other powers of the soul became inordinate. Accordingly, the privation of original justice, whereby the will was made subject to God, is the formal element in original sin; while every other disorder of the soul's powers is a kind of material element in respect of original sin. Now the lack of order in the other powers of the soul consists chiefly in their turning inordinately to mutable good; and this lack of order may be called by the general name of concupiscence. Hence orginal sin is concupiscence materially, but the privation of original justice formally. (S.T. I-II,82,3c)

How are we to repair the wound inflicted on our nature; how are we to obtain the help to fulfill our desires for things above our natural powers? As theology has pointed out the end of man as the Beatific Vision, so it points out the remedies for these difficulties: divine grace. Consequently, original sin and divine grace are elements that we must take into consideration if we are to establish a science of ethics that is applicable to man as he exists. As we have said when treating of the end of man, these are matters of revealed truth, of belief; we can accept them or deny them. If we deny them, we cannot understand man as he really exists; we cannot establish an ethics for man. For this reason a completely philosophical ethics is impossible. As Maritain writes:

The moralist works on human life. His experience of man is that of real men—and they are in no pure state of nature. In the measure in which experience plays a part in moral philosophy (and it does so in great measure, and is fundamental), and in the measure in which the philosopher respects the data of experience, something more than that which is purely natural will enter into his philosophy: though in an obscure and implicit way, because he is not able to discern it. If he seeks to conceptualize and systematize it all in a texture of pure reason, with the sole aid of philosophy, he will construct in fact, not a purely philosophical moral philosophy dedicated to a homo possibilis, but a false philosophy, designed for a man as he is but with his axis awry. (Science and Wisdom, p.167)

Readings

Aristotle, *Nicomachean Ethics*, bk I, c. 13.
———— *De Somnis*, cc. 3-5.
Farrell, W., *A Companion to the Summa*, cc. 5-7.
Klubertanz, George, *The Philosophy of Human Nature*, cc. 9, 11.
Leibell, J. F., *Readings in Ethics*. "The passions," Arthur Devine, pp. 207-213.
McDougall, *Body and Mind*, pp. 312-329.
———— *Energies of Man, passim.*
Maritain, J., *Science and Wisdom*, pp. 48-59.
Moore, T. V., *The Driving Forces of Human Nature and Their Adjustment*, pp. 105-114; 115-144; 340-356.
Morgan, Clifford T., and Stellar, Eliot, *Physiological Psychology*, pp. 340-356.
Noble, H. D., *Les Passions dans la vie morale.*
Plato, *Republic*, bk. IV, *Timaeus*, pp. 70.
Renard, H., *The Philosophy of Man*, pp. 161-175.
St. Thomas, *Summa Theologica*, I-II, qq. 23-48.
Wild, John, *Introduction to a Realistic Philosophy*, pp. 109-115.
Woodworth, Robert S., *Experimental Psychology*, pp. 234-241.

CHAPTER V

THE MORALITY OF HUMAN ACTS

1. *The Meaning of Morality*

We now know that the last end of man is perfect happiness in the possession of God. We know, too, that human acts are the means to attain this end. We have discussed both the end of man and the essential elements of the human act as well as the circumstances which may affect its voluntary character. We must now discuss how the means are to be related to the end. We might put the problem in the form of a question: If human acts are the means to obtain perfect happiness, does it make any difference whether these acts are good or bad?

No one has ever said that it makes no difference. No matter whose ethical theory we study we have to conclude that everyone insists that only good human acts, the good life, are the means to perfect happiness. The ethical theorists, in truth, are reflecting the common conviction of all men. The expressions "good morals" and "bad morals," "acting like a man" or "acting in an inhuman way," are frequently used both in ordinary conversation and in public discourse about questions concerning public and private interests. Treason is not good moral action, patriotism is; lying is not good moral conduct, honesty is. These concepts are part and parcel of man's intellectual make-up. There may be, and often is, wide disagreement on what is morally good or bad, but there is no man who does not make a distinction between actions in terms of the good and the bad, the moral and the immoral. Those who perform the good acts are praised because their acts are approved; those who act in a bad manner are condemned because their acts are judged to be reprehensible. Because of this distinction which all men make between the moral and the immoral, we must conclude that men do judge that there is a wrong kind of human action that will not bring us to our last end, as well as a right kind which will.

From this common observation, then, we must conclude that all are agreed that *morality is a quality of human acts by reason of which some acts are called good and others bad.* But is this conviction of mankind, namely, that there is a right and a wrong of human actions, a true judgment? Why, in fact, are some actions considered right and others wrong, and why should we accept this distinction between the right and wrong of human actions? This is the problem of the present chapter.

2. *The Meaning of Good*

To solve this problem, we must consider the meaning of good and evil. In considering this, as well as in the whole of ethics, St. Thomas appeals to metaphysics so that ethics may be integrated with a theory of being. It was by showing how man is part of the whole system of being and subject to the metaphysical laws of action that we found the specific purpose of his being and his actions. Just as all beings have a definite purpose in their being and their activities, which purpose is always some good, so man as a part of the whole system of being works for a purpose. It is, then, by considering moral good and evil in relation to good and evil in being itself that we learn what moral good and evil are. Let us see what St. Thomas says about good and evil in general in order that we may follow this up with an inquiry into what moral good and evil are.

We must speak of good and evil in actions as of good and evil in things, because such as everything is, such is the act that it produces. Now in things, each has so much good as it has being, for good and being are convertible, as we stated in the First Part. But God alone has the whole fullness of His Being in a manner which is one and simple, whereas every other thing has its proper fullness of being in a certain multiplicity. Therefore it happens with some things, that they have being in some respect, and yet they are lacking in the fullness of being due to them. Thus the fullness of human being requires a composite of body and soul, having all the powers and instruments of knowledge and movement; and so if any man be lacking in any of these, he is lacking in something due to the fullness of his being. Hence, as much as he has of being, so much has he of goodness, while so far as something is lacking in the fullness of his being, so far does this fall short of goodness, and is said to be evil. Thus a blind man is possessed of goodness inasmuch as he lives, and of evil, inasmuch as he lacks sight. That, however, which has nothing of being or goodness, could not be said to be either evil or good. But since this same fullness of being is of the very notion of good, if a thing be lacking in its due fullness of being it is not said to be good absolutely, but in a certain respect, inasmuch as it is a being; although it can be called a being absolutely, and a non-being in a certain respect, as was stated in the First Part. . . . We must therefore say that every action has goodness in so far as it has being, whereas it is lacking in goodness in so far as it is lacking in something that is due to its fullness of being; and thus it is said to be evil, for instance, if it lacks the measure determined by reason, or its due place, or something of the kind. (S.T. I-II,18,1c)

A human act is only one of the many things that is qualified as good or bad. We apply the same adjectives to material things as to things of the mind. Do the terms goodness and badness have the same connotation in all cases? We say that a coat, an automobile, a watch is good. Why? If we analyze our reasons for saying so, we shall find out that in all cases it is because the things we qualify as good fulfill the end or purpose which by their nature, their makers, their purchasers they were intended to fulfill. And if we go further and ask, why do they so fulfill their end or purpose, we find out that it is because they possess that fullness of being, that complete-ness, that their nature calls for; that they are what they are supposed to be. Thus the end or purpose of a watch is to keep time. If it does so, it is because nothing is lacking to it which its nature demands. And so of other things. Their goodness, therefore, consists in hav-ing all the reality of being that their nature demands. Evil, then, is a lack of some portion of this reality.

We must, then, say that a thing is good in so far as it has being, or, contrariwise, a thing is a being in so far as it is good. Goodness and being are one. But although good and being are one, yet not all being is perfect good, or as St. Thomas puts it, not all being is good *simply* and *absolutely*. A man may have good hearing and good locomotive powers, that is, he may be good with qualifications, but he is not a good man unless he has all of that being that is natu-rally due to a man. Furthermore, all objects have an appetite for that perfection that is proper to their nature; that is, a plant to be perfect in its own species must have all that which the species re-quires, and so on through the different kinds of being: each has a tendency to be perfect in its own species, and if it does not arrive at the perfection proper to its nature it is because it has been pre-vented from achieving that end which in the proper conditions it would achieve. Hence, the good of any object is to be what it ought to be in its own species, to attain its natural perfection. This natural perfection is called the fullness of being. Hence a thing has fullness of being when it possesses all those perfections and parts and pos-sesses them in a way that is up to nature's standards. It is evident that only God is Absolute Being and Absolute Good, since He alone possesses all of the being that his nature demands.

If anything is lacking in any of the perfections which are natu-rally due to a thing, that thing is bad in so far as it lacks perfections. To be bad, therefore, it is not necessary that everything in an object be lacking; it is sufficient that it lack something which causes it to fall short of the standard of perfection set by nature. If complete absence of good were necessary to make a thing bad, then it would be impossible to speak of bad, for since bad is a lack, if everything were lacking it would be nothing. Consequently, to be bad an ob-ject must be good and lacking some goodness. Hence, whereas we can speak of two kinds of goodness, i.e., relative good and absolute good, we can never speak of absolute bad. And if we say that an object is bad if it falls short of the natural standard in any degree we have given the full meaning of the qualification bad. Consequently, we can say a thing is bad if it does not possess the fullness of being; we cannot say a thing is good without qualification unless it be all good. Thus a blind dog may be a good watchdog, but it is not a good dog; it may be good with qualification, but we do not say it is absolute good, but rather we say that it is a bad dog because it lacks its fullness of being.

Just as good is fullness of being, so human good is fullness of human being. A man to be good must have all the parts that belong to man naturally and must act in the way that is befitting to that nature which man possesses. Now parts are of many kinds. There are *integral parts*, e.g., hands, feet, head, etc., and there are *potential parts* or powers, e.g., vegetative, sensitive, rational, etc. All these parts, integral and potential, are necessary for the perfect man, and these are what we call the goods of man. As is clear, some of these have been given by nature, i.e., from the beginning, and in so far as man possesses them he is good. But others of these, i.e., the potential parts, although good, require exercise before they are perfect. Thus, for example, man has received a digestive tract, but its perfection is acquired only through exercise and this, together with other potencies of nature, is not directly under man's control; other potencies or potential parts, however, are under man's control, such as the acquisition of knowledge and the attainment of the real goods of life which finally lead to happiness. These are the goods of human acts and these alone are the subject of ethics. Since, therefore, good means the possession of being, it follows that moral good is that which bestows upon man moral being. In other words, the goodness of the human act is the fullness of the being that is proper to a human act. When a human act possesses that being which it should have then that human act is a good human act.

What, then, is the fullness of being that is proper to the human act? Human acts are for the purpose of attaining perfect happiness. If, therefore, they are of such a nature, of such a degree of perfection, as to lead man to his last end, they are rightly called good;

otherwise they are called bad. As a watch is not good if it fails to keep time, the end or purpose of its existence, so a human act is not good if it fails to advance a man along the way that leads to his ultimate end. And as man will have perfect being when he obtains his ultimate end, for he will have his perfect good, so an act that leads to man's ultimate end is good for it adds to his being.

We started this discussion of good by saying that good is that being which a thing should have in order that it may be what it should. Perfect good, then, is that being which a thing possesses in such wise that it is complete. Now since man is perfect as man only when he shall have reached his ultimate end, for only then does he possess his fullness or completeness of being, we must say that any act that helps him along the way to the acquisition of this perfect good is a good act. Here, then, we have a way of knowing whether a human act is good or not: whether it is a means to perfect happiness or not.

But here a difficulty arises. How do we know a human act leads to man's ultimate end? How do we know when a human action is good in itself? How can we know whether an act helps or hinders man in his pursuit of perfect happiness? If we could see men before us actually reaching their last end, we could examine how they did it and use the same means ourselves. But we cannot; as we see men passing out of life, we do not know who reach their last end and who miss it, nor do they come back to tell us which acts they found successful in gaining the end and which they found harmful. Hence the need of discovering some norm or measure of the goodness and badness of human acts.

3. The Meaning of and Need for a Norm

If we were to ask whether the act of cutting wood is good for a wood saw, or keeping time good for a watch, or producing oranges good for an orange tree, I am sure that we would all say that such actions are good for the agents that produce them. The reason we should give for our answer is that if things act the way they ought to act, the way their natures demand, or, as the physical scientists say, if things follow the law of their natures, they are acting well. Hence, if we know the nature of a thing, we can know what is good for that thing. The measure of the goodness of action is the nature of the thing that acts. An act, therefore, has something within itself by reason of which it is conformed to the nature of the agent that acts. Such acts are not determined good or bad by something outside the act, but rather by the nature of the acts themselves. Their goodness is intrinsic to the acts because the acts are the result of what the nature should do.

However, when we come to man and his acts, there is more than a little disagreement about how we determine the goodness or badness of human acts. What is the norm by which we determine whether the human act is good or bad? No one can doubt that all who have thought about the matter of good and bad of moral acts have admitted a norm, but the problem is: What is the correct norm? Let us see if we can find a norm.

A norm is a standard or measure or rule. It is something that remains fixed and constant with which we compare other things whose quality, size or nature we wish to know. A norm of morality, then, is a rule or measure of the goodness or badness of human acts.

A norm may be proximate or ultimate. We can recall that when we were studying arithmetic we learnt that if we wished to know whether a space or quantity was a yard wide or long, we must apply a yardstick to it. But we also learnt that the yardstick we used was not its own measure, but that the truth of its being a yard was to be measured by an official yardstick kept in London or Washington. The yardstick we used was, we may say, a proximate norm for measuring; it was something handy; something immediately applicable to the space or quantity we wished to measure. The yardstick in Washington or London was the ultimate norm, the reason why the yardstick we used was what it was, namely, a yard. Both of these norms are needed. The ultimate norm is required to guarantee the truth of the proximate norm; the proximate norm is required so that we may have a practical and immediate standard of judging.

We must also have a norm for morality. We have shown that man's ultimate end is the possession of God and that human acts are the means to obtain this end. However, not all acts are means to this end. It is only the good acts which will lead us there. But, unless we wish to make a mockery of life and to reduce all of man's life to confusion, we should have some way of determining what actions are good and will bring him to his end and what actions are bad and will not bring him to his end. There must be a proximate norm which we can use for judging of the goodness and badness of our moral acts; there must also be an ultimate norm which will guarantee the truth of the proximate norm. Our problem, then, is to discover these norms. Let us see whether we can.

4. *The Norm of Morality*

The means that we must use in discriminating right from wrong is the *human reason*. The reason for this statement seems to be clear, for if the highest good of man is the highest act of reason in a life of contemplation, to be prepared for and obtained by deliberately and freely performing acts in this world, then it is through reason that we discover and measure the goodness and badness of human acts.

Or to put it in another way. We know that a morally good act is one which makes towards progress of human nature on the part of him who does it, and one which is done freely. In like manner, a morally evil act is freely done and it is a hindrance to progress of human nature. Now, only that act can make for progress of human nature which befits human nature and suits it in its best and most specific character. What is best in man, what characterizes and makes a man a man, is his reason. Reason, then, is the norm or standard by which we can judge the morality of human acts. Progress in human nature is progress along the lines of reason. To make progress along the lines of reason, to be morally good, an act must be done deliberately and freely in accord with reason—not blindly as plants act, nor brutishly or on the impulse of passion as the brute animals act, however pleasant and beneficial the effects may be.

It appears, then, that if an act is done according to reason the act is good; if it is done contrary to reason the act is bad. Reason, then, is in some sense the norm of what is good and bad in human acts. However, reason is a power of man and it may be used rightly or wrongly. We surely cannot say that merely any reason is the norm or morality. We must say that only *right* reason is such a norm. But how are we to know when reason is right?

Since we are dealing with the norm of morality, it must be a question of right reason in the practical order. Now we know that in this order the end is primary and so right reason must be concerned with the ultimate end of man and the acts which are ordered to this end. We reason rightly, then, in this order when we judge rightly of the end with the intention to will according to this reason.

But such reasoning is not the result of the whims of the one who reasons; rather right reason about the goodness or badness of human acts depends on true knowledge, in the speculative order, of nature and its end. In the speculative order reason does not create or make its own truth or object. It does not manufacture truth; it merely discovers truth. It can accordingly be right or wrong, true or false. The only way that reason can discover truth is to be conscious that its judgments are in agreement with reality. Consequently, if we wish to discover whether human acts are good or bad we must know man's nature and his end. Knowing these, practical reason is the norm of morality if it reasons about them.

We have said that an act is good if it has that fullness of being by which it can lead man to his end. But how do we know that a human act may lead to man's ultimate end? How do we know when it is good? In the same way that we know whether the act of keeping time is good for a watch or the act of producing oranges is good for an orange tree: if they act the way their natures demand or, as the scientists say, if they follow the law of their natures. Hence, acts are good if they are conformed to natures, bad if they are not.

The same is true for man. If we know man's nature we know what human acts are good, what human acts are bad. Thus human nature is one norm of morality.

5. *The Proximate Norm of Morality*

But what is the meaning of human nature? Let us recall that we are concerned with the moral good, the highest good of man. There are many goods which man may enjoy, such as the sense good or the useful good, but these are goods only in a certain sense, goods with qualification. The moral good, however, is that which is befitting man without qualification, in the highest sense of the term; it is that which is befitting man as a unitary being, because it is that good which is befitting him precisely as a rational animal. Consequently, the norm of morality is not this or that aspect of man, but man considered completely in all his essential parts and in all of his essential relations.

Man's nature is more complex and the norm of morality must be discovered in this multiplicity of parts. Man has essential parts which may be said to be metaphysical, i.e., animality and rationality, or may be called physical, i.e., body and soul. He also possesses integral parts such as members and organs of his body. All these parts must be kept in harmony if man is to act as a unitary rational being. Such harmony means that the powers must be kept in their proper hierarchy: the lower powers receiving their needs but also contributing to the higher powers as is befitting reason. Thus, as Plato writes: the moral man "should ever so speak and act as to give the man within him in some way or other the most complete mastery over the entire human creature. He should watch over the many-headed monster like a good husbandman, fostering and cultivating the gentle qualities and preventing the wild ones from growing; he should be making the lion-heart his ally, and in common care of them all should be uniting the several parts with one another and with himself." (*Rep.* IX,598)

Besides the parts, man also has essential relations which must be included in the norm of morality. Man must preserve harmony not only within himself but also with other beings with whom he must work out his destiny. Man is not an isolated being but a part of God's creation all of which is moving towards its end under divine guidance. Man, then, must take his proper place and perform his proper function that is required of him by his nature, so that God's purpose in creation shall be attained. Man does thus by acknowledging that he is a creature and so has duties to his Maker; that he is a social being and must recognize not only his own rights but also his duties to his fellow men; that he is a proprietary being who must use the good of the universe in a rational manner.

Man is a *contingent* being. The adequate reason for his existence is not found in man himself, but in God, the supreme and most excellent Lord of all creation. Towards God man has the duties of religion. To refuse to fulfill these duties is to declare oneself self-sufficient and to subvert the order of dependence of the creature upon the Creator.

Man is a *social* being. Not only is man born into the society of the family, but he must also live in the society of men, wherein by mutual cooperation he obtains his proper physical, intellectual, and moral development. To refuse this cooperation is a hindrance to his own development as well as to that of others. Hence, all that contributes to such cooperation is good for man; all that prevents such cooperation is bad.

Man is a *proprietary* being. He must possess the material things of the universe in some way, in order that he may use them in a manner befitting his rational nature. Such possession or even dominion, however, is not absolute and unlimited but restricted by the perfect dominion of God, who intends that the material goods of life be used as a means of bringing man to his ultimate end. Hence, to possess the material goods and use them properly is good for man; to use and think of them as the ultimate good of man is bad.

In view of all these elements of human nature we might sum them all up by defining the proximate norm of morality as *human nature taken completely in all its parts and relations.* It follows, then, that a human act is good if it is perfecting or befitting a rational animal, created by God, living in the society of men, and using the material goods of the universe. A morally bad act is one not perfecting or befitting such a being. It also follows that because man possesses a hierarchy of powers the order of subordination of the vegetative and sentient to the rational must prevail in any conflict between them. Similarly, the hierarchy of relations must always be maintained so that in a conflict the relation of man to God must come first, the relation of man to society second, the relation of man to material goods third.

6. The Ultimate Norm of Morality

We have concluded that a proximate norm is one directly applicable to the things to be measured; we have also shown that human nature is the most direct rule by which we can measure the goodness or badness of human acts. But human nature cannot be the ultimate norm, for human nature is not the ultimate reason why human nature is what it is, nor the ultimate reason why human acts are good or bad. If, then, a human act is good or bad because it is befitting or unbefitting human nature, we may further inquire where human nature gets its goodness. The proximate norm must be guaranteed by an ultimate norm.

This need of an ultimate norm of morality should be evident or, at least, acceptable to one who considers the postulates on which the science of ethics is built. We know that God is the Creator of the universe. But God cannot be the Creator unless, first of all, he knows how he may imitate the divine essence and unless, secondly, he wills that it be so imitated. Ultimately, then, things are what they are because the divine reason knows the divine essence can be imitated in a certain way and God wills that it be imitated in this way. Now the divine reason and will directed towards created things is the eternal law. Hence, just as human nature is what it is because of the eternal law, so the goodness and badness of human acts are what they are because of the same law. The divine reason, then, is the ultimate norm of morality.

St. Thomas puts the whole matter of the norm of morality in a different way, but the meaning is the same. He writes:

In those things which are done by the will, the proximate rule is the human reason, while the supreme rule is the Eternal Law. When, therefore, a human action tends to the end, according to the order of reason and of the Eternal Law, then that action is right; but when it turns aside from that rectitude, then it is said to be a sin. Now it is evident from what has been said before that every voluntary action that turns aside from the order of reason and of the Eternal Law, is evil, and that every good action is in accord with reason and the Eternal Law. (S.T. I-II,21,1c) . . . Now it is from the Eternal Law, which is the Divine Reason, that human reason is the rule of the human will, from which the human will derives its goodness. (S.T. I-II,19,4c)

According to the Thomistic view *right reason* is the norm of moral goodness and evil. As *reason* is present in God, it is the ultimate and unchanging moral standard. As it is found in man, in the particular status known as right reason, it is the proximate moral standard. This statement might appear to be in opposition to what we have said about human nature in all its parts and relations being the norm or morality. It is not; rather it contains a difference in emphasis. What does St. Thomas mean? First, it is beyond dispute that free choice of the will pertains to the essence of a moral act. It is also beyond dispute that free choice is impossible unless there be knowledge. The rational and the voluntary, then, are the marks of the moral act in such a way that the human agent wills his acts according to what he knows. An act, then, is moral if it is a willed act subject to reason.

But St. Thomas insists that we will good moral acts only if the will is subject not to merely any reason but rather to right reason. In this instance right reason does not mean reasoning in a logical fashion but it means reason that is rectified, aimed straight at or properly disposed towards some end. The reason is thus right because in the practical order the end is primary and reason and will must be concerned with acts as ordered to an end. Hence, we reason rightly in this order when we judge rightly of the end with the intention to will accordingly. Such right reason, obviously, since it has to do with acts which will be done, is primarily in the will since it is the will that must be properly disposed towards the end if reason is to judge properly about it and about actions ordered to it.

Now right reason can develop and the will can be oriented towards good ends and towards actions which are ordered to these ends. This development takes place as reason acquires a greater knowledge of man's nature and his ultimate end. As a consequence of possessing a more exact or true knowledge of these, reason apprehends in greater detail the moral acts which are befitting or not befitting man. Hence, it is human nature taken completely in all its parts and relations which is the proximate norm of morality as a measure of the good and bad of moral acts.

The ultimate norm is the eternal law. For that is the ultimate rule of morality with which the dictate of reason must agree in order to be right, and which itself does not need to conform to any other rule. Such is the eternal law. For reason is not a measure of morality except inasmuch as it is right, and it is right only when it squares with divine reason, according to which all things are made and according to which all things should act.

7. Intrinsically Good and Bad Acts

Because human nature is what it is, actions are either conformed to this nature or they are not. Consequently, there is a natural distinction between good and bad acts, i.e., good and evil are not arbitrary and changing with our passing whims and desires, but some actions in themselves are good and some are bad.

To discuss this question, let us say that it is universally admitted that all actions are not of the same moral value. All men, too, make a distinction between morally good and morally bad actions though they may not agree that the same actions are morally good or bad. Moreover, it is a matter of common assent that there are actions which, indifferent in the abstract, become morally good or evil because of the command or prohibition of legitimate authority. All would agree, for example, that the action of driving an automobile on the right side of the street is indifferent in itself, but becomes good by reason of law. All would agree that the eating of pork is an indifferent action, yet it became bad when God commanded the Jewish people not to eat such meat.

But these agreements being granted there remains quite a difference of opinion concerning the question whether there are certain actions which are good, others which are evil, independently of all law, so that such actions are permanently, unchangeably, intrinsically good or evil. Our conviction is that certain actions are good, others are evil by the very nature of man himself. Just as God could not have created man with a different nature, so he could not have created man for whom it could be good and proper and befitting to blaspheme, to perjure himself, to steal, to abandon himself recklessly to lust, or anger, or any other passion. God need not have created man at all, but he could not have created him with other than human necessities. Some, as the Nominalists and Cartesians, have denied this view and have said that all distinction between good and evil is founded on the arbitrary will of God; but such a doctrine is destructive of all science and philosophy. Others, as the Evolutionists and Pragmatists, found their distinction of good and evil on the results of man's social evolution and on utility. Others again, as Rousseau and Hobbes, declare that the State determines the good and evil of human actions.

While we admit that in certain conditions, because of changing times and customs, some things are declared evil by the will of God, some by the State, and some by the conditions themselves, and that good is correspondingly determined, nevertheless not all distinction between good and evil is so determined; otherwise natures would have no meaning at all. Natures are constituted with certain exigencies and appetites and that which is in accord with these is good, that which is otherwise is bad; and no circumstance of time, place, or person can alter this difference.

While denying these different theories about the constitution of all moral good and evil, namely, that good and evil are determined by something outside the acts themselves, we must note that when we say some actions are intrinsically good and bad, we do not say that there is an obligation of performing or omitting them independently of law. Obligation necessarily implies law and a lawgiver. Many actions, moreover, are morally good and praiseworthy though they are not at all obligatory, e.g., heroic acts of charity. Nor do we maintain that actions which are intrinsically good have their full moral value independently of the binding will of God, or that they are of themselves meritorious. We merely assert that there are

some actions which, even if they were not commanded or prohibited, would nevertheless have some intrinsic goodness or badness,
and it is, as we shall see, by reason of this inherent goodness or evil
that they are necessarily commanded or prohibited by God. Hence,
they are commanded or prohibited by God because they are in
themselves good or bad; they are not good or bad because they are
commanded or prohibited. Even if we were to make the impossible
supposition that God has never commanded or prohibited these
actions, it would nevertheless be morally good for man to do those
which are intrinsically good, and morally evil to do those which are
in themselves bad.

8. *The Moral Determinants of an Action*

By applying the proximate norm of morality we can tell
whether a certain kind of human act is morally good, bad, or indifferent. If it agrees with human nature taken completely in all its
parts and relations, the act is good; if it disagrees, the act is bad;
if it neither agrees nor positively disagrees but is neutral, it is morally indifferent.

Now ethics is a practical science, and there is always a question
of an individual, concrete act, not a question of universal acts which
differ just in the fact that they are good or evil. Even so, nothing in
the concrete is merely specific and neither are man's acts. Man's acts
do not differ one from another merely by reason of goodness or
badness but rather by reason of some particular goodness or badness. Why, for instance, is treachery different from stealing? Both
are bad and yet they differ. Why can we say that laziness is not as
evil as blasphemy? Both are bad acts, yet they are bad with a determined badness and in this they differ. In other words, good and bad
acts not only differ specifically but differ also in kind or class. The
question arises, then, what is there in a concrete moral act which
determines it to have a determined conformity or nonconformity
between the act and the norm of morality? To answer, we must
distinguish the parts of the human act in a way differing from our

previous analysis of the human act. We are now considering those elements which can be the sources of the conformity or nonconformity.

This effort requires us to distinguish between the act itself, i.e., the reason why an act is the kind of act that it is, the circumstances in which the act is done, and the intention of the agent in acting. Two men may perform the same act but from different intentions, or different acts from the same intention, or different acts from the same motive and in the same circumstances. In each instance the acts have different morality because of a different combination of these three elements.

Following the terminology of St. Thomas we may call these three determinants of morality, the *object*, the *end*, and the *circumstances*. By *object* is meant the kind of action willed, the act which the will chooses to perform. By *end* is meant the purpose for which the act is willed and performed; this, we may recall from our discussion of end in Chapter II, is either the purpose the act is naturally fitted to accomplish (*the end of the work*), or the purpose the agent wishes to accomplish by willing the act (*the end of the worker*). By *circumstances* are meant the various accidental surroundings of the act.

But before going on to consider these three determinants of morality, we shall say something of the distinction of moral acts into different kinds and species. Let us recall animal, man, and brute, with their various kinds. Animal is a genus; man and brute are species; races of men and breeds of brutes are classes or kinds, not species. In much the same way, moral acts are the genus; good and bad acts the species; while charity and justice, murder and adultery, etc., are classes or kinds, not species.

Moral acts are constituted by the fact that they proceed from the intellect and the will and are capable of a twofold division of good and bad because they have an aspect in common, i.e., voluntary, and an aspect which is not common and by reason of which they are contradictorily opposed to each other, i.e., good and bad. Consequently, we have a genus, i.e., human acts, and a species good and bad. These species in turn admit of different classes or kinds, i.e., as containing individuals which have the same common aspect (i.e., good or bad) but are different by reason of a degree of badness or goodness. There are no different species of men, though there are different classes or races of men, and they differ not because they possess a different essence but because they have different character-istics of the same essence. So there are no different species of good and bad acts, but only different kinds or classes. Man and brute are different as species because they contain essential notes which are mutually contradictory as well as notes which are similar. But justice and charity, for example, are not different species of good acts, be-cause they do not differ in an essential characteristic, for both are good; yet they differ by reason of their particular characteristic of good. They are of the same genus and species, i.e., they are volun-tary acts in conformity with human nature; they are different be-cause they portray different aspects of conformity.

Different species must have different essences; different classes have the same essence but different accidents. No human act can be-long to different species, but the same act can belong to different classes. One act cannot be of two species, at the same time good and bad, though it may be an act of two kinds, charity and justice—as when one owes five dollars and gives ten; or as when the same act is both thievery and revenge, e.g. one stealing from another in order to injure him in retaliation for injury.

Now the object, the end, and the circumstances of an act not only specify a moral act, but they also determine an act to be in a definite class of moral act. In other words, these three not only de-termine that an act is in harmony or disharmony with human na-ture, and therefore determine an act as good or bad, but they also place the act in a definite class of good or bad. To show this is our present purpose.

The *object* of the action is the kind of act that is performed; the action itself. Morality resides in the will, in its consent to what is presented to it by the intellect as morally good or bad. The will cannot just will; it must will something, to do or omit some act which is therefore the object of the will's consent. Since we have proved that there are some acts which are good or bad by their very nature, it is evident that the consent of the will derives its morality first and foremost from the kind of act the will consents to. As we have said earlier in this chapter, a thing is good in so far as it has the being that it ought to have; an act is good in so far as it has the being that it ought to have, in so far as it adds to the being which acts. Hence, the very being of an act, the form of an act, is either good or bad, if it adds to the being of the agent which places it, or detracts from it. Now it is this being, this good, or this lack of being, this evil, which the will wills; if the act willed is bad of its very nature, the willing of it is bad; if the act willed is good of its very nature, and if there is nothing else about it to render it evil, the willing of it must be good. Consequently, the act itself is responsible for the willed act being in a certain class and species of morality. As St. Thomas writes:

As was stated above, the good or evil of an action, as of other things, depends on its fullness of being or its lack of that fullness. Now the first thing that belongs to the fullness of being seems to be that which gives a thing its species. And just as a natural thing has its species from its form, so an action has its species from its object, just as does movement from its term. Therefore, just as the primary goodness of a natural thing is derived from its form, which gives it its species, so the primary goodness of a moral action is derived from its suitable object; and so some call such an action good in its genus, e.g., to make use of what is one's own. And just as, in natural things, the primary evil is when a generated thing does not realize its specific form (for instance, if instead of a man something else be generated), so the primary evil in moral actions is that which is from the object, for instance, to take what belongs to another. Furthermore, this action is said to be evil in its genus (genus here stands for species, just as we apply the term mankind to the whole human species). (S.T. I-II,18,2c)

This point seems so obvious that it hardly needs expression. But we must call attention to the fact that ethics studies acts not in the physical but in the moral order. What may seem to be mere circumstances in the physical order can belong to the very essence of the act in the moral order. We distinguish seizure and theft, killing and murder, speaking and lying. The first of each pair indicates only the physical act, which may be right or wrong; the second means an act which is morally wrong in its nature. Theft is not mere seizure, but the seizure of another's property against his reasonable will; murder is not mere killing, but the direct killing of an innocent person; lying is not mere speaking but the saying of what one knows to be untrue. At first sight these added qualifications may seem to be mere circumstances: whether what I take is mine or another's property, whether the man I kill has lost his right to life or not, whether the words I utter express my thought or contradict it. But in the moral order these points are essential. They do not merely add to a morality already present, but give the act its moral quality and go to make up the very essence of the act in the moral order.

Since the object of the act specifies the moral act, it follows that because of the object of the action some acts are in conformity with the nature of man, others are not. From this we can conclude that if the act of itself is bad, man is never morally permitted to place such an act: blasphemy, e.g., is evil in itself and so it is never permitted. But the like—that they are always permitted—cannot be said of acts which by their object or nature are good, for even granting that the end of the action is good it is possible that it becomes evil by reason of the end or the circumstances in which the action is placed.

To understand this possibility we must consider the *end* of the action. By the end of the action is meant the intention or purpose which the agent has in view in placing the act. That the intention does enter into the morality of an act and does specify the morality of an act can be concluded from the nature of the moral act. A moral act is an act which proceeds from the intellect and will. Consequently, a moral act is an act which is performed with a knowledge of the end which is freely chosen and a knowledge of the means to obtain the end. When, therefore, a man directs his act to some consciously intended purpose, he deliberately wills this purpose together with the act, and both are voluntary. The act itself is used as the means to accomplish this end. When a man deliberately uses a means to an end, in the one and the same act he wills both the use of the means and the attainment of the end. As the act itself can be morally good, bad, or indifferent, so can the end to which it is directed by the will of the agent. Therefore, in addition to the morality which the act has by its own nature, the act also derives morality from the motive with which it is performed.

In a certain true sense, the end is more important than the object itself in a human action, for since a man intends the end more than the means, the end is the principle moral element in the act; it is the energizing element. But since the end is intended then the means are intended, for the end has no meaning without the means, nor has the means any meaning without the end. The motive may give an indifferent act its first moral quality, either good or bad; thus one who borrows money with the firm intention of never returning it is not a borrower, but a thief. The motive may strengthen or weaken in degree the same species of morality the act already has; a clerk who pilfers a little money each day in order to build up to a predetermined sum cannot excuse himself by the smallness of each single theft. The motive may give to an already specified moral act quite a new species of morality; one who steals money to have the means of seducing his neighbor's wife is, as Aristotle observed (*Nic. Ethics*, V,2,1130a,24), more of an adulterer than a thief.

The disposition of things as to goodness is the same as their disposition as to being. Now in some things the being does not depend on another, and in these it suffices to consider their being absolutely. But there are things the being of which depends on something else, and hence in their regard we must consider their being in its relation to the cause on which it depends. Now just as the being of a thing depends on the agent and the form, so the goodness of a thing depends on its end. Hence in the Divine Persons, Whose goodness does not depend on another, the measure of goodness is not taken from the end. Whereas human actions, and other things, the goodness of which depends on something else, have a measure of goodness from the end on which they depend, besides that goodness which is in them absolutely. (S.T. I-II,18,4)

The end or intention is what lies nearest to a man's heart; it is that, as St. Thomas writes, which gives meaning or form to the act of the will, and man in willing the end must also will the means. Now, if these means are actions which, by definition or nature, are not conformed to human nature, then the act of the will in willing the end must also will the acts as means; if these acts are in harmony with human nature, then the act of the will in willing the end must also will the acts as means. We should remember, and we have said this before, that, though the end is the last in the order of execution, it is first and foremost in the order of intention. Therefore, the end in view enters into morality more deeply than any other element of the human act. It is not, however, the most obvious determinant, because it is the last point to be gained, and often the means are more obviously the determinant of morality.

But we must not stress the end or intention too much. If morality were determined by the end in view, and by that alone, the doctrine would hold that the end justifies the means. That doctrine is false, because the moral character of any human act depends on what is willed, on the objects of volition, according as they are or are not befitting objects for human nature. Now the objects of the will, as we have shown, are not only the end in view, but also and necessarily the means chosen to this end. Besides the end, the means are also willed. Indeed, in a different sense and a true sense, the means are willed more immediately even than the end for they have to be taken first in the order of execution.

A good action, like any other good thing, must possess a certain fullness of being, proper to itself. As it is not enough for the physical excellence of a man that he have the bare essentials, a body with a soul animating it, but he needs also to have a certain grace of form, color, powers, and other accidental qualities, so for a good act it is not enough that it be a proper means to a proper end for man, but in addition the proper means and proper end must be taken by a proper person, at a proper time and place, in a proper manner, and with many other proper circumstances. In other words, *circumstances* enter into the fullness of being of a moral act, as do the accidents in the fullness of being of any form or existing essence.

On the contrary, the Philosopher says that a virtuous man acts as he should, and when he should, and so on, according to the other circumstances. Therefore, on the other hand, the vicious man, in the matter of vice, acts when he should not, or where he should not, and so on with the other circumstances. Therefore human actions are good or evil according to circumstances. . . . I answer that, in natural things, it is to be noted that the whole fullness of perfection due to a thing is not from the mere substantial form, that gives it its species, for a thing derives much from supervening accidents, as man does from shape, color, and the like; and if any of these accidents be out of due proportion, evil is the result. So it is with action. For the fullness of its goodness does not consist wholly in its species, but also in a certain addition which accrues to it by reason of certain accidents; and such are its due circumstances. Therefore, if something be wanting that is requisite as a due circumstance the action will be evil. (S.T. I-II,18,3c)

Circumstances are accidents morally affecting the act by way of object or by way of the agent. They do not belong to the essence or substance of the act, but the will wishes these, not on their own account and primarily, but on account of the object and secondarily. A convenient way of listing the circumstances is to ask the familiar questions: *who? where? when? how? to whom? by what means? how often? and the like.* (S.T. I-II,7,c)

Some circumstances have no bearing on morality for they affect the act only physically: whether one poisons with strychnine or cyanine, steals with his right or left hand. But other circumstances do affect morality: whether one robs a rich or a poor man, murders a stranger or a parent, commits sin with a married or unmarried person. These latter circumstances are the only kind we consider.

Some circumstances so affect the act as to put it into a different moral species. Getting drunk in a church is not only drunkenness but also a sacrilege. Intimate relations between persons married but not to each other are sins of injustice as well as of unchastity. Perjury in a law court is not merely lying but also a violation of religion and justice. Circumstances which thus change the species of the act are called *specifying* circumstances.

Other circumstances only change the degree of goodness or badness in the act while leaving it in the same moral species. Such circumstances exist in good acts but have no particular name, while in bad acts they are *aggravating* or *extenuating* circumstances. Theft is still theft whether one steals a large or a small sum of money; drunkenness is still drunkenness whether one has had five or fifteen too many.

Obviously, human act can have its morality colored by the circumstances in which it is done. Because no act is done in the abstract, every human act is performed in definite circumstances of quantity, place, time, manner, frequency, and by a definite person or persons. Such circumstances can be known and willed in the choosing of the act. Thus, they enter into the morality of the act by either giving the moral act a new species or a new kind of morality within the species.

To sum up what we have said about the moral determinants of acts. Three things must be considered in a moral act: object of the act, end of the agent, and circumstances of the act. An act is good when all three are good. An act is bad when any of the three is bad. The fact that a human act is good in object is far from settling its morality. A wrong intention can make the best thing in the world wicked. The fact that an act is bad in object also settles the question, for the best intention in the world cannot make a good of an evil act. If the circumstances are evil, then the act is also evil.

Nothing hinders an action that is good in one of the ways mentioned above, from lacking goodness in another way. And thus it may happen that an action which is good in its species or in its circumstances, is ordained to an evil end, or vice versa. However, an action is not good simply, unless it is good in all those ways: since evil results from any single defect, but good from the complete cause, as Dionysius says (Div. Nom. iv). (S.T. I-II,18,4, ad 3)

9. The Morally Good and Evil Act

Nothing seems to be clearer than this: human nature in all its concrete reality is the norm whereby we determine our action to be morally good or evil. Yet, at the same time, nothing seems to be clearer than this: although two men may place actions that are contradictorily opposed to each other, nevertheless, if both act from good will both are placing morally good acts. Thus, one man will think the claims of his country to be just as opposed to those of another country; another man will be equally certain that the first man and his country are unjust. Both men act from a sincere good will. Both men are morally good and are certain of it. Yet, both cannot be right! We shall attempt to answer this difficulty.

As we have said, St. Thomas has integrated his ethics with his metaphysics. This means that ethics is based upon the study of the nature of man, who is created with a definite part to play in the scheme of God's creation. Consequently, man is a concrete reality, constituted with certain definite essential notes and in definite relations to God, to himself, and to his fellow creatures for the purpose of attaining a definite ultimate end. Moreover, man, when he acts deliberately, performs the acts in definite circumstances for definite purposes. These acts and circumstances are just as real as the man who performs the acts for a definite purpose; they have in themselves a relationship of conformity or nonconformity to the nature of man just as the essential notes of man in themselves are hierarchically ordered among themselves. All this being true, ethics, the science of human acts, is based upon a fact, a reality which exists in a definite manner and independently of the mind's apprehension of and judgment about it.

We can look upon this relation of man and his activity in a two-fold manner: *objective* and *subjective*. The first depends altogether on the nature of man himself and on the order of reality in which he acts: the second adds to the first the further circumstances of reception into the intellect. The objective fact that man exists with certain essential characteristics and relationships is something established by nature itself, or more properly by the Author of Nature, and, as such, it is a fact which exists antecedently to and independently of man's mind regarding it. The subjective fact is objective order grasped and recognized by the mind, that is, it is knowledge based upon this objective reality.

Now it so happens that men's minds accidentally differ. Because of the very contingency of matter and the essential limitation of the created intellect no human mind grasps reality in all the fullness of its complexity. Some minds can and do grasp the order of reality in a more or less perfect manner, subject to the innate limitation of the human intellect, and in so far as they do they are in conformity with reality and, consequently, that which they possess intellectually is true. Other minds, for some accidental reasons, be they lack of education, the influence of environment, the power of the emotions, etc., do not grasp reality as it is, and in so far as they do not they are in error. Because of this difference of grasping reality we have differences in the practical judgments of men about what is morally good and evil.

In the practical judgment some theoretical knowledge is always involved, namely some consideration referring to the reality of things, to what things are and to what they will be: in the example about men judging about the justice of their country's claims, both apprehend in different ways the reality of their countries' claims to be just. Depending on this theoretical judgment, each of the men makes the practical judgment that he must fight against the other in defense of his country and of justice; both judge that in acting thus they place a morally good action. The theoretical judgment in one consideration, let us say, is wrong, and let us say it is later proved to be wrong; yet we must say that he who acts in this way because of the knowledge he possesses certainly makes a true decision in his practical judgment and certainly places a good moral act even though he is opposed to the man who acts from a theoretical judgment that is true, that is based upon the correct apprehension of the reality of things.

There is a difference in the theoretical knowledge which is the foundation of the practical judgment. Now, because a human act and, therefore, a moral act, is that which is the result of knowledge and will, the certainty of the practical judgment is not a theoretical truth but a practical truth; it is not the truth of cognition, but the truth of direction, of means to an end or of ends; it does not consist in a relation of conformity between mind and things, but rather in a relation of conformity of the mind perceiving an end to be attained and the will to pursue the end. Whatever the theoretical truth may be, owing to the intellect's inability to grasp reality, when one makes a decision honestly, in full accord with the demands of a good will, his decision is what it ought to be, it is true, even if, for lack of a clearer knowledge, it implies assumptions that reality will not and cannot substantiate. A man, then, acts morally good or bad not because reality is as it is, but because he sincerely and honestly follows the knowledge that he possesses of reality; if he acts prudently, that is, does what he thinks he ought to do to attain the end he thinks good, he acts in a good moral manner.

Because of the interdependence of the theoretical and practical judgments we have to say that reality, the *norm* of morality, is not morality but the basis of morality. Morality consists in the good or bad will which follows the apprehension of this order of reality. Hence, a man can be good although he puts a bad act; he can be bad although he puts a good act, meaning by that that he can judge that a certain act is in conformity with his nature in a certain way, when actually it is not; or, on the contrary, he can judge that an act is not conformed with his human nature in a certain way, when actually it is conformed in this way. A man can say what is not true and think that it is right; the practical judgment is true, the theoretical judgment is false. Or he can tell the truth and think that it is a lie; his practical and theoretical judgments are both wrong.

Because, then, good morality is essentially a good will, that is, a will which chooses what the intellect presents as good, must we admit that morality is wholly subjective? But that admission would certainly make our wholly metaphysical foundation of ethics useless and meaningless. Man's practical judgments of what is good or evil must be founded upon reality, upon theoretical truth, somehow. We will look into this matter of practical judgment in a more detailed manner in the chapter of the natural law. But we may say right here that ultimately and essentially every practical judgment is based on a theoretical judgment that is true. Everyone apprehends the order of reality to the extent that he knows that it is good to act in accord with his nature and, therefore, judges that the good must be done and the evil avoided. Moral good, then, is not wholly subjective but is founded upon reality which all apprehend in the same way in its broader aspects, though not in the fullness of detail or complexity. If the will follows the intellect's apprehension of the good, then such a will is a good will and it is in conformity to what this order of reality demands in its most ultimate and universal demands.

It must be said, then, that there is no such thing as subjective morality pure and simple, for fundamentally everyone's judgments about what is good and to be done, what is evil and to be avoided, are derived from the judgments that good must be done and evil must be avoided, and these judgments are based upon the true and certain theoretical judgment that nature is to be followed. Reality of nature, then, is the solid foundation upon which man builds his practical judgments. There may be differences of opinion as to what nature demands in certain details, but in certain general aspects there is no difference.

But in connection with this we must remember that my way of thinking, your way of thinking, when they fail to square with the objective order of things, is a contradiction in terms in the theoretical order of reason. Error is not truth in the theoretical order, and although a good will does make an action flowing from such untrue theoretical knowledge good and true morality, nevertheless the man who possesses such untrue knowledge is still wrong. A man may say that two times two are five, and he may adhere to this statement with all the power within him. He may be subjectively convinced, but he is still wrong. And so a man may say that divorce and remarriage are good and right, and he may hold to this opinion with all sincerity and act accordingly. He is morally true and good; his practical judgment is good and will lead him to the end of human life. But on the level of knowledge he is still wrong because his mind does not conform to reality, and when he becomes conscious of this lack of conformity the obligation arises of squaring his practical judgment with reality.

The man whose morality is not in agreement with reality, who does wrong without scruple, may be in one of three classes. (1) He may be an idiot, and he is then no more responsible for his acts than brute animals; in fact there is no question of morality, since there is a lack of knowledge. He deserves no reward for his acts however apparently virtuous they may be; he deserves no blame for what would be otherwise reprehensible. (2) He may be the victim of ignorance, of ignorance in no way imputable to him, of ignorance that can with no amount of reasonable endeavor be shaken off. In this case, if any such exists, he is again not responsible for his condition, nor for all the wrong it occasions. In neither of these two cases do the acts performed cease to be what we may call objectively immoral or wicked, that is, such acts do not conform to that which the order of reality demands in itself, and which the more enlightened mind would know is demanded by the real order. Of course the insane and the ignorant are not responsible before God for their deeds, that is, they are not held accountable for that which is unknowingly done and not conformed to the order of reality, for God is to judge according to one's conscience, that is, according to that which is done knowingly and willingly, which is moral action. (3) Last of all, a man may be the willing victim of an ignorance that he could have easily remedied at some point in his life, that he, on the contrary, fostered and encouraged by every means at his disposal. Such ignorance is of course inexcusable, and the morality, or immorality, based on it is deserving of punishment.

10. *Moral Evil*

Moral goodness consists in the will electing those acts which are intellectually recognized as conformed to human nature and which, therefore, are means to the final end of man. To place a morally good act, then, the will follows the rule or measure recognized by the intellect; and the act elicited by the will in following the rule of the intellect adds goodness or being or perfection to man, because it bestows upon man that which is lacking to him in so far as it advances him along the way of the perfection of his form or nature.

Moral evil, consequently, consists in the will eliciting those acts which are intellectually recognized as difformed to human nature and which, therefore, are not means to the final end of man. To place a morally evil act, then, the will elects not to follow the rule or measure recognized by the intellect and the act elicited by the will in so refusing to follow the rule does not add goodness or being or perfection to man because it lacks that which helps human nature along the way to the perfection of its form. As St. Thomas writes:

That which formally constitutes the fault of moral evil comes into being in this, that without concurrent consideration of the rule, the will proceeds to the act of choice. (On Evil I,3)

Now since evil does not exist in itself, but in what is good, for evil is an absence of good, we must say that in order that an evil act might be, the evil must exist somehow in an act which is good, and, therefore, the act of the will which is good is also that in which the moral evil exists. Without entering fully into this question, we can say that the moral act which is morally evil is also under one aspect good, and hence the moral evil does exist in a positive entity, that is, the act which is good. But since this act possesses a defect which it should not possess, the act is evil in that respect. To explain: the act, in so far as it is positive, tends towards some object under the aspect or formality of good, for it is impossible to elicit an act that tends towards an object under the aspect or formality of evil. Now precisely under the formality of good, the act of the will, and therefore the moral act, is good or possesses positive entity, and does confer a perfection on some aspect of man. But in so far as the same act tends towards an object which the intellect recognizes as not conformed to human nature adequately considered, and therefore, possessing evil, the will not conforming itself to the rule of the intellect elicits an act that possesses evil in relation to the final end of man and to man's nature. Such an act is morally evil because it cannot and does not confer perfection or goodness on human nature completely considered. It is the choice of an act that lacks the goodness it should have, i.e., conformity to the rule of reason, that is moral evil. Although, then, in such an act of the will there is moral evil, i.e., nonconformity, nevertheless the evil exists in the positive act of the will, i.e., the conformity to some aspect of human nature.

Readings

Bourke, V. J., *St. Thomas and the Greek Moralists*, pp. 21-29.

Brosnahan, T. J., *Prolegomena to Ethics*, pp. 12-13; 167-173.

Cronin, Michael, *Science of Ethics*, vol. I, pp. 318-366; 89-114.

Farrell, W., *A Companion to the Summa*, vol. II, pp. 65-82.

Gilson, E., *Moral Values and the Moral Life*, pp. 79-90.

Kendzierski, Lottie H., "Object and Intention in the Moral Act," *Proceedings of the American Catholic Philosophical Association*, XXIV (1950), pp. 102-110.

Leibell, J. F., *Readings in Ethics*. The following articles are most informative:

"The norm of moral rectitude," V. Cathrein, pp. 156-162.

"The moral determinants of an action," Michael Cronin, pp. 165-167.

"Are there any indifferent acts?," Michael Cronin, pp. 168-171.

"Does the end justify the means?," John Gerard, pp. 193-207.

"Ethical implications of the law of habit," William James, pp. 272-279.

"The limitations of habit," John MacCunn, pp. 279-282.

Maritain, J., *St. Thomas and the Problem of Evil.*

Murray, T. B., "Reason and Morality according to St. Thomas," *The Month,* CLI (1928), pp. 417-423.

O'Brien, Sr. M. Consilia, "Recta Ratio in Relation to Moral Truth," *Proceedings of the American Catholic Philosophical Association,* XVII (1942), pp. 120-126.

Rickaby, Joseph, *Moral Philosophy,* pp. 31-41.

Rommen, H., *The State in Catholic Thought,* c. 6.

Simon, Y., *The Nature and Function of Authority,* pp. 22-30.

St. Thomas, *Summa Theologica,* I-II, qq. 18-21.

CHAPTER VI

LAW IN GENERAL

1. *Reason Judges of the Good and Evil of Actions*

Human reason taken completely in all its parts and relations gives us a basis for distinguishing between good and bad moral acts. But it does not of itself oblige us to perform good moral acts. Yet we are conscious of an obligation to perform such acts. What, therefore, is the reason for this obligation? This is the problem of law, for law accounts for obligation. Without law there is nothing more than the knowable relationship between human acts and human nature, a relationship between means and end. Without law we can know what acts will bring us to our end, because we can know what acts are conformed to human nature, but such knowledge does not of itself oblige us to do the good and to avoid the evil. At most such knowledge would give us the hypothetical imperative about which Kant speaks: If you want to be moral, human nature shows us how to do it. But such knowledge does not oblige us to be moral. The obligation to be moral arises from law. Law commands: You must be moral; you must see to it that your acts are conformed to your nature and to your end.

The ethician, then, knows of an exterior source of good actions, a principle which regulates and obliges man from the outside to a definite course of action. This source is law. But, although law is exterior to man, nevertheless it is not something foreign and opposed to his self-determining nature. Rather it is precisely of the same order as reason, the inner principle from which human activity gets its human end, and therefore its moral character. That law does not destroy but rather is the very source of freedom, as reason itself is, requires some explanation. Of necessity this explanation will be a repetition of much that we have said so far, yet it will at the same time clarify the close union of will and reason in our moral acts.

Up to the present we have defined the general principles and conditions of morality. We began by accepting the fact of consciousness that man acts because he desires ultimately to obtain perfect happiness. This desire, as we know, is a metaphysical, finalistic ordination of the intellect towards a knowledge of the quiddity of things, not of effects only but also of causes, and so eventually of the First Cause. This desire is to be fulfilled, God is to be possessed, by means of human acts that are morally good.

The human act, then, is a means to the ultimate end of man. But since the human act is a most complex act, we have tried to make the nature of this act clear. Essentially it is a willed act, which means that it is an act that proceeds from the will under the direction of reason. Because the will is an appetite, a tendency towards an object, the will has no object other than the good. The good is that which we desire; we desire only the good; these are equivalent statements. But the will is a reasoned desire, that is to say, it desires only that good which is known by reason.

The will acts, consequently, only when some good has been proposed by the intellect. Without entering into the mixed character of every act of the will, we should understand, nevertheless, that the will can, in our reasoned acts, be the reason why our faculties operate. I will to walk, to feel, to know; I will to will. The will makes use of all the other faculties and of itself at its pleasure. The will sets them in motion, or keeps them from acting, so much so that, in the last analysis, it is because we have a will that we can always will or not will what we do will or do not will. Yet the will can never determine the nature of the act. The will is a tendency which of itself is blind, and it becomes voluntary or reasonable only at the moment when reason proposes to it several objects among which it may choose. An act is voluntary because the will wills it, but the will takes *this* object rather than *that* because reason offers it as good and as *this* good rather than *that* good; and it is the presentation of reason, making known to the will the different possible objects— walking, thinking, loving God, lying, etc.—from which it can make its choice, that moves the will towards *this* object rather than towards *that* other. It is the will that causes me to will, but it is the intellect that causes my will to will what I will; hence in this sense my intellect acts upon my will as my will acts upon my intellect.

Because of this close union of intellect and will in the human act, several necessary elements enter into it, and we have dealt with them. Because the will is a self-determining power, no external force, or violence, can be imposed on it. Because the will is dependent on knowledge, ignorance can, and does, limit the voluntary character of the human act. So too, the passions can interfere with calm deliberation and as a consequence can circumscribe the willed act.

All this leads to one conclusion, namely, that the willed act is present with, and only with, an inner principle of action, plus knowledge of the end pursued. That is to say, the human act and the willed act are one and the same. And this leads to the further conclusion that morality and the willed act are one and the same, for just as a morally good act is a rational good that is willed, so a morally evil act is an irrational good, that is, an evil that is willed. As Augustine writes, "It is by the will that a man's life is made righteous or sinful." (*Retract.* I,9,4) From this identification of the willed act with morality it might appear to some that we are reducing morality to a subjectivistic system. But this is not the truth of the matter.

We have explained the principles by which morally good and evil acts are constituted and distinguished. By integrating man with a system of being and with the metaphysical laws of action we have found the laws of his activity. As a result of these, we have said that the moral good is fundamentally the metaphysical good. That is to say, moral good is to be determined by concrete human nature acting for its end, perfect happiness. This is true, because good is an aspect of being, and good acts, which are means to perfect happiness, and ultimately perfect happiness itself, are the highest expressions of man's being and therefore the highest good. A morally good act is aimed at an object fit for man in view of his nature; an evil act, on the other hand, does not aim at an object that is fit for man in view of his nature. Or, in other words, from a consideration of the nature of man and good, we have concluded this much: an action is good when it strives for an object which man should seek; it is evil when the object at which the action aims is not what the nature of man requires. And what is the nature of man? It is reason. Consequently, an action is morally good when the will under the direction of reason wills to act in conformity to reason.

Now in human actions, good and evil are predicated in relation to the reason, because, as Dionysius says, the good of man is to be in accordance with reason. For that is good for a thing which suits it according to its form; and evil, that which is against the order of its form. It is therefore evident that the difference of good and evil considered in reference to the object, is an essential difference in relation to reason, i.e., according as the object is suitable or unsuitable to reason. Now certain actions are called human or moral inasmuch as they proceed from the reason. (S.T. I-II,18,5c)

Because the object of the will must be presented to it by reason, the good towards which the will is inclined, which is willed, is dependent upon reason. Consequently, although some acts or some objects in themselves, for example, may or may not be befitting human nature in its more precise and particular detail, nevertheless because they must be known by reason as conformed or not conformed before they can be presented to the will, as an object of good or evil morality, it is reason which basically establishes them as good or bad, as moral or immoral. It is reason which establishes differences in morality for different persons.

As we have stated above, the goodness of the will depends properly on its object. Now the will's object is proposed to it by reason. For the understood good is the proportioned object of the will, while the sensible or imaginary good is proportioned, not to the will, but to the sensitive appe-

tite; for the will can tend to the universal good, which reason apprehends, whereas the sensitive appetite tends only to the particular good, apprehended by a sensitive power. Therefore the goodness of the will depends on the reason in the same way as it depends on its object. (S.T. I-II,19,3c)

It is clear, then, that the morality of acts is not established by a unilateral agreement of human reason with an object, for then morality would have to be in practice universally the same morality, and there would be no place for an erring reason, since the metaphysical relation of object to intellect is always the same. Rather, reason helps to establish morality as much as and more than the object itself, for the will acts well or evilly only on condition that the reason present an object to it. And an object is an object only in relation to the faculty that understands it. And since different intellects can understand the object in different ways they can present the same object to different wills in different ways. Consequently, it is the intellect that is the most immediate or proximate arbiter in morality, for it determines an act as fitting or not fitting to human nature. The agreement of an object, then, with reason, and the consequent subjection of the will to reason, which is the moral characteristic of acts, determines the morality of acts. If reason, in a hypothetical case, is correct, and the will does not follow it, the will is wrong; and the will is equally wrong if, when reason is mistaken, it refuses to follow reason.

For in matters of indifference, the will that is at variance with erring reason or conscience is evil in some way because of the object on which the goodness or malice of the will depends; not indeed because of the object according as it is in its own nature, but according as it is accidentally apprehended by reason as something evil to do or to avoid. And since the object of the will is that which is proposed by the reason, as we have stated above, from the very fact that a thing is proposed by the reason as being evil, the will by tending thereto becomes evil. And this is the case not only in indifferent matters, but also in those that are good or evil in themselves. For it is not only indifferent matter that can receive the character of goodness or malice accidentally; but likewise that which is good can receive the character of evil, or that which is evil can receive the character of goodness, because of the reason apprehending it as such. . . . Consequently, if it be proposed by the reason as something evil, the will tends to it as something evil; not as if it were evil in itself, but because it is evil accidentally, through the apprehension of the reason. Hence the Philosopher says that, properly speaking, the incontinent man is one who does not follow right reason; but accidentally, he is also one who does not follow false reason (Ethic. VII,9). We must therefore conclude that absolutely speaking, every will at variance with reason whether right or erring, is always evil. (S.T. I-II,19,5c)

Thus we reach the conclusion that in moral acts, the goodness of will depends principally upon the goodness of purpose, i.e., upon that which the intellect proposes. For the will to follow reason, be it true or false, is to be guided towards an end which reason proposes and to use the means in view of the end. If, therefore, good and evil depend upon the object as apprehended by the reason and if it is the object that directs all action towards itself, it follows that it is the desired object which primarily gives the element of good or evil to a willed act. Thus, for example, if we should propose the virtue of purity to ourselves and use the means to practice it, the object of the will, purity, is good because understood by the reason as good, and the means are good because understood by the intellect as good means to this end. Thus it is that the object desired establishes the actions as good. In every instance in which the object desired is bad, the act of the will, choosing this object and the means, is bad because it is impossible to do good while understanding it to be bad. This statement is true because, as we have said, acts are specified by their objects; hence, if the object of the will presented by the intellect is bad, the act of the will subsequent to this presentation is bad.

But even if the purpose is good, the act of the will which follows in choosing the means does not, because of the purpose, become good; for if the will chooses an evil means, which is presented to it by the reason, the act of the will is evil; yet the intention or purpose does give to the act of the will something of its own goodness. For example, to will to steal in order to help an indigent friend is less evil and therefore better than to will to steal in order to fornicate. Hence, the purpose is not the whole of the willed act but it does enter largely into the willed act and gives to it much of its own goodness or badness. Morality, then, is based upon purposes, but the morality of an act is not reduced to the purpose which motivates the act. For if the purpose is bad, the will willing the purpose and the means to it will be bad and so the act will be morally evil; but if the purpose is good, the will must still choose means which are something of reason and apprehended as good or bad. And even when the means are chosen, the will must still take account of the circumstances, which are of reason, too, for the object of the will must be conformed to reason not only in the abstract but in the concrete. Thus, although the purpose does permeate all the elements of the moral act, it does not constitute the whole act. Consequently, to be a good moral act, the willed act must be directed by reason apprehending the purpose, the means and the circumstances as good; otherwise the moral act is bad.

2. *Reason Dictates the Good and Evil of Acts*

What is most clear in the mutual cooperation of the reason and will in the moral act is that since the will is a blind faculty it cannot operate unless reason presents an object to it. By virtue of his reason, man is capable of surveying the whole range of truth and goodness, of deliberating about values it contains, and of judging that here and now this value or this good is desirable and to be pursued; and the will chooses or refuses to choose the good so presented. Apart from this previous deliberation and judgment, there is no free act. And every free act is an obedience to a judgment of reason. (This, of course, is not rational determinism: we are considering only one point here, not explaining how the will can and does enter into the free act of deliberation and judging.) Because and only because the will is obedient to reason is the will free; i.e., only because the reason can deliberate about particular goods and judge them desirable and present them to the will for acceptance is the will free to choose or not to choose.

But there is something more in this judgment of reason as far as it concerns the moral act. Not only does it state what is good and what is evil, but it also dictates that the evil is to be avoided and good done. The judgment of reason in the moral act manifests itself as an imperative of reason, prescribing to the will what it must seek and what it must turn away from, in order that man may reach his last end, his proper perfection or good. This demand of reason is what we mean by law—*an order of reason.*

Experience tells us that we know ourselves to be under some necessity of performing or omitting certain actions, right or wrong. This necessity, for example, constrains us to tell the truth in difficult circumstances, or to abstain from stealing another's money even though there is no likelihood of our being found out. We are quite accustomed to what we call necessities in the physical order. An unsupported body *must*, we feel, necessarily fall. Water *must* seek its own level. Gasoline *must* ignite, if a match is applied to it. The fact to be explained in ethics is the moral necessity laid on the will by reason, in virtue of which we realize that we *ought* to do such and such a thing, even though we do not wish to do it, or that we *ought not* to do something else, however much we may feel inclined to it.

3. *The Meaning of Law*

Law is one of those words which we are constantly using, the exact meaning of which we might find difficult to state. There are laws of the United States and the laws of the physical sciences; there are laws of parliamentary procedure and laws of diplomatic protocol; there are laws of learning and laws of heredity; there are laws of etiquette as well as economic laws. Clearly, there is some difference of meaning in these various uses of the term. But if there is a difference there must also be a common element in the various uses; otherwise the use of the term would be perplexing to the point of absurdity. The common element is that all these different laws signify uniformity of action. The difference lies in the manner in which the different laws signify uniformity. Some of them indicate a uniformity to which civilized people have agreed as accepted procedure; some signify a uniformity which men have observed in things; some signify a uniformity which is imposed upon things.

In the proper sense law is a rule or measure of action imposed on others directing them to their proper ends (*S.T.* I-11,90,4). Law imposes some kind of necessity on the beings it directs. It may be of two kinds: (1) physical law, imposing physical necessity; (2) moral law, imposing moral necessity.

Physical law directs nonfree beings to uniform action towards their ends by an inner necessity of their nature. The uniform manner of action affords a place for science to establish its laws, which are not normative (imposing a necessity) but pure and simple declarations. The laws of physics, chemistry, biology, and allied sciences are formulas expressing how bodies are observed to act, but they do not speak of the necessity with which the natures of things must act. In other words, such scientific physical laws are statements of the constant method of actions. Thus it is said, for example, that falling bodies fall with velocity accelerating thirty-two feet per second every second. But there is another way in which we can speak of physical laws. It is a philosophical way of speaking and complies in a true sense with the definition of law. The philosopher recognizes that the observed uniformity does not happen accidentally. It is the very nature of the bodies and the structure of the universe that necessitates them to act as they do. In this sense, physical laws are the nature or the permanent inclinations inherent in natural objects by reason of which their actions are ruled. Thus the natures are the laws of natural things because the natures are the principles which direct their common method. Consequently, the philosophical law is different from the scientific law in so far as the philosophical law is concerned with the cause of the actions in natural objects, i.e., the natures; whereas the scientific law is concerned with the effects produced by the natures. Scientific laws declare the constant and uniform action in certain natural beings and they formulate this action. Since the scientific laws are concerned with the mere compilation of statistics, if these were the only laws admitted—and many there are who admit only such laws—they would certainly be opposed to the philosophy of St. Thomas, who bases his laws on a metaphysical finality. But we will deal with this matter later; for the present we will note that a scientific law is not strictly a law but a declaration of a constant method of action; a philosophic physical law is the rule or measure of action, and in physical objects this rule is the nature of things. It is obvious that nonfree beings cannot rebel against their own very nature, and that disobedience to physical law is impossible. Not so with moral law.

Moral law directs free beings to act towards their ends by imposing obligation on the free will. This obligation or duty or oughtness is called moral necessity. Since it is imposed on free beings, it is not physically compelling, but it is not less demanding than physical law, since free beings must reach their ends just as thoroughly as nonfree beings. Hence moral laws *can* be broken by the beings bound by them, but they *ought not* to be broken, and moral necessity means precisely this: that they *ought not* to be broken. All other acts are regulated by physical law, but human acts are governed by moral law.

4. *The Definition of Moral Law*

In the strictest sense law means moral law, the law that rules and measures human action. St. Thomas gives us the classical definition of it: "It is nothing else than an ordinance of reason for the common good, made by him who has the care of the community, and promulgated." (*S.T.* I-II,90,4) Our first business is to have a clear conception of law by explaining the various parts of the definition.

AN ORDINANCE

This distinguishes a law from a mere counsel, a piece of advice, which has no real binding force. An ordinance is an order, a command, imposing obligation. It is the imposition of the superior's will on the will of the inferior, and must be expressed in a mandatory form.

Law, though imposed by the superior's will, is formulated by his intellect as the planning and directing faculty. As directing beings to their ends, law must be no arbitrary whim but a dictate of right reason. Or we may put the same in other words: since the purpose of law is to indicate the means that inferiors are to use to obtain an end, for things act only for the sake of an end, and since reason alone is competent to devise means to an end, it follows that law is primarily a function of reason:

Law is a rule and measure of acts whereby man is induced to act or is restrained from acting; for lex (law) is derived from ligare (to bind), because it binds one to act. Now the rule and measure of human acts is the reason, which is the first principle of human acts, as is evident from what has been stated. For it belongs to the reason to direct to the end, which is the first principle in all matters of action. Now that which is the principle in any genus is the rule and measure of that genus; for instance, unity in the genus of numbers, and the first movement in the genus of movement. Consequently, it follows that law is something pertaining to reason. (S.T. I-II,90,1c)

In what sense does law belong to reason? Evidently, it belongs to practical reason and within practical reason to the final end of things which, as we shall see when we treat of obligation, is the one principle capable of binding rational beings. But though law belongs essentially to practical reason, we must distinguish two reasons in which it dwells. Preeminently law dwells in the directing reason of all things, God, for it is this reason which primarily and essentially apprehends the end and the means to the end of all things. Nevertheless, law dwells in created beings by participation. The law of the divine reason which apprehends the end to be attained by all creatures, which apprehends the natures and functions of the creatures which are to attain the end, dwells first of all in the reason of God and then, by participation, in all creatures thus directed to their ends. In irrational beings, the law of divine reason is within, identified with the very inclinations of their irrational forms, physically necessitating them to definite lines of action. In rational creatures it is within, in the very inclination of man's reason to judge of and to command about the good and the evil of his acts. Because rational creatures can apprehend their end and so know the necessary means to that end, man through his knowledge imposes a necessary manner of action on his will in view of his end. Since, then, law is something of reason, it is essentially in the divine reason and human reason; but in irrational creatures in the broader use of the term. This relation or extension of the law of the divine reason to created reason and to things devoid of reason is of extreme importance in ethics and will be considered at greater length when we come to speak of the eternal and natural laws and their relation to each other.

Since law is a kind of rule and measure, it may be in something in two ways. First, as in that which measures and rules; and since this is proper to reason, it follows that in this way law is in the reason alone. Secondly, as in that which is measured and ruled. In this way, law is in all those things that are inclined to something because of some law; so that any inclination arising from a law may be called a law, not essentially, but by participation as it is. (S.T. I-II,90,ad1)

But although law proceeds from reason, it is also related to the will. For law, being a rule of action, has two elements, among others: it is a plan in which end and means are apprehended, and this is of reason; it is also a command imposed on subjects, and this is of reason, but only on condition that the will wills the end to be obtained by law.

Hence, law is a function of both the intellect and the will. Yet primarily, law is a function of reason, for it is reason which devises the means to the end, which is the purpose of law, and it is reason that commands, but only because the will wills the end. Hence, in the Divine Lawgiver, law belongs primarily to reason, for it is his reason that conceives of the end of creatures which moves his reason to impose his law upon creatures. In the same way in rational creatures, participating in the divine law, reason is the primary element of law, for it is the reason which obliges the will to a certain line of action, but only because the will wills an end, perfect happiness.

Because law is something of right reason, it must, therefore, be reasonable. To be reasonable every law must have certain characteristics. It must be *consistent*, both with itself and with other laws, for no one can keep contradictory laws or obligations; *just*, respecting existing rights guaranteed by higher laws and distributing burdens equitably; *observable*, for no one can do the impossible or be reasonably expected to do what is too harsh and difficult; *enforceable*, otherwise only the good will keep the law and the wicked, who need to be restrained, will go free; *useful*, for a law is a means to an end and needless restriction of liberty serves no purpose.

FOR THE COMMON GOOD

The purpose of law is to get people to act together. You have only to watch a number of people struggling to get in at a door from which others are struggling to get out to realize the need of a regulation or "order" of some kind. You feel instinctively that it would be to everyone's advantage, the common good, if those going in kept to one side and those coming out to the other. Thus a law differs from a command, order, precept, or injunction laid on an individual person. The latter may bind a person quite as strongly as a law, for a son must obey his father no less than a citizen must obey the state, but the two have different functions.

A law looks always to the common good, the benefit of the community as a whole, not to private or personal good. This is true because law, being a reasonable rule of action, must aim at some good. Now the only good at which actions ruled by law aim is either the good of the individual or the good of the whole community. But law aims directly and primarily at securing the common good, because the common good alone can bind the individual to a definite course of action. When we consider the source of obligation we will see that the only object capable of binding the human will in each individual act is final happiness and, consequently, since law imposes such an obligation the source of its obligation is final happiness. Because, then, final happiness is the common end or common good for all men, law is the rule of action ordained for all men.

Moreover, because the individual good or the individual welfare is good only in so far as it is conducive to the final perfection or happiness of the individual, which is the common good, law aims only indirectly at the individual good, i.e., only in so far as the individual good secures the universal good. We may emphasize this point by saying that because every part is ordained for the whole, and because man is a part of the whole universal community of mankind, law must be ordained primarily for the common good, for the good of the individual is secured only if the good of the whole is secured.

Therefore, it is right that we should regard law as a rule of action given to a community: for the good of the community is higher than that of the individual, being related to the individual good as the whole is related to the part. And moreover, since the individual cannot be bound to a definite course of action except it lead to the final perfection of man, and since the final perfection of man is a common good, law is primarily for the common good. A law is not laid down for an individual, except so far as his action is of importance to the community. The private concerns of one man do not afford scope and room enough for a law. Neither do the domestic affairs of one family. A law aims at a deep, far-reaching, primary good, which is the ultimate perfection of man. But the private good of an individual, and the domestic good of a family, are not primary goods, inasmuch as the individual and the family are not primary but subordinate beings; not complete and independent, but dependent and partial; not wholes but parts. The individual is part of the family, and the family is part of a higher community. It is only when we come to some community which is not part of any higher that we have found the good which is the aim of law. Such a community, not being part of any higher community in the same order, is in its own order a perfect community. Thus, in the temporal order, the individual and family are parts of the state; in the spiritual order, they are parts of the church. These are perfect communities, containing within themselves the means to reach their own perfections, and so the ultimate perfection of man or the common good. Their ends, though subordinate to the ultimate happiness of man, are necessary means for this end, and consequently their ends are the common good of man. Such perfect communities can make laws, for such laws are for the common good; and the good of these communities is of more consequence than the good of the individual. The good of the individual, then, is a matter of law in so far as it is subservient to the good of these societies, just as the good of the individual is matter of law in so far as it is subservient to the good of the universal happiness of mankind.

As we have stated above, law belongs to that which is a principle of human acts, because it is their rule and measure. Now as reason is a principle of human acts, so in reason itself there is something which is the principle in respect of all the rest. Hence to this principle chiefly and mainly law must be referred. Now the first principle in practical matters, which are the objects of the practical reason, is the last end; and the last end of human life is happiness or beatitude, as we have stated above. Consequently, law must need concern itself mainly with the order that is in beatitude. Moreover, since every part is ordained to the whole as the imperfect to the perfect, and since one man is a part of the perfect community, law must need concern itself properly with the order directed to universal happiness. (S.T. I-II,90,2c)

We should, however, remark in explanation of our theory that although the end of law is the good of the community, nevertheless not all laws are meant to bind the whole community or are meant to lead directly and immediately to the good of the whole community. Many laws bind only a part of the community and directly benefit no more than a part. Thus, those who drive automobiles are bound by the laws concerning driving; those only who are engaged in religious work enjoy the benefit of the law freeing them from paying taxes on their income. But persons who come under the laws of the community come under it as *parts* of the community, and the law which guides them must be regarded as part of the general scheme for the securing of the common good. If rules are made for individual conduct only and in no wise pertain to the common good, they are not laws. As St. Thomas writes:

Since law is chiefly ordained to the common good, any other precept in regard to some individual work must need be devoid of the nature of law, save in so far as it regards the common good. Therefore every law is ordained to the common good. (S.T. I-II,90,2c)

MADE BY HIM WHO HAS THE CARE OF THE COMMUNITY

Because law is a rule binding the subjects to follow a definite course of action for the common good, only the authority that has the care of the community can make a law. The individual may regulate his actions for his own individual welfare; but the individual lives in society and is a member of the community in which he must be directed in view of the whole community of which he is a part. Although the individual is qualified to guide his actions for his own personal good, he is not qualified to guide his actions for the good of the community of which he is a part, and to subordinate these actions to it, because as an individual he has not the care of the community as such, and as an individual his direction would conflict with the other individuals who are his equals and so instead of order we would have confusion. Hence, there is need of an authority outside of himself to guide those actions to the common good which is the proper goal or business of the community. Here, we may say, is the basis for the exteriority of law as far as the individual is concerned. Law must be imposed by an authority whose purpose it is to guide to the common good and who, therefore, has the right as well as the duty to bind wills to certain definite actions.

PROMULGATED

Promulgation is the making of the law known to those whom it binds. Obviously it is not enough that the lawmaker know and will a law; the law must be known by those who are subject to the law. Since law is to direct subjects to an end by indicating what means are to be used, the law must come to the notice of the subjects in some way. Promulgation, however, need not succeed in bringing the law under the notice of every subject, but it must be such that every subject can know of the law's existence. In regard to the promulgation of human laws, it is sufficient that every subject have the opportunity to acquaint himself with its existence and provisions—through public announcement, through the press, through notices in public places, and the like. A certain time is always allowed to elapse before a new law, after promulgation, comes into force. At the end of that time, it is taken for granted that the law is known, and ignorance of it is not admitted by the human judges as a valid excuse for its violation. But though this is true of human law, still, in order that a law may bind the individual conscience formally—that is, in order that its violation may be regarded as, properly speaking, a transgression—it must be known with certainty or knowable by the individual, since for formal wrong, sin, it is necessary that a man do wrong knowingly and willingly. And this is true of all laws of God: unless they are known with certainty or knowable, they do not bind, and their infraction cannot be said to be a sin.

5. *The Necessity Imposed by Law*

We said earlier in this chapter, in inquiring of the meaning of law, that law imposes upon man an obligation, a necessity. Although we will deal with the notion of obligation later, we should note that law is concerned with a necessity laid on the will. The only necessity to which the will can be subject is that arising from an end to be attained. If I wish to be in Chicago by a certain time and can go only by train, and if there is only one train which will get me there on time, I *must* take that train. This necessity, arising from the end intended, may carry with it a number of other necessities which will modify my conduct: earning enough money to make the trip, packing my valise, going to the station, etc. But these necessities are *hypothetically necessary*, that is, they depend on whether I wish to be in Chicago on time. These necessities are *final* necessities, because they arise from the *finis* or end in view. And this is the kind of necessity that is imposed on the will by reason: a final necessity is imposed on the will because it desires an end proposed by the reason.

Most final necessity is *hypothetical*: it depends on an "if." If I wish to keep the appointment in Chicago, I must take these means. But the end in view here, being in Chicago, is subordinated to another end: a monetary advantage, a football game, or whatever it may be. Consequently, I may reject it, rejecting at the same time the further end. The reason why I may reject it is that it is not ultimate. If my object is money, I may tell myself that money is not the be-all-and-end-all of life and that I will be just as happy without this money. But if there is an end which is *absolute* and *ultimate,* which is desired for its own sake and not because it leads to anything else, then the necessity arising from it will be *absolute* and not hypothetical. In the first chapter of this book we saw that there is such an end, a thing which all men desired for its own sake, the natural object of the will, which comes from the possession of the good: happiness. This ultimate end is not of man's choosing; he is made that way. There is no question of an "if" in regard to it. He must desire happiness, and all his actions are tending to it. Hence the necessity which the end lays upon the will is not a hypothetical but an absolute necessity. And as in hypothetical necessity a certain necessity is laid upon the will to take certain means which will insure the possession of the end, so from the natural desire of the ultimate end there arises a necessity of taking some, at least, of the means that lead to it and of avoiding what leads away from it. In other words, when man acts he acts because he knows happiness is his ultimate end and he necessarily desires it, and there is the consequent necessity of taking means to obtain it. But the means which lead man to his perfection or last end are good acts, bad acts being those which lead away from it. Hence, from this ultimate end, and knowledge of it, there arises a necessity of performing good acts and avoiding evil acts. Man knows that he must do good and avoid evil because he necessarily desires ultimate perfection. This necessity is not *hypothetical,* but *categorical* or absolute. It springs from the very nature of the will itself as having for its formal object the good. The will must follow the reason proposing the means to obtain the final end. Hence, if the will is to be employed, a rational will must be obedient to reason dictating the good to be done and the evil to be avoided.

The reason, then, judging of the good and evil and prescribing to the will what is good and evil, is what is known as law, or an order of reason. Thus the fact of freedom of the will appears as an obedience to the order of reason and its concrete demands. It is in this sense that Leo XIII wrote:

The radical reason for man's need of law is to be found in his own faculty of free choice—that is, in the need for harmony between the will and right reason. It is a complete perversion and inversion of the truth to imagine that, because man is by nature free, therefore he should be free from law. If this were the case, it would follow that liberty, in order to be liberty, would have to be loosed from all vital relation with reason. As a matter of fact, the very opposite is true: because man is free, therefore, he must be subject to law. (Libertas, p. 100)

Because the reason can know what is good and evil for the ultimate perfection of man, the will is free to choose. But because the reason can know what is good and evil the will is morally necessitated to choose the good and to avoid the evil. Hence it is that law is an ordination of reason, a dictate ordering things to an end, and in case of man, proximately a dictate of his reason ordering the will to choose those means that are necessary to his final perfection, the good acts. Consequently, when the will submits to this ordering of reason, it does not submit to an alien force, to an unworthy heteronomy, that violates its very nature, but it submits to reason which is the source of its freedom. Law, then, does not impose needless restrictions or unreasonable burdens on people, but it tends to make men good by directing them to their ultimate end and by indicating to them the means whereby they may obtain this end. It promotes liberty by pointing out the way man ought to act if he wishes to possess his ultimate good, but it also leaves him free to accept or reject this direction, for law does not destroy man's free will.

In spite of what countless numbers might think liberty is, it is not a license to commit evil, but the power by which we can direct ourself with the help of law to do good and ultimately reach our true goal of life. A sick man, who is ignorant of medicine, is not free to regain his health because he does not know what medicine he should take. A doctor will not destroy his freedom; rather the doctor will free the man from the necessity of remaining sick. The sick man is free to follow the doctor's advice, but if he refuses he will suffer the consequence of his refusal: continued sickness. Similarly, laws direct us to our end; we have the free will to choose to follow them or reject them, but the penalty of refusal is a failure to reach our ultimate goal.

6. Kinds of Law

There are many different classifications of laws, but we will divide them according to how we shall treat of them. Consequently, we will divine laws by reason:

(1) Of their *duration*, into eternal and temporal. Since God governs his creation by a decree of his intellect and will which are identical with his essence and since his essence is eternal his decree is called the *eternal* law. Other laws, since they are made in time, are called *temporal* laws.

(2) Of their *mode of promulgation*, into natural and positive. The *natural law* is promulgated in the very natures of the beings it directs. Thus, the natural law includes both the moral law of rational beings and all the physical laws. We shall restrict the term *natural law* to that law which governs man and the term *law of nature* to physical laws. *Positive laws* are promulgated by some sensible sign, such as the written or spoken word. Examples of positive laws are ecclesiastical and civil laws.

(3) Of their *origin*, into divine and human. God is the lawgiver when there is question of a *divine law*. *Human laws* are made by human legislators. Obviously, the eternal and the natural law as well as the laws of nature are divine laws. Human laws must be both positive and temporal. But there can be divine positive laws by which God immediately imposes laws on men. The Ten Commandments are examples of such positive divine laws; so are the laws which God imposed on the Jews of the Old Testament times regulating their dietary habits and ritual, etc. But let us note that the Ten Commandments are merely statements of the Natural Law, and that the difference between natural law and positive law is not in the content of the law but in the manner of promulgation; the Ten Commandments are positive law since they were given by God to Moses by means of an external sign. The same may be said of

many of civil and ecclesiastical laws: in content they are natural laws, but in their mode of promulgation positive.

We have, then, made these divisions of laws because this is to be our manner of treatment. We began this chapter by noting the fact of obligation to perform or to omit actions and we have said that law is the source of this obligation; in the next four chapters we will consider how these several kinds of law are the origin of obligation and what is the nature of this obligation.

Readings

Adler, M., "The Doctrine of Natural Law," *University of Notre Dame Law Institute Proceedings,* vol. I, pp. 65-84.

——— "A Question about Law," in *Essays in Thomism,* ed. Brennan, pp. 206-236.

Blackstone, W., *Commentaries on the Laws of England.* Introduction, section II. This famous work begins by putting law on a solid ethical basis.

Bourke, V. J., *Ethics,* pp. 162-166.

Cronin, Michael, *The Science of Ethics,* vol. I, pp. 203-244.

Davitt, T., *The Nature of Law, passim.*

Farrell, W., *A Companion to the Summa,* vol. II, c. 18.

Gilson, E., *The Spirit of Medieval Philosophy,* c. 16.

LeBuffe, F. P., and Hayes, J. V., *The American Philosophy of Law,* c. 2.

Leibell, J. F., *Readings in Ethics.* The suggested readings are:

> "The nature of law," Thomas Slater, pp. 301-302.
> "The effects of law," St. Thomas Aquinas, pp. 302-303.
> "Classification of laws," V. Cathrein, pp. 303-306.
> "Major divisions of law," F. P. LeBuffe, pp. 306-313.
> "Moral law," Timothy Brosnahan, pp. 325-326.

Rommen, H., *The Natural Law,* cc. 8-12.

Suarez, Francisco, Selections from his *De Legibus (On Laws)* are given in J. B. Scott, *The Classics of International Law: Selections from Three Works of Francis Suarez.* Read bk. I, cc. 3-7; 9, 2; bk. II, cc. 1-4.

St. Thomas, *Summa Theologica,* I-II, qq. 90-108 *(Basic Writings.* Read pp. 90-93).

CHAPTER VII

THE ETERNAL LAW AND THE NATURAL LAW

1. *The Meaning of the Eternal Law*

In Chapter IV we discussed how right human reason is the proximate norm of morality, and how God's reason is the ultimate norm. We also pointed out that the norm, as norm, does not account for obligation; obligation is caused not by the norm of morality, but by law. In this chapter we will consider how both the divine reason and human reason are the sources of law. As a result we will have to say that the divine reason and human reason are not only the norm of morality but also the sources of law or obligation.

When we are speaking of the eternal law there is question of the divine reason and will establishing definite lines of actions which God's creatures must follow. The first and most fundamental need of law is found in the mind of the Creator. To create is not to bring things in to being capriciously. For the creative act is a rational act, and so deliberate and purposeful. Rational actions are necessarily teleological. And when the end or purpose is necessary, as it obviously must be in the act of creation, the Creator cannot be indifferent whether or no his creatures act for the end set for them. Whence arises the need for law or rules of action mandatory in character whereby created things may so act as to fulfill the purpose of their existence.

Just as there must exist in the mind of the legislator of a civil society a plan whereby he directs all the members of that society to their common good, so there must exist in the mind of God, the Creator, a plan whereby all the things which he has created are guided to their common purpose, the divine goodness. All beings, created by God and maintained in existence by his will, can be regarded as one huge society in which all of us are members, along with animals and even with things. There is not a single creature, animate or inanimate, which does not act in conformity with certain ends and ultimately with the last end, the divine goodness under the direction of God whose purpose in creating will certainly be obtained. All the laws of nature and all the laws of morality or of society ought to be considered as so many particular cases of one single direction or law, divine law. Now God's plan for the guidance and rule of the universe is, like God himself, necessarily eternal. Thus the name of eternal law is given to this first law, the sole source of all others. Putting it in another way, the world is governed by God and a detailed plan of that government, which we call providence, exists in the mind of God; the root of that providence and government, the universal principles from which providence proceeds to its detailed conclusions and to the execution of those conclusions, we call the eternal law.

St. Thomas expresses his proof for the existence of the eternal law twice, and for greater clearness we give both:

Law is nothing else but a dictate of practical reason emanating from the ruler who governs a perfect community. Now it is evident, granted that the world is ruled by Divine Providence, that the whole community of the universe is governed by Divine Reason. Wherefore the very Idea of the government of things in God the Ruler of the universe, has the nature of a law. And since the Divine Reason's conception of things is not subject to time but is eternal, according to Proverbs 8,23, therefore it is that this kind of law must be called eternal. (S.T. I-II,91,1c)

Just as in every artificer there pre-exists a type of the things that are made by his art, so too in every governor there must pre-exist the type

of the order of those things that are to be done by those who are subject
to his government. And just as the type of the things yet to be made by
an art is called the art or exemplar of the products of that art, so too the
type in him who governs the acts of his subjects, bears the character of a
law, provided the other conditions be present which we mentioned. Now
God, by His wisdom, is the Creator of all things in relation to which He
stands as the artificer to the products of his art. Moreover He governs all
the acts and movements that are to be found in each single creature.
Wherefore as the type of the Divine Wisdom, inasmuch as by It all
things are created, has the character of art, exemplar or idea; so the type
of Divine Wisdom, as moving all things to their due end, bears the
character of law. Accordingly the eternal law is nothing else than the type
of Divine Wisdom, as directing all actions and movements. (S.T. I-II,93,
1c)

We may, then define the eternal law as "the type or exemplar
of divine wisdom, as directing all actions and movements." Verbally, though not essentially, this definition may differ from the definition which St. Augustine gives. St. Augustine defines the eternal
law: "That law by which it is just that all things be most perfectly
ordered." (De Lib. Arbit. I,6) He also defines it as: "The divine
reason or the will of God commanding that the natural order of
things be preserved and forbidding that it be disturbed." (Contra
Faustum, XXII,27)

2. The Eternal Law Is a Law

But in order that it may be clear how this exemplar of divine
wisdom may be a law, let us expand the thought of St. Thomas
somewhat. This expansion may be phrased in the following remarks:
God, being intelligent, has a plan in creating the world. According
to this plan he directs all things to the end he has given them.
God cannot be indifferent whether this plan is carried out or not,
otherwise he would both will it and not will it. He must will that
creatures carry out his plan as he intends it. This plan of God's in-

tellect carried out by the decree of his will is what we call the eternal law. It can be easily shown that: (1) It is a law, and (2) It is an eternal law.

It is a law, for it has all the elements required by the definition of law: (a) It is an ordinance, a command, for God in creating wills that creatures follow a definite line of action so that they will certainly attain to the end he has in view. This, then, is no mere counsel or wish on the part of God, but a rule of action which he decrees to guide creatures. (b) It is an ordinance of reason, for it is God's reason which conceives creatures and their purposes and the means to that purpose. (c) It is for the common good, because it establishes order and harmony in creation, by which each being, accomplishing its purpose, will enable the whole universe to achieve the end God intends. (d) It is from authority, for God is the supreme ruler of the universe he has created. (e) It is promulgated, because God has embedded it in the very nature of the creatures governed by it, and has thus enabled them to observe it. Since, however, the promulgation must be adapted to the nature of the creature, irrational creatures have it promulgated in the very necessity of their natures by which they must act in certain and definite ways; rational creatures, since they are capable of understanding, have the promulgation of this law through knowledge.

It is an eternal law, for God is eternal, and his intellect and will, which are identified with his essence, are likewise eternal and unchangeable. This law is the plan of God's intellect carried out by the decree of his will, and since God cannot have accidents, whatever is in him is identified with him. Therefore such a law, identified with God himself, is properly called eternal.

3. The Promulgation of the Eternal Law

A difficulty is often brought up about the eternity of the promulgation. Since a law is for its subjects, promulgation is an essential part of law. But how can the eternal law, which is for creatures, be promulgated to creatures when the creatures do not yet exist?

This difficulty is only apparent. There are several answers that can be given. Promulgation does mean that the law is made known to someone. But the divine plan directive of all creatures was made known for all eternity in the Eternal Word. As St. Thomas puts it:

Promulgation is made by word of mouth or in writing, and in both ways the eternal law is promulgated, because both the Divine Word and the writing of the Book of Life are eternal. (S.T. I-II,91,1)

Or we may answer the difficulty by distinguishing between active and passive promulgation. Active promulgation is God's decree to make the law known to creatures when they exist; this must be eternal, for the plan of the universe existed eternally in God's intellect and the decree to activate this plan existed eternally in God's will. Passive promulgation is the actual knowing of the law by the creatures; this is not eternal, for, until creatures exist, they cannot know or keep a law. Since the eternal law by definition means the law in the Lawgiver rather than the law in the subject bound by it, it is obvious that active promulgation is the only kind such a law can have.

But it is still objected that active promulgation of this kind is not sufficient to justify it receiving the name of law, for law to be law must be passively promulgated, known to those who are to be guided by the law; otherwise the law would not have subjects and would, thus, be meaningless. Again, this difficulty is only apparent. For just as this plan must have eternally existed in the divine mind, so also all creatures for whose direction it was intended must have existed ideally in his mind, and thus the law always had subjects. Clearly the law was not promulgated to them in the sense of being made known to them, but it was promulgated in the sense of a divine and, therefore, immutable decree to be manifested in time, i.e., when the subjects of the law were destined to be given existence.

Those things that are not in themselves exist with God, inasmuch as they are foreknown and preordained by Him, according to Romans 4,17: Who calls those things that are not, as those that are. Accordingly the eternal concept of the Divine law bears the eternal concept of the eternal law, in so far as it is ordained by God to the government of things foreknown by Him. (S.T. I-II,91,1)

Then, too, we should see that if a law is only for the good of the subjects, that is, for the good of something beyond itself, then promulgation before the subjects exist is meaningless. However, the eternal law is not a means to anything beyond itself. Consequently, it can be promulgated before the subjects exist. Let us expand this. Human laws are means to an end outside of the legislators and the subjects, because they are rules of right reason which both the legislators and the subjects use to obtain what they do not already possess, namely, the common good. The eternal law, however, is not a means to something outside of God, nor is it a means used by creatures to obtain their own good. Rather, the eternal law is the divine intellect and will as a directive principle for creatures, directing creatures to their end which is God. Hence, the end of the eternal law is God himself. Though the eternal law produces effects outside of God, it is true, it is not for the purpose of the creatures but it directs the creatures to the end which is God. Even before created things existed, therefore, the eternal law has reached its end, i.e., the ordering of all things to the divine goodness. Consequently, though a human law without subjects is meaningless because a human law is a means for the creatures to obtain a good both distinct from the human legislator as well as from themselves, the eternal law without subjects is not meaningless since this law is its own end, i.e., God.

4. The Scope of the Eternal Law

Since the eternal law is the divine wisdom in so far as it contains the plan of the universe and directs all actions and movements of all creatures, the totality of creation, of both free and determined things, is subject to it. It comprises the laws of physical nature and the action of physical causes, no less than the moral law and human acts. It is the primeval and most fundamental law underlying the whole order of the universe, antecedent to it and coeternal with God. Because of this law everything is ordered to an end in accord with its nature. But this subjection of creatures to the eternal law is not the same in all creatures. Things which are without reason are subject to it because they possess inward principles of action by which they necessarily act to attain definite ends in accord with law, but they do not recognize the law. Man, however, is subject not only to this law but also to the commands of this law; that is, he is conscious of it and his moral rectitude consists in accepting them voluntarily. Consequently, man's subjection to the eternal law is twofold: first, as a natural being man is subject to the rule of God, as are all creatures, that he has a natural appetite to do what is right and good to attain his end and thus act according to his nature; second, as a rational being he can recognize this law that rules him and thus share in the divine reason that directs him.

Man, then, can voluntarily subject himself to the eternal law; he can also voluntarily refuse to so subject himself, but only temporarily for in the end he will be forced to subject himself. The good man, consequently, is he who with knowledge of the divine law acts according to it as he knows it and thus shares in the good that is given as a reward of observing the law. The evil man, on the other hand, is he who knowing the eternal law violates it and thus tries to avoid it. His attempt, however, is futile, for although he meets with a little success in enjoying his own temporal pleasure in the violation of the divine law, he must, nevertheless, make right the order of justice by suffering to atone for this pleasure acquired by the violation, this pleasure he should not have had.

There are two ways in which a thing is subject to the eternal law: first, by partaking of the eternal law by way of knowledge; secondly, by way of action and passion, i.e., by partaking of the eternal law by way of an inward moving principle. In this second way, irrational creatures are subject to the eternal law. But since the rational nature, along with that which it has in common with all creatures, has something proper to itself inasmuch as it is rational, consequently it is subject to the eternal law in both ways. For each rational creature both has some knowledge of the eternal law, and it also has a natural inclination to that which is in harmony with *the eternal law; for we are naturally adapted to be recipients of virtue, as it is said in Ethics ii.* [Nic. Ethics II, i, 1103a 25]

Both ways, however, are imperfect and to a certain extent destroyed in the wicked; because in them the natural inclination to virtue is corrupted by vicious habits, and, moreover, the natural knowledge of what is good is darkened in them by passions and habits of sin. But in the good, both ways are found more perfect, because in them, besides the natural knowledge of what is good, there is added knowledge of faith and wisdom; and, again, besides the natural inclination to what is good, there is the added interior motive of grace and virtue.

Accordingly, the good are perfectly subject to the eternal law, as always acting according to it. But the wicked are subject to the eternal law, imperfectly as to their actions, since both their knowledge of what is good and their inclination thereto are imperfect; but this imperfection on the part of action is supplied on the part of passion, in so far as they suffer what the eternal law decrees concerning them, according as they fail to act in harmony with that law. (S.T. I-II,93,6c)

A great point with many modern thinkers is the inviolability of physical nature. The difficulty lies in their conception of law. For these moderns, law is a mere systematic expression of fact (see the preceding chapter), a scheme established with no objective norm. To such a statistical summation of concrete cases, the modern thinkers claim that any exception is impossible and so claim that miracles are impossible. St. Thomas has a different view of law. To him law is a principle of action and hence in the physical order of things the repeated occurrence of an event is not the law but the expression or effect of law. Consequently, in relation to the eternal law natures or tendencies are the laws of physical natures.

Because there are no exceptions to these physical tendencies, for they are the natures of things, there cannot be exceptions which are not provided for in the eternal law itself. If these tendencies do not always produce their ordinary effects there is no exception to these tendencies but there is exception to the ordinary course of nature, that is, to the production of effects, which exception is provided for in the eternal law. The law of gravitation, for example, is equally fulfilled in a falling body, in an airplane held in the air by an engine and air flow, and in a body borne up by the power of God. The law of corruption of matter is equally fulfilled in a corpse, in the raising of the body of Lazarus, and in the Resurrection of Christ from the dead. There is no law to the effect that a supernatural force shall not intervene. Even if, as may be done perhaps in the greatest of all miracles, God suspends His concurrence, so that the creature acts not at all, that event would be no violation of the physical law of the creature's action: for all that such a law provides is that the creature, if it acts at all, shall act in a certain way, not that God will always give the concurrence which is the necessary condition of its acting at all. The laws of physical nature, then, are, strictly speaking, never violated, although the course of nature is sometimes altered by supernatural interference, and continually by free human volitions. Because God knows of these exceptions and the laws of physical nature, as well as of free natures, all are based upon the eternal law that guides all things to their proper ends. Consequently, every law—whatever be its origin, divine or human, physical or moral—and all exceptions to the carrying out of the law have their source ultimately in the divine eternal law. The reason is obvious: since the eternal law is the plan in the Supreme Ruler of the universe, all other laws or subordinate rules must be derived from this law, for the eternal law is the master plan to which all other subordinate plans must be conformed.

As was stated above, law denotes a kind of plan directing acts towards an end. Now wherever there are movers ordained to one another, the power of the second mover must need be derived from the power of the first mover, since the second mover does not move except in so far as it is moved by the first. Therefore we observe the same in all those who govern, namely, that the plan of government is derived by secondary governors from the governor in chief. Thus the plan of what is to be done in a state flows from the king's command to his inferior administrators; and again in things of art the plan of whatever is to be done by art flows from the chief craftsman to the undercraftsmen who work with their hands. Since, then, the eternal law is the plan of government in the Chief Governor, all the plans of government in the inferior governors must be derived from the eternal law. Therefore all laws, in so far as they partake of right reason, are derived from the eternal law. Hence Augustine says that in temporal law there is nothing just and lawful but what man has drawn from the eternal law. (S.T. I-II,93,3c)

5. The Knowledge of the Eternal Law

The existence of the eternal law is a necessary consequence of our knowledge of a personal God. Just as any human authority guides his subjects by first knowing and willing an end and the means to this end and then by directing the subjects to the end in accordance with this knowledge and will, so God guides all creatures to their respective ends in accordance with the divine knowledge and will which he has of these ends and means to these ends. Such is the eternal law: the eternal plan by which God directs all things to the end which he wills. Moreover, just as any human authority promulgates his law or guiding principle by imprinting it on things or by making it known to the intellects of his subjects, so God imprints his guiding principle or law on irrational creatures and makes it known to rational creatures through their intellects. The eternal law, then, as it is promulgated to creatures is the natural law.

We must, then, say that the eternal law is the exemplar of the natural law. However, we should note that although the eternal law is ontologically prior to and is the cause of the natural law, yet the natural law is known before the eternal law, and through it we come to a knowledge of the eternal law. This should not be a surprise if we have followed the way of philosophy, even though we have dealt with the eternal law first. Just as we come to know the existence of God, who is the efficient cause of all things, from the existence of finite beings, so from the existence of the natural law we come to a knowledge of God as the Lawgiver and of the existence of the eternal law. Just as the existence of finite things requires God's efficient causality, so the natural law existing in finite beings requires another law which is its cause, in which it participates, of which it is the reflection.

Since the divine wisdom, which is the truth of God, is beyond the comprehension of any created intellect and since such knowledge is simply incommunicable, no creature can directly know the eternal law, which is the divine wisdom. Nevertheless, any knowledge of moral truth or of the necessity in physical things which man attains is a participation in the eternal law. Now, all those who have the use of reason, because they are able to form the common principles of the natural law as well as of being itself, have attained some knowledge of moral and physical truth. This limited knowledge is a participation in the eternal law. In this manner all rational beings attain to some knowledge of the eternal law.

6. *The Existence of the Natural Law*

When the divine plan or eternal law is actualized or promulgated through the creative act, a multitude of beings, rational and irrational, come into orderly existence. Each has its place in the whole; each is related in certain fixed and unchangeable ways to the others. The sum total of these immutable relations constitutes the natural order of things. This order is maintained because each creature, following the modes of activity with which it has been endowed by the Creator, not only attains its own particular end, but so conspires with all others that the end of the whole is attained. Each observes the *law of its nature*.

Let us dwell upon this. In all things in nature there are constant and uniform inclinations to attain definite ends. It is natural for the sun to light and heat the earth, for flowers to grow and bloom, for fish to swim and birds to fly, for man to think his thoughts and share them with his fellows. They are simply obeying the law stamped on their natures by their Creator. Here we see the eternal law at work in creatures, the divine reason and will guiding them to their ends. Here we see the temporal effects of the eternal law. Here we see the natural law at work, for the temporal effect of the eternal law showing itself in creatures is what we mean by the natural law. We call it natural law because it is grounded in nature itself, and manifests itself through the nature or essence or constitution of things. St. Thomas writes:

Law, being a rule and measure, can be in a person in two ways: in one way, as in him that rules and measures; in another way, as in that which is ruled and measured, since a thing is ruled and measured in so far as it partakes of the rule and measure. Therefore, since all things subject to divine providence are ruled and measured by the eternal law, as was stated above, it is evident that all things partake in some way in the eternal law, in so far as, namely, from its being imprinted on them, they derive their respective inclinations to their proper acts and ends. Now among all others, the rational creature is subject to divine providence in a more excellent way, in so far as it itself partakes of a share of providence, by being provident both for itself and for others. Therefore, it has a share of the eternal reason, whereby it has a natural inclination to its proper act and end; and this participation of the eternal law in the rational creature is called the natural law. (S.T. I-II,91,2c)

There is an axiom that whatever is received is received according to the manner or capacity of the recipient. This axiom applies to the manner in which creatures participate in the eternal law. That they must participate in this law in some manner follows from the fact that since the eternal law is the rule according to which God, in his providence, guides all things to their natural ends, this law must somehow be imprinted in, imposed on, the creatures which are to be guided by the eternal law.

The great multitude of creatures are wholly necessary agents. Even in man, in a free agent, much of what is in him, and much that proceeds from him, is necessary and beyond the control of his will. In inorganic matter, the tendency of each individual object is to preserve its own existence, to exercise its own proper functions —i.e., to assume a certain form, to possess certain chemical attractions and repulsions, to exhibit a certain odor, weight and color; these acts are possible only if such matter has inclinations to perfect its own nature. In the organic world, plants are moved by an inner inclination to take in moisture, to assimilate, to grow and to reproduce; animals are moved to seek food, to assimilate, to grow, and to reproduce by conscious impulses of nature according to which they act in determined and definite manners; such conscious impulses we call instinct. In man, too, these same inclinations to assimilate, to grow, and to reproduce are present. And although they are fundamentally sensuous and, therefore, conscious appetites, they are under the control of his reason. All of these inclinations are the means which nature uses to attain certain necessary ends; without them neither the individual nor the species could continue to exist. These appetites or inclinations are part of the natural constitution of things. They are the law of nature, the rule that natures must follow.

We must remember that God does not move and govern His creatures by some external directive impulse, as a billiard player imparts motion and direction to the cue ball, or a baseball pitcher to a baseball, but that God directs all things by an inclination and impulse which He has implanted in the very constitution or essence of things. Let us here recall the distinction which we have made between a philosophical and a scientific law. The scientific law is the concrete expression of these inclinations and in their turn the inclinations are the philosophical law. Both are expressions of the eternal law.

As nonrational creatures have guiding principles within their very being by which they live and act for their several purposes, so man himself has similar guiding principles. However, man works towards his end by a knowledge of what is good for him and by choosing the known good. Consequently, man is not necessitated by blind impulse or instinct; he must work his own way by picking and choosing what he knows is good for him. But like all creatures, he must have guiding principles by which he regulates his human actions, by which he can know what is good and so choose. Such principles must evidently be consonant with his freedom; that is, they direct him but they do not physically necessitate him.

Let us put it in another way. All irrational creatures have implanted in their natures certain guiding principles which physically determine them to definite lines of action by which they attain their purposes. Man cannot be an exception to this generality; he, too, must have certain guiding principles, natural impulses by which he is directed to his purpose. For if irrational creatures have inclinations to act according to their natures to attain the purposes

which God wills, man must have inclinations to act according to his
nature. Now, because it is by reason and will that God directs
man to his final end, man must have the inclination to judge what
is necessary for his perfection and the power to choose what is
necessary for this. Hence, man must have an impulse, an inborn
inclination, a power, to judge about his actions, whether they are
conducive or not to his final end. Man must make judgments
about his actions, whereby he recognizes what is good and what is
evil. Man, therefore, possesses a power to judge that some actions
are good and to be done, that others are evil and to be omitted;
and the sum of these judgments is the natural law. This is the eternal
law as made known to man, whereby he is to regulate his free acts.
It is a reflection of and a participation in the eternal law: as God
judges of means to an end for man by the eternal law, so man judges
of means to an end by the natural law.

By the natural law, we mean the temporal effects of the eternal
law as shown in creatures. We call it the natural law because it is
grounded in nature itself, and manifests itself through the nature or
essence or constitution of things. The part of the natural law governing irrational creatures is the *natural physical law,* because it physically necessitates; it is the *law of nature,* and the part of the natural law governing rational creatures is *natural moral law.* It is customary to use the terms *natural law* and *moral law* interchangeably.

It is called the natural law, first, because it is found more or
less perfectly expressed in all rational creatures, at least in the most
general form: Do good and avoid evil. It belongs to their specific
nature, for all men are conscious that good must be done and evil
must be avoided. Moreover, this law points to something which any
rational nature must necessarily encompass within itself in order to
obtain the perfection of its own being. Again, this law is natural in
much the same sense that speech, walking, and seeing are natural to
man. One who has no trace of it would be below the standard of
mankind, something abnormal, so much so that if one did not have
it he would not be capable of human action. But like many natural endowments the natural law will depend for its development
on education, training, and environment. Every rational creature,
then, knows that there is a difference between good and evil, and

every rational creature is conscious that as he distinguishes between good and evil, the good is to be done, the evil to be avoided. Wherefore we can define the *natural law as the rule of action that reason itself discovers as necessary to perfect happiness.* From what we have said it is apparent why St. Thomas defines it as "the rational creature's participation of the eternal law." (*S.T.*I-II,91,2c)

Francis Suarez (*De Legibus* 1, II, c. 5) says that the "Natural Law may be said to be that certain rule of action which is essentially inherent in the very nature of every creature. The law of all creatures' actions is rooted in their very nature, or it results from the very constitution of their essence. Creatures have no actions, and can have none, except in accordance with the law originally implanted in them at their creation." This is, of course, essentially the same as what we have said. The natural law can be said to exist in some form or other in all creatures. It is present in plants, in animals, in men. But the natural law of animals and plants falls far short of the full conception of law. For law is an activity of reason, whereas animals and plants have no reason. In them, the eternal law is indeed, received or participated in, but it is received in a modified form only, and not as a rule of reason. The natural law of plants and animals, therefore, though it results from or reflects the eternal law, is rather of the nature of an irresistible force than law. But in man the natural law is law in the true sense of the word. It is a dictate of man's reason, as the eternal law is a dictate of God's divine reason. For, even though the natural law does not proceed from or originate in the reason of man ultimately, yet man's reason is the proximate source of it, and unlike both plants and animals man guides himself to his final end by means of it. The natural law, then, in man is law in the fullest and truest sense of the term. Consequently, the natural law is that aspect of the eternal law that is impressed on rational creatures to direct them to their final end.

Even irrational animals partake in their own way of the eternal reason, just as the rational creature does. But because the rational creature partakes thereof in an intellectual and rational manner, therefore the participation of the eternal law in the rational creature is properly called a law, since a law is something pertaining to reason, as was stated above. Irrational creatures, however, do not partake thereof in a rational manner, and therefore there is no participation of the eternal law in them, except by way of likeness. (S.T. *I-II*,91,2 ad 3)

Rational creatures, as we have said, have perfect happiness as the end of their activity. Inasmuch as God created them for this purpose, he must efficaciously desire that this end be attained by them, in a manner consonant with their nature. Their nature is a free nature; hence they can be moved to act only if the intellect proposes to the will a good to be attained; they can be moved to act with any amount of necessity only if the good is recognized as something of obligation, i.e., as leading to perfect happiness for which they are striving, for which man is striving. What the good is we have proven in Chapter III on The Moral Act: it is what is conformed to human nature. Consequently, there must exist in man a power of mind enabling him to know what he must do and what he must avoid to obtain perfect happiness. Man must not only do what is in harmony with his nature; he must also avoid what is at discord with it. He must, therefore, be able to detect this harmony and discord and at the same time recognize an obligation to do the good and avoid the evil. The good and evil so known, with the consequent obligation of performing the one and avoiding the other, constitute the natural law.

God, then, is bound so to construct the human reason that it will, with ease, formulate particular, obligating judgments with regard to conduct. For, since it is by reason that man is led by God to fulfill his part in the plan of creation, reason must have a native capacity to form these practical, obligating judgments which are a reflection or a promulgation of the eternal law of God commanding that the natural order be observed and forbidding its disturbance. These judgments give direction and motion to the will towards man's final end. They give direction because they express what will lead to this end; they give motion to the will because they show the necessity of doing the good and avoiding the evil.

We have proved *a priori* that there is a natural law. A consideration of human history in all its variety of time, place and condition ought, therefore, to give us *a posteriori* verification of the fact that all men are conscious of an obligation, of a necessary way of acting and, therefore, that they participate in the eternal law. All men know something of this law and its universal prescriptions for honesty, fairness, and courage. C. S. Lewis in his book, *The Case for Christianity*,* has put the matter most clearly:

True, some people say that the idea of a Natural Law known to all men is unsound, because different civilizations and different ages have had quite different moralities. But they haven't. They have only had slightly different moralities. Just think of what a quite different morality would mean. Think of a country where people were admired for running away in battle, or where a man felt proud for double-crossing all the people who had been kindest to him. You might just as well try to imagine a country where two and two made five. Men have differed as regards what people you ought to be unselfish to—whether it was only your own family, or your fellow countrymen, or every one. But they have always agreed that you oughtn't put yourself first. Selfishness has never been admired. Men have differed as to whether you should have one wife or four. But they have always agreed that you mustn't simply have any woman you liked. People are constantly appealing to this law of nature in common life and constantly attempting to justify their conduct before it.

Thus, everyone has heard people quarrelling. Sometimes it sounds funny and sometimes it sounds merely unpleasant; but however it sounds, we can learn something very important from listening to the kind of things they say. They say things like this: "That's my seat, I was there first"—"Leave him alone, he isn't doing you any harm"—"Why should you shove in first?"—"Give me a piece of your orange, I gave you some of mine"—"How'd you like it if anyone did the same to you?"—"Come on, you promised." People say things like that every day, educated people as well as uneducated, and children as well as grown-ups.

Now what is so interesting about all these remarks is that the man who makes them isn't just saying that the other man's behavior doesn't happen to please him. He is appealing to some kind of standard of behavior which he expects the other man to know about. And the other man very seldom replies, "I am not interested in your standard!" Nearly always he tries to make out that what he has been doing doesn't really go against the standard, or that if it does, there is some special excuse. He pretends there is some special reason in this particular case why the person

* Lewis, C. S., *The Case for Christianity*. New York: The Macmillan Company, 1945, pp. 3-5.

who took the seat first should not keep it, or that things were quite different when he was given a piece of orange, or that something has turned up which lets him off keeping his promise. It looks, in fact, very much as if both parties had in mind some kind of Law or Rule of fair play or decent behavior or morality, about which they really agreed. And they have. If they hadn't, they might, of course, fight like animals, but they couldn't quarrel in the human sense of the word. Quarrelling means trying to show that the other man's in the wrong. And there would be no sense in trying to do that unless you and he had some sort of agreement as to what is right and wrong, just as there would be no sense in saying that a football player had committed a foul unless there was some agreement about the rules of football.

The most remarkable thing about all this is that whenever you find a man who says he doesn't believe in a real right and wrong, you find the same man going back on this a moment later. He may break his promise to you, but if you try to break one to him he will be complaining, "It's not fair" before you can say Jack Robinson. A nation may say treaties don't matter; but then, the next minute, they spoil their case by saying the particular treaty they want to break was an unfair one. But if treaties don't matter, and if there's no such thing as right and wrong—in other words, if there is no Natural Law—what is the difference between a fair treaty and an unfair one? Haven't they given away the fact that, whatever they say, they really know the Natural Law just like anyone else? We seldom hear a subjectivist reply which repudiates the standard. Outside academic walls and classrooms men are not relativists and subjectivists. Both parties know something of the Natural Law and accept it as real, obligatory, with authority over them, as they certainly would not accept any merely human invention. So nearly always what the other man does is to try to justify himself.

Even primitive peoples and children have some knowledge of the natural law. This law obliges us because it is based not on any human opinion or desire but rather on the very nature of man and of the universe he inhabits. Hence of all our faculties reason alone, which apprehends things exactly as they really are, is able to apprehend its prescriptions.

As soon as we understand the nature of any finite thing we also understand the general kind of activity or treatments which perfect that thing. What is good for one thing is not good for another. What perfects a fish will kill a tree, and vice versa. We can gain some general understanding of the nature of man; hence we can gain some general understanding of the pattern of activity which will perfect this nature and the instruments it requires. This understanding is purely theoretical and is accessible to any human mind. But when it is united with a metaphysical natural desire to perfect man's nature, it is transformed into a set of practical principles for the direction of human action. These are the principles of the natural law—a rational determination, founded on nature, of the end which perfects man and of the necessary means to this end.

This law is not made up or constructed by any man or human groups: it is rather discovered by reason as embedded in the very nature of things and is caused by God who has produced human nature and the natural world of which man is a part. This law is not, as we will see, a mere empty form of universality lacking all concrete content, for human nature possesses distinctive notes and demands a distinctive perfection and modes of activity. Hence this law is not *a priori* in the modern subjectivistic sense: it can be discovered only by an empirical examination of the real nature of man as he actually exists. Finally, this law is universal in the sense that it applies not merely to this group or that, but to all men whatsoever, and wherever they may be. It does not describe the way in which they must act or the way in which they do act, but rather the way in which they *ought* to act: the way they *must* act if they are to perfect their nature. These judgments, therefore, of good and evil of actions are a part of the consciousness of the human race. Men have constantly and universally judged that there is a difference between right and wrong in human behavior and that there is an obligation to do the right and to avoid the wrong—so judged because man's reason has been impressed by God, the Author of Nature, with a capacity and an impulse so to judge under the conditions proper for the exercise of this capacity and impulse. Nothing can explain the constancy and universality of these judgments except a cause as constant and universal as the judgments themselves. Obviously this cause can only be human reason.

7. How Reason Discovers the Natural Law

Our business now is to study the content of this law. This can be inferred from the role which the natural law plays as the regulator of man's activity. Just as all knowledge is derived from the first principles of being intuitively known to us, so all desire for the means to perfect happiness is derived from our innate desire for perfect happiness; and since it is the natural law that directs man to perfect happiness, it is from this law that the obligation of performing or omitting actions is derived.

Certain elementary moral principles, therefore, belong naturally to the human mind in the sense that certain elementary theoretical truths belong to the human mind. They are natural, not in the sense of being innate, but because the mind comes quickly and easily to acquire them. These principles may differ in words between one mind and another, but they are fundamentally the same. The commonest type of them is to be seen in such elementary judgments as that good should be done, evil avoided, parents should be honored, benefactors requited, evildoers punished, etc. In regard to these the question arises: What is their origin?

The question belongs primarily to psychology, not to ethics. However, we must treat of it for ethical purposes. St. Thomas writes:

The precepts of the natural law are to the practical reason what the first principles of demonstration are to the speculative reason because both are self-evident principles. Now a thing is said to be self-evident in two ways: first, in itself, secondly, in relation to us. Any proposition is said to be self-evident in itself, if its predicate is contained in the notion of the subject; even though it may happen that to one who does not know the definition of the subject, such a proposition is not self-evident. For instance, this proposition, Man is a rational being, is, in its very nature, self-evident, since he who says man, says, a rational being; and yet to one who does not know what a man is, this proposition is not self-evident. Hence it is that, as Boethius says, certain axioms or propositions are universally evident to all; and such are the propositions whose terms are known to all, as Every whole is greater than its parts, and Things equal to one and the same are equal to one another. But some propositions are self-evident only to the wise, who understand the meaning of the terms of such propositions. Thus to one who understands that an angel is not a body, it is self-evident that an angel is not circumscriptively in place. But this is not evident to the unlearned, for they cannot grasp it.

Now a certain order is found in those things that are apprehended by men. For that which first falls under apprehension is being, the understanding of which is included in all things whatsoever a man apprehends. Therefore the first indemonstrable principle is that the same thing cannot be affirmed and denied at the same time, which is based on the notion of being and nonbeing: and on this principle all others are based, as is stated in Metaph. iv [Aristotle, Meta. III,c,1005b,29] Now as being is the first thing that falls under the apprehension absolutely, so good is the first thing that falls under the apprehension of the practical reason, which is directed to action (since every agent acts for an end, which has the nature of good). Consequently, the first principle in the practical reason is one founded on the nature of good, viz., that good is that which all things seek after. Hence this is the first precept of law, that good is to be done and promoted and evil is to be avoided. All other precepts of the natural law are based upon this; so that all things which the practical reason naturally apprehends as man's good belong to the precept of the natural law under the form of things to be done or avoided.

Since, however, good has the nature of an end, and evil, the nature of the contrary, hence it is that all those things to which man has a natural inclination are naturally apprehended by reason as being good, and consequently as objects of pursuit, and their contraries as evil, and objects of avoidance. Therefore, the order of the precepts of the natural law is according to the order of the natural inclinations. For there is in man, first of all, an inclination to good in accordance with the nature which he has in common with all substances, inasmuch, namely, as every substance seeks the preservation of its own being, according to its nature; and by reason of this inclination whatever is a means of preserving human life, and of warding off its obstacles, belongs to the natural law. Secondly, there is in man an inclination to things that pertain to him more specially, according to that nature which he has in common with other animals; and in virtue of this inclination, those things are said to belong to the natural law which nature has taught to all animals, such as sexual intercourse, the education of offspring and so forth. Thirdly, there is in man an inclination to good according to the nature of reason, which nature is proper to him. Thus man has a natural inclination to know the truth about

God, and to live in society; and in this respect, whatever pertains to this inclination belongs to the natural law: e.g., to shun ignorance, to avoid offending those among who one has to live, and other such things regarding the above inclinations. (S.T. I-II,94,2c)

The "origin" of these primary moral precepts or principles may mean several things: (1) The original sources whence man in ages past received these moral precepts; (2) the logical grounds upon which these moral judgments are based; (3) the beginning of these judgments in the mind of a child today. It is the last with which we are now concerned, but it will necessarily imply the second. What is the source of a child's moral judgments? Do they come to a child by unaided reason? Are they the result of reason helped by tradition? Or are they due to tradition alone?

We are of the opinion that these primary moral judgments are self-evident truths. A self-evident truth, according to St. Thomas, is a truth which is evident to anyone who knows the meaning of the terms; that is, a truth that is apprehended without reasoning, a proposition on the mere consideration of which it is seen that the predicate is contained in the subject. It is apparent that some truths in the speculative field of knowledge are self-evident. No one reasons to the conclusion that the whole is greater than the part, that being is not nonbeing. These truths are immediately evident to anyone. However, there are some self-evident truths whose truths are understood by only the wise; for example, that an angel is not circumscriptively in space because it has no body.

As it is hardly necessary to point out, it does not follow from what has been said that whatever propositions or judgments are known to all men are therefore self-evident. For some truths in both the theoretical and practical orders of knowledge are known to all and yet are not self-evident. Such is the case, for example, with many of the precepts of the natural law. They are known to all men, not because they are self-evident, but because the reasoning process involved in arriving at them is so simple that the mind cannot help performing the process if it thinks at all. Hence, these truths are not self-evident but are still known to all men.

Now it is clear that some moral principles must be self-evident, for many of our moral principles are deduced from other principles, and all deduction must ultimately begin with principles that are self-evident. If any deductive science were without self-evident principles it would be impossible to reason in such a science. For all reasoning, like all movement, must begin from a fixed point, and in the case of reasoning the fixed point is the principle or group of principles which the human intellect accepts without the need of reasoning and on the ground of their own intrinsic evidence. Hence, there must be some self-evident moral principles.

Because they are self-evident all men know them and such knowledge is not entirely dependent on tradition, that is, on the teaching of parents and masters. Few today would maintain the extreme view that such principles are due solely to tradition. That they are something due partly to teaching may be readily admitted. Tradition plays a part in much of what we accept intellectually. Children, long before they are able to reason or to express their thoughts with any clarity, have already been instructed in moral truths, i.e., they have in the first instance accepted these truths on the ground of tradition alone. Even children of savage tribes, from their very earliest years, are taught the particular religious and moral persuasions of their tribes, so that from the beginning their moral principles are developed under pressure of religious, moral, and political training.

The child may begin with tradition, but by the time the use of reason has asserted itself the child holds some of the principles not merely on the testimony of his parents or teachers but because he sees them as true; some of these as self-evident truths, some as reasoned truths. The child who has reached the age of reason knows that two and two are four not merely because the printed book or his teacher tells him so but because of the inner conviction of the truth. And he would refuse to believe you if, with no matter how great an apparatus of learning, you tried to prove to him that two and two make five. Similarly he may be taught that many things are good, many things are bad, but at the age of reason he knows that the good must be done and the evil must be avoided not because he has been taught this but because he sees the reason for it.

The reason and origin of this is that God has endowed man

with the ability and the impulse to form many concepts, principles, or judgments. When man comes to the use of reason he forms, by a natural necessity based on the apprehension of being, certain general principles of theoretical reason which are the bases of all his reasoning in the speculative sphere of knowledge. These are self-evident principles. Such self-evident truths are: the same things cannot be affirmed and denied at the same time; that which begins to be must have a cause; etc.

And in the practical order, in the order of activity which is directed to the good, as soon as reason can judge, by a necessity of nature, it forms the concept of good and evil, i.e., the opposed concepts of something which is proper to the reasoner—as a rational creature, as a child of these parents, as a student of this teacher, as a member of this church, etc.—and worth striving for, and of something which is unbecoming and therefore to be avoided. And so by nature the child is attracted by what is good and repelled by what is evil. Thus he necessarily forms some self-evident judgments, as: good must be done, evil must be avoided, good is to be returned to benefactors, evildoers are to be punished.

However, because the will is necessarily inclined towards good and repelled by evil, the first self-evident principle is that the good must be done and the evil avoided. But not only is it self-evident that good is to be done and evil is to be avoided but, since good is that which is befitting an appetite, that which we desire by a natural appetite is good. Thus no man can fail to recognize that food is good, that society is good, for all men are moved by natural appetites to food and society. Such goods are self-evident, for to know an appetite is to know the fulfillment of that appetite is good. This does not mean, however, that the pursuit of the objects of these appetites is always good. For even when reason apprehends that certain things are good for a particular appetite, it also recognizes that such objects must be pursued in due manner, i.e., according as reason recognizes the relationship of subordination of one appetite to another. Thus, every man recognizes that eating is good, but that it is not good to the extent that it injures one. The determination of such relationship requires, at times, much reasoning, but the object of the appetites is recognized as good.

Because there is a hierarchy of appetites which incline men to different goods, the self-evident goods may be divided according to this hierarchy. Thus, man in common with other substances has an appetite for self-preservation, and since good is the object of appetite, one's own continual existence is a self-evident good. In common with animals, man has certain natural appetites for food, for sexual intercourse, and for the care of offspring; hence the good of these is self-evident. Other appetites are proper to man, like the appetite for society, i.e., for a life of peaceful relations and mutual help; hence to help and not to injure those with whom we live is a self-evident good.

These are examples of some of the self-evident truths in the practical order of knowledge. As soon as man becomes conscious of the appetites or inclinations which he possesses he knows that the fulfillment of these is good. True, man does not possess a simple but rather a most complex nature in which there are almost countless appetites seeking satisfaction. The order of satisfaction is a complicated problem: it is not easy at times to determine what appetite should be satisfied and which should not. Such knowledge requires a profound study of human nature and its hierarchy of appetites, and such a study will result in a more detailed knowledge of the precepts of the natural law. This study will be undertaken in the next chapter, but for the present we must say that human reason without any reasoning apprehends that the appetites are good and their fulfillment is equally good. But more than this: for simultaneously with this discovery man is conscious of a necessity, an obligation, to place actions in conformity with them, to omit actions difformed to them. He is conscious, in other words, that the good must be done, the evil avoided. Such is the first self-evident truth in the sphere of morals. This is the first principle of the natural law and is known to all men.

Readings

Aristotle, *Nicomachean Ethics*, bk. I.

Cronin, Michael, *The Science of Ethics*, vol. I, pp. 225-244.

Doheny, Wm. J., C.S.C., "The Eternal Law Background of Natural Law," *University of Notre Dame Natural Law Institute Proceedings*, 1947, pp. 104-142.

Farrell, W., A *Companion to the Summa*, vol. II, pp. 365-411.

Hart, Chas., "The Natural Law and International Relations," *Proceedings of the American Catholic Philosophical Association*, XXIV (1950). Papers by various authors.

Leibell, J. F., *Readings in Ethics*. The following articles are informative.

"The eternal law," Joseph Rickaby, pp. 313-317.
"The natural law," Walter McDonald, pp. 317-320.
"The natural law," V. Cathrein, pp. 320-323.
"The Kantian ought," Timothy Brosnahan, pp. 383-400.

McKinnon, Harold J., *The Higher Law*.
—— "Natural Law and Positive Law," *University of Notre Dame Natural Law Institute Proceedings*, 1947, pp. 85-103.

Maritain, J., *Man and the State*, pp. 80-107.
—— "Natural Law and Moral Law," *Moral Principles of Action*, ed. Ruth Nanda Anshen, pp. 62-76.
—— "On the Philosophy of Human Rights," *Human Rights*, a symposium, ed. UNESCO, pp. 72-77.
—— *The Rights of Man and the Natural Law*, pp. 59-64.

Plato, *Republic*, bk. IV; *Laws*, bk. VII; *Gorgias*.

Rickaby, Joseph, *Moral Philosophy*, pp. 126-132; 184-215.

Rommen, H., *The Natural Law*, pp. 161-269.

Suarez, Francisco, *De Legibus*, bk. II, cc. 5-8; 13-15.

St. Thomas, *Summa Theologica*, I-II, pp. 93-95.

CHAPTER VIII

THE PROPERTIES OF
THE NATURAL LAW

In the preceding chapter we began to study the content of the natural law. The purpose of this present chapter is to continue this
same study by a consideration of the properties of this law. We
mean by a property that which necessarily flows from or accompanies an essence but is not the essence. Traditionally these properties have been attributed to the natural law: *unity, universality,
clarity, immutability,* and *sanction.* We will deal with these five
properties in the order mentioned.

With regard to the natural law three questions may be asked.
First, with respect to a single individual, is the natural law one unified whole? Secondly, with respect to all men and in all places, is it
one unified whole? Thirdly, is it also such a unified whole with respect to all times and every condition of human nature?

1. *The Unity of the Natural Law*

The first of these questions deals with the property of *unity.*
By imputing unity to the natural law we mean that with respect to

an individual the natural law is one unified whole. This means that although there are many principles of the natural law, nevertheless, all can be referred to one common or single principle in which, as it were, they are all united, and from which all the duties of man's moral activities can be derived. This single principle which all men naturally and infallibly have in common in regard to their moral activity is that *good must be done and evil must be avoided.*

We can infer this principle from the role which the natural law has as regulator of man's activity towards his ultimate end. We have said something about this in the preceding chapter, but a more detailed exposition will be profitable. In this exposition we must consider the meaning of a self-evident proposition. In the speculative order of knowledge, it is not possible to prove everything by demonstration. Things that are so proven are not principles but conclusions. There must be principles that are known by some other kind of act than that of discursive reasoning. Now besides discursive reasoning, there are two other acts of the human intellect: simple apprehension and judgment. By simple apprehension, a simple concept is conceived, say, the concept of "being," or "thing." By the simplest of judgments the intellect of man knows that "a thing is a thing," or "a thing is a being," or "a being is not a nonbeing." No reasoning is involved in this judgment, but such a judgment is certainly a known truth, and a knowledge of the truth that "being is being" or that "being and nonbeing are not the same" is the very foundation of all discursive reasoning of the speculative intellect. How does the human intellect know these first truths unless it has a special quality by which it can, without reasoning, know the concepts included in the judgment? The reason why the intellect can make such judgments is that it sees, without reasoning, that the predicate "being" is included in the essence of the subject "being," or that the predicate "nonbeing" is not included in the essence of the subject "being." In other words, the intellect sees that the proposition is self-evident, indemonstrable. The quality of the intellect by which the intellect is able to know these self-evident principles is called the *habit of first principles,* or *understanding.*

These judgments about being are so simple and so true that

everyone makes them as soon as he reaches the age of reason. And having been made, they are the very foundations of, and included in, every demonstration of the speculative intellect, for unless the judgment of "being is being" is implied in every demonstration, the demonstration is no demonstration. The reason, of course, is that the formal object of the intellect is being as being. This knowledge of being and nonbeing enables the intellect to infer by analytical derivation the other fundamental principles of the speculative intellect.

Now, just as the speculative intellect cannot arrive at any truth unless it first make the judgment about the nature of being—or, in other words, unless it perceive the self-evident and indemonstrable truth that "being is being"—so the practical intellect, which is concerned with action, must have some first principle or self-evident truth upon which it may base its reasoning about action. The practical intellect has such a principle based on its apprehension of good as desirable. The reason why the knowledge of the good as desirable belongs to the practical rather than to the speculative intellect is that the speculative intellect is ordered to the contemplation of truth, and unlike the practical intellect, it does not look to action. It cannot, of course, be denied that the speculative intellect can and does speculate upon the nature of good, but the apprehension of good as desirable looks to the appetite and therefore looks to action at least as a remote possibility. Now every agent must act for an end, and the end must be viewed as good and desirable. Hence action presupposes knowledge of the good. From this knowledge of the good as desirable, the intellect forms the first principle of the practical reason. This first principle is expressed thus: *The good is that which all desire and seek.* The judgment by which the intellect forms this principle is immediate, that is, there is no demonstration involved, since anything desired and sought is desired and sought under the formality of good. Nothing is desirable, nothing is sought except under the formality of good. Hence, "the good is that which all seek." From this principle follows the first principle of the natural law: *The good must be done and evil must be avoided.* From this first principle follow others.

Now a certain order is to be found in those things that are apprehended by men. For that which first falls under apprehension is being, the understanding of which is included in all things whatsoever a man apprehends. Therefore, the first indemonstrable principle is that the same thing cannot be affirmed and denied at the same time, which is based on the notion of being and nonbeing: and on this principle all others are based, as is stated in Metaph. IV. [Metaph. III,3,1005b,29] Now as being is the first thing that falls under the apprehension absolutely, so good is the first thing that falls under the practical reason, which is directed to action (since every agent acts for an end, which has the nature of good). Consequently, the first principle in the practical reason is one founded on the nature of good, viz., that good is that which all things seek after. Hence this is the first precept of law, that good is to be done and promoted, and evil is to be avoided. All other precepts of the natural law are based upon this; so that all the things which the practical reason naturally apprehends as man's good belong to the precepts of the natural law under the form of things to be done or avoided. (S.T. I-II,94,2c)

To recapitulate this discussion. Just as from the apprehension of being by the speculative intellect there follows the judgment that *being is being*, which is a self-evident proposition, and upon this judgment there follow other self-evident propositions analytically contained in this, such as *a thing cannot be and not be at the same time*, so from the apprehension of good there follows the judgment of the practical intellect that *good must be done*, and upon this judgment there follow other self-evident propositions that are analytically contained in this. And just as all discursive reasoning of the speculative intellect implies its first self-evident proposition, so all discursive reasoning of the practical intellect implies its first self-evident proposition.

This principle of the natural law is self-evident to all, for the terms of the proposition—"good" and "must be done," "evil" and "must be avoided"—are understood by all men. That the predicates "must be done" and "must be avoided" belong to the nature of the subjects "good" and "evil" is explained in the following manner. It is the nature of an appetite to move to action when attracted by its object, by that which is suitable for, or perfective of, the appetite. An appetite naturally seeks, or is naturally inclined to, its own good. Now reason naturally understands that the good is that towards which nature tends by its appetites, for the good is that which is suitable for human nature, and which disposes man to his end. Evil, on the other hand, is that which causes man to deviate from the end. Evil is, therefore, the contrary of good. Hence reason understands that the good must be sought, precisely because it is the perfection of nature, and that the evil must be avoided because it is opposed to the good. As soon, therefore, as the intellect knows the appetite, it knows that good must be sought and evil avoided. Consequently, the first principle of the natural law is not only absolutely true but also self-evident.

Although this principle, "the good must be done, the evil must be avoided," is the first and fundamental principle of the natural law, it is not the only self-evident principle; rather there are many such indemonstrable principles. The reason is that since the natural law is to direct man towards his ultimate good, it must direct him to the complete good, the whole good. This, of course, is happiness. But happiness, as a whole of goods, as the possession of all good things, is constituted by an order and variety of partial goods, each of which is a part of the end and may, therefore, be regarded as an end or as a constitutive means to *the* end. Hence, the natural law may be expressed in a single principle or in several principles, according as the end is conceived as the whole itself or as the orderly structure of the parts constituting the whole. "Do good" is analytically equivalent to "do every kind of good which is essential to the constitution of happiness." Precisely because human happiness is itself a complex unity, the natural law can be expressed in a single principle which derives its singleness from the unity of the end, or in several principles which derive their multiplicity from the complexity of the end. When it is said in response to the first objection (*S.T.*I-II,94,a,2) that the several principles are reducible to one, or flow from that one, what is indicated is not that the many are deducible from the one—for then the several principles would be conclusions, whereas they are as genuinely indemonstrable as the single principle—but rather that the one and the many are analytically equivalent expressions of the same truth.

Let us make this point clear, for it will be most useful in regard to the universality, clarity, and immutability of the natural law. Every man's will is necessarily fixed upon the good and necessarily repelled by the evil. Man cannot help but seek the good; he must necessarily seek happiness. Since it is the practical intellect which must direct man in seeking happiness, whatever it apprehends as the good must be sought and done; and, on the contrary, whatever the practical intellect understands to be bad for man must be avoided.

The principle is clear, self-evident. The real crux of the matter, the point to be established, is this: How can we discover in the concrete what is the good, what is happiness for man, and what are the true means to such happiness so that man may seek it? If happiness were a simple thing, all there would be to the natural law would be *the good must be done and the evil avoided.* But happiness is very complex, the object of many different desires, and these desires must be directed by specific principles of the natural law. How, then, are we to discover what the good is for these desires, so that we may know the principles of the natural law which must be observed to obtain happiness? St. Thomas answers very simply that the good will be understood from a consideration of the things to which man has a natural inclination. Consequently the order of principles of the natural law will be discovered in accordance with the order of natural inclinations.

The point to be established is: How can we discover in the concrete the good of human nature, that is, not only true happiness, but also the means to such happiness and, consequently, what the natural law prescribes? The answer is that "reason naturally understands" that the good of human nature must be manifested by a natural inclination, that is, by an inclination of man's specific nature. Hence, first of all, we must understand, not merely by observation but by a reflection upon man's nature, what these inclinations of nature are. From these inclinations we shall become certain that certain actions are good and their contraries evil, and consequently that we must do those actions towards which we are naturally inclined in accordance with our specific nature, because they are good and sometimes necessary means which dispose us towards the last end. On the other hand, we must always avoid the contrary of our natural inclinations, because being evil, they frustrate nature.

This answer, of course, implies an amazing trust in the natural rectitude of the intellectual nature of man. It declares that the natural inclinations must always be towards the good of nature. Such a position as regards this rectitude of man's rational nature is obviously poles apart from such errors as that of the completely vitiated nature proposed by Luther, of the predeterminism of Calvin, and of the pessimism of Jansenius. St. Thomas is a realist for whom nature is a principle of action ordered to its last end and, therefore, a principle which must be naturally inclined to the necessary means.

Let us now examine these fundamental natural inclinations of man in order to formulate the other primary principles of the natural law. As we have said, the end is the good of nature, and evil is opposed to this good. Now nature being necessarily inclined to its end, must be naturally inclined to those things which are good, that is, which dispose it to the end. Consequently, the things to which the rational nature of man is inclined must be proposed by the practical intellect as good and as something to be sought by action. For the same reason, those things which are contrary to the natural inclinations are opposed to the good of nature, and therefore, are to be avoided. Hence, the order of the principles of the natural law will be discovered in accordance with the order of the natural inclinations. Now as we examine the natural inclinations of man we distinguish three fundamental tendencies of nature according as the nature of man is a substance, an animal, and a rational being. From these three inclinations we discover the primary principles of the natural law.

In common with all existing substances, man naturally seeks to preserve his existence which is his life. Hence, a principle of the natural law is: *Seek the things necessary for the preservation of life; avoid those which destroy life; preserve life; do not destroy life.*

In common with all animal nature, there is in human nature a strong inclination to the procreation and education of offspring. Hence, a principle of the natural law is: *Foster offspring; unite with the opposite sex in a union of love; avoid anything that would be contrary to the natural use of this power of procreation, that would be contrary to the natural attraction existing between male and female, etc.*

In man, according to the nature of reason and the spiritual perfection we find an inclination to communicate with God and to have peaceful social intercourse with rational creatures. Hence, a principle of the natural law is: *Reverence the Supreme Being; seek the social good; do good to others; avoid injuring others; render to each his own; follow reason; do unto others as you would have others do to you,* etc.

These principles of the natural law are not in themselves of equal perfection, since their respective foundations in nature vary in perfection. The third, of course, is the highest, being founded on a rational nature. Moreover, we should note that the negative aspects of all three degrees of principles, such as destroying life, interference with the natural inclination to procreate, denial of God, are intrinsically evil because directly opposed to the rational appetite, and therefore such negative principles must always obligate man. Nevertheless, the positive aspects of these principles need not always oblige, for the lesser goods may at times be sacrificed for the higher, for example, the precepts about preserving life may, at times, be sacrificed for the higher precept to safeguard one's family, etc. Hence, the general precept or principle that the good must be done does not mean that all possible good must be done, but every good the omission of which would be evil.

We have, then, several principles of the natural law founded on the diverse inclinations discovered in rational nature. However, these principles are as self-evident as the most fundamental principle *do good and avoid evil.* This self-evident character of these principles appears from the following summary of our analysis: Because man seeks the good in every action the single principle *good must be done and evil avoided* has been shown to be self-evident and implied in every action. According to this principle the natural inclinations of nature according to its specific inclinations manifest the good, the happiness, which is desired and sought. From this knowledge of the natural inclinations and their various objects, the practical intellect draws other primary judgments about action. Each of these judgments is self-evident because the predicate is contained in the notion of the subject of the judgment. For example, this particular good of nature (e.g., to be just) must be obtained by an action because such a specific good is a perfection, an object of desire, of man's social inclination. The contrary particular evil (e.g. and unjust act) must be avoided because it is a frustration of this same inclination. Upon these self-evident judgments about the good of the diverse inclinations of nature are founded the self-evident principles of the natural law. Consequently, the natural law may be expressed in a single first principle or in several, according as we express the unity of the good or happiness that must be sought or the orderly structure of the parts that constitute the whole good or happiness. But whether we express it in one principle or in several they are all self-evident, because in the several we do no more than analytically express what is contained in the one. The several primary principles of the natural law, then, have unity in the single self-evident principle *good must be done and evil must be avoided.* Thus we return to the question with which we began. Is the natural law one unified whole? We must give an affirmative answer as far as the primary principles are concerned, and we shall have to say the same as far as other derived principles are concerned, for all have their source, either analytically or synthetically, either immediately or mediately, in the one fundamental principle *good must be done and evil must be avoided.*

2. The Universality and Clarity of the Natural Law

The second question relative to the natural law is whether it is one unified whole with respect to all men and in all places. The answer to this question seems to be self-evident, for if one grants that the natural law is founded on the common natural inclinations of human nature, the proposition that the natural law is the same for all men will seem a foregone conclusion. Yet we must take great care to indicate exactly how this truth is to be understood. In treating of this question the third property of the natural law, that is, its *clarity* or the knowledge that all men have or can have of it, will be involved along with the *universality*.

In regard to this matter, St. Thomas distinguishes between *rectitude* and *knowledge,* and applies this distinction to the principles of speculative and practical knowledge. The distinction helps in the clarification of the problem and its solution. St. Thomas writes:

> As we have stated above, to the natural law belong those things to which a man is inclined naturally; and among these it is proper to man to be inclined to act according to reason. Now it belongs to reason to proceed from what is common to what is proper, as is stated in Physics I [Phys. I, 1,184a,16]. The speculative reason, however, is differently situated, in this matter, from the practical reason. For, since the speculative reason is concerned chiefly with necessary things, which cannot be otherwise than they are, its proper conclusions, like the universal principles, contain the truth without fail. The practical reason, on the other hand, is concerned with contingent matters, which is the domain of human actions; and, consequently, although there is necessity in the common principles, the more we descend towards the particular, the more frequently we encounter defects. Accordingly, then, in the speculative matters truth is the same in all men, both as to principles and as to conclusions; although the truth is not known to all as regards the conclusions, but only as regards the principles which are called common notions. But in matters of action, truth or practical rectitude is not the same for all as to what is particular, but only as to the common principles; and where there is the same rectitude in relation to particulars, it is not equally known to all.
>
> It is therefore evident that, as regards the common principles whether of speculative or of practical reason, truth or rectitude is the same for all, and is equally known by all. But as to the proper conclusions of the speculative reason, the truth is the same for all, but it is not equally known to all. Thus, it is true for all that the three angles of a triangle are together equal to the two right angles, although it is not known to all. But as to the proper conclusions of the practical reason, neither is the truth or rectitude the same for all, nor, where it is the same, is it equally known by all. Thus, it is right and true for all to act according to reason, and from this principle it follows, as a proper conclusion, that goods entrusted to another should be restored to their owner. Now this is true for the majority of cases. But it may happen in a particular case that it

would be injurious, and therefore unreasonable, to restore goods held in trust; for instance, if they are claimed for the purpose of fighting against one's country. And this principle will be found to fail the more, according as we descend further towards the particular, e.g., if one were to say that goods held in trust should be restored with such and such a guarantee, or in such and such a way; because the greater the number of conditions added, the greater the number of ways in which the principle may fail, so that it be not right to restore or not to restore. (S.T. I-II,94,4c)

We should distinguish, on the one hand, between *knowledge* and *rectitude* of the principles of the *speculative* and *practical* intellect, and, on the other, between the *common* principles and the *particular* conclusions which are particular applications to given cases. Now because the speculative reason deals with necessary truth, both the principles which are the beginning of the reasoning process and the conclusions which are derived from these principles are true even though an individual may not know these conclusions. For example, that God is a being of infinite perfection is a necessary and true conclusion from the fact that all created beings possess act and potency, which is based on the self-evident principle that a thing cannot be and not be at one and the same time. All men know this self-evident principle and it is universally true for all men. But not all men know the conclusion even though it is true. Consequently, the common principles and their particular conclusions of the speculative reason are universally true because they deal with necessary truth, but the conclusions are not known by all men.

The same cannot be said of the practical reason which deals, not with necessary matters, but often with contingent matters, that is, with human acts. The better to understand this we can distinguish between several grades of the natural law. We have discussed the primary or common indemonstrable principles of this law. We have seen that they can be variously expressed as "Good must be done and evil avoided," "Right reason must be followed," "Do to others as you would have them do to you," etc. Because they are founded on the fundamental inclinations of human nature they are always right, always true. Moreover, such principles are equally known to all men, because they are not the result of rational demonstration but of an immediate insight into the nature of an appetite and its good. But we should note that although all men know these common self-evident principles as universally true, nevertheless, the intellect needs, and all men possess a special quality in the practical intellect by which it acquires such knowledge. In thomistic terminology this quality is called *synderesis*. Just as the human intellect requires a special quality or habit, called *understanding*, in order that it may know the first principles of the speculative order, so it needs this other quality or habit to grasp the first principles of the practical order. These primary or fundamental principles so grasped may be called the *common principles* of the natural law, being the principles from which other principles for moral action are derived by rational demonstration.

Using these primary or common indemonstrable principles as premises, the practical intellect derives other principles which are either necessary conclusions or contingent general determinations of these necessary conclusions. The necessary conclusions may be either proximate or remote, depending, of course, upon the complexity of the reasoning process involved. We may, following the traditional division, distinguish two kinds of proximate conclusions: the *law of nations* (*jus gentium*) and *secondary principles* for the individual.* The law of nations means, in the ethics of St. Thomas, those general and necessary conclusions of the primary principles which are concerned with the demands of justice between the individual citizen and his fellow citizens, between the citizens and their civil authority. Such laws can be expressed as: "Institute a division of property," "Be just in buying and selling," "Do not kill," "Revere civil authority," etc. The law of nations, then, is those proximate conclusions of the natural law relative to justice in the political body, whereas the secondary principles of the natural law per-

---

* The law of nations is not the same as international law, although most modern writers use the term to signify international law. Since the collapse of a united Christendom in the sixteenth century and the consequent loss of a common court of appeal acceptable to all sovereign nations, there has been a continuous attempt on the part of the sovereign nations to draw up a common code of conduct governing the relations between nations. By common agreement nations have accepted certain rules governing warfare, treaties, alien property, citizenship, etc. These rules voluntarily accepted by sovereign states constitute what is known as international law. Such laws are good but they are not all necessary conclusions of the natural law. They may be such conclusions and they may be only contingent determinations. In any case, they are not what has been called the law of nations.

tain to what may be said to be individual morality. Such principles may be expressed as: "Honor thy father and thy mother," "Do not commit adultery," "Adore God," etc. All the proximate necessary conclusions of the natural law are summed up in the Decalogue.

But what shall we say of the knowledge and of the rectitude of these principles? They are not only universally true; they are also known to all men. They are universally true, because they are so obviously connected with the common principles, so intimately related to the fundamental inclinations of human nature. They are known to all men, because the full and adequate formulation of them requires such a fundamental and easy reasoning process that they almost partake of the nature of self-evident principles. Were it possible for men to be ignorant of such principles, we would have to conclude that the natural law, a necessary means for man's attaining of his ultimate end, has not been properly promulgated by the Divine Legislator and Creator.

By a still further reasoning about the nature of man, the practical intellect can arrive at further detailed and necessary conclusions of the natural law. Here the reasoning process is very complex. This does not mean that there is anything doubtful about these conclusions; the conclusions are certain and the logic perfect, but the reasoning is long and involved as in a difficult theorem in geometry. Untrained minds cannot follow it and even trained minds can become sidetracked through confusion or prejudice. Such principles are derived not only from the law of nations but also from the secondary principles for individual morality. Such principles, for example, prohibit suicide, mercy killing, duelling, divorce, polygamy, contraception. We may express some of the principles in the following manner: "Do not perjure yourself," "Do not blaspheme," "Keep holy the names of God," "Return borrowed articles," "Do not commit unnatural sin," etc. Some modern writers call these the tertiary *principles* of the natural law; others, more in accord with St. Thomas, call them *secondary*; to avoid confusion we shall simply call them *remote* conclusions.

Are these remote conclusions of the natural law always right, always true? To this question we must answer that generally these conclusions are universally true, but in particular instances it may be injurious and therefore unreasonable to act in accordance with them. The reason is that because of a change in the circumstances the specification of the act has been so affected that its goodness or badness has been modified in relation to the law or principle of action. An example will make this clear: It is in accordance with justice that I should return to another what I have borrowed from him. This is a universal principle of action and its truth or rectitude is absolute. A right action may seem to be an exception to this universal law, when, for instance, I refuse to return a gun to its owner who wishes to commit murder with it. But clearly, the present circumstances change the specification of the act. For the object is no longer returning what belongs to another, but returning it to another who wishes to commit a crime with it. What would be right and just generally becomes unreasonable and therefore evil because of the change in the specification of the act.

As regards the knowledge of a particular remote conclusion, it is an observable fact that, because of the state of civilization, because of prejudice, of education, of passion, of habit, or of some other obstacles to knowledge, men sometimes err in evaluating properly the rectitude of a particular conclusion of this kind. Hence a true knowledge of the natural law is not always had by all men as regards the more remote conclusions. But inasmuch as such ignorance is the result of a depraved will and the rejected light of reason, it is vincible and culpable, not only in its first authors, but also in those who have erred because of the teaching of the first authors by having deliberately rejected reason in such matters, or in those who have unknowingly been led into error, when the opportunity to learn what is right presents itself.

In order to avoid confusion we should note that although we have been distinguishing between principles and conclusions we do not mean to imply that the conclusions are any less mandatory than the principles. The distinction between principles and their conclusions is based on the immediacy by which man's intellect knows their obligatory character, not upon the kind or degree of obligation which they impose on man. All these various levels of knowledge or knowability of the natural law are concerned with precepts or principles of this law which bind the individual human will absolutely once they are known.

We ought also to notice that just as there are several levels in man's knowledge of the natural law, so there can be mistakes in the application of the proximate and remote conclusions or principles. But this should not be a matter of surprise. Just as some of the principles of the natural law are self-evident while others are known only after a most complex and difficult reasoning, so at times the principles of the natural law are quite easy to apply and at other times most difficult because of the actions or cases to which they are applied. Mature ethically knowledgeable men may err in their reasoning about the application of these principles to concrete cases. Such mistakes do not mean that they do not know these principles of the natural law, but only that they do not clearly understand the concrete case in all its existential ramifications and conditions and so cannot apply these principles unerringly. In like manner a medical doctor may have a full grasp of the laws or principles of medicine yet make mistakes about the application of these principles to a sick man.

We conclude: The natural law as a dictate of the practical reason admits of various degrees of clarity and universality. Although the primary principles are universally true and are known by all men, and although the proximate conclusions are of the same universality and clarity, it happens that men may err in their knowledge of the remote conclusions and sometimes the universality of these conclusions is defective. As we will deal with these same problems implicitly in the question of the immutability of the natural law, let us leave matters for the present with a quotation from St. Thomas:

We must say that the natural law, as to the first common principles, is the same for all, both as to rectitude and as to knowledge. But as to certain more particular aspects, which are conclusions, as it were, of these common principles, it is the same for all in the majority of cases, both as to rectitude and as to knowledge; and yet in some few cases it may fail, both as to rectitude, and as to knowledge. But as to certain more particular aspects, which are conclusions, as it were, of these common prin-

ciples, it is the same for all in the majority of cases, both as to rectitude and as to knowledge; and yet in some few cases it may fail, both as to rectitude, by reason of certain obstacles (just as natures subject to generation and corruption fail in some few cases because of some obstacle), and as to knowledge, since in some the reason is perverted by passion, or evil habit, or an evil disposition of nature. Thus at one time theft, although expressly contrary to the natural law, was not considered wrong among the Germans as Julius Caesar related. (S.T. I-II,94,4c)

3. The Immutability of the Natural Law

The property of immutability is concerned with the third question which we have proposed concerning the natural law, namely, whether the natural law is a unified whole with respect to all times and every condition of human nature. Can there be, in other words, change in the natural law? Let us first refer to St. Thomas. He writes:

A change in the natural law may be understood in two ways. First, by way of addition. In this sense, nothing hinders the natural law from being changed, since many things for the benefit of human life have been added over and above the natural law, both by the divine law and human laws.

Secondly, a change in the natural law may be understood by way of subtraction, so that what previously was according to the natural law, ceases to be so. In this sense, the natural law is altogether unchangeable in its first principles. But in its secondary principles, which, as we have said, are certain detailed proximate conclusions drawn from the first principles, the natural law is not changed so that what it prescribes be not right in most cases. But it may be changed in some particular cases of rare occurrence, through some special causes hindering the observances of such precepts, as was stated above. (S.T. I-II,94,5c)

If the natural law can be changed, how can it be changed? First of all it can be changed by addition. An addition in the precise sense here understood is a law derived from the more general or common principles of the natural law. There are, however, various ways by which a law could be derived from the natural law. Some laws are necessary and are formally, either mediately or immediately, contained in the common principles. In the preceding section we spoke about the proximate and remote conclusions of the natural law. Such conclusions are necessary conclusions from the common principles. But since the proximate conclusions are not generally spoken of as additions, because of the immediacy with which they are derived, we shall confine additions to the more remote conclusions. Consequently, some laws are necessary remote conclusions. Thus, for example, the law that one should not murder is a conclusion from the more general principle of the natural law that one should be just to others. Thus, too, the law of monogamous marriage is a necessary conclusion from the more general principle that one should not commit adultery. Such laws or principles of morality are derived from the common principles as *conclusions* from principles. Other laws are not formally contained in the natural law, but are *determinations*. Such determinations are not necessary conclusions but rather useful interpretations depending upon time and place. For example, the law establishing the kind of punishment for murders, or the law establishing the minimum age for marriage, or the traffic law.

Evidently such additions, either by way of conclusions or determinations of the natural law are useful for all men taken as a whole so that they may live the more peacefully among themselves and the more surely guide their conduct in their pursuit of human happiness. Such additions are called *positive law*. We will treat of these laws in a more detailed manner in the next chapter. Here it suffices to say that they are additions of the natural law and, as such, changes in the natural law.

But the remote principles of the natural law may change not only through addition but also in some cases through subtraction. By subtraction we mean that a law which at one time prohibited or commanded a particular action no longer prohibits or commands that particular action.

That the determinations of the natural law may change seems to be fairly obvious: since a determination is useful only for definite circumstances of time, place, or condition, the authority may and should change such a law when its time of usefulness has passed.

However, it does not seem to be so obvious that remote conclusions of the natural law, that is, necessary conclusions, should change through subtraction. Nevertheless, at times they do. The ultimate reason for such variations is the changeable character of the matter or the circumstances, changes in which change the specifications of the acts with which these principles or laws deal. If the whole natural law down to its last conclusion dealt with beings that were unchangeable and with circumstances which were unvariable the law would be unchangeable in every respect, but since it deals with beings which are changeable, we must expect some change in the law. The thought of St. Thomas in this matter is that the natural law of unchangeable beings is as unchangeable as the beings which it regulates. But that which is natural for changeable beings participates in their changeableness. (*S.T.* II-II,57,2) Now since the principles of the natural law and their most proximate conclusions govern a universal, unchangeable aspect of human nature and its relations to a universal object or matter, namely, the pursuit of good through reason, there can be no change either in the principles or in the matter. But the other principles which are derived from these principles as remote conclusions from a principle, and which deal with matter which is contingent and variable, may change in certain circumstances because of the matter, which is a means to man's end and which may change according to the conditions of persons, time, or place.

Not only may the natural law undergo changes by reason of God changing the specification of the act which usually falls under the law, but human reason, too, may cause such a change. As St. Thomas writes, the derived principles may fail because of knowledge, since reason can be perverted by passion, evil habits, dispositions of nature, and error. The natural law like any other law is a general rule of action, and even though it be true and known as true it will not apply exactly in every particular circumstance except in its more general expression. In the science of physics, for example, there is the universal law that falling bodies fall with a motion accelerated by thirty-two feet per second each second. Yet this law is not fully realized in many cases of falling bodies, because there is always the margin of error due to the contingency of matter. So, too, in the natural law which deals with the free acts of man. The remote conclusions will change at times because of the different specifications of the acts to which they apply. Thus, for example, there is the principle that borrowed goods must be returned; hence, if a man leaves a knife with me for safekeeping, I am bound in natural justice to return it to him on demand; but if he returns roaring drunk, not only am I not obliged to return the knife, I am instead forbidden to do so. The material of the act has changed.

In like manner, the remote conclusions of the natural law will change because of some defect in the person who is applying the law. Thus, because of perverted education, custom, passion, or error, a law which is universally true will not be true because an individual man does not know the matter to which the law should be applied. Divorce, for example, is not permitted except by God's authority. Whole groups of people, however, because of perverted education think it permissible by civil authority. These people know of the existence of a law against divorce, but they are ignorant of the act that is forbidden by the law, namely, divorce by human authority. Others, again, are ignorant of the very law against divorce.

We may conclude, then, that while the common and more proximate principles of the natural law are always true and known by all men who have the use of reason, the remote conclusions are not always true nor always known. The reason for this is that since the natural law is a measure of human actions it must be in harmony with the thing it measures. In order that the natural law be in harmony with the thing it measures, i.e., with human acts, it must not only take into account man's unchanging nature and his constant desire for ultimate happiness, but also the facts that man as he exists is an individual, concrete, contingent, and variable creature and that he lives in a variable and contingent world. The natural law has this harmony and is commensurate with both man's stability and his changeableness. As to stability: Man is a rational animal with a natural desire for ultimate happiness, and these things do not change. As corollaries to this unchangeableness there are the common principles of the natural law which are immutable. The obligation to act according to reason which recognizes the fundamental inclinations of nature and the good of these inclinations is applicable to every moral action. As to changeableness: On the other hand, the remote conclusions of the natural law share with man the variableness and contingency of this world. Man as he actually exists is not being itself; he is being concreted. He is contingent, variable, singular, with all the properties which go to make him an individual person who will obey the law and in so doing fulfill the requisites of his nature. The natural law, then, is consistent with both man's changeableness and his unchangeableness: the common and proximate principles correspond to man's stability; the remote principles to his variability.

Readings

Adler, M., "A Question about Law," in *Essays in Thomism*, ed. Brennan, pp. 205-236.

Cronin, Michael, *The Science of Ethics*, vol. I, pp. 225-244.

Doolan, Aegidius, O.P., *Order and Law*, cc. 8 and 9.

Farrell, W., A *Companion to the Summa*, vol. II, pp. 379-390.

Gilson, E., *Moral Values and the Moral Life*, pp. 193-218.

Leibell, J. F., *Readings in Ethics*. The following are recommended:

"The eternal law," Joseph Rickaby, pp. 313-317.
"The natural law," Walter McDonald, pp. 317-320.
"The natural law," V. Cathrein, pp. 320-324.
"Moral law," Timothy Brosnahan, pp. 325-326.
"International law," W. G. Smith, pp. 1011-1015.
"International law," Timothy Brosnahan, pp. 1015-1016.
"The law of nations," Alfred O'Rahilly, pp. 1016-1032.

Lottin, Odon, "La loi en général. La définition thomiste et ses antécédents," *Psychologie et Morale*, II (Problèmes de Morale, première partie), pp. 11-47.

———— *Principes de morale*, vol. I, pp. 121-146; II, 33-54.

Manion, Clarence E., "The Natural Law Philosophy of Founding Fathers," *University of Notre Dame Natural Law Institute Proceedings*, 1947, pp. 30-65.

Maritain, J., *The Rights of Man and the Natural Law*, pp. 64-68.

Meehan, Francis X., "Absolute and Relative in the Moral Order," *Proceedings of the American Catholic Philosophical Association*, XXII (1947), pp. 53-79.

Mullahy, B. I., "Practical Knowledge and Relativity," *American Catholic Philosophical Association*, XXII (1947), pp. 151-166.

Palmer, Ben W., "The Natural Law and Pragmatism," *University of Notre Dame Natural Law Institute Proceedings*, 1947, pp. 30-65.

Rickaby, Joseph, *Aquinas Ethicus*, vol. I, pp. 83-287.

—— *Moral Philosophy*, pp. 144-152.

Rommen, H., *The Natural Law*, c. 13.

Sertillanges, A. D., *La philosophie morale de saint Thomas d'Aquin*, pp. 91-114.

Suarez, Francisco, *De Legibus*, bk. II, cc. 13, 17, 19.

St. Thomas, *Summa Theologica*, I-II, 94, 99, 100.

CHAPTER IX

SOME CONSEQUENCES OF THE NATURAL LAW

1. *Law and Freedom*

One of the thorniest problems of ethics is the explanation of the idea *I ought*. Stated in the form of a question, the problem may be expressed thus: "Why must I be moral? Why may I not be bad if I choose? Why must I choose good and avoid evil?" Everyone admits that if there is a law then those subject to the law are in some way necessitated or bound to keep it. But there is no general agreement about this necessity nor about the source of the necessity. Since we have been studying the natural law and its obligation we must now see how law can impose a necessity upon man, how it can bind man to be moral.

In its broadest sense freedom means absence of necessity or bonds. Let us recall from the science of psychology or the philosophy of human nature that when the problem of free choice was examined and proved a distinction was made between three kinds of freedom and their corresponding bonds.

We may, first of all, think of those physical bonds which restrict our bodily movements, such as handcuffs, prison bars, ropes, etc. Such bonds force us to act contrary to our inclination. They are

248

extrinsic physical bonds which impose an extrinsic physical necessity by compelling us to act. Such bonds cannot, however, force the will to act, because the cause of the movement resulting from such bonds is extrinsic to the agent who is necessitated to act. Freedom from such bonds is called freedom of *spontaneity*. A dog running loose in the street and a criminal escaping the hangman's noose have such freedom because they are under no extrinsic necessity. Generally, speaking strictly, such freedom implies intrinsic necessity.

Another bond is that which is imposed by a being's own nature. The necessity of the proper or specific activity of material beings (by which an orange tree produces oranges and not apples, or a stone falls to the ground) is an intrinsic physical necessity. All beings which do not possess free will must, by the necessity of their own natures, act in definite predetermined ways; they cannot but be subject to their natural tendencies and must perform the acts their natures prescribe. These intrinsic physical necessities are what we have described as the laws of nature. Freedom from the bonds of such necessity is called freedom of *choice*. Freedom means lack of both intrinsic and extrinsic necessity and implies act. The lack of external constraint or extrinsic necessity alone, which is called spontaneity, is freedom only in the improper sense of the term. Freedom is found only when in the absence of both intrinsic and extrinsic necessity an act occurs. It is in this sense that we say a human act is performed voluntarily and freely.

Unlike these two physical bonds which impose either an extrinsic or an intrinsic necessity upon beings, there are moral bonds which impose necessity upon the free will of rational beings. Such moral bonds are laws in the strict sense as we have explained in Chapter VI, Law in General. Moral laws have their origin in the causality of an agent other than the agent so bound; their origin is in the lawgiver who has a right to command subjects by reason of his authority. Moral laws impose moral necessity, duty, or obligation. Freedom from moral necessity or obligation is called freedom of *independence*. In this sense God alone possesses freedom of independence because He is not subject to a law of a higher authority.

Having distinguished among these three kinds of freedom and their corresponding bonds, we are now interested only in the moral necessity which law imposes upon rational beings. Since moral necessity binds without any extrinsic or intrinsic physical necessity, our problem is to discover how laws can impose a necessity upon the will. What is the source of the obligation which law imposes?

There are many opinions about this. The social utilitarians think that the origin of obligation is the need that man has of promoting the social good. If a proposed action would contribute to the good of the social body of which he is a part, man is obligated to perform the action. If the action is destructive of this social good, man is obligated to refrain from it. The moral positivists think that the origin of all obligation is the state. In this opinion, then, civil law is the cause of all obligation. These theories of obligation are based on a denial of a natural law. While there are many who are willing to accept these opinions, the prevalent theory of obligation is that of Kant. For this reason let us consider the opinion of Kant.

2. Kant's Theory of Obligation

Kant thinks that in the world of morality man is a completely independent being: he is not bound by the will of any other being in the universe; he is subject only to the laws of his own giving; the lawgiver obligating and the subject obliged are one and the same. Kant arrives at this notion of law and obligation because he maintains that a law should of its nature be universal, applicable to every man, and it should also be absolute, binding unconditionally and without exception.

But law, he contends, cannot be grounded in objects outside the will, for objects are sought only as means to inner pleasure and since inner pleasure varies in individuals, the law itself would vary; furthermore, since objects are not universally good but vary according to the individuals, law cannot have its source in any object outside the will. This being true, Kant contends that law must be founded on the will itself; not upon any inclination of the will, for inclinations of men differ, but upon an *imperative* of the will.

What is the nature of this imperative of the will? The sole right that belongs to each individual in virtue of his human nature is liberty or autonomy. Consequently, there are no moral necessities or bonds imposed upon man's freedom by nature, but such bonds must be placed by man himself, because if each individual acted without regard to his fellow men, liberty itself would be destroyed in the consequent clash of actions. Hence man must so act externally that his freedom may co-exist with the freedom of others. These limitations on his freedom which the individual's reason recognizes as necessary for the continued peaceful existence of the individual among his fellow men are law. If these limitations are of such a nature that all men should accept them they are laws, for the will of the individual as well as the will of every man should command that they be obeyed.

But how do we know that a limitation of our freedom is a law? We can determine this by asking ourselves the question: Can this limitation of my freedom, this maxim or principle, become a universal law morally obligating all? If I can will that this limitation or this maxim bind my will, then it should be willed by all other men to bind their wills. An example will make this clear. Suppose I ask the question: May I, when in a difficult position, make a promise with the intention of not keeping it? The answer is determined by my answer to a universal question: May every one make the same kind of promise? Asking this question makes us realize that although we may will to lie, nevertheless we cannot will that lying should become a universal law. With such a law there would be no promises made. Consequently, my maxim that I may lie cannot be made a universal law. Hence I must accept the contrary maxim "I must not lie," and I must will that this maxim obligate my will, and all men must will the same.

Law then, in the opinion of Kant is that which the will commands as something that can and should become universal for all men. The cause of this obligation or binding of the will is twofold: (1) man's reason recognizes that its subjective reasons for acting or, as Kant calls them, maxims, can and should become the ways of acting for all men; and (2) the will of each individual man obligates itself to act in this way. So, the will commands nec-

252 · Some Consequences of the Natural Law

essary rules of action, binding in all circumstances, because reason recognizes the need of limiting freedom for the good of the whole. These dictates of the reason and will are called *categorical imperatives*, i.e., categorical because they are unconditionally binding on all; imperatives because they are commanded by the will.

But if it is the will that makes the laws for itself, what makes an act moral? Acts are morally good not because they are according to law nor because of the end to which they lead. Acts are morally good only when they are performed from the motive of duty.

It is impossible to deny that Kant has said much that is worthwhile. His insistence on the necessity of acting from motive of duty shows his high regard not only for the moral law but also of the demands of right reason. But such worthwhile elements should not lead to overlooking the defects in his theory of obligation of the natural law.

First of all, Kant seems to identify intrinsic physical necessity with moral necessity. But evidently there is a difference between the necessity of acting in accord with the physical laws of one's nature and the moral necessity of freely subjecting one's will to the obligation which moral law places upon the will. As we have said, the natural necessity of acting according to one's nature has its origin with the agent itself, but moral necessity or obligation has its origin outside the agent.

And more, Kant thinks that the will can bind or obligate itself and this binding is nothing arbitrary which the will may or may not subject itself to: the will must will the moral law and it must also submit itself to the law which it wills. In other words, the will must will that the maxims become universal laws and it must subject itself to the categorical imperatives or universal laws which it wills the maxims to be. If this necessity is founded on the very nature of things demanding that its physical laws be obeyed we do not have moral obligation or necessity but physical necessity. If this necessity does not originate outside the will itself it is not the moral necessity of moral law.

Finally, Kant says that unless an action is done from the motive of duty it cannot be a moral act. From this it follows that we cannot predicate morality for the acts of a mother who takes care of her child not from a sense of duty but from her mother's love and devotion. True, a mother could care for her child from a pure sense of duty, but it is the general opinion of men that it is love and not duty which makes such acts of the mother so appealing to men. The same is true of heroic acts such as that of a national hero who has given his life for his country or that of the lover who gives his life for the beloved, for "greater love no man has, than that a man lay down his life for his friends." Are such acts the acts of strict duty? Do men approve of them because they are acts which are motivated only by duty? Or do men judge them the noblest and best of human acts because they go beyond the call of duty?

To conclude, we must admit that the moral law does command us with a categorical imperative and assuredly Kant emphasizes this very well, but it does not seem that his explanation of this absolute obligation squares with the facts, with the meaning of moral obligation. Let us, then, look at what St. Thomas has to say about moral obligation.

3. *Saint Thomas' Theory of Obligation*

Although St. Thomas does not treat of this question explicitly, his thought on the matter is easily evolved from his opinions on the nature of law and on the nature of the will.

Obligation is moral necessity, imposed on a free will. Now the only necessity that can be laid on the will is that which arises from an end or good known by the intellect. As we know from Chapter VI, most necessities of the will are hypothetical, that is, if we desire the good or end, we must take the means to acquire it. Such hypothetical necessity can be removed by removing our desire for the good. But evidently the necessity of the will is dependent on the good desired. Besides the hypothetical necessity that might be placed upon the will, there is a categorical necessity imposed on the will because of the absolutely final good or end of man. Man is not free to seek his ultimate good, happiness; he must seek it. Because he is categorically necessitated to seek this end, he is also categorically necessitated to seek the means to this end. Such categorical necessity is the essence of moral necessity, and such necessity arises not from the will of man but from an object outside the will of man which the will must seek.

Let us put the matter in this way. One cannot will an end and at the same time not will the means to the end. If there are several means to the same end, there is no necessity of willing one group of means rather than another, for the use of either will bring us to the end. But if there is only one means to an end, he who is obliged to attain the end must use this means. Now we have shown that there is only one means to man's end, for the good must be done and the evil must be avoided. If, then, man is categorically necessitated to reach his end, it follows that he must, that he is categorically obligated to do the good and avoid the evil. From what we have said about man's last end, we know that this end is not something that he is free to seek or not to seek but something he must seek, for it is his ultimate end, his highest good. Man's last end, then, is the source of his obligation, the origin of the necessity of the moral law. All of this, however—namely, the necessary connection between men's last end and his observance of the moral law, and man's last end as absolutely necessary—is determined by God Himself. Consequently, we must say that the proximate source of man's obligation to observe the moral law is man's ultimate end, but the ultimate source is God himself, who by a command of his intellect carried out by his will establishes this moral order for man. It can be said more simply: The eternal law is the ultimate source of man's obligation.

Our obligation of observing the natural law, then, comes proximately from the necessity that we have of seeking our ultimate good, but in this context is our ultimate good to be taken in its subjective or objective sense? Are we under a moral necessity because of the happiness we are to experience in possessing God or because of God Himself, the Highest Good? To answer this question we must consider the meaning of sanction.

4. Sanction of the Law

There is no adequate equivalent in St. Thomas of the word *sanction*. In the present acceptation of the word, *sanction* generally means those rewards and punishments which make it advisable to observe the law. This implies that the real reason for observing the law is to obtain some reward or to avoid a punishment. It is this very meaning of the word *sanction* that Kant rejected. Kant was of the opinion that the man who thought the whole reason for observing a law was to get something out of it was not really a good man. He thought that one should do good just because it is good. Now, although St. Thomas has erected his ethics on altogether other principles than Kant, he could have agreed with Kant that a man is not a perfectly good man if he acts wholly from the motive of getting a reward or avoiding a punishment.

St. Thomas, indeed, speaks of rewards and punishments, but he explains that to be rewarded is to reach one's end, and to be punished is to miss it. (*S.T.* I-II,5,7) Just as in a certain sense Thomistic morality is a morality without obligation, i.e., without a necessity whose source is in the arbitrary will of God or the will of man, but is derived from human reason perceiving the ultimate good, so in a certain sense it is a morality without sanction, i.e., without rewards and punishments imposed by the arbitrary will of the legislator, God. It makes sanction not an extrinsic reward or punishment, but the effect of man's intrinsic action, under the providential guidance of God.

Once we grant that good acts are the rational means to happiness, and bad acts the irrational rejection of these means, we are bound to conclude that good acts procure happiness, which is a reward, and bad acts procure unhappiness, which is punishment. Because good acts are the subject matter of the right observance of law, and, consequently, of the preservation of order, good acts will necessarily lead to the perfection of human nature which is happiness. In like manner, because bad acts are a deordination to the end, they will necessarily lead to unhappiness. Such a notion of rewards and punishments follows from the metaphysical notions of potency and act, and St. Thomas always keeps his morality in line with his theory of metaphysics: just as the perfection of a potency is caused by the ordered actualization of that potency, so the perfection of human nature, which is a potency in relation to perfect happiness, is caused by the ordered actualization of that nature, which consists in good acts; unhappiness, consequently, is the necessary result of a violation of this ordered actualization.

Now because the ordered actualization of man's nature is accomplished on three different levels or in three different spheres, we can expect three different rewards; likewise three different punishments for a violation of this ordered actualization.

Man can be punished with a threefold punishment, corresponding to the three orders to which the human will is subject. In the first place, a man's nature is subject to the order of his own reason; secondly, it is subject to the order of another man who governs him either in spiritual or in temporal matters, as a member of the state or of the household; thirdly, it is subject to the universal order of the divine government. Now each of these orders is disturbed by sin, for the sinner acts against his reason, and against human and divine law. Therefore he incurs a threefold punishment: one inflicted by himself, viz., remorse of conscience; another inflicted by man; and a third inflicted by God. (S.T. I-II,87,1c)

Although St. Thomas says nothing about the rewards we can conclude what they are from his notion of the nature of man and his notion of act and potency. Consequently, because man finds himself in three different orders in which he must do the good and avoid the evil, there are three natural results of his actions: (1) *The rewards and punishments which affect him precisely as an individual.* In this order, which consists in the subordination of the lower appetites to the dictates of right reason, the rewards or punishments are approval or remorse of conscience, the enjoyment or loss of mental or bodily health, etc. (2) *The rewards and punishments which affect a man in so far as he is a social being.* In this order, which consists in the essential relations of man to his fellow men, the rewards or punishments are the social good or evil that follow upon the attention or disregard of these relations. Virtue is followed by esteem, vice by contempt or by the punishment inflicted by human authority. (3) *The rewards and punishments which affect a man in his relation with his Creator.* In this order, which consists in the proper subordination of all of man's powers to his Creator and his last end, the rewards or punishments are final happiness or final unhappiness.

These are the principles of what may be called the Thomistic theory of sanction. Its fundamental notion rules out all recompense or punishment which is extrinsic to the effect of action, and it identifies it with the normal result of the natural outcome or end of our actions. Just as law is the voice of reason commanding actions to be done, a natural outcome of reason, so sanction is a natural outcome of the actions that are done. Just as man, in the view of St. Thomas, should observe the law because it is the reasonable thing to do, so he is obliged because it is reasonable, because his highest good, taken in itself, is the reasonable thing to be sought after. True, man's highest good is a reward and the loss of this good a punishment, nevertheless, this good should not be sought precisely because it is a reward, but because it is a reasonable good. It is true that the two are inseparable, that is, man's enjoyment of his highest good and the highest good, but the second is prior to the first. God deserves our obedience, not because he is good for us, but because he is good in himself. The natural law is not "If you do this, you will be happy," but rather "Do the good." This command is unconditional, categorical: the good must be sought because it is the reasonable thing to do; hence, our moral obligation comes from our last end because it is good in itself and not precisely because it is good for us.

It is a misunderstanding of Thomistic rewards and punishments to say that the moral law should be observed because we are going to get something out of it. The receiving of a reward or punishment is the natural result of the moral goodness or evil of a human act. The norm of the moral goodness or evil of human acts is determined not so much by the reward or punishment which are natural consequences of the human act, but by the act's relation to right reason. If we also know that over and above the motive of seeking and doing the good because it is the reasonable thing to do, there is another motive for performing good acts, namely that it brings rewards and prevents punishment, we have a secondary motive for performing good acts. Because St. Thomas knows that man should do everything he can to reach his ultimate happiness, he further recognizes, and in this he does not agree with Kant, that it is good to act morally well because it will bring a reward. But St. Thomas does not think that man's primary motive in observing the natural law should be the hope of a reward but his primary motive should be that it is the reasonable thing to do.

However, we must know that all men are not so in love with reason that they will always seek the good because it is the reasonable thing to do. Not all men keep their obligation out of a sense of reasonableness. To such, the lawgiver must have another appeal. He must propose another motive sufficiently strong to attract his subjects to obey the law. This way is sanction: an appeal to the subjects of the law that they keep the law because of the hope of a reward or because of fear of punishment for violating it.

In this meaning of the word, sanction may be considered *actively*, that is, as the promise of reward for keeping the law or the threat of punishment for breaking it, or both; *passively*, that is, as the rewards or punishments so established. The purpose of sanction is twofold: (1) to induce people to keep the law and to dissuade them from breaking it; (2) to restore the order of justice after the law has been kept or broken.

As laws may be either natural or, as we will see in the next chapter, positive, so may sanction. A *natural* sanction follows from the very nature of the act performed, as sickness from intemperance, lack of trust in a person who has a habit of lying, etc. A *positive* sanction is decided by the will of the lawgiver and has no necessary or natural connection with the act, as a fine for speeding or ten years in prison for theft. Clearly, the rewards and punishments which naturally follow the observance of the natural law are natural sanctions in the Thomistic sense of the word.

A sanction may be more or less perfect according to its capacity for fulfilling its purpose. A *perfect* sanction is both *adequate*, in that it provides a rational will with a sufficient motive for keeping the law, and *proportioned*, in that it sets up equality between merit and reward, demerit and punishment. An *imperfect* sanction is in some measure either inadequate or unproportioned or both.

Obviously, as ethicians, we must ask and answer the following questions about the natural law: (1) Has the natural law any sanction in the present life? (2) Has the natural law a perfect sanction? Let us answer these questions by combining St. Thomas's rewards and punishments with the above notions of sanctions. Of all the sanctions mentioned as rewards and punishments in the individual, social, and universal orders by St. Thomas, it is only those of the universal order which we can properly call perfect, i.e., sufficient of themselves to move a rational will to observe the natural law, and proportionate to the good or evil acts performed in observing or breaking this law. Because of the inequalities of life, the uncertainties of remorse of conscience, of ill-health, of loss of esteem, of virtue receiving its reward, such rewards and punishments, such sanctions are not of themselves sufficient to insure the observance of law by all. In fact they do not, as we well know, and if this life were all, if all were to end with the grave, if there were not a term of our actions in the supreme good or supreme evil, there would be little reason for most people to observe the law. But final happiness and unhappiness—which are the terms of man's free activity, the sanctions of the next life, the sanctions which give meaning and persuasion to the other sanctions—are adequate of themselves and proportionate of themselves to move a rational will to practice virtue.

There are some who declare that the earthly results, interior and exterior, of virtue and vice are sufficient to satisfy us, that they give sufficient reason to observe the law. But they are not sufficient, because they are precarious, because moral laxity co-exists with moral effort, and because the good often suffer and the bad possess an abundance of goods in this life. Virtue is not its own reward, but virtue is meant to serve; it is a means, not an end. We respect life because of its value, we guard life because we value it, we take care of health because we value it, we study because we value knowledge, we are just because we value peace. Similarly, we act virtuously because we value happiness.

The outcome of our actions in this world, the arrival of means at their end, is too limited and precarious to satisfy our moral conscience or our idea of order. We must reject such a theory of the outcome of virtue, just as we must reject Aristotle's moral optimism, for they are theories which depend too much on chance, which are valid only for a few fortunate ones, and then only for fleeting moments. We substitute a Christian optimism that is thoroughly philosophical, yet dependent upon revelation for a more perfect knowledge of that happiness which is a certain outcome of all who practice virtue. The fact that there is a providential God is a divine guarantee that virtue will be rewarded, while the existence of a future life makes possible that ultimate and perfect happiness which we cannot find in this world, which the world cannot give.

5. Merit and Demerit

We get the reward by keeping the law and the punishment by breaking it. But what is there in the observer of the law that entitles him to a reward, and in the violator of the law that makes him liable to punishment? In Thomistic ethics, rewards and punishments follow as the natural consequences of the observance or nonobservance of the law; authorities establish rewards and punishments to induce subjects of the law to observe it, but over and above these we also feel that such rewards or punishments are in some sense due him who keeps or breaks the law. There is something in the human act by reason of which the observer of a law has a right to the reward, and something in the human act by reason of which the lawbreaker must undergo punishment. This quality or essential consequence of a human act is called *merit* when there is question of a reward and *demerit* when there is question of punishment.

Because merit and demerit belong to human acts they are closely connected with *responsibility* and *imputability*. These two words express the same relation between an agent and his act but from different aspects. We say that an agent is responsible, accountable for his acts, and that the act is imputable, attributable to the agent. Imputability is the relation of ownership between a man and his act, and the consequent attributing of it in praise or blame to him as a cause. In the strictest philosophical sense, the word imputable is applied to actions which are regarded as morally good or bad. And those acts are morally imputable to the person who freely chooses them. Wherefore we may define imputability as that quality in a man's free acts by reason of which they may be attributed to him in praise or blame.

From the moral imputability of an act follows the responsibility of the agent. If an act is imputable to an agent he is also responsible for the act. Responsibility is the condition of the agent, imputability is the character of the act, by reason of which an act can be attributed to an agent in praise or blame. Responsibility, therefore, is that condition of the agent by reason of which he is so regarded as the cause of his actions that he is held accountable for them and answerable for their consequences. Freedom of choice is the basis both of imputability and responsibility.

An act is said to deserve praise or blame from its being imputed to the agent, since to praise or to blame means nothing else than to impute to someone the malice or goodness of his act. Now an act is imputed to an agent when it is in his power, so that he has dominion over it; and this is the case in all voluntary acts, because it is through his will that man has dominion over his acts, as was made clear above. Hence it follows that, in voluntary acts alone, good and evil constitute the nature of praise or blame. (S.T. I-II,21,2c)

Now if the act imputed to an agent tends to the advantage of another, the natural idea of equality or justice carries with it, as a consequence, the idea of compensation, which strikes a balance between him who confers and him who receives the benefit. On the other hand, if the act imputed to an agent injures another, equality demands some retribution which strikes a balance between him who injures and him who is injured. This necessity of equality is derived, as we shall see when we treat of justice, from the order and symmetry that presides in the moral as well as in the physical order. Applied to free acts, this order of justice shows that there ought to be equality between what is given and what is received, for otherwise a due proportion would not be observed—there would be an excess on one side and a deficiency on the other. The order of justice, therefore, implies a proportion or balance between what is given and what is received by free creatures.

But justice applies either directly or indirectly to all human acts, because every good or bad moral act has some good or evil consequence for some other being other than the agent. Thus, merit or demerit, as demands for rewards or punishments, are consequences of every human act. As we shall see later on when we deal with justice at length, there are several kinds of justice which entail merit or demerit. At the present time we shall merely mention them.

There is that kind of justice which is concerned with an agent and another individual considered as an individual. Now, some of man's acts have merit or demerit because of a benefit conferred or an injury inflicted on another as a private person. This is the area of commutative justice.

There is also that justice which is concerned with an individual agent and the civil or marital society of which he is a member, and that which is concerned with an agent and the society of all men who are working for their ultimate end under the government of God. Every human agent is a member of a civil society and of the society of mankind under God. Wherefore, if an agent benefits another citizen of his own civil society, or even himself, by a good act, he merits a reward from the civil society, because he has benefited that civil society by benefiting one of its members. In like manner, he demerits by an evil act. The same is true of an agent who benefits another man or God (in an analogous sense), even if this other man is not a fellow citizen of the same civil society; the agent merits before God, because God is the Governor of the whole society of mankind. Every good and every evil act, then, has some social merit or demerit either in the sight of men or in the sight of God—in the sight of God, because he is the Ruler of the whole society of mankind, and because he is the ultimate end of all human acts. This is the field of distributive justice.

St. Thomas writes of these two ways:

We speak of merit and demerit, in relation to retribution, rendered according to justice. Now retribution according to justice is rendered to man, by reason of his having done something to another's advantage or hurt. It must, however, be observed that every individual member of society is, in a fashion, a part and member of the whole society. Wherefore, any good or evil, done to the member of a society, rebounds on the whole society; thus who hurts the hand, hurts the man. When, therefore, anyone does good or evil to another individual, there is a twofold measure of merit or demerit in his action: first, in respect of the retribution owed to him by the individual to whom he has done good or harm; secondly, in respect of the retribution owed to him by the whole society. Now when a man ordains his action directly for the good or evil of the whole society, retribution is owed to him, before and above all, by the whole society; secondly, by all the parts of society. Whereas when a man does that which conduces to his own benefit or disadvantage, then again is retribution owed to him, in so far as this too affects the community, forasmuch as he is a part of society: although retribution is not due to him, in so far as it conduces to the good or harm of an individual, who is identical with the agent: unless, perchance, he owes retribution to himself, by a sort of resemblance, in so far as man is said to be just to himself. (S.T. I-II,21,3c)

Merit and demerit, then, are measured by justice. However, justice in relation to merit has some peculiarities and we should look at them. We may define merit as that quality of a free act having a beneficial bearing on another person by reason of which the agent deserves a reward or recompense from him in whose behalf the action is performed. Now because justice is based on the due proportion or equality that should exist between persons we may distinguish three kinds of merit relative to the three ways in which a reward is due: (1) *Condign merit in the strictest justice.* (2) *Condign merit but not in the strictest justice.* (3) *Congruous merit.*

Condign merit is merit in justice, i.e., a reward is due to the agent who acts in a way beneficial to another. But this reward may be due either in strictest justice or not in strictest justice. *Condign merit in the strictest justice* excludes all favor or grace or liberality of any kind and is based upon the strict law of contract, so that by reason of the act performed or the work done a reward is due. Thus, if a man by reason of a contract for a definite wage has performed a certain work, the wage is due him by reason of the work done. In order that such merit may be present, we will readily agree, the following conditions are necessary: (1) The one meriting should have conferred a benefit, which he was free not to confer, for merit is a part of justice and hence related to human acts. (2) There must be a formal agreement or contract between the agent meriting and the person benefiting regarding the benefit to be conferred and the reward to be given; (3) There must be a proportion of equality between the action and its reward, i.e., *vi operis*, there is a connection between the work and the reward so that the one meriting only has to point to the work to claim his reward. If this proportion does not exist, that is, if the reward given is of more value than the action, the merit is not *condign* but *congruous*; if the action is of greater value than the reward, the reward is not a reward, but an injustice. (4) Prior to the payment of the reward there must exist an imbalance in the order of justice between the person meriting and the person benefiting by reason of which the latter is a debtor and the former a creditor, which imbalance can be removed only by giving the reward due. (5) The person rewarding is deprived of that by which he pays the reward, otherwise due proportion would not be maintained.

Condign merit but not in the strictest justice binds in justice, but there is also the element of grace or liberality present. Although a reward is due in justice and the one meriting can, *vi operis*, point to the work done as a claim to the reward, nevertheless, there is the element of grace which is the ultimate basis for the power or the right to perform the work. Thus, if the athletic board of a school offers a monetary prize for the winning of a race, he who wins the race has a right to the prize. He has a right in view of the work done, *vi operis*, and yet the liberality of the board is the ultimate reason why he has a right.

Merit and reward refer to the same, for a reward means something given anyone in return for work or toil, as a sort of price for it. Hence, just as it is an act of justice to give a just price for anything received from another, so also it is an act of justice to make a return for work or toil. Now justice is a kind of equality, as is clear from the Philosopher, and hence justice exists absolutely between those that are absolutely equal; but where there is no absolute equality between them neither is there absolute justice, but there may be a certain manner of justice, as when we speak of a father's or a master's right, as the Philosopher says. And hence, where there is justice absolutely, there is the character of merit and reward absolutely. But where there is nothing absolutely just, but only relatively, there is no character of merit absolutely, but only relatively, in so far as the character of justice is preserved there: since the child merits something from his father and the slave from his lord. (S.T. I-II,114,1c)

Congruous merit is merit in justice, but in justice in an imperfect manner. In merit of this kind there is no question of a contract nor of liberality nor of grace, but rather of gratitude or propriety. An example will explain this. Suppose that I, while walking along the lake shore, hear a man crying for help. I swim to his rescue. There is no question of a reward to be given me by him in strict justice: there has been no contract between us; there has been no promise of a favor to be given. Yet there is an obligation of gratitude, of propriety or of humaneness, for I, by endangering my life, have allowed him to use me as an instrument for his own preservation, and in so doing have disturbed the order of equality existing between men. I merit not by reason of what I do, for I cannot point to the action done as a title to a reward, since the action itself demands no reward either by reason of a contract or a promise. But other considerations do demand a reward, namely, love of fellow men, friendship, gratitude that I have endangered my life for him.

The different kinds of merit having been defined, the questions arise, can man merit with God as a consequence of his good acts, or is the final end of man a pure gift? If we can merit with God, what kind of merit is it? St. Thomas writes:

Man's meritorious work may be considered in two ways. First, as it proceeds from free choice: secondly, as it proceeds from the grace of the Holy Ghost. If it is considered as regards the substance of the work, and inasmuch as it proceeds from free choice, there can be no condignity because of the very great inequality. But there is congruity, because of an equality of proportion; for it would seem congruous that, if a man does what he can, God should reward him according to the excellence of His power.

If, however, we speak of a meritorious work inasmuch as it proceeds from the grace of the Holy Ghost moving us to eternal life, it is meritorious of eternal life condignly. For thus the value of its merit depends upon the power of the Holy Ghost moving us to eternal life. . . . Furthermore, the worth of the work depends on the dignity of grace, whereby man, being a partaker of the divine nature, is adopted as a son of God, to whom the inheritance is due by right of adoption. (S.T. I-II, 114,3c)

To answer our question, does man merit with God, we must distinguish. If there is question of man's final end as the Beatific Vision, we must answer that as far as man's free act is concerned, there can only be a question of congruous merit. If, however, we consider the free act as done with the aid of grace, we must say that man merits condignly, but not in the strictest justice. Moreover, if we prescind from the fact that man's ultimate happiness is the Beatific Vision, and consider man's end of complete happiness on the purely natural plane, here too we must say that man's merit with God is condign but not in the strictest of justice.

We do, then, merit with God condignly, for perfect happiness is not something that is given as though it has no connection with our good acts. It is not given to us by considerations other than our acts, but *vi operis* we can claim the reward. There is, in other words, a necessary connection between our acts and the perfection of these acts, for the acts are ordered to man's ultimate happiness and are perfectly actualized in it. But we do not merit with God condignly in the strictest justice, for it is not a question of a reward which excludes grace and liberality, since the first reason why we can merit with God at all is that He has endowed us with a human nature ordained for happiness, and further enriches and elevates this nature with divine grace, which is essentially ordered to man's supernatural end.

But in order that we may see how this is true, let us run through the five conditions for condign merit. These conditions can be perfectly fulfilled between man and man, but imperfection and limitation are implied in all of them when they are applied to man's merit with God.

(1) We cannot strictly give God a benefit because to give a benefit to someone implies a lack in the one who receives. But there is nothing that God lacks. We say our good deeds glorify God, contributing to his external glory, which adds nothing to his intrinsic perfections. But from our side it is a benefit in the sense that we by our free will can refuse it. When we will to do a good deed for God, we offer him what would be a benefit, were he not too perfect to need it.

Man merits, inasmuch as by his own will he does what he ought: or otherwise the act of justice whereby anyone discharges a debt would not be meritorious. . . . God seeks from our goods not profit, but glory, i.e., the manifestation of His goodness; even as He seeks it also in His own works. Now nothing accrues to Him, but only to ourselves, by our worship of Him. Hence we merit with God, not that by our works anything accrues to Him, but inasmuch as we work for His glory. (T.S. I-II,114,1 ad 1 and 2)

(2) There can be no contract or formal agreement between God and ourselves, for this would mean that God is bound by a law superior to himself. Yet there is implanted within us by nature and grace a promise that ultimate happiness will be the reward of a morally good life. Our human acts, elevated by grace, have an exigency for a reward of perfect happiness. Since, therefore, nature and grace are gifts from God, God owes it to himself to fulfill his promises. Furthermore, because it is God who has freely given us nature as well as grace there can be no question of merit in the strictest justice.

(3) Between this reward and the actions which we place there is not a proportion of equality, but there is a proportion of teleology, i.e., the proportion that exists between a nature and its final end in which its activities naturally issue. There cannot be a proportion of equality between God and us any more than there can be a proportion of entitative equality between an acorn and the mighty oak into which it grows, but just as there is a proportion of teleology

between the acorn and the oak tree, for this is the natural end of the acorn, so there is a proportion between man's good moral acts and his perfect happiness.

Now it is clear that between God and man there is the greatest inequality; for they are infinitely apart, and all man's good is from God. Hence there can be no justice of absolute equality between man and God, but only of certain proportion, inasmuch as both operate after their own manner. Now the manner and measure of human virtue is in man from God. Hence man's merit with God exists only on the supposition of the divine ordination, so that, namely, man obtains from God, as a sort of reward of his operation, what God gave him the power of operation for, even as natural things by their proper movements and operations obtain that to which they were ordained by God. There is a difference, however, since the rational creature moves itself to act by its free choice; and so its action has the character of merit, which is not the case in other creatures. (S.T. I-II,114,1c)

(4) God does not become our debtor as a consequence of our good actions as though he had received some increase in his possessions or being. Neither do we become his creditors as though we had given something which was not due to him. Our acts are already due him by the facts of creation and elevation. Rather God becomes in a sense his own debtor, that is, God is necessitated by his own attributes of wisdom, sanctity, and justice to give us the happiness which he has promised. And God does not postpone the payment as a debtor does, for we have not fully earned the reward until death.

Since our action has the character of merit only on the presupposition of divine ordination, it does not follow that God is made our debtor absolutely, but His own, inasmuch as it is owing that His will should be carried out. (S.T. I-II,114,1 ad 3)

(5) Finally, God by giving the reward does not diminish his own possessions, since the reward is union with himself, and a friend loses nothing by bestowing friendship and knowledge on another. Human rewarders do lose something by their material payments, but God loses none of his happiness by giving man perfect happiness in the possession of himself.

6. Punishment

Little need be said about demerit and punishment. As merit and reward are consequences of morally good acts, demerit and punishment are consequences of morally evil acts. Merit, as we have seen, is the right to have restored the natural equality among persons that has been disturbed by a person freely placing an act that is beneficial to another. Demerit and punishment arise from the need of restoring the natural equality that has been disturbed by a person freely placing an act that is harmful to another. Since the order disturbed may be threefold, viz., the order of the individual, of human society, of universal government of God, the punishment can be threefold corresponding to the order disturbed by the evil.

In relation to justice, then, demerit and punishment are built upon the same foundation and follow the same law as merit and reward, namely, the foundation and the law of justice. There is, however, this difference: reward can be given when there is not a question of strictest justice, but that of gratitude or liberality, but no one should be punished unless he deserves it in strictest justice. No one should, nor can one, be punished unless he has committed a moral evil.

It is by a transfer from the natural things to human affairs that whenever one thing rises up against another, it suffers some detriment therefrom. For we observe in natural things that one contrary acts with greater intensity, when the other contrary supervenes; and for this reason hot water freezes rapidly, as is stated in Meteor. i 12. Therefore we find that the natural inclination of man is to repress those who rise up against him. Now it is evident that all things contained in an order are, in a manner, one in relation to the principle of that order. Consequently, whatever rises up against an order is put down by that order or by its principle. And because sin is an inordinate act, it is evident that whoever sins, commits an offense against some order. Hence he is put down, in consequence, by that same order; and this repression is punishment. (S.T. I-II, 87,1c)

The essential element in punishment is the infliction of pain upon one who has wrongfully enjoyed pleasure, a pleasure unduly received at the expense of another by breaking a law. This other, as we have said, may be God, society, or an individual, for all have rights which may be violated.

Accordingly, man can be punished with a threefold punishment, corresponding to the three orders to which the human will is subject. In the first place, a man's nature is subject to the order of his own reason; secondly, it is subject to the order of another who governs him either in spiritual or in temporal matters, as a member either of the state or of the household; thirdly, it is subject to the universal order of the divine government. Now each of these orders is disturbed by sin, for the sinner acts against his reason, and against human and divine law. Therefore, he incurs a threefold punishment: one, inflicted by himself, viz., remorse of conscience; another, inflicted by man; and a third, inflicted by God. (S.T. I-II,87,1c)

Accordingly, then, punishment is essentially retributive, retrospective, because it has in view the restoration of the disturbed natural equilibrium of possessions which one has freely and wrongfully disturbed for his own selfish pleasure. Not all, however, are in agreement with this opinion, particularly when the question concerns punishment in human society. There are those who say that we punish only for good of him who has done an evil, or in order that others may be deterred from doing the same evil act.

Because of this difference of opinion about the primary purpose of punishment, particularly with regard to that given by human authority, it would be well to consider punishment in greater detail.

The sum of all the opinions is that punishment has three purposes: one looks to the past and two to the future. As looking to the past punishment is called retributive or vindicative: *retributive* because it restores the order of justice which has been disturbed by an evil act; *vindicative* because it upholds the law by putting down the one who has risen up against it by his evil act. As looking towards the future, punishment has two purposes. It is *corrective* if its purpose is to reform or improve the evildoer; it is *deterrent* if its purpose is to prevent others from committing the same evil by showing them what happens to such evildoers.

There is complete agreement about the need of punishment

being corrective and deterrent, for unless it were human society would be impossible. But many, particularly at the present time, deny that punishment is retributive. The reason for their denial is that such punishment is vengeance or revenge and so it is immoral.

Against this view that punishment is only corrective and deterrent is the view that it must also be retributive. Those who hold the retributive character of punishment urge the three following arguments in their favor:

(1) In the popular conception, punishment is always retrospective. It is always regarded as inflicted on account of evil freely done.

(2) Punishment must always be proportioned to the crime. Were the corrective and deterrent purposes the reason for punishment, the punishment should be proportioned not to the evil done but to what is necessary for the improvement of the evildoer or for the example of others. On this basis we should be justified in punishing the wrongdoer far beyond his deserts if doing so were necessary for his reform or for the purpose of preventing others from committing the same action. We are opposed to this kind of punishment because the evil does not deserve it.

(3) If punishment were primarily corrective and deterrent, it would be immoral and useless to punish a hopeless recalcitrant. Furthermore, capital punishment makes correction impossible for the criminal. Granted that the corrective element is impossible in these cases, the deterrent element is present, the defenders of this opinion maintain. But is deterrence the primary element of punishment? If it were, we would have no justification for punishing Pilate, who unjustly condemned Christ to death. Such a condemnation cannot be repeated in the history of man, yet such a crime does demand punishment.

Punishment, then, is primarily retributive. It cannot be inflicted unless an evil act has been done. But public authority in inflicting punishment will always have before its mind's eye not only the restoration of justice but also the good of the individual who is punished as well as of those who have need of an example in order to be deterred from committing similar acts. Governments, indeed, cannot inflict pain on an individual merely for his own good. But granted that a person has already put himself in the power of the government so that it becomes right for the government to punish him on account of some crime, it is then the right as well as the duty of the public authorities to punish him and so to choose the kind of punishment that will provide not only that justice be administered but also that the personal improvement of the offender be aided and that potential criminals be deterred from their wrongdoing.

We are saying, then, that the ideal punishment should produce all three effects, but this combination is most difficult to attain. Some criminals are stubbornly defiant and will not reform. Capital punishment just cannot correct the offender. Some punishments will not be a deterrent for there are those who always think that they can get away with it.

Retribution, then, is the only element which can be found in every punishment. Such retribution is not revenge, because to take revenge is to punish an offender with the intention of harming him as the dominating motive. Retribution, on the other hand, is concerned with justice and not with the pleasure that one may or may not receive in dealing out punishment.

Let us conclude this consideration of punishment by summarizing what has been said. To punish is moral only when an evil act has been done. Punishment inflicted to restore the order of justice is moral, whether or not the evildoer is reformed or others are deterred from evildoing. Consequently, retribution is the primary purpose of punishment and the corrective and deterrent purposes are secondary at best. Nevertheless, human rulers should not disregard the corrective and deterrent purposes of punishment. Neither should they, influenced by sentiment, overemphasize these purposes so that they lose sight of the retributive purpose.

7. *The Immanence of the Natural Law*

From what has been said about the nature and properties of the natural law, it should be clear that the natural law is an intrinsic law, a law immanent in man, not something imposed upon man from the outside. St. Thomas says that by the natural law man becomes a partaker and dispenser of providence; by it man looks out for the welfare of himself and others, so that man is his own legislator. (*S.I.* I-II,91,2)

But this should be evident. The world, as we have accepted from metaphysics, is governed by an intelligent finality. God directs all things to their respective ends by a form proper to their kind, so that even what is inanimate is ideal, in the sense that it has form, which is a sort of soul. Consequently, all action is directed by an intrinsic or immanent law. And this law, immanent in creatures, is a reflection, a participation, of the transcendent law, the eternal law, which is in God. All things are, in this sense, directed to their ends by two laws: the eternal law which is transcendent; the law of nature and the natural law, which are immanent. The clearest example of the immanence of law is found in living things. No one will deny that there is an organic plan, a direction in them. Now, an organic plan has the character of law, a necessary manner of action, a command of nature. The carrying out of this plan is left to the form or nature of things. Coming to man, we find that in a certain respect he is like the lower living things, and indeed like all natural things. The forms of his activity are the result of the ideality immanent in him. But he differs in an all-important respect: the form or immanent end which determines his activity is not entirely given. He himself is partially responsible for it; he can apprehend nature and form a practical judgment, a judgment wherein he chooses what he is to do to gain his end. He is his own lawmaker in so far as he, under the guidance of reason, perceives his own end and chooses the means to his end. Reason indicates the inner agreement of actions with his rational nature, i.e., reason recognizes the natural inclinations and so proposes what is to be done and what is to be avoided. This dictate of reason is the natural law, the obligation of which flows necessarily from human nature itself.

But can man oblige himself? As regards obligation, St. Thomas' morality is not a legalism like that of Kant and of some Catholic philosophers. For Kant, the good is obligating because we so conceive it, and impose it upon ourselves as obligatory, by an autonomous will, i.e., by a will that does not depend on anything outside itself. For certain others, like Duns Scotus, the good is obligatory because God so willed it. For St. Thomas, the good is obligatory because reason judges it to be the means whereby man may be truly man, and may reach his end. Man's end, though freely sought after, is just as imperative to him as physical necessity is to other beings; though man freely pursues his end, he is necessitated to that end and in view of that end chooses. This knowledge of the end is the source of his obligation. The obligation, therefore, that man recognizes is not something that is proximately imposed upon him from the outside by the will of another. Law is a thing of reason, not of will; its obligation is from reason, not from will. And it is for this reason that God can no more abrogate nor dispense from the general principles of the natural law than He can change the nature of man, the eternal truth within Himself, for if human reason recognizes the conformity of actions with nature, they must be done.

God's will does not, as Scotus thought, turn what would be otherwise indifferent into something obligatory, but it makes things to be obligatory because they are conformed to human nature. In making things obligatory because of the nature of man, God acts more as a Creator than as a legislator, or if you prefer, he is a legislator because he is a creator, because for God to impose a law is to impose an end, and to impose an end is to impose a nature, i.e., to create. And by the very fact that he creates, the autonomy of reason is left intact, because in creating, God entrusts each being to itself, and does not absorb it, does not by an arbitrary will make it, as it were, a slave, which should and must act as he wishes. Law and being depend upon God, but law is only a consequence of being. Once God has created the being, in the present case the being of man, man must follow the rule of his being which is the law of reason. In this sense, then, obligation does not come from without, but from human reason.

Putting it quite simply, human reason recognizing the essential order of things is the proximate source of obligation of the natural law. Because human reason, recognizing that it must always act for good (which is the end set by nature), perceives a certain act as necessary for this end, reason obligates the will and this is the proximate source of obligation. The obligation of the natural law, therefore, does not depend for its efficacy on a knowledge either of God or of God's will. For in the impossible hypothesis that God might not will the natural law, it would nevertheless become known to man and would oblige man in the same way as now, because human nature would be constituted in the same way as now by the command of Divine Reason, and both human nature and its act would be ordained to the last end. The essential order of things, more particularly the rational good of man, is the proximate source of the obligation of the natural law. It is a secondary but true cause in the moral order, producing a true effect, a true obligation. Ultimately, of course, the efficacy of this secondary cause of moral obligation, which simply results from the necessity of an act in relation to an absolutely necessary end, depends on the first and supreme cause, God and his eternal law. Obviously, if there were no God, nothing would exist, and hence there would be no natural law of any kind. Yet the obligation of the natural law no more demands a knowledge of God as a legislator for its efficacy than do the first principles of the speculative order for their validity. This obligation arises from a first principle, the principle of finality, which like the other first principles has ontological value.

But, as Farrell writes, "that the Natural Law does not demand an idea of God for its efficacy does not mean that God is a superfluity in the moral order. I do not need a knowledge of God to fry eggs; but without God there would not only be no frying done, there would be no eggs and no cook. The efficacy of the second cause does not exclude dependence on the first cause. If the first cause should cease to exist, the second cause would lose all causality; it is only in reducing the undoubted causality of the second cause to the first cause that this secondary causality is entirely explicable and intelligible. The proximate source of the obligation of the Natural Law is indeed the essential order of things as understood by natural reason and proposed to the will of man; but the supreme and first cause of this obligation is the Eternal Law and its author, God." (*A Companion to the Summa*, vol. II, p. 385) The natural law, then, is not an extrinsic regulator, like the command of a superior, but is a participation in the eternal law, an immanent law, and, consequently, makes the reason autonomous.

Readings

Aristotle, *Nicomachean Ethics*, bk. V, VII, cc. 2, 3.

Brosnahan, T. J., *Prolegomena to Ethics*, appendix A. Also pp. 217-226, 273-275.

Cronin, Michael, *Science of Ethics*, vol. I, cc. 8, 9, 14.

Davitt, T., *The Nature of Law*. Contrasts the intellectualist or Thomistic with the voluntarist or Scotistic interpretation of obligation.

Farrell, W., *A Companion to the Summa*, vol. I, pp. 633-652; vol. II, pp. 384-389.

LeBuffe, F. P., and Hayes, J. V., *The American Philosophy of Law*, ch. IX.

Leibell, J. F., *Readings in Ethics*. The following are worth reading:

"The immortality of the soul," Michael Maher, pp. 77-88.
"Freedom of the will," Michael Maher, pp. 89-98.
"The precepts of the natural law," Joseph Rickaby, pp. 323-324.
"The moral law," Timothy Brosnahan, pp. 325-326.
"Altruism," Timothy Brosnahan, pp. 380-383.
"The Kantian ought," Timothy Brosnahan, pp. 383-400.

Manion, Clarence E. "The Natural Law Philosophy of Founding Fathers," *University of Notre Dame Natural Law Institute Proceedings*, 1947, pp. 30-65.

Paton, H. J., *The Moral Law, passim.*

Rickaby, Joseph, *Moral Philosophy*, pp. 109-125; 159-176.

Suarez, Francisco, *De Legibus*, bk. II, c. 9.

St. Thomas, *Summa Theologica*, I, 82, 1, 2; I-II, 10, 1, 2; 13, 3, 6; 21, 3, 4; 86; 87; 114.

——— *Summa Contra Gentiles*, bk. III, c. 10.

CHAPTER X

POSITIVE LAW

1. *The Need for Positive Law*

All men are governed by the natural law. However, we have seen that this law is known naturally to all men only in its most general principles; it is not known with equal clarity by all men in many of its more detailed principles. Such obscurity does not argue any defect in the natural law, but is rather implied in the very concept of this law, for since the natural law is discovered by reason we should expect that as reason is gradually developed the knowledge of the law itself should grow and become gradually more and more detailed. Now, because the majority of men either have not the inclination or the ability or the opportunity to develop a detailed knowledge of the natural law, the knowledge which all men have of the general principles must be supplemented by other laws which are more detailed expressions of the natural law.

Such laws are *positive laws*. Even though we grant that man has a natural capacity for drawing true conclusions from self-evident principles, nevertheless, this power is limited both in the speculative and in the practical orders so that not all the details of truth are or can be known by every man. Just as man, therefore, needs the help

277

of others to arrive at certain and true conclusions in the speculative order, so he needs the help of others to arrive at conclusions in the practical order so that he may lead a safe and certain upright life befitting him as a rational being. If these conclusions in the practical order are drawn and established by authority they are positive laws.

We may divide positive law into two kinds because of the authority issuing such commands: *divine* and *human*. There are few who deny that God has made such positive laws, no matter how much the various peoples of various religions may dispute the content of these laws. Blackstone writes:

This has given manifold occasion for the benign interposition of the divine Providence, which in compassion to the frailty, the imperfections and the blindness of human reason, hath been pleased at sundry times and in diverse manners, to discover and enforce its laws by an immediate and direct revelation. (William Blackstone, Commentaries on the Laws of England; Introduction, Section 1)

Man needs divine positive law. The supreme concern of every enlightened man must ever be to reach God, by whom and for whom he was made. He cannot, unless he acts rightly; and rightly ordered action means action in accordance with just and reasonable laws. Now man, though free and intelligent, can observe laws only to the degree in which he knows them. To attain his final end with security he would have to understand the law and its application perfectly. But man does not so understand them. On the contrary, men differ greatly in their knowledge and interpretation of law, and hence of the rightness and wrongness of human acts. They set up laws that are contrary to one another, even contradictory. Therefore in order to be certain of what is right and what is wrong in all essential matters, it is necessary that God promulgate to men laws that are infallible rules of right conduct.

Man also needs human positive law. Man must live in political society in which differences of opinion must be set aside for mutual cooperation. Consequently, man needs the help of authority to determine the truth of the practical order for his own good as well as for the good of the community of which he is a part. This need for human positive laws may be mainly referred to deficiencies in the superior powers of the soul, the reason, and the will.

Owing to weakness of intellect in apprehending and to feebleness of reason in following out principles to their legitimate consequences, many men are incapable of applying the general principles of the natural law with truth and certainty even in many practical matters that necessarily concern both their own good and the good of the political society of which they are members. Such individual members of the state would err in their duty to themselves and to others through ignorance; still more impossible would it be for them to prescribe for themselves safe or just rules of conduct in matters concerning which even the most prudent need counsel and direction. Therefore, man needs law as rules for the direction of his life owing to ignorance and weakness of his reason.

There is also a need for positive law arising from the disorderly inclinations, passions, and vices which many persons permit to control their lives. Being ruled by selfish feelings, and devoid of moral rectitude in action, the conduct of many persons would be injurious both to themselves and to the community; hence, positive laws are needed, not only to declare what is good and right, but to restrain evil, and compel obedience to necessary duty towards the public.

We have stated above, man has a natural aptitude for virtue; but the perfection of virtue must be acquired by man by means of some kind of training. Thus we observe that a man is helped by diligence in his necessities, for instance, in food and clothing. Certain beginnings of these he has from nature, viz., his reason and his hands; but he has not the full complement, as other animals have, to whom nature has given sufficiently of clothing and food. Now it is difficult to see how man could suffice for himself in the matter of this training, since the perfection of virtue consists chiefly in withdrawing man from undue pleasures, to which above all man is inclined, and especially the young, who are more capable of being trained. Consequently a man needs to receive this training from another, whereby to arrive at the perfection of virtue. And as to those young people who are inclined to acts of virtue by their natural disposition, or by custom, or rather by the gift of God, paternal training suffices, which is by admonitions. But since some are found to be dissolute and prone to vice, and not easily amenable to words it was necessary for such to be restrained from evil by force and fear, in order that, at least, they might desist from evildoing, and leave others in peace, and that they themselves, by being habituated in this way, might be brought to do willingly what hitherto they did from fear, and thus become virtuous. Now this kind of training, which compels through fear of punishment, is the discipline of laws. Therefore, in order that man might have peace and virtue, it was necessary for laws to be framed: for, as the Philosopher says, as man is the most noble of animals if he be perfect in virtue, so he is the lowest of all, if he be severed from law and justice. [Pol. I, 1, 1253a, 31] For man can use his reason to devise means of satisfying his lusts and evil passions, which other animals are unable to do. (S.T. I-II,95,1c)

Because divine positive laws can be known only by revelation we shall now limit our discussion of positive law to human positive law. However, we should bear in mind that divine positive law is not useless for man's human conduct nor incidental to it. Such laws are necessary for several reasons. As man is now situated he is ordained for an ultimate end which far exceeds his natural ability. To be surely and safely directed to this end, man needs more than the natural or human laws. Man's judgments, too, are subject to error in contingent and particular matters. Divine positive laws give man help to free him from such uncertainties. Again, human law cannot forbid nor punish all evil without at the same time doing away with much good. Divine positive law is able to legislate against the evil without at the same time prohibiting the good. Further, human positive law is so limited in character that much evil would go unpunished and much good unrewarded unless divine positive law intervened to forbid the one and to command the other, and so establish perfect sanctions. Finally, the function of law is to make men good. Now men are good or bad, not merely because of external acts, but also because of such internal acts as envy, jealousy, unchaste or unjust thoughts or desires. Human law can regulate only those actions which human legislators know; and since they can know only external actions, it follows that a law is necessary having power to regulate internal as well as external acts. But this is the divine positive law; for only God can know the hearts of men.

Besides the natural and the human law it was necessary for the directing of human conduct to have a divine law. And this for four reasons. First, because it is by law that man is directed how to perform his proper acts in view of his last end. Now if man were ordained to no other end than that which is proportionate to his natural ability, there would be no need for man to have any further direction, on the part of his reason, in addition to the natural law and humanly devised law which is derived from it. But since man is ordained to an end of eternal happiness which exceeds man's natural ability, as we have stated above, therefore it was necessary that, in addition to the natural and the human law, man should be directed to his end by a law given by God.

Secondly, because by reason of the uncertainty of human judgment, especially on contingent and particular matters, different people form different judgments on human acts; whence also different contrary laws result. In order, therefore, that man may know without any doubt what he ought to do and what he ought to avoid, it was necessary for man to be directed in his proper acts by a law given by God, for it is certain that such a law cannot err.

Thirdly, because man can make laws in those matters of which he is competent to judge. But man is not competent to judge of interior movements, that are hidden, but only of exterior acts which are observable; and yet for the perfection of virtue it is necessary for man to conduct himself rightly in both kinds of acts. Consequently, human law could not sufficiently curb and direct interior acts, and it was necessary for this purpose that a divine law should supervene.

Fourthly, because, as Augustine says, human law cannot punish or forbid all evil deeds, since while aiming at doing away with all evil, it would do away with many good things, and would hinder the advance of the common good, which is necessary for human living. In order, therefore, that no evil might remain unforbidden and unpunished, it was necessary for the divine law to supervene, whereby all sins are forbidden. (S.T. I-II,91,4c)

Now to return to human positive law, which we will deal with exclusively from this point on. Without such laws to control their actions as members of a civil society, men would not only be in constant danger of losing their own personal liberty but they would also be constantly threatening this liberty of others; not only would they live amid uncertainties and chaos but they would also be lacking that cooperative activity which is required for any society. Without such laws, dishonesty, theft, sexual immorality, and murder would be widespread. Consequently, there are several important reasons why human positive laws are necessary. They are the following:

(1) *The demands of the natural law may be unknown to some persons.* We have seen that the natural law in many of its detailed applications and in its remote conclusions is not known to all men and neither are these conclusions true for all men. There are some persons with defective or perverted moral education in every civil society. In order that these might know what right reason in accordance with the natural law demands there is need for legislators, who make laws in accordance with the requirements of the natural law for these concrete circumstances of the particular civil authority.

(2) *The changing conditions of civil society.* Although the principles of justice remain eternally the same, yet the circumstances to which these principles are to be applied are constantly changing. Consequently, there is a constant need of positive laws to explain or clarify the obligations of the natural law regarding the duties and rights between individuals and between individuals and their governments.

(3) *The need of cooperative actions.* The natural law often permits the choice of many alternatives for its fulfillment. Each person, then, in his own individual ordering of himself to his ultimate end may morally choose any good means. However, civil society requires cooperative action between the governed and the governors for its continued existence. Consequently, there is need of a choice of means which all must use to promote the common good of civil society. Human positive laws indicate this mutual cooperative activity.

(4) *The need of earthly sanctions.* As we have discussed, the natural law does have perfect sanctions, but these are reserved for the future life. Such sanctions are not sufficient to move the great multitude of men, simply because they are in the next life and are not experienced in this. Numberless men do not believe in a future life and others can be influenced only by what they experience. If

civil society relied only on these perfect sanctions of the natural law it could not continue to exist. Consequently, there is a necessity of human positive laws whereby definite manners of actions are laid down and definite punishments are established for the violations of these laws.

2. *The Meaning of Human Positive Law*

The need of positive law for the good of society as well as for the good of the individual is clear. We shall now look into the meaning of human positive law. St. Thomas writes:

Augustine says (De Lib. Arb. I,5) that which is not just seems to be no law at all; therefore the force of a law depends on the extent of its justice. Now in human affairs a thing is said to be just, from being right, according to the rule of reason. But the first rule of reason is the law of nature, as is clear from what has been stated above. Consequently every human law has just so much in the nature of law, as is derived from the law of nature. But if in any point it deflects from the law of nature, it is no longer a law but a perversion of law.

But it must be noted that something may be derived from the natural law in two ways: first, as conclusions from premises, secondly, by way of determination of certain generalities. The first way is like to that by which, in science, demonstrated conclusions are drawn from the principles: while the second mode is likened to that whereby, in the arts, general forms are particularized as to details: thus the craftsman needs to determine the general form of a house to some particular shape. Some things are therefore derived from the general principles of the natural law, by way of conclusions; e.g., that one must not kill may be derived as a conclusion from the principle that one should do harm to no man: while some are derived therefrom by way of determination; e.g., the law of nature has it that the evildoer should be punished; but that he be punished in this or that way, is a determination of the law of nature.

Accordingly both modes of derivation are found in the human law. But those things which are derived in the first way, are contained in human law not as emanating therefrom exclusively, but have some force from the natural law also. But those things which are derived in the second way, have no other force than that of human law. (S.T. I-II,95,2c)

Every human law has just so much of the nature of law as it derives from the natural law. A human law is a rule of action that is imposed by legitimate civil authority. Such a law, however, is a law only in so far as it has been derived from the natural law. There are two reasons for this limitation. First, the natural law is, as we know, the fundamental rule of action which rational beings must follow in order to arrive at their ultimate end, the perfection of their nature. Every law, then, must be conformed with this law, must perfect rational beings; must, in some way or another, be derived from this law. Secondly, man is a social being by his very nature and can, therefore, perfect himself only by being a member of civil society. Civil society, however, requires an authority to direct the members by cooperative activity to its common good. The rational nature of man, then, requires that man be subject to civil authority. Hence, civil authority in the natural order is entrusted by the natural law to guide men to their common end by directing them in their observance of the natural law. Such direction, evidently, must be an interpretation or a derivation of the natural law.

Because human positive law must be derived from the natural law it is possible to distinguish two kinds of positive laws by reason of the manner in which they are derived from the natural law: *declarative* and *determinative* positive law.

A *declarative positive law* may be defined as a law which commands or prohibits that which is deduced as a necessary conclusion from the principles of the natural law. Let us recall what we have said about the law of nations. It is those general and necessary conclusions of the primary principles which are concerned with the demands of justice within civil society. We use these general conclusions as principles about the requirements of justice in civil society. Thus, from the general and necessary principle "Institute a division of property," the state draws the necessary conclusion that it must establish laws for such an institution. Or, from the general principle "No one should harm another," the state prohibits murder. Such laws, although derived from the natural law by civil authority, are necessarily derived and so are to be considered as natural law and derive all their obligating force from this law. The reason why civil authority must establish such necessary conclusions as rules of action for the members of society has been adequately expressed in the preceding section, where we dealt with the need of positive law.

A *determinative positive law*, on the other hand, may be defined as a determination, or application, of the natural law to the particular circumstances and needs of a particular society. For example, the law of nations prohibits one from harming another; a necessary conclusion of this general principle is the law which forbids stealing, or taking what belongs to another. But this law does not clearly determine in every case when a thing first belongs in fact to another. Such a determination, then, has to be made by human positive law. Determinative positive laws, then, are useful interpretations of the natural law for particular circumstances. There are numerous laws of this kind. The laws about contracts, taxes, buying and selling, about different kinds of punishments are examples of determinative laws. They are what we may call *civil laws* pure and simple. Evidently, the source of their obligation is immediately to be found in the civil authority which establishes them.

Let us be clear about these two kinds of positive laws. Declarative laws have the force of both the natural law and the positive law. On the other hand, those parts of the positive law arrived at by a determination of the human lawmaker have only the force of human law. This means that it is an offense against the natural law, as well as state law, to murder. But it is not a direct offense against the natural law, but only against the state law, to break a traffic law.

3. *The Qualities of Human Law*

Some human positive laws, then, are determinations of the natural law. Since such laws are civil laws we shall confine ourselves to these laws. Among the many questions which may be raised about civil law we shall consider a few of the most important. The first is, how can we know whether a civil law is a law? The answer, following St. Thomas, may be put most simply: It is a law if it makes men good in some way. But let us clarify this answer by expanding it.

These are a most practical question and answer in a society such as ours, where men are almost always discussing such subjects as freedom and rights. There are some who, while admitting the necessity of law, are so insistent upon freedom that they restrict the field of law to vague generalities which would in no way interfere with one's personal freedom. There are others who, fearful of the utter anarchy which would follow from such a view, demand that law enter into almost every detail of men's lives.

Between these two extreme opinions about the place of civil law in society is the more moderate opinion of Aristotle and St. Thomas. Without civil law at all, vice will be the order of the day and chaos will reign. But state control which would completely regulate men's lives so as to exclude all vice and reduce man to a mere cog in a vast civil machine would not be law. History has shown that men will not long endure state interference with their private lives, their families, their professional and business activities, except when the common good requires. Aristotle has written some words which are just as pertinent today as the day in which he wrote them:

But it is difficult to get from youth up a right training for virtue if one has not been brought up under right laws; for to live temperately and hardily is not pleasant to most people especially when they are young. For this reason their nature and occupations should be fixed by law; for they will not be painful when they have become customary. But it is surely not enough that when they are young they should get the right nurture and attention; since they must, even when they are grown up, practice and be habituated to them, we shall need laws for this as well, and generally speaking to cover the whole of life; for most people obey necessity rather than argument, and punishments rather than the sense of what is noble.

This is why some think that legislators ought to stimulate men to virtue and urge them forward by the motive of the noble, on the assumption that those who have been well advanced by the formation of habits will attend to such influences; and that punishments and penalties should be imposed on those who disobey and are of inferior nature, while the incurably bad should be completely banished. A good man (they think), since he lives with his mind fixed on what is noble, will submit to argu-

ment, while a bad man, whose desire is for pleasure, is corrected by pain like a beast of burden. (Nic. Eth. X, c.9,1179b, 31-1180a,12)

The purpose of law, then, is to help to make men good, to help them live together amid peace and harmony. St. Thomas, as we know, is of the same opinion, for as it has been noted he says that laws must be framed in order to secure peace and virtue. In this, as well as in other moral matters, St. Thomas maintains that goodness consists in order. Whatever is rightly ordered is good and whatever is disordered is bad. Moral goodness, then, is rightly ordered acts. Man lives the good life when his actions are rightly ordered to everything and everyone.

Now it is the purpose of law to secure such order for man. It is an ordinance of reason whose purpose is to direct or order man to his good by indicating to him the ways in which he should deal with other creatures about him. Civil law, too, is an ordinance of reason whose purpose it is to indicate the order which ought to exist in human relationships. There is, in fact, no civil law which does not concern itself with order, with controlling the relationship between buyers and sellers, employers and employees, government and individuals, etc. To regulate these relationships is to make good citizens, to secure the needed cooperation among the citizens. Civil law, then, must limit its sphere of operation to these human relationships and be content with making good citizens.

To assure that this purpose of civil law be attained it must have the elements or qualities which St. Isidore enumerated as far back as the sixth century. St. Thomas reaffirms these qualities when he writes:

Whenever a thing is for an end, its form must be determined proportionately to that end; as the form of a saw is such as to be suitable for cutting. Again, everything that is ruled and measured must have a form proportioned to its rule and measure. Now both these conditions are verified in human law, since it is both something ordained to an end, and it is also a rule or measure ruled or measured by a higher measure. Now this higher measure is twofold, viz., the divine law and the natural law, as was explained above. But the end of human law is to be useful to man, as the Jurist states. Therefore Isidore, in determining the nature of law, first lays down three conditions, viz., that it foster religion, inasmuch as it is proportioned to the divine law; that it be helpful to discipline, inasmuch as it is proportioned to the natural law; and that it further the common welfare, inasmuch as it is proportioned to the utility of mankind.

All the other conditions mentioned by him are reduced to these three. For it is called virtuous because it fosters religion. And when he goes on to say that it should be just, possible to nature, according to the customs of the country, adapted to place and time, he implies that it should be suitable to discipline. For human discipline depends, first, on the order of reason, to which he refers by saying just. Secondly, it depends on the ability of the agent, because discipline should be adapted to each one according to his ability, taking also into account the ability of nature (for the same burdens should not be laid on children as on adults); and it should be according to human customs, since man cannot live alone in society, paying no heed to others. Thirdly, it depends on certain circumstances, in respect of which he says, adapted to place and time. The remaining words, necessity, useful, etc., mean that law should further the common welfare; so that necessary refers to the removal of evils, usefulness, to the attainment of good, clearness of expression, to the need of preventing any harm ensuing from the law itself.(S.T. I-II,95,3c)

From this quotation, we can see that every civil law must be ultimately derived from the natural law. But this should be evident from what we have said about how civil laws are determinations of the natural law. Moreover, since the natural law is a participation in the eternal law, it follows that civil laws are true laws in so far as they share in the perfection of the eternal law. Now, since it is the eternal law which is the Divine Rule by which God guides and orders all things to their respective ends, every civil law, to be a law, must guide and order men so that they may obtain their proper end, their good in some sense. Such laws would, of course, help men to be good and virtuous, for they would command or prohibit that which would promote or hinder the order that should be found in human relationships. If civil laws are capable of doing this they possess the qualities of religion and discipline, for they not only are guides for virtue in man, they are also according to reason and justice.

The last quality of civil laws, namely, that they are for the common good, is frequently the reason why so many men find dissatisfaction with numerous laws which civil authority promulgates. Most laws, so the dissatisfaction expresses itself, do not consider the individual and his particular needs. If it were possible to find a group of legislators who were endowed with an angelic or, better still, a divine knowledge and a corresponding consummate good will, who could individually direct each citizen in the way of virtue to reach the end of the state, there would be no need for civil laws, for each individual citizen, under the direction of such a guide, would be individually directed in the best way possible both for his own good and the good of others. There can be no doubt that wisdom would be the rule of action in such circumstances. But the fact is that we do not live in such an angelic society. We cannot find such a large number of men who could and would direct every individual citizen with perfect wisdom and good will. It is far easier to find a few prudent men to legislate for the community taken as a whole. But because such human legislation is for the community and not directly for the individual citizen, certain limitations are found in civil laws.

Civil laws regulate general situations and not specific circumstances. Means should always be proportionate to the end, and as the end of these laws is the common good, that is, the good of the many citizens who are endowed with different characteristics, engaged in different activities at different times, interested in diverse personal goods, it is necessary that laws be made for the whole community and for the foreseeable future of the community. Civil laws, then, must be framed along general lines and should not be so definite or particularized that they may be applicable to every and each individual case. It is the duty of the judge to interpret and apply the law properly to each individual case.

Whatever is for an end should be proportioned to that end. Now the end of law is the common good, because, as Isidore says, law should be framed, not for any private benefit, but for the common good of all the citizens. Hence human laws should be proportioned to the common good. Now the common good comprises many things. Therefore law should take account of many things, as to persons, as to matters, and as to times. For the community of the state is composed of many persons, and its good is procured by many actions; nor is it established to endure for only a short time, but to last for all time by the citizens succeeding one another, as Augustine says. (S.T. I-II,96,1c)

As it is, civil law aspires to such noble purposes: it does want to make the citizens good. But are we to conclude that civil law not only proposes to eliminate all iniquity and vice but also to promote all virtue? If civil law has the qualities which Isidore has said and which St. Thomas has reiterated, must it not legislate against all possible evil in civil society? St. Thomas presents the view of one of his objectors: "The intention of the lawgiver is to make the citizens virtuous. But a man cannot be virtuous unless he forbear from all kinds of vice. Therefore, it belongs to human law to repress all vices." (S.T. I-II,96,2, obj. 2)

Were this the purpose of civil law we can easily imagine what the results would be. Not only would civil laws have to regulate contracts between buyers and sellers, to legislate against slander, ill-treatment of fellow citizens, injury to property and life, but it would also be obligated to make laws against every kind of intemperance and cowardliness in thought, word, and deed. As a result of this view civil authorities would have to see to it that no one was idle, uncharitable in thought, or untruthful in speech. A policeman would have to be appointed as a personal watchman for each citizen to prevent any evil action or thought.

Against this view, St. Thomas maintains that the purpose of civil law is to promote the external good of society. He writes:

As was stated above, law is framed as a rule or measure of human acts. Now a measure should be homogeneous with that which is measured, as is stated in Metaph. X [Meta. IX,1,1053,24], since different things are measured by different measures. Therefore laws imposed on men should also be in keeping with their condition, for, as Isidore says, law should be possible both according to nature, and according to the customs of the country. Now the ability or facility of action is due to an interior habit or disposition, since the same thing is not possible to one who has not a virtuous habit, as is possible to one who has. Thus the same thing is not possible to a child as to a full-grown man, and for which reason the law for children is not the same as for adults, since many things are permitted to children, which in an adult are punished by law or at any rate are open to blame. In like manner, many things are permissible to men not perfect in virtue, which would be intolerable in a virtuous man.

Now human law is framed for the multitude of human beings, the majority of whom are not perfect in virtue. Therefore human laws do not forbid all vices, from which the virtuous abstain, but only the more grievous vices, from which it is possible for the majority to abstain, chiefly those that are injurious to others, without the prohibition of which human society could not be maintained. (S.T. I-II,92,2c)

Civil law, then, does not legislate for the practice of all virtues but only those which are concerned with the external actions of the citizens in their dealings with their fellow men. It would not be prudent for civil legislators to try to suppress all vices, for in their attempts to do so they would be imposing such burdens on the majority of citizens that civil life itself would be impossible. Circumspection and caution are to be the virtues of civil legislators in the ruling of society, for they are not to think that it is their duty to suppress all vices but only those which are the more vicious and injurious to the common good of society. In point of fact, human legislators cannot prescribe or prohibit every virtue or vice; much of such legislation has to be left to God who in his divine providence rules and governs each individual act of man. Only the Divine Law of Love can compel men to be subject to this rule of God; only Divine Justice can vindicate his law. Human law, writes St. Thomas, falls short of the eternal law in that it must be limited to the more vicious of external actions; hence it must rightly allow some vices, by not repressing them. And he concludes, quoting St. Augustine, "the law which is framed for the government of states, allows and leaves unpunished many things that are punished by divine providence." (S.T. I-II,96,2, obj. 3).

4. The Obligation of Civil Laws

So far we have defined human positive laws and have described some of their qualities; we have still to consider two serious problems: (1) How far do these laws obligate a person's conscience?

(2) In what cases and on what grounds is it permissible to change the laws of the state?

We shall begin with the examination of the first question. There is a difference of opinion about the obligation which civil law places upon man. Some say categorically that all such laws bind the conscience of the citizens to perform or refrain from performing what the law commands or prohibits. Others, on the contrary, distinguish between civil laws and purely penal laws, and while admitting the binding force of the civil laws in conscience, deny this obligation in regard to penal laws. They define a penal law as a law which *does not bind in conscience to do or omit something,* but which *obliges the subject either to obey or to accept the penalty for not obeying.* If a man is willing to accept the penalty he may disobey the provisions of the law. The obligation of accepting the penalty does not mean that one has to give oneself up after he disobeys the law; nor does it mean that he may not invoke his right to legal defense. It only means that he must pay the penalty when it is imposed by civil authority. Those who favor such laws give as examples the ordinances which pertain to the external order of the community, i.e.: police orders about traffic; fire and health rules for conduct in public buildings in regard to smoking and hygienic measures; ordinances about hunting and fishing; statutes about taxes and military service in time of peace.

Many ethicians maintain that the legislator has authority to enact such laws. They support their opinion by two main reasons. Their first reason is that the authority has control over the nature of the obligation he wishes to impose upon his subjects. Because he can determine that a law framed about gravely important matter obligate the subjects only lightly, so he can decide that the obligation refer to the acceptance of the penalty and not to the observance of the law. The second reason given by the supporters of penal law is that the good of civil society can often be better secured by such laws than by laws which impose a moral obligation to observe the provision of the laws. More men, they observe, are moved to obey a law out of fear of the penalty than out of reverence for the law or out of fear of moral guilt.

We must recall that a law imposes an obligation upon the subject. A penal law, then, must carry some obligation. A civil enactment which would carry no obligation either to obey or to accept the penalty for its nonobservance would not be a law. Consequently, civil legislators must either explicitly or implicitly have the intention of binding their subjects to obey the law or to accept the penalty.

Without pretending to arbitrate this difference of opinion about penal laws, it is important to point out several difficulties which the concept of penal law provokes. As we have seen in the preceding chapters on law, law as a command of the practical reason necessarily implies an obligation arising from the necessary connection between the act commanded and the end for which the act is commanded. If the end, then, is of obligation, the act leading to the end is likewise obligating. Let us put it in another way. Human law is derived from the natural law, which, in its turn, is derived from the eternal law. Now, just as the mind and will of God are the supreme source of obligation, so the positive law of human authority is law only in so far as it participates in this moral obligation. But the moral obligation binding the human will arises from God commanding a definite action to be done as a means to man's end. Such a law binds in conscience. If civil law participates in this obligation it would follow that it, too, binds in conscience to perform the action prescribed.

The obligation of a penal law rests upon the citizen's willingness to undergo the penalty for not observing the law. There is no question of a law indicating a necessary means to an end, for then the law would oblige the citizen to perform or to refrain from an action; rather, it is a question of binding the will to accept the penalty. It appears that it is not the action of obeying or not obeying which promotes or hinders the common good, but the penalty itself. It would appear, however, that the imposition of penalties promotes the common good because it vindicates law. But the refusal to obey a penal law does not imply an infraction of law since penal law does not bind the citizen to perform an action.

If it is conceded that there is an obligation in a penal law, it must also be conceded that the obligation is almost nothing. It amounts to this: the citizen must pay the penalty if he is caught. As we have said, there is no obligation that the violator of the law make his violation known or that he give up his right to civil defence. If he is not apprehended, or if he is successful in the prosecution of his case in a court of law, he is freed from all moral responsibility and accountability. The sanction of such a law seems to be almost nothing, for the moral obligation of accepting the penalty is extremely tenuous.

This is not to say that civil authority may not frame enactments which carry no morally binding force to obey them if the citizen is willing to accept the penalty, but these are not laws. In the mind of St. Thomas a law that does not bind in conscience is no law, for a law which lacks obligation lacks order to an end which is the very meaning of law. And to lack order is to lack justice. Human laws, then, are either just or unjust. They are just if they answer the definition of law: an ordination of reason for the common good by him who has the care of the community. The only question, then, that arises in regard to the binding force of a law is the question of its justice or injustice. How then are we to decide whether a law is just or unjust? To discover this, let us refer to St. Thomas:

Laws framed by man are either just or unjust. If they are just they have the power of binding in conscience from the eternal law whence they are derived, according to Prov. 8,15: By Me kings reign, and lawgivers decree just things. Now laws are said to be just, both from the end (when, namely, they are ordained to the common good), from their author (that is to say, when the law that is made does not exceed the power of the lawgiver), and from their form (when, namely, burdens are laid on the subjects according to an equality of proportion and with a view to the common good). For, since one man is part of the community, each man, in all that he is and has, belongs to the community; just as a part, in all that it is, belongs to the whole. So, too, nature inflicts a loss on the part in order to save the whole: so that for this reason such laws as these, which impose proportionate burdens, are just and binding in conscience, and are legal laws.

On the other hand, laws may be unjust in two ways: first, by being contrary to human good, through being opposed to the things mentioned above:—either in respect of the end, as when an authority imposes on his subjects burdensome laws, conducive, not to the common good, but rather to his own cupidity or vainglory; or in respect of the author, as when a man makes a law that goes beyond the power com-

mitted to him; or in respect of the form, as when burdens are imposed unequally on the community, although with a view to the common good. Such are acts of violence rather than laws, because as Augustine says, a law that is not just seems to be no law at all. Therefore, such laws do not bind in conscience, except perhaps in order to avoid scandal or disturbance, for which cause a man should even yield his right according to Matt. 5,40-41: If a man . . . takes away thy coat, let go thy cloak also unto him; and whosoever will force thee one mile, go with him other two.

Secondly, laws may be unjust through being opposed to the divine good. Such are the laws of tyrants inducing idolatry, or to anything else contrary to the divine law. Laws of this kind must in no way be observed, because as is stated in Acts 5,29, we ought to obey God rather than men. (S.T. I-II,96,4c)

There is little doubt in St. Thomas' mind, as this passage bears witness, that laws justly framed by civil authority obligate a person's conscience. Now, to be just, a law should be rightly ordered in respect to three things: (1) its *end*, that is, it should be for the common good. A law opposed to the common good would be one, for example, in which the legislator promulgated an enactment for the good of a certain group to the detriment, either direct or indirect, of the rest of the citizens; (2) its *author*, that is, the law should not exceed the legislative power of the ruler or rulers. A law could be invalid for this reason if the legislator, for example, enacted a law compelling children to attend schools of which the parents do not approve on religious grounds; (3) its *form*, that is, the burden imposed by the law is not properly distributed. When we are speaking of the burden imposed by law, we should remember that a law is for the common good and an individual is obligated by the law not as an individual but as a citizen; hence it is possible that a law which furthers the common good may at times be burdensome to the individual as an individual, yet the individual is still obligated. Thus a law may be passed compelling citizens to enter military service in time of war, which will result in the death of many individuals—a greater burden in the temporal order cannot be conceived—yet the individuals as citizens are still obligated.

Of course, it is conceivable that the legislator pass an unjust law. In such a situation, if the law does not command what is intrinsically evil, the individuals are bound in conscience to obey it, not because it is a law (for it is opposed to the common good), but because disobedience would be the cause of greater evil, such as scandal or revolution. Because we are essentially social and political beings, we must for prudential reasons, at times, and for the good of the whole society, obey even an unjust law but not an intrinsically evil law; for disobedience cannot be justified unless it is for the purpose of promoting the good of society.

In this connection, the question may be asked: Are all men compelled to obey the laws of a country? The word *compelled* is used broadly and analogously, it is true, but let the answer be yes, with three exceptions, and the exceptions will clarify the analogy of the word. We are compelled to obey civil laws or human positive laws except: (1) A man is obligated to obey only the laws of his country, for a law of a community of which he is not a member is not a law as far as he is concerned. (2) If an official of a community frames a law from which a higher authority has already dispensed us, we do not have to observe the law of the lower authority. (3) Although law is for all, it really compels only the wicked. Good men are not really compelled by law, because they recognize that laws help them to live good lives. The wicked, however, are compelled by law because their desires are for evil and law obliges man to gain the good. But anyone who thinks that law interferes with liberty lacks the most fundamental notion of liberty. If a citizen's will is good, it should and will be inclined towards the end for which just laws are made; the whole purpose of law is to give the individual citizen opportunities to exercise his liberty as a means to his own perfection. But a wicked citizen, simply because he is not thinking of his own true perfection and, consequently, the perfection of the civil society in which he lives, always thinks that law interferes with his freedom. A law for the wicked, then, is always coercive and it should be. But the wicked citizen would never seriously plead in a court of justice that law has hindered his freedom and violated the justice due him. The good citizen, then, knows that laws always help him to accomplish what he wants, namely, his own perfection, for they are helps for him to be a better human being; the bad citizen, however, is coerced by law, because laws make him live a rational life which he does not desire to lead.

5. Change in Civil Law

One more question about civil law must be answered. The question was proposed several pages back, namely, in what case and on what grounds is it permissible to change the laws of the state? Because civil laws depend on the ever varying conditions of the state, they possess neither the universality nor the invariability of the natural law upon which they are ultimately based. Because these laws are made for the good of the citizens, they should be such that they may promote this good. Conditions do change and legislators should frame laws in order to keep up with the varying needs of their subjects. As civil societies continue in their existence both the legislators and the citizens perceive improvements which could be made in laws so that the good of the community might be the better promoted.

But here as in all other questions, St. Thomas is directed by prudence and indicates the caution and circumspection which legislators must exercise in changing civil laws. A change in law should not fly into the face of custom. Custom is a powerful help in observing laws, because it gives the citizens a facility, but a change in law destroys the custom and brings difficulties and confusion into the citizens' actions. A change of law, then, should occur not because the legislators see some abstract betterment of law in such a change, but only because it is for the good of the citizens. Law, after all, is an order of reason for the common good, and so any change which would result in the loss of much good for the community by disrupting custom should be avoided even though there be a theoretical betterment in the law itself. Custom should be changed only when some very great and evident advantage for the community results, for a change should not lead to greater evil than the evil the law intended to combat.

As stated above, human law is rightly changed in so far as such change is conducive to the common welfare. But, to a certain extent, the mere change of law is of itself prejudicial to the common welfare, because custom avails much of the observance of laws, seeing that what is contrary to general customs, even in slight matters, is looked upon as a rather serious offense. Consequently, when a law is changed, the binding power of law is diminished, in so far as custom is abolished. Therefore human law should never be changed, unless, in some way or other, the common welfare be compensated according to the extent of the harm done in this respect. Such compensation may arise either from some very great and very evident benefit conferred by the new enactment; or from the extreme urgency of the case, due to the fact that either the existing law is clearly unjust, or its observance extremely harmful. Therefore the *Jurist* says that in establishing new laws, there should be evidence of the benefit to be derived, before departing from a law which has long been considered just. (S.T. I-II,97,2c)

St. Thomas, true to his principles about the origin of law, says that custom can be law, can abolish and interpret law. Because law is a dictate of the practical intellect, the legislator may make his law known by acts as well as by words. Wherefore, if a legislator allows a custom to spring up in a civil community and he in no way manifests his displeasure, the custom becomes a law; for silence is taken for his approval. The custom might take the form of a continual violation of an existing law, or it might in no way take such a form; in either case the legislator, by not imposing any sanction for the violations or by not disapproving of the actions, indicates his practical judgment that the custom is law. The very repetition of an action by a community shows that the action does not spring from mere caprice of reason and when the legislator accepts this manner of action it becomes law.

Custom, then, must have the consent of the lawgiver to become law. In a state where the people themselves are the legislators, custom can more easily become law than in a state where the power to frame laws has been handed over to one person or to a group of persons. But in either kind of government custom has the force of law only when it is approved by the legislators, for custom of itself is not and cannot be law. As the custodian of the welfare of the state no legislator can recognize a customary immoral action as a law, for certainly no unreasonable act can become law. By the same token a legislator may not permit a custom to abolish a useful law even though the custom in itself is not immoral, for to do so would be to defeat the purpose of law.

To round out St. Thomas' treatment of human positive law, let us remember that he insists upon the common good as being the purpose of any law. It is the spirit or the reason for the law and not the letter that is imposed upon the subjects. When, then, the letter of the civil law in a particular circumstance is interfering with the common good, the law is not to be followed, because the legislator is not primarily interested in the observance of the law but rather in the common good of the citizens. However, if the circumstances do not arise suddenly and unexpectedly and recourse to the legislator is possible, recourse for a dispensation must be made to the legislator. It is evident that if a legislator has the power to make laws he also has the power to abolish them or to dispense individuals from obeying them providing such abolition or dispensation does not interfere with the common good.

6. Conclusion

We have now completed the Thomistic explanation of law. It portrays a balance of judgment about the notion of law which is foreign to the legalistic view of law which has a very widespread acceptance today. This legalistic attitude looks upon law as a restraint upon liberty, a burden which man must accept because he cannot escape it, a rule of action whose fundamental motivation is the fear of punishment. We have said it before, but it can bear repetition, such an attitude towards laws is based upon an ignorance of the meaning of law. Contrary to this concept, St. Thomas presents law in its true light. Law is something of reason; it is not foreign to man but is the result of man's highest power and perfection; it is not something which is forced upon his will wholly from the outside, but man's reason itself imposes law upon his will. Law flows from man's reason not in order that it may enslave and compel the will but in order that man himself may be led the surer and the safer to his ultimate perfection, which is complete and unending happiness.

Readings

Corwin, Edw. S., "The Natural Law and Constitutional Law," *University of Notre Dame Natural Law Institute Proceedings*, 1950, pp. 47-84.

Cronin, Michael, *The Science of Ethics*, vol. I, pp. 544-558.

Farrell, W., *A Companion to the Summa*, vol. II, c. 14.

Ford, John C., S.J., "The Fundamentals of Holmes' Juristic Philosophy," *Fordham Law Review* (Nov. 1942), pp. 2-28.

Howe, Mark, "The Positivism of Mr. Justice Holmes," *Harvard Law Review*, vol. 64 (Feb. 1951), pp. 529-546.

LeBuffe, F. P., and Hayes, J. V., *The American Philosophy of Law*, cc. 8, 10; *Jurisprudence*, cc. 4, 8.

Leibell, J. F., *Readings in Ethics*. The article by O'Rahilly will contribute much to an understanding of the different kinds of law. The student should read: "The law of nations," Alfred O'Rahilly, pp. 1016-1032.

Lottin, Odon, *Le Droit Naturel chez Saint Thomas d'Acquin et ses prédécesseurs*.

Messner, J., *Social Ethics*, bk. I, pt. III.

O'Sullivan, Richard, "The Natural Law and Common Law," *University of Notre Dame Natural Law Institute Proceedings*, 1950, pp. 9-46.

Rickaby, J., *Aquinas Ethicus*, vol. I, pp. 253-266.

———— *Moral Philosophy*, pp. 156-176.

Rommen, H., *The Natural Law*, c. 14.

Ryan, J. A., and Boland, J., *Catholic Principles of Politics*, c. 14. This is a revised edition of Ryan and Millar, *The State and the Church*, where the same matter is found as c. 11. Leibell reprints it in *Readings in Ethics*, pp. 326-341.

Suarez, Francisco, *De Legibus*, bk. II, cc. 16-20; bk. III, c. 1; bk. IV, cc. 9. Besides, the whole of Book VII is on custom.

St. Thomas, *Summa Theologica*, I-II, 95-97.

Vitoria, Francisco, *De Jure Gentium et Naturali*, translated in J. B. Scot, *The Spanish Origin of International Law; Francisco de Vitoria and his Law of Nations*, appendix E.

CHAPTER XI

CONSCIENCE

1. The Fact of Conscience

Nothing is clearer to anyone than this fact of consciousness: every time one acts, knowingly and willingly, he acts so that he may be happy, because of the desire for happiness of which all men are conscious. We began our study of ethics with this fact; we have tried to explain the fact; we have laid down rules and laws which, if followed and obeyed, will bring us to happiness. No one will deny that this has been a long drawn-out job. At times the reasoning has been acute, exacting, and deep; at others clear cut, almost self-evident or seemingly unnecessary.

Yet there is another and equally clear fact of consciousness; the fact of conscience. This fact, too, has to be explained, for it is intimately connected with man's happiness and his pursuit of happiness. In fact, it is, as we will show, the paramount means that man possesses to arrive at the happiness he is seeking.

Conscience exercises several functions, and it exercises them without regard for our will or our desires. There exists, to adopt the words of Matthew Arnold, "a something within us, not ourselves, which makes for righteousness." Conscience brings our faults before us and rebukes and scolds us about them and passes sentence upon us coldly and impartially without fear or favor, as if it were not part of us or had no dependence on us at all. Conscience bears upon it every mark of supremacy; it assumes a tone of command which is absent from all our other powers or acts, and it imposes its dictates even upon the autonomy of the free will—not in such a way as to deprive it of its power of choice, but in such a way as to claim obedience as right, and to censure and condemn disobedience as wrong.

Conscience, in a word, has its own authority and its own guarantee that it has the right to try and to condemn us, so that it causes us to experience grief, regret, joy, or satisfaction; it excites in us approbation or blame for actions which we call right or wrong; it has the right to legislate for us, so that it is ever forcing us by threats and by promises to follow the right and avoid the wrong. We know that we cannot evade it, that it is sometimes accompanied by painful emotions, confusion, foreboding, self-condemnation; it sheds upon us a deep peace, a sense of security, a resignation, and a hope.

None will deny that conscience is present, that it always is legislating for us, blaming us, approving us. It fears nothing from us, and delivers its judgments unsympathetically, but always in such a way as to gain our instant submission. We may disobey it, but we know that we ought not do so. Conscience, apparently, lays upon us an obligation whence arises the feeling of necessity to avoid the evil and to perform the good, the feeling of shame or exaltation, of condemnation or approbation which we experience after freely placing our actions.

2. The Nature of Conscience

But what is the nature of conscience, whose presence we so intimately experience in its many-sided expression of praise or blame, of command or prohibition, of approbation or condemnation? The word *conscience* is in that group of words which are posing the great contemporary problem of semantics. Its meaning, especially in the much used and much abused phrase "freedom of conscience," is something impossible to determine; and frequently the term has no meaning at all, no ethical meaning, being practically synonymous with individual good pleasure, that acknowledges no regulation by any ethical standards, that fails to explain the conscious facts of praise and blame, of necessity, which we experience about our actions. Yet the traditional ethics of Christianity has defined the concept very exactly, in itself and in its premises.

The premises have already been established. We have said that man is a rational being and, hence, that he can be governed only by reason and can be free only under the order of reason. Man is and must be governed by law like any other creature, yet he is not governed by a law that is imposed from the outside; otherwise he would be under coercion, which would mean a denial of freedom. Consequently, man must give the law to himself. The doctrine of conscience is a synthesis of these two principles, i.e., that man is governed by law which is imposed upon him, yet man gives the law to himself; hence conscience resolves this seeming contradiction. It is not the function of conscience to create law for human life, any more than human reason creates God or human nature; yet it is conscience which imposes the law and directs man necessarily to a certain line of action. There are certain realities which are given— God, and human nature in all its concrete reality—and with these is given the law which man must follow. Man is, therefore, under a heteronomy. On the other hand, being endowed with reason and will, the human person is autonomous, master of his acts; and his autonomy must be respected even under the control of a heteronomous regime of law. To resolve this dilemma, it is necessary that law, remaining law, should become somehow interior to man. As we have seen in the last two chapters, man must give law to himself, but as a law given to himself.

He does this by conscience. What then is conscience? Is it a faculty or a power or a habit? It is none of these; it is an act. St. Thomas, in an often quoted passage, has this to say about conscience:

Properly speaking conscience is not a power, but an act. This is evident both from the very name and from those things which in the common way of speaking are attributed to conscience. For conscience, according to the very nature of the word, implies the relation of knowledge to something; for conscientia may be resolved into cum alio scientia (knowledge applied to an individual problem). But the application of knowledge to something is done by some act. Therefore from this explanation of the name it is clear that conscience is an act.

The same is manifest from the things which are attributed to conscience. For conscience is said to witness, to bind, to incite, and also to accuse, torment, or rebuke. And all these follow the application of knowledge or science to what we do. This application is made in three ways. In one way, in so far as we recognize that we have done or not done something: Thy conscience knoweth that thou hast often spoken evil of others (Eccles. 7,23); and according to this, conscience is said to witness. In another way, in so far as through the conscience we judge that something should be done or not done; and in this sense, conscience is said to incite or to bind. In the third way, in so far as by conscience we judge that something done is well done or ill done, and in this sense conscience is said to excuse, accuse, or torment. Now, it is clear that all these things follow the actual application of knowledge to what we do. Therefore, properly speaking, conscience denominates an act (S.T. I,79,13c)

From this passage we are to conclude that conscience performs the function of applying law to one's particular action in a threefold manner: (1) Conscience confronts us with our past actions in order to pass sentence on them; conscience *witnesses*. (2) Conscience declares that the act which it has imputed to us has been well done, and thus causes joy, or that it has been ill done, and thus causes remorse: conscience *accuses* and *excuses*. (3) Conscience commands an act here and now, or it prohibits an act; conscience *incites* or *binds*. Because conscience exercises all these functions we have the long but complete definition of conscience: *An act by which man applies the natural law or some certain general principle of rectitude to a particular action, and concludes that the action is good and therefore to be done, or evil and therefore to be avoided, or if the action has been performed, either blames or approves.*

We have, therefore, defined conscience as an act. Such a definition is far from being acceptable to all, for there are some who are of the opinion that conscience is a power, a perceptive sense, a feeling, or a sentiment; others think that conscience is a spiritual power distinct from human reason or even a divine power transcending yet dwelling in human nature. Not to refute these several opinions explicitly, the opinion that conscience is an act of the intellect appears the more reasonable. It is not a special faculty nor power nor principle distinct from the intellect. Otherwise our judgments about the rightness or wrongness of our individual acts would be nonintellectual, nonrational, the product of blind instinct or of a power not our own. Conduct of this kind would not be an object of ethics, neither would it be worthy of one whose chief characteristic is rationality. Conscience is but the intellect itself in a special function of judging the moral rightness or wrongness of our individual acts.

But let us be more precise about the function and the definition of conscience. We know that man can and does understand the general principles and conclusions of the natural law in various degrees, that he possess a knowledge of the universal rules of good and bad human conduct. However, since man does not live in a vacuum in which he does no more than contemplate truth, but must employ himself in practical acts, in acts which have a bearing on his ultimate end, he must therefore know whether the acts he performs are according to or in violation of the natural law. He must be able to apply the law to his particular acts. For if man is to attain to his ultimate end, he must do so by reasoning, by understanding how this particular act which he proposes to do falls under the general law. We know from our own experience that the rightness or wrongness of our human conduct is not presented to the human intellect as facts are, immediately and intuitively, so that we know each and every action which falls under the law. Neither, on the other hand, is the human mind directed to the fulfillment of law as animals are by compulsion of inner instincts. In the case of man the application of law to conduct here and now invariably implies reasoning. Hence, conscience is simply an act of the intellect by which one judges the rightness or wrongness of an individual action as a result of reasoning from some general principle of morality. The conclusion or practical judgment, let us say, *I should pay this debt of $50*, which is the result of reasoning from the universal law *Give to each his due* is the application of knowledge to one's moral action. Since this judgment is done with knowledge (*cum scientia*, i.e., *conscientia*), it is, as St. Thomas points out, what we mean by *conscience*.

With reference to the time at which conscience deals with the act we can distinguish two elements or kinds of conscience, which some ethicians call *antecedent* and *consequent* conscience. From our own experience we know that we may accept the fact that we have performed a certain action and by applying general principles of morality arrive at the conclusion that we should have or should not have performed the said action. Thus conscience is said to witness, to excuse or accuse. This experience is what people generally mean when they say that their conscience "hurts" them or that they have a "prick of conscience." Clearly, this judgment is properly called *consequent conscience,* since it is a moral judgment that follows the performance of an action. As a result of this judgment of past actions there may be a feeling of remorse, grief, or exaltation, but these feelings are not conscience.

Antecedent conscience, however, is a practical judgment about an action that is not yet performed. It is a judgment by which one knows the action which he should or should not perform. In arriving at this judgment about actions which are not yet performed we reason from some general moral principle to this conclusion. Thus conscience is called a guide or instigator of actions. Since we are interested in conscience as a moral director of human acts, we shall confine our treatment of conscience to this antecedent conscience which instigates and directs acts.

3. *Conscience and the Judgment of Choice*

By means of conscience, which is simply an act of knowledge, we judge what we ought to do in a particular case. Does it follow that we do here and now what we judge we ought to do? Experience proves that we do not always do what we know we should. Our experience shows that we may not do what we know we should. Only too often, perhaps, we have, as we say, acted "against conscience." But how does this occur? By distinguishing between *conscience* and the *judgment of choice* we can better understand not only this problem but also the function of conscience.

Since we have no immediate or intuitive knowledge of the morality of our individual human acts, we must acquire this knowledge by a process of reasoning which begins with the intuitive principles of the natural law or with other mediately derived general rules of conduct and conclude to a knowledge of the morality of an individual act. We know from our study of logic that all discursive reasoning is either explicitly or virtually syllogistic in form and its purpose is the demonstration of a definite conclusion. However, we should note that the syllogism which we studied in logic and the syllogism which we use to form our conscience have two important differences. The first difference is that the conclusion of the practical syllogism is completely and wholly singular, whereas the conclusion of the syllogism used in logic as well as in other sciences is universal. The second difference is that the minor premise of the practical syllogism which is used for the formation of conscience is a particular judgment and not a universal as it is in all sciences.

Now we must observe that the reason directs human acts in accordance with a twofold knowledge, universal and particular: because in conferring about what is to be done, it employs a syllogism, the conclusion of which is an act of judgment, or of choice, or an operation. Now actions are about singulars: wherefore the conclusion of a practical syllogism is a singular proposition. But a singular proposition does not follow from a universal proposition, except through the medium of a particular proposition: thus a man is restrained from an act of parricide, by the knowledge that it is wrong to kill one's father, and that this man is his father. (S.T. I-II,76,1c)

The reasoning of the practical intellect, then, has for its conclusion a particular action. But since this conclusion may have two distinct purposes, we must distinguish between two practical syllogisms. The first syllogism is for the purpose of knowledge. In this the reasoning and the conclusion arrived at are made by the intellect alone, not in the sense that the will may not cause the reasoning process, but in the sense that the will does not directly enter into the process. The conclusion of such a reasoning process is conscience itself; its sole purpose is knowledge, that is, to know what must or must not be done in a concrete circumstance. To clarify this, let us return to our example. The judgment that I should pay the debt of $50 is based upon the objective principle which I know to be true, that all debts must be paid for justice demands it. We may illustrate this in a syllogism:

Major: Justice demands that debts be paid. (mediate universal rule of conduct)
Minor: This $50 is a debt. (particular judgment)
Conclusion: This $50 debt must be paid. (judgment of conscience)

As we will speak of an erroneous conscience, we can now illustrate a false conscience because its judgment is derived from a faulty syllogism:

Major: Gambling is unjust. (mediate universal rule of conduct derived from a misconception of the law of justice)
Minor: This game of cards is gambling. (particular judgment)
Conclusion: This game of cards is unjust (judgment of conscience)

In both of these examples, conscience, the practical judgment about one's moral action, is the result of syllogistic reasoning in which there is a major premise that takes the form of some general principle of conduct, a minor that is a judgment by which a particular fact is included in the extension of the major, and a conclusion, the judgment of conscience. This judgment of conscience is merely a judgment of one's obligation here and now in the light of a general principle of morality; it is a knowledge of what one should or should not do, but it does not necessarily lead to action, for one may still refuse to pay the debt or still play cards even though conscience makes it known that one's duty is otherwise.

If such knowledge leads to action it is because of another syllogism. This is the syllogism which concludes in the judgment of choice, the second kind of syllogism of the practical reason. This judgment of choice is an act of the practical reason made in conjunction with the act of choice of the will. This judgment is an act which flows from both the intellect and the will, for it is made under the influence of appetite. But, first of all, we can illustrate an instance of the judgment of choice:

Major: This $50 debt must be paid. (judgment of conscience)
Minor: I owe this debt to this man. (judgment of act)
Conclusion: I will pay this $50 debt to this man. (judgment of choice)

Like the judgment of conscience, the judgment of choice is preceded by a reasoning process; yet the two differ. The judgment of conscience establishes the manner in which one should act, while the judgment of choice leads to the actual performance of the action which conscience shows is obligatory or to the refusal to perform the action. One may refuse to pay the debt or may pay it, but in either case the judgment of conscience remains: *I should pay the debt.* If one pays the debt it is because something else besides the intellect is at work, namely, his will (which is now controlling the concupiscible or irascible appetites); one's appetites and intellect are in conformity with each other; if one refuses, it is because his appetites are in conflict with his judgment of conscience.

The judgment of conscience and free choice are partly different and partly alike. They are alike to the extent that both are concerned with a particular act; but the judgment of conscience applies to it in so far as it examines the particular act. On this point the judgment of both differs from the judgment of synderesis. And the judgments of conscience and free choice differ from each other because the judgment of conscience consists simply in knowledge, whereas the judgment of free choice consists in the application of knowledge to the affection of the will, and this is the judgment of choice.

Therefore, it happens that the judgment of free choice goes wrong, but not the judgment of conscience. Thus when one examines something which should be done here and now and judges, still speculating as it were in the realm of principles that it is evil, for example to fornicate with this woman. But when he begins to apply this to the act, many circumstances which are concerned with the act present themselves on all sides, for example, the pleasure of fornication, and this desire so contains reason that its dictate does not result from choice. As a result he acts contrary to conscience and he is said to act from an evil conscience in so far as the act which is done does not agree with the judgment which is based on knowledge. Thus it is clear that it is not necessary that conscience be the same as free choice. (De Ver. q. XVII,1, ad 4m.)

Evidently, then, the judgment of choice is not the effect of the intellect alone, but the effect of both the intellect and the will. Hence, just as the judgment of conscience is the result of a reasoning process, so the judgment of choice is a like result, but with the difference that the former is caused immediately by the intellect alone, whereas the latter is caused immediately by both the intellect and will.

It is in the judgment of choice, let us note, that the virtue of prudence exercises its influence. St. Thomas writes:

Prudence is right reason applied to action. Hence that which is the chief act of reason in regard to action must needs be the chief act of prudence. Now there are three such acts. The first is to take counsel, which belongs to discovery, for counsel is an act of inquiry. The second is to judge of what one has discovered, and this is an act of the practical reason. But the practical reason, which is directed to action, goes further, and its third act is to command, which act consists in applying to action the things counselled and judged. And since this act approaches nearer to the end of the practical reason, it follows that it is the chief act of the practical reason and consequently of prudence. (S.T. II-II,47,8c)

Because we have proven that man can be good only if he lives according to right reason, it follows that he must not only know the good but also perform the good. Now, since it is prudence by which man has the habit of so knowing, so choosing and so doing, prudence is necessary for man to live the good life. But of the three acts required for living a prudent life, as St. Thomas writes, only the third, command, is not included in the reasoning process which precedes the judgment of conscience. Counsel and judgment are certainly required for the formation of conscience according to right reason, but the third act, command, belongs to prudence or the judgment of choice by which he chooses or wills to act in accordance with right reason.

4. Kinds of Conscience

Because conscience is an act of the practical intellect judging that a particular action is right or wrong, it is possible to distinguish several kinds of conscience depending upon whether we base the distinction on epistemological or psychological grounds.

Considering conscience from the point of view of epistemology, conscience is not infallible; man may err in his judgment about moral matters, as he may err in his judgment about other matters. And just as we determine any judgment of the intellect as a purely speculative power to be true or false by the conformity of the intellect to the things themselves about which it is judging, so we can distinguish two kinds of conscience in so far as reason or conscience judges of the object as it is in itself or does not judge of the object as it is in itself: (1) *True conscience* in which the judgment accords with the objective order of things. (2) *Erroneous conscience* in which the judgment is not in accord with the objective order of things. Such error may be the result of a faulty knowledge of the general principles of morality (not however of the primary principles of the natural law, for synderesis cannot be in error about these self-evident principles; but of the derived principles) or it may be the result of a faulty application of these principles by the practical reason.

Error of this kind may be, of course, voluntary or involuntary. If conscience is the director of our moral actions the questions of whether an erring conscience binds or whether it excuses may arise. For the present let us leave these questions and go on to the description of the various kinds of conscience.

For various reasons, peculiar to the individual who is making the judgment, the psychological attitude about the judgments may be of various kinds because of the firmness or certainty with which the individual adheres to the judgments of conscience. Consesequently, there are (1) *certain conscience*, and (2) *doubt*.

(1) In *certain conscience*, the mind so adheres to the judgment that all prudent fear of the opposite judgment is excluded. An example of such certainty is given by a boy who lies to his father about some happening about the house in order to avoid a reprimand, thinking that he should lie to avoid this unpleasantness. He is so sure that lying is here and now what he should do that he never doubts that he should not lie. It is clear that a certain state of mind may be present in both a true and an erroneous conscience: one

may be just as certain that lying is good as another is certain that it is wrong.

A certain conscience excludes a *prudential* fear. To understand this, let us distinguish between what is known as metaphysical and moral certainty. Metaphysical certainty is that which excludes all possibility of error, e.g., that $2 + 2 = 4$. There is no possibility of their being otherwise. Moral certainty, prudential certainty, on the other hand, is that which is not absolute so as to exclude all error, for it does admit of exceptions. Such certainty is relative and not absolute or universal, but the exceptions are few. Such certainty is sufficient for moral matters, sufficient for a prudent man to act with. It is impossible, practically speaking, for man to obtain metaphysical certainty upon all matters, particularly upon moral matters, in which man must act without time to discover or weigh absolutely all the conditions of actions, simply because he cannot know all of reality. If man had to delay his action until he was certain in an absolute sense of every condition he could never act. For example, during the war recently waged, the enemy soldiers often played possum, lying down, pretending to be wounded, but when the American soldiers approached to take them prisoners or to administer aid to them, the enemy suddenly began to fight them. Now, it is certain that it is immoral to kill a wounded soldier. But each time the American soldiers approached a prostrate enemy soldier they were uncertain whether the man was wounded or just pretending. Should the American have held his fire and approached the enemy to learn whether the man was wounded or not? If such were the solution, it would have become too late for many Americans to defend themselves, which they certainly had a right to do. Consequently, after a number of times, after learning through sad experience that frequently the enemy soldiers were only pretending, the American soldiers became humanly, morally certain, that the apparently wounded soldiers were not wounded but fighting men, and so treated them as opponents in war. It is true that sometimes the enemy soldiers may have been wounded, but this was the exception; the Americans were morally certain that they were not. Such certainty must be sufficient to act, for it is the only certainty that man can generally have in human conduct.

(2) Another state of mind that might be present relative to conscience is *doubt*. In doubt the mind sees probable reasons both for and against a manner of action, and so the mind wavers between two opposing sides of an action—suspending its decision, unable to favor either side of the solution of the problem. As a result of doubt, then, the agent can make no judgment of conscience. What should one do who is in doubt as to how to make a judgment of conscience so that he may act? We shall answer this question presently.

5. *The Obligation of Conscience*

As we have said before, man being a creature of God is really governed by law, by a law that is *given* to him; yet, on the other hand, being endowed with reason and will, man is autonomous, master of his acts, and his autonomy must be respected even under the heteronomous regime of law. We have mentioned that this apparent contradiction is resolved in the doctrine of conscience wherein law, while remaining something external to man, becomes something interior to man. The solution of this dilemma is the purpose of the present section.

Because man is rational nothing seems to be clearer and more certain than that man cannot be bound nor obligated by anything, by law, unless that law is known as binding in general as well as in individual cases, i.e., unless the law is promulgated. It is equally clear and certain from what we have said that the law is known and known as binding in a particular case only through conscience. It follows, then, that conscience makes a law known and binding in a particular case.

But whence arises the binding force of a certain line of action? Whence arises the law which reason uses to form the judgment of conscience? The law must be given and yet it must be man's own. Law is given because man recognizes that he is necessitated by his nature to seek happiness. By reason man discovers and understands the "order of reason," the relation of himself to God, his Creator and Last End, and the relation that all his free actions have to the attainment or loss of that end. Man discovers that the possession of God is man's highest good, the only Absolute Good, to be willed of necessity, for its own sake, above all things and in all things. And in this discovery man discovers the principle of right reason, the principle of the order of reason, and the norm whereby to make true judgments of value. Man recognizes that if a choice of actions is given, one of which will advance him towards his goal of perfect happiness, and the other of which will not bring him to this goal, he is free to choose either action, but he is not free to determine which will be a means to his happiness. Man's judgments, formed in the light of this order of reason, not only state what is good and what is evil; they also dictate that the evil is to be avoided and the good is to be done. Consequently, man recognizes a necessity not born of himself which obliges him to perform the action which will lead him to God, his happiness. Such a necessity arises from the order of reason which man recognizes as requiring means to an end. This is law. We have expressed it in its most general terms of "good must be done; evil must be avoided." Man is not free to set this law aside; it is given to him; he must act in this way. This is, of course, a reflection of the eternal law of God, and is the norm of every other law, the first principle upon which man forms his conscience.

Yet law, in order to safeguard man's autonomy, must be given by man to himself. Man thus gives himself law by the act of the practical judgment, which is conscience, whereby man judges that a concrete act is good or bad and, consequently, to be done or avoided. In this act of judgment, the law is so mediated to man that it becomes his own law. In other words, man is necessitated to seek happiness and, hence, obligated to perform acts which are necessarily connected with this happiness. It is man, however, who judges—in the light of his intellectual apprehension of the concrete order of things—which act is to advance and which is to impede his progress towards happiness. But this judgment of reason is not only an act which weighs the particular good and judges it desirable, but it appears also as an imperative of reason, prescribing what is to be done in order that man reach his happiness. Such a judgment expresses itself in the particular judgment that a certain action is what must be done in certain particular circumstances. Thus, it is man who judges that a particular concrete act of supporting his children in a specific particular way is good for him as the father of the family. In this act of judging what is good for him, he recognizes an obligation of so acting in order that he may advance towards happiness. That he must necessarily seek happiness is certain; that he must seek it in this particular way is imposed upon himself because he apprehends reality in this manner. It is conscience, then, that binds or obligates man; it is conscience that imposes an obligation on man.

However, conscience is not the norm of its own rightness; it does not arbitrarily establish that right or wrong is to be done or avoided; it cannot inverse the law; conscience only judges what is right or wrong and in so judging brings the law upon the agent. Conscience is regulated by a higher norm, not of its own making: the eternal law of God, which ultimately establishes the obligation, for it orders man's nature to its end which is the source, as we have said, of all obligation. The natural law, too, is a norm of man's conscience, for it is this law which is, in the first place, the concrete origin of man's obligation, for this law, which is born of man's judgment of the order of reason, is the principle of man's judgments about particular actions, and the principle of man's individual obligation in relation to particular actions. Determinations of the natural law as laid down by legitimate authority are also a norm of conscience. All these are higher norms of conscience, for in the light of them man judges of the obligation of concrete actions, and through his conscience the law is applied to such particular actions. Consequently, it is conscience which makes the external law interior to man.

In his moral action, therefore, man preserves the autonomy proper to him as a rational being, because in it he obeys a dictate of his own conscience. At the same time, he remains under the heteronomy likewise proper to his rational nature, because the dictate of his own conscience ulitmately demands obedience, not because it is his own dictate, but because it applies the dictate of the eternal law. So conscience stands, as it were, between the objective law and the freely chosen act. Its function is essentially mediatorial, that of conforming itself to the order of divine reason, in order that it may conform human action to this order.

As a matter of fact, the nature and function of conscience are admirably summed up in the traditional metaphor: "Conscience is the voice of God." This statement immediately cuts between two extreme false positions. First, it asserts that conscience is the *voice* of God; it is not God himself as some ethicians have contended. Hence, conscience is not the final arbiter of truth and falsity, right and wrong. Man is indeed judged in the light of his conscience, but it is God who judges conscience. Only God is law in its source; conscience is law in its application. On the other hand, conscience is the voice *of God*; it is not merely a human voice. Hence its commands come to us vested with a divine authority that may not be disregarded under the penalty of wrongdoing. Conscience is a sacred and sovereign monitor; for in its utterances we hear God himself speaking. The same has been summed up in another manner.

Conscience is God's voice in the sense that from the attestations of conscience we may learn God's law. Conscience is that function of the practical reason by which we establish moral conclusions. As a faculty it is not in any way different from that which directs a man in the other practical concerns of life, political, economical, and commercial. Now, if the practical reason be used aright it must be true. If it is not used aright, it will go wrong. But just as the speculative reason, when true, is in perfect harmony with the objective order which it represents, whether mathematical, metaphysical, or physical, so when the conscience is true is expresses and accords with the facts of the moral world. Now, God's intellect is always true; nay, from Him all truth proceeds. Hence, the true conscience which harmonizes with objective truth, is in exact replica of God's mind on morality. In this sense, therefore, conscience is the voice of God, viz., as truly representing God's mind on human good and duty. Thus, conscience claims from us reverence and submission, not from what it is in itself, but because through it we can come to know God's law in our regard. Directly and immediately, therefore, conscience only tells us what is good and what is duty. But indirectly it tells us also what is God's mind in our regard. (Michael Cronin, The Science of Ethics, vol. i, p. 474)

Conscience, therefore, is the voice of God in so far as it acquaints us with the dictates of the moral law. However, being a human power, conscience is fallible. We know that human reason is not infallible; the possibility of erroneous judgments is native to it, not indeed as a perfection of reason, but as its essential imperfection. As a created reason, it is of its nature defectible; as a human reason, it is dependent on matter and sense; it is obliged to proceed in concepts, which are partial views, and difficult to combine; and it is subject at every step to the influence of sentiment and passion. Consequently, in its function of being a light to the will, reason can at times lead the will into darkness and in obedience to its leading the will can go astray after the good which is delusory. Are we to say that such a conscience is the voice of God? Should such a conscience be obeyed?

6. An Involuntary Erroneous Conscience Must Be Obeyed

To the question, "Must one follow an erroneous conscience?" we must answer, "yes, with some reservations." The will can choose only it, and therefore man can act morally only if the intellect presents some good to the will. Now the fact that man's reason in practical matters of morality can be erroneous, that it can command what is actually wrong and forbid what is actually right, is too obvious to escape anyone who has ever thought about conscience. Human reason has almost unlimited possibilities of being deceived, and especially of deceiving itself, notably in its own case, and even more notably in its moral judgments. Men confuse right with wrong, error with truth; and the confusion is nonetheless real because it is often entirely sincere. A man's sincerity, however, proves only that he is sincere; it does not prove that he is wise, or even right, for he may be sincerely ignorant or sincerely wrong. Moreover, God has commanded us not only to be sincere but also to do what is right and avoid what is wrong. The question arises therefore, whether conscience can oblige us to do what is wrong or avoid what is right. Historically, some have thought that man should not follow such a conscience. It seems to be an impossible opinion, but let us give St. Thomas' account of it:

Since conscience is a kind of dictate of the reason (for it is an application of knowledge to action, as was stated in the First Part [S.T. I,79,13], to inquire whether the will is evil when it is at variance with erring reason is the same as to inquire whether an erring conscience binds. On this matter, some distinguish three kinds of acts: for some are good of their nature, some are indifferent, some are evil of their nature. And they say that if reason or conscience tell us to do something which is of its nature good, there is no error; and the same is true, if it tell us not to do something which is evil of its nature, since it is the same reason which prescribes what is good and forbids what is evil. On the other hand, if a man's reason or conscience tell him that he is bound by precept to do what is of itself evil, or that which is in itself good is forbidden, then his reason or conscience errs. In like manner, if a man's reason or conscience tell him that which is in itself indifferent, for instance, to lift a straw from the ground, is forbidden or commanded, his reason or conscience errs. They say, therefore, that reason or conscience, when erring in matters of indifference, either by commanding or by forbidding them binds; so that the will which is at variance with that erring reason is evil and sinful. But they say that when reason or conscience errs in commanding what is evil in itself, or in forbidding what is good in itself and necessary for salvation, it does not bind; and so in such cases the will which is at variance with erring reason or conscience is not evil. (S.T. I-II,19,5c)

It seems to be true to say that man must follow an erroneous conscience. From what has been said about the nature of the will and its relation to the intellect which is essentially a mediator between the will and its object, it is quite clear that the will, being as it were a blind faculty, is attracted towards good only provided the intellect proposes a good; it can reject a good only provided the intellect proposes a good. The choice of the will, therefore, depends immediately upon what the intellect apprehends to be good or evil. Now, because a moral act is an act which is performed with knowledge and freedom, if the will is obedient to what the intellect presents as good, the act of the will can be only good; if it rejects the reasoned good the will can be only evil. Or again, if man by law must do good and avoid evil, he can do only what he knows to be good or evil. It is perfectly true that the intellect through ignorance or lack of attention, or sentiment, may judge wrongly of the good and evil, but since the reason is that through which the will of man is attracted to the good and through which the will is obligated by law, if the will is obedient to reason, which it ought to be, the will can do only moral good; if it rejects the known good it can do only evil. And because it is only through reason that man can be obligated by law, the will can be obligated only by what the reason knows as law.

In matters of indifference, the will at variance with erring reason or conscience is evil in some way because of the object on which the goodness or malice of the will depends; not indeed because of the object according as it is in its own nature, but according as it is accidentally apprehended by reason as something evil to do or to avoid. And since the object of the will is that which is proposed by the reason, as we have stated above, from the very fact that a thing is proposed by the reason as being evil, the will by tending thereto becomes evil. And this is the case not only in indifferent matters, but also in those that are good or evil in themselves. For it is not only indifferent matters that can receive the character of goodness or malice accidentally; but likewise that which is good can receive the character of evil, or that which is evil can receive the character of goodness, because of the reason apprehending it as such. For instance, to refrain from fornication is good, and yet the will does not tend to this good except in so far as it is proposed by the reason. If, therefore, the erring reason propose it as evil, the will tends to it as to something evil. Consequently, the will is evil because it wills evil, not indeed that which is evil in itself, but that which is evil accidentally, through being apprehended as such by the reason. In like manner, to believe in Christ is good in itself, and necessary for salvation; but the will does not tend thereto, except inasmuch as it is proposed by the reason. Consequently, if it be proposed by the reason as something evil, the will tends to it as to something evil; not as if it were evil in itself, but because it is evil accidentally, through the apprehension of the reason. Hence the Philosopher says that, properly speaking, the incontinent man is one who does not follow right reason; but accidentally, he is also one who does not follow false reason. (Eth. VII,9,1151a,33) We must therefore conclude that, absolutely speaking, every will at variance with reason, whether right or erring, is always evil. (S.T. I-II,19,5c)

If, therefore, conscience or reason commands or forbids a particular action, one is strictly bound to follow it, and not to act against it. The reason, again, lies in the very nature of man. In making human nature rational, God made it subject to the laws of rational nature; and one of these laws is that a law must be properly promulgated, must be known by man, and, therefore, must be imposed upon him by practical reason. There is no other way, in keeping with the dignity of man, whereby his obedience to the laws of his nature can be secured, save by the practical dictates of reason, which procure obedience, and a rational obedience. It is, therefore, a law of nature that one of the functions of reason is to mediate between the eternal law of God and the will of man. Reason may perform this function badly; it may mistake for law what is not law; it may be blind to what really should be law. But, even when performing its function badly, it is still performing its function, for reason cannot destroy its own function nor alter the law that it is a mediator between the will of God and the will of man. St. Thomas has this general law in mind when he expresses a principle and illustrates it from St. Augustine with an example:

The saying of Augustine holds good when it is known that the inferior authority prescribes something contrary to the command of the higher authority. But if a man were to believe the command of the proconsul to be the command of the emperor, in scorning the command of the proconsul he would scorn the command of the emperor. In like manner, if a man were to know that human reason was dictating something contrary to God's commandment, he would not be bound to abide by reason; but then reason would not be entirely erroneous. But when erring reason proposes something as being commanded by God, then, to scorn the dictate of reason is to scorn the commandment of God. (S.T. I-II, 19,5 ad 2)

7. Ignorance and the Erroneous Conscience

An erroneous conscience, therefore, is a practical judgment about a moral act, that is formed in ignorance of the full realities of the case, and that, as a matter of fact, is wrong. So, to take an obvious example, one might judge that divorce-and-remarriage is not only licit but also a matter of religious observance, in ignorance of the fact that it is contrary to the natural law. Ignorance is at the root of the error found in this judgment. It follows immediately, therefore, that the moral status of the erroneous conscience—the right of the obligation that we have to follow it—will depend on the nature of ignorance which caused it. What we have said about ignorance in dealing with the moral act in Chapter III must be applied to this matter of conscience; so we may summarize here. In general, two kinds of ignorance may be distinguished: *vincible* and *invincible*.

First, we may suppose the case of a man who is in ignorance, but who knows that he is in ignorance, because he has consciously fostered such ignorance either from the desire to plead ignorance when he does do wrong, or from his failure to acquire knowledge when the opportunity presented itself. This has been called vincible ignorance. The question is whether a conscience formed as a consequence of such ignorance is a right norm of moral action. Obviously the answer is no. A man cannot follow such a conscience, since the judgment resulting from such vincible ignorance is a judgment which he knows to be wrong.

Just as in syllogistic arguments, granted one absurdity, others must needs follow, so in moral matters, given one absurdity, others must follow too. Thus suppose a man to seek vainglory, he will sin, whether he does his duty from vainglory or whether he omit to do it. Nor is he in a dilemma about the matter, because he can put aside his evil intention. In like manner, suppose a man's reason or conscience to err through inexcusable ignorance, then evil must needs result in the will. Nor is this man in a dilemma, because he can lay aside his error, since his ignorance is vincible and voluntary. (S.T. I-II, 19,6 ad 3)

We may, again, suppose the case of a man who is in ignorance, but who has a more or less strong suspicion that he is in ignorance. To some degree, he is conscious of the fact that he is assuming a position, making a judgment, that is not entirely reasonable, but rather "rationalized"; he assumes it for reasons that are, as the moderns put it "good reasons," but not the "real reasons." He achieves certainty of a kind, but it is only on the surface; he is at least dimly aware that he has not got to the bottom of the matter. His ignorance is real enough, therefore, but vincible. It can be overcome because it is somehow recognized as ignorance. The defect of knowledge has not escaped the man, and he perceives it as possibly leading to an error of judgment. Yet he makes the judgment, which turns out, in fact, to be erroneous. This, too, is a state of mind which is called a vincibly erroneous conscience. The question is whether such a conscience is a right norm of moral action.

Again obviously, the answer is no. A man may neither follow such a conscience nor act against it, since for all practical purposes this is a doubtful state of mind and because of it conscience can give no proper command nor prohibition. In this state of mind, a man's obligation is to rid himself of his ignorance and get at the realities of the case by a process of consultation and study. In the meantime, no action can be placed. We will treat of this more fully shortly.

Finally, we may suppose the case of a man who is in ignorance, but who likewise is not in a position to get out of his ignorance, because he does not suspect that he is in it. His position was reached after serious thought and the ready available means of arriving at a correct judgment. He is quite certain that the judgments he makes are true and, therefore, the action he contemplates is good; there is neither doubt nor disquiet nor any thought that he may perhaps be wrong. His ignorance, in a word, is invincible; for the starting point for overcoming it, namely, suspicion of ignorance, is lacking. Yet the practical judgment made in consequence of the ignorance is actually erroneous. Is the practical judgment resulting from this ignorance a norm of moral action? Obviously, again, yes. This answer is evident from the preceding section: an involuntary erroneous conscience must be followed.

Whereas the previous question is the same as inquiring whether an erring conscience binds, this question is the same as inquiring whether an erring conscience excuses. Now this question depends on what has been said above about ignorance. For it was said that ignorance sometimes causes an act to be involuntary, and sometimes not. And since moral good and evil consists in an act in so far as it is voluntary, as was stated above, it is evident that when ignorance causes an act to be involuntary, it takes away the character of moral good and evil; but not, when it does not cause the act to be involuntary. Again, it has been stated above that when ignorance is in any way willed, either directly or indirectly, it does not cause the act to be involuntary. And I call that ignorance directly voluntary to which the act of the will tends, and that, indirectly voluntary, which is due to negligence, because a man does not wish to know what he ought to know, as we have stated above.

If, therefore, reason or conscience err with an error that is voluntary, either directly or through negligence, so that one errs about what one ought to know, then such an error of reason or conscience does not excuse the will, which abides by that erring reason or conscience, from being evil. But if the error arise from the ignorance of some circumstance, and without any negligence, so that it cause the act to be involuntary, then that error of reason or conscience excuses the will, which abides by that erring reason, from being evil. For instance, if erring reason tells a man that he should go to another man's wife, the will that abides by that erring reason is evil, since this error arises from ignorance of the divine law, which he is bound to know. But if a man's reason errs in mistaking another for his wife, and if he wish to give her her right when she asks for it, his will is excused from being evil; for this error arises from ignorance of a circumstance, which ignorance excuses, and causes the act to be involuntary. (S.T. I-II,19,6c)

8. Doubt and Conscience

We have said that doubt cannot be a norm for moral action. This is true because conscience cannot give a command or prohibition when doubt is present, simply because a man in doubt is aware that he lacks knowledge and is aware that any judgment he makes about his actions may lead to error of judgment. In other words, his conscience does not make a clear, positive, certain answer as to the morality of an act contemplated, but rather reasons both for and against an action are present, and conscience's answer is "perhaps" and "perhaps not." Because conscience cannot make a judgment when doubt is present, lacking knowledge, it cannot, obviously, be a rule of right moral action, and an action done in such a state of mind would be morally wrong, for it would be a practical affirmation of indifference towards the law of God, and a wilful exposure of oneself to the risk of offending him. If a man, in other words, is under the general law of doing good and avoiding evil, he cannot act in a state of doubt, for then he would, at least implicitly, consent to evil, making his choice with this understanding: I doubt whether this action is right or wrong, but whether right or wrong I will do it.

Of itself, this state of mind imposes the obligation of a search for further truth. Although man may never act in a state of doubt, nevertheless he very frequently feels that he would like to act, and sometimes he knows he must act even though he is in doubt and recourse to further knowledge is impossible. What is he to do? Must he remain inactive? This is impossible. Must he suppose that there is an obligation forbidding him to do what he would like to do? May he suppose that there is not any obligation whatsoever and so he is morally free to do whatever he wishes?

Doubt, as we know, is something subjective and peculiar to oneself. It turns on a matter of fact, which others know full well though another doubts it, or on a point of law, dark to one but clearly known by the learned. The doubt may arise, in general, about two different matters: (1) There may be doubt about the existence of a law which is necessary to obtain one's final purpose in life; there may be doubt about the application of a law, whose existence is certain, to an action which could, if done, cause harm to another. (2) There may be doubt about the existence of a law, which is not absolutely necessary to obtain one's final purpose; there may be doubt about the application of a law, whose existence is certain, to an action which, if done, would cause no harm to another.

The solutions of these two doubts, so that one may act with a certain conscience, must be made in accordance with the distinction which we have made. These two solutions are called the *direct* and *reflex* solution.

THE DIRECT SOLUTION

Since man cannot act in a doubtful state of mind. he must always have such certainty for actions as would merit the assent of a prudent man. Since man cannot obtain absolute certainty, it is sufficient, as we have said, that we have prudential certainty in proportion to the gravity of the matter of the act contemplated. One must use all reasonable diligence to discover the truth. We know that if any-one had perfect knowledge there would be no doubt, for if we knew all the facts of a situation as they objectively exist, and all the laws that might enter into the case, and the full and accurate appli-cation of all these laws to the facts, there would never exist any doubt. There is no such thing as anything being objectively doubtful; everything in point of fact is or it is not. But neither is there any human mind so perfect as to grasp always the full reality of things as it is and grasp it firmly to the exclusion of all doubt. All due in-quiries, therefore, may fail; the fact may remain obscure; the argu-ments of learned men conflict. The application of direct knowledge fails. Even after due investigation which the gravity of the matter necessitates, a man finds that the doubt is still present. Since, there-fore, we may act only with prudential certainty, the question arises, must we abstain from action after such direct inquiry fails? Or can we, in spite of positive, theoretical doubt, arrive at the certainty re-quired for action, and thus change doubt into certainty? In other words, can our practical reason be morally certain in spite of the fact that our speculative reason is doubtful? It is by having recourse to a reflex principle that conscience can be formed to certainty in circumstances in which the direct solution is impossible.

THE REFLEX SOLUTION

In this solution of doubt we have recourse to certain principles of conduct that have application in which direct knowledge of the right and wrong of the matter cannot be obtained. By these prin-ciples, the individual conscience leaves the doubt—the direct, specu-lative doubt—unsolved, i.e., there is no attempt made to determine what one should do who has a thorough knowledge of the facts and the law as they are in themselves, for these are impossible to know in the doubt of which we are speaking. These principles are applicable in these particular circumstances of doubt. They are called reflex principles, because without knowing the proper objective solu-tion, the one who is to act accepts another principle which is objec-tively true, and with this as a starting point for reasoning concludes to the right or wrong of a contemplated action.

An example of such reflection: When the testimony in a criminal suit before the court affords only a *doubtful* proof, the jury is instructed that "one accused is entitled to the benefit of the doubt, and if there is doubt about the defendant's guilt, the verdict should be not guilty." This is a principle of civil law. Suppose a man has been tried and the testimony points only doubtfully to his guilt. Therefore, it is doubtful whether he is guilty or not. The jury cannot act in doubt, yet cannot retry the case to discover the realities, for this is impossible. So the jury has recourse to this certain principle: one is innocent until proven guilty. Since the guilt of this person is only doubtfully proven, therefore, the accused person is not guilty. Here we have a certain conclusion of the practical judgment which is based on certain premises. The doubt, whether the defendant is guilty or not, will always remain a doubt in the speculative reason, for there are not enough facts to judge of the question with speculative certainty. But these doubts are put aside, and another premise for arriving at a certain conclusion in the practical reason is introduced. Beginning with such a certain principle, the conclusion is also certain as well as sufficient and correct for being a norm for the right moral action of freeing the defendant. It is the same with the following principles to be used in a practical doubt. The principles are certain and, consequently, the conclusions drawn from them are certain.

Two kinds of doubt have been distinguished; hence there are two principles applicable to them. In regard to the first kind of doubt, namely, a doubt about the existence of a law which is necessary to obtain one's final purpose, or about the application of a law whose existence is certain to an action which if placed would cause harm to another, the principle to be followed is: *the safer course of action is to be chosen*. The reason for this principle as a solution of such a doubt is simple. If there is question of a law which demands something that is absolutely necessary to obtain perfect happiness, the goal of life, the reasonable thing to do is to perform that action even though there may be doubt about its necessity. If we do not perform such an act, and it is necessary, we will miss our final end; if it be not necessary, we shall not harm ourselves by performing the action. Suppose, for example, that someone doubted the necessity of baptism for the supernatural vision of God. That baptism is a necessary means is known by the learned. If one in doubt were not baptised he would act unreasonably by not using the safer means, for he would run the risk of endangering his final purpose in life.

The same is true in a doubt not about the existence of the law, but about its application to an action which if done would perhaps harm another. If the safer course were not followed in such a doubt and there were danger of harming another, then one would be indifferent and careless about the rights and life of another. Suppose, for example, that Dr. Smith is attending a patient. He has a medicine which will most probably cure the patient; another medicine of which he is not sure; at least the probability of cure using the second is less than that using the first. He is in doubt which medicine to try. It would be unreasonable to use the second, for his action would manifest an indifference to human life which is wrong in itself.

In regard to the second kind of doubt, namely, a doubt about the existence of a law which is not necessary for one's final purpose, or about the application of a law whose existence is known to an action which would not cause harm to another, the principle to be followed has been variously expressed by different ethicians. Several moral systems have been proposed as a means of forming conscience with certainty in such doubt. One is the system of *probabilism*, as it is called. According to this system, if there is doubt about a law or the application of a known law which does not endanger the rights of others, one need not obey such a law or refrain from such an action. In other words, if there is a good and solid reason, one may act in the manner one chooses. Suppose, for example, that one is in doubt whether he is obliged to undergo a serious operation. Here there is no question about a means to eternal life, nor about harm to another, but only of taking care of one's own life. In such a doubt one may use the principle that since he is not certain of the existence of a law obligating him, he may do what he wishes. The reason why such a principle is applicable in these circumstances is founded upon the nature of man and of law. A law cannot bind a rational creature unless it is promulgated, and a doubtful law means the absence of knowledge. Therefore, we may formulate the principle: *a doubtful law does not bind*. A law by its very nature restricts liberty to which we have a certain right by nature. This right cannot be limited unless the limiting law has a right to do so. Now, in the case of a doubtful law, there is a doubtful right to limit, which is no right. For if a doubtful right to limit could actually limit, we might say that the effect is greater than the cause, which is contrary to the principle of causality. Consequently, the principle that a doubtful law does not bind may be followed in all circumstances where there is a doubt about the licitness of an act.

9. Conscience and the Eternal Law

The fact that we have said conscience is the voice of God and a norm of action appears to be the basis for an objection either against the divine eternal law upon which we have insisted so much as the eternal plan of God directing all creatures to their ends, or against the rational basis of law in creatures. We have said several things in treating of law and conscience. We have said that God has an eternal plan according to which all creatures must direct their actions in order to reach their various ends. Because God's knowledge is always true, the law which man must follow must harmonize with the knowledge of God and, therefore, with the eternal law of God in order that it may express God's knowledge and will; in order, in other words, that it may be God's voice or expression. We have also said that if man does what reason proposes as right he will be acting as a rational creature should act, will be acting in a way that will lead him to his final end. We have said that the law to be law for man must be recognized as an obligatory rule of action, and since reason is subject to error, reason can apprehend an obligatory manner of action in different ways, so that which the law demands for one will not be that which is demanded of another. Finally, we have said that even though conscience be involuntarily erroneous it must be followed. St. Thomas, as we have seen concludes with what is the universal law of nature:

Wherefore it must be asserted, as an absolute principle, that the voluntary act which is out of harmony with reason, whether reason be right or erroneous, is always evil. (S.T. I-II,19,5)

Again, St. Thomas has taken cognizance of this particular difficulty and has expressed it:

Further, the will is always good when it abides by the commandment of God and the eternal law. But the eternal law and God's commandments are proposed to us by the apprehension of the reason, even when it errs. Therefore the will is good even when it abides by erring reason. (S.T. I-II, 19,6, ad 2)

And St. Thomas answers the difficulty in a most summary fashion by saying:

The eternal law cannot err, but human reason can. Consequently the will that abides by human reason is not always right, nor is it always in accord with the eternal law. (S.T. ibid.)

Man's reason, according to St. Thomas, is not always in accord with the eternal law and the will that follows such a reason is not always right. Yet we also know that God wills that man follow his conscience, which is not always right. Evidently, therefore, we must speak of two wills of God here. Initially, there is his supreme will that the reason of man and its practical judgments should be in harmony with the eternal order of reason which exists in his divine mind; in other words, God wills that man's conscience should always be right and true. There is also his will that the voluntary acts of man should be in harmony with man's own reason and its practical judgments; in other words, God wills that man should act according to his conscience. But at times these two wills of God are not simultaneously observed. In acting according to conscience, man at times acts against the eternal order of reason, being in ignorance of it; his act, therefore, is in harmony with his conscience, but his conscience is not in harmony with the eternal reason or law of God. This is, of course, an eccentricity in the moral order, which illustrates at once the dignity as well as the misery of conscience. In the face of it, to keep our moral thinking straight, we must maintain two principles. On the one hand, even when conscience is erroneous, it must be followed. On the other hand, even though we must follow an erroneous conscience, it still remains erroneous. These two principles must be maintained, lest we either assent that conscience is God, or deny it is the voice of God.

We can explain this seeming contradiction between the eternal law and the individual conscience in another way. First of all, to put the difficulty clearly. God certainly wills that natures act in conformity with themselves. God, therefore, wills that the practical intellect of man, or conscience, judge that those acts must be performed which are conformed to the essential natures of things. God does not will that a man, for example, judge it good that he must hate his enemies. This seems to be clear, for why should God create natures unless he wills that such natures act in harmony with themselves and with the natures with which they are essentially related? Moreover, God must will and, therefore, must oblige rational creatures to place acts which are in harmony with their rational natures, for God, as we have seen, must necessitate natures somehow, otherwise he cannot direct things to their proper ends, which direction is necessarily implied and included in the act of creation.

We must conclude, therefore, that human nature ought to follow the essential order of things to reach its end. Conscience, therefore, which is the source of moral action, ought to be in harmony with the order of reality. At the same time we know that conscience is not always in such conformity with reality nor with the eternal law, because the human intellect can err, yet it is the norm of moral action and actions resulting from an erroneous conscience that will lead man to his end.

We must affirm that conscience, even though it be mistaken, is a means to the end of man, and if man, with good will, follows an erroneous conscience he will attain his end. This is a fact. To deny it will mean that the attainment of man's end is not dependent upon man himself, his knowledge and good will, but upon something outside of man's rational nature, the essential order of things. If, therefore, God wills by the eternal law that the essential order of things be followed, it can only be that he wills this order in an absolute sense, with his absolute will, i.e., antecedently to the operations of natures. He wills such natures to perform acts which are conformed to the order of reality as it is constituted by natures; but by his conditional will God must will that this order be followed, provided—in the case of man—man's intellect apprehends it as it is. Consequent to the acts of man, God wills that the good conscience be followed. In the eternal law, therefore, God wills essences to be followed and, therefore, that man's conscience be conformed to the essential order of things, but he also wills that this order be followed by man only if man knows it.

If, therefore, we speak of the eternal law as the will of God obligating man to follow the essential order of things, we must say that an erring conscience is not in conformity with this law, but at the same time we must say that God also wills by the same law that such a conscience formed in good will be followed, for in creating human man liable to err, God willed that the practical judgment of man is to be the proximate measure of his moral action. There is, therefore, this peculiarity in the moral order, and it will not be found in any other order: God wills that man's conscience be conformed to the reality of things—and this is the eternal law; but he also wills that man follow his conscience even though it is not in conformity to the order of reality—and this, too, is the eternal law. But the basis of the peculiarity is to be found in the nature of man in relation to knowledge and the object of knowledge. God wills natures and the essential order of these natures. He also wills, among these natures, human nature which is not always right and true in its apprehension of these natures and their relations. Yet, God must will that human nature follow its apprehension and judgment about reality. But since the order of reality is the evidence for truth in knowledge, conscience always has a check for its judgments, and God must always will that man, as far as he can, approach the perfection of agreement between his conscience and reality, and in so doing man participates perfectly in the absolute eternal law of which the order of essences is a reflection.

Sometimes man's conscience dictates actions to be done or avoided which are in agreement with reality. In so doing the intellect reflects the law of God correctly and as it is discovered in the natures of things. Conscience in this instance is the voice of God because it acquaints man with the order of reality which God wills to be followed in an unqualified sense, as well as with the obligation which can be derived from the reality of things. At other times, conscience commands or prohibits that which is not conformed to reality. But here, too, conscience is the voice of God, because it is the eternal law, which is the mind of God, that human reason be the measure of moral action, and in following reason, even though it be mistaken, man is following the law of God. Even though conscience commands what is objectively wrong, being ignorant of the truth, it commands with an authority which is sacred and inviolate and in so doing participates in the eternal law, the source of all authority.

A corollary of the relation of conscience and the eternal law is that good will or its absence establishes moral right or wrong. We have discussed this in a summary way when we spoke about law. But its repetition will help to clarify the present problem of conscience and the eternal law. Let us begin by asking the question: "When is a practical judgment of conscience true?"

10. Good Will and the End of Man

The answer to this question is not too difficult even though it may not be as clear as we might desire. Aristotle in his *Ethics* (*Nic. Ethics* VI,5,6) and St. Thomas in the *Summa* (*S.T.* I-II,57; II-II, 47-56) have given the answer by their consideration of the meaning of truth in scientific knowledge and in a practical judgment. Science is a judgment about things that are universal and necessary and about conclusions of demonstration. Consequently, in science there is perfect conformity between the mind and the object, so that the judgment made about these objects is certain and universally true. Practical judgment, however, is concerned with the human acts which are to be performed for the good life, and so it deals with things that are variable and, consequently, not universally true.

We can, for example, attain to a conclusion of science with which all scientists agree, simply because science involves demonstration based upon first principles which are universal and necessary.

But the same is not true of a practical judgment. Many men of high intelligence and of perfect good will, for example, will not agree about a course of action to be followed in a specific circumstance, simply because a judgment of this kind does not involve a demonstration based upon invariable principles. Consequently, we cannot expect to have the same universality and certainty in a practical judgment that we have in a scientific judgment. This means, in other words, that a statement as regards a manner of action might be entirely true, yet the truth cannot be universally made known, whereas a statement of a scientific truth can be made known in a universal manner.

There is, therefore, a difference between the truth of the practical judgment and the truth of the speculative judgment. The former does not have the universality and invariability of the truth of the latter. Yet is it not possible to have in our practical judgments some intellectual principle which will lead men to truth in their activity, just as we have an intellectual principle in our scientific judgment which will lead men to truth in science?

That certain intellectual principles which will lead to truth in our moral actions can be had is evident, provided we consider the meaning of the term *prudent*. We call men prudent who deliberate well about what is good and necessary for them to lead the good life as men. We also know that when a man has made a decision after an honest and sincere deliberation proportionate to the gravity of the contemplated action, then he not only is intellectually convinced that the decision is good but also that it is true, and as far as the known evidence of action is concerned the judgment cannot be invalidated regardless of what may later follow as a result of his decision.

Let us take the following example. A man, the father of three children, decides that he should divorce his present wife in order to marry another woman. Since he knows that such a step is most significant both for himself and his children, he has weighed the matter carefully. He has, let us say, been educated in the best nonsectarian college, a college where divorce has been looked upon not as a violation of the law of God or of any religious law but rather as a strain upon and a danger to the social body and as an act which from a so-called humanitarian point of view should be the last resort of a married man. In fact, he has been taught that divorce should be permitted only to save either one's own good name and life or those of others. More than this, he realizes that his present wife is an alcoholic who not only neglects but is a scandal to the children, while the woman he wishes to marry is, as far as he has been able to discover, a kind, considerate and motherly woman who has for the last two years treated the children with the greatest show of affection. Taking all these and many more reasons into consideration, the man honestly and sincerely decides to divorce and remarry. He does, and the second woman, far from possessing the character he thought she had, is found to be a scheming, selfish, ease-loving person. Not only does she neglect the children but she also looks on them as obstacles in her search for freedom from responsibility and as hindrances to the fulfillment of her desires for luxury, and she considers her husband an improvident and thoughtless spouse because he will not satisfy her every irrational wish. The second marriage has proven anything but a betterment for the family good. Yet, it cannot be said that the father's decision was bad or unreasonable because of the future events which he could not foresee, which he did not want, and against which he took every precaution that was humanly possible. Although he could not prevent or rationally discard (and what human could?) the possibility of these future evils, the decision was certainly reasonable, right, and good. His action was, as a matter of fact, a very good action done with the best intention, performed with the best means that he had at his disposal.

Yet, on the other hand, there is something about that decision that is false. The man's decision to marry was based upon a judgment which was proven false, namely, that this marriage would be good. As a matter of fact the remarriage is not good; it is anything but good.

And thus we are led to recognize that there is, in the practical judgment, a twofold truth. In the practical judgment, some theoretical consideration is always involved, namely some consideration referring to the reality of things, to what the things are and to what the things will be; in the example the theoretical consideration was that the marriage was to be a good thing. This theoretical judgment proved to be untrue: the following course of events showed that it was not in conformity with what was to happen in fact. The truth of the theoretical consideration implied in the practical judgment cannot be established with an entire certainty because we are unable to overcome the mysteries of contingency, because we are unable to foresee the future with certainty. However, we are all convinced that a decision may be certainly true despite the inability to foresee with certainty its possible consequences. The certitude of the practical judgment does not concern the theoretical assumptions implied in it, but the very practical aspect of the practical judgment; we do not refer to its conformity with the reality of things—this conformity cannot be perfectly ascertained—we refer to its conformity with the requirements of a will which is supposed to be sound, healthy, honest. According to the so enlightened view of Aristotle, the certain truth of which the practical judgment is capable is not theoretical but a practical truth; it is not the truth of cognition, but the truth of direction; it does not consist in a relation of conformity between the mind and things but in a relation of conformity between the judgment of the mind and the requirements of a right appetite of the end to be pursued. Whatever the factual consequences of a decision will be, owing to the unpredictable interference of contingent causes, one who made a decision honestly, in full accord with the exigencies of a virtuous will, has not to repent: his decision was what it ought to have been; it was true, undoubtedly true, even if, for lack of knowing things that we could not know, it implied some assumptions that the factual course of events invalidated. (Yves Simon, The Nature and Functions of Authority, pp. 24-26)

Thus, the practical order, in spite of the variability of the objects with which it deals, has a principle of truth for its decisions, just as the speculative or scientific order has its principle of truth: the principle of the practical order is the good will; the speculative order has the principle of primary truth of being. And so, while our conscience may be good and true and may not possess the goodness and truth of the speculative order, it may be opposed to the order of essential being and that absolute will of God which orders this essential order, it may be opposed to the eternal law regarded as the rule of essences, yet the practical intellect will be in harmony with the order of ends which depends upon the apprehension of the human intellect, which may accidentally err, but being the result of the honest intellect and a good will it is conformed to the eternal law of God which obliges man to follow his intellect for it is this intellect which reveals this same eternal law to man.

If man, therefore, is of good will, he will not only act in a practically good manner, but also in a practically true way, even though in a theoretical way he is not only bad but also wrong. But since the practical intellect is an act of the intellect (and the intellect is made for the truth of the speculative order as well as the truth of the practical order), the first and lifelong objective of conscience is, of course, that of educating itself so that its judgments may involve judgments which are speculatively true. The voice of God initially speaks with clarity and universality only about the distinction between right and wrong, and on the duty of doing right and avoiding wrong. It must be taught all else; and the process of teaching and learning is extraordinarily difficult. Cardinal Newman puts the situation very well:

But the sense of right and wrong, which is the first element of religion, is so delicate, so fitful, so easily puzzled, obscured, perverted, so subtle in its argumentative methods, so impressible by education, so biassed by pride and passion, so unsteady in its course, that, in the struggle for existence amid the various exercises and triumphs of the human intellect, this sense is at once the highest of all teachers yet the least luminous. (Letter to the Duke of Norfolk, in Difficulties of Anglicans)

How shall it be made luminous? First, the education of conscience demands the cultivation of that measure of moral science which the individual requires to meet and make successfully the moral decisions which occur in his own life—family, business, and individual life. Obviously, the acquisition of this moral science demands consultation of the best moral thought of humanity throughout its history; it is more than ordinarily fatal for the individual to do his moral thinking in isolation. Again, the education of conscience demands cultivation of the virtue of prudence, whereby the conclusions of moral science are applied to particular cases, with a certain readiness of concrete judgment. But above all, the educated conscience is acquired at the price of high moral discipline—the discipline of the moral virtue, whereby reason is rescued from the dominion of pride and prejudice and passion, and from the subtle influence of self-deception or evil habit, and from the general darkness in which sin and lack of sincerity always obscure the light of reason.

Readings

Cronin, Michael, *The Science of Ethics*, vol. I, pp. 472-505.
D'Arcy, M., *Christian Morality*, pp. 73-101.
Humphrey, G., *Conscience and Law*, c. 2.
Kendzierski, Lottie H., "Wisdom, Synderesis and Practical Principles," *Proceedings of the American Catholic Philosophical Association*, XXVI (1952), pp. 168-179.
Lehu, L., "La recta ratio de s. Thomas signifie-t-elle la conscience?" in *Revue Thomiste*, n.s. VIII (1925), pp. 159-166.
Leibell, J. F., *Readings in Ethics*. The following articles should be read:

"The norm of morality," Thomas Slater, pp. 156-162.
"Synderesis," Thomas Slater, pp. 341-364.

Maritain, J., *Existence and the Existent*, pp. 50-61; 85-122.
Murray, John C., "Freedom of Religion," *Theological Studies*, VI (Jan. 1945), pp. 229-286.
Newman, John Henry, *Grammar of Assent*, pp. 105-112.
O'Neil, C. J., "Practical Knowledge and Liberty," *Proceedings of the American Catholic Philosophical Association*, XXIX (1955), pp. 1-13.
—— "Prudence, the Incommunicable Wisdom," *Essays in Thomism*, ed. R. E. Brennan, pp. 185-205.
Rickaby, Joseph, *Aquinas Ethicus*, vol. I, pp. 281-285; 303-307.
—— *Moral Philosophy*, pp. 133-143; 152-158.
Rommen, H., *The Natural Law*, pp. 27-38.
Sertillanges, A. D., *La philosophie morale de saint Thomas d'Aquin*, pp. 385-401.
Simon, Yves, *The Nature and Functions of Authority*, pp. 17-30.
St. Thomas, *Summa Theologica*, I, q. 79; I-II, q. 19.

CHAPTER XII

VIRTUE

1. *The Need of Habit*

Besides the exterior principles of the moral life which we have studied in the chapters on law, there are interior principles or virtues which are necessary for the moral life. If we were to study the interior principles of human acts in an exhaustive manner we would have to consider not only the intellect and will which are specifically required for the moral act, but all the other principles which are presupposed by them, such as the soul itself, the sensitive powers, etc. A moral act is, in truth, the effect of all of man's powers. But such a study would take us too far afield from our purpose. We will, then, limit ourselves to the study of virtue in the present chapter.

But to repeat a little of what has been said in the philosophy of man. The soul is not, of course, like God, a pure act and, therefore we cannot find in it any act which is essential to it. Consequently, because the soul is not pure act, all that it has in the way of existence has been given to it. Although the soul, therefore, is the form of an organized body, it still does not possess of itself the powers by which it can exercise its functions of vegetation, sensation, and intellection, but must receive them. For this reason the powers of the

338

soul are not the soul itself; rather there is a real distinction between them as between substance and accidents. These powers or active principles are given to the soul; they are something distinct from the soul, given to the soul in order that it can be a principle of action besides being the form of the body. These powers, then, are the immediate principles of all acts, the moral acts included.

It is impossible to admit that the power of the soul is its essence, although some have maintained it. For the present purpose this may be proved in two ways. First, because, since potency and act divide being and every kind of being, we must refer potency and its act to the same genus. Therefore, if the act be not in the genus of substance, the potency which is said in relation to that act cannot be in the genus of substance. Now the operation of the soul is not in the genus of substance, for this belongs to God alone, whose operation is His own substance. Therefore the divine potency or power which is the principle of His operation is the Divine Essence itself. This cannot be true either of the soul or of any creature, as we have said above when speaking of the angels. Secondly, this may be also shown to be impossible in the soul. For the soul by its very essence is an act. Therefore, if the very essence of the soul were the immediate principle of operation, whatever has a soul would always have actual vital actions, as that which has a soul is always an actually living thing. For, as a form, the soul is not an act ordained to a further act; it is rather the ultimate term of generation. Therefore, for it to be in potentiality to another act does not belong to it according to its essence as a form, but according to its power. So the soul itself, as the subject of its power, is called the first act, with a further relation to the second act. Now we observe that what has a soul is not always actual with respect to its vital operations. Hence it is also said in the definition of the soul that it is the act of a body having life potentially; which potentiality, however, does not exclude the soul. Therefore it follows that the essence of the soul is not its power. For nothing is in potentiality by reason of an act, as act. (S.T. I,77,1c)

But even with the soul possessing these powers it must still have other principles of action. The reason why this is necessary is the same as the reason why it must possess these distinct powers: the soul with its powers is not, as God is, wholly in act: the soul with its powers needs determination for acting; it needs some inner principles, halfway between powers and acts. Clearly the soul with its powers is not wholly in act, as is God who lacks nothing for action. Neither is the soul with its powers one of the natural elementary forms, such as fire or cold, etc., which are everything they can be and need nothing besides themselves for action. Neither is the human soul a particular natural form of a body, as a vegetative or sensitive form, which needs nothing further for its action. The human soul with its powers, however, is not wholly in act but is indetermined to any particular act both in its power of intellect and of will. Take, for example, the will. Although the will is by nature determined to the good in general, yet it would never pass from this simple potency of desiring to the concrete particular goods which it desires, if it were not somehow disposed to desire the particular good. With this primary disposition the will can be further disposed towards other goods. The same is true of the intellect, which by its nature can know all things. Yet it would never pass from this simple capacity of knowing to the concrete facts which it knows, if it were not first of all disposed to the first principles of knowledge from which it goes on to acquire other truths. With this primary determination the intellect goes on to build up the sciences by which it is more and more specified in its acts.

Evidently these particularizing principles of action are not the soul, neither are they the powers of the soul, for they are added to them. Consequently, they are dispositions to use the powers in a determined manner. When one of these dispositions is so engrafted on the soul or its powers that it becomes something permanent, difficult to change, and a property of the soul, then we call it a *habitus*. Such a *habitus* is clearly necessary in order that the soul may use its powers to perform moral as well as other acts.

2. The Meaning of Habit

A habit, therefore, has relation to act in such wise that as a result of habit a permanent manner of action is added to the potentiality in which it is. Now because act depends not only on the powers of the soul which are the immediate principles of act, but also upon the nature itself which is the ultimate principle of act, both these principles or potentialities are subject to habit. Consequently, habit is defined as *a disposition whereby that which is disposed is well or ill disposed either in regard to itself or in regard to another.*

To have relation to an act may belong to a habit both in regard to the nature of habit, and in regard to the subject in which the habit is. In regard to the nature of habit, it belongs to every habit to have relation to an act. For it is essential to habit to imply some relation to a thing's nature, in so far as it is suitable or unsuitable to it. But a thing's nature, which is the end of generation, is further ordained to another end, which is either an operation, or some product of operation, to which one attains by means of operation. Therefore habit implies relation, not only to the very nature of a thing, but also, consequently, to operation, inasmuch as this is the end of nature, or conducive to the end. And so it is also stated in the definition of habit, that it is a disposition whereby that which is disposed, is well or ill disposed either in regard to itself, that is, to its nature, or in regard to something else, that is, to the end. (S.T. I-II,49,3c)

We may distinguish, then, two kinds of habit: *entitative habit,* which disposes the nature itself in such a way that it is perfected or impaired in its being, e.g., health, beauty, sickness, etc.; *operative habit,* which disposes the powers of the soul in such a way that they operate ill or well. Because habits reside in potentialities whether they be potentialities for the perfection of being or of operation, we may inquire whether habit resides in the soul or in the body.

To consider operative habits first. As we have said before, if a body has a natural form which is necessarily determined to one course of action, no further disposition or habit is possible; neither is habit possible in those beings, such as brutes, which possess natural forms and natural instincts which are ordained to one thing. Habits, then, can be possessed only by a rational being whose soul, while being the principle of act in the body, is not disposed to a particular act. Because it is the soul that is the principle of action, it is in the powers of the soul that the habits reside, although we can say that in a secondary and subordinate way the habit is in the body in so far as the body is rendered easily subject to the movements of the soul. For example, the habit of swimming is principally in the soul, for it is the power of the soul which is habitually disposed to produce the acts that move the body muscles to such movements, but the body has become used to responding to such acts. In regard to the entitative habits, as health, beauty, sickness, etc., which perfect or impair the manner of being, such habits are principally in the body, though in a way they also reside in the soul in so far as by them the soul can perform acts with a greater facility of difficulty. For example, the powers of the soul are more disposed to perform the acts of a healthy man if it is united to a healthy body than to a sick body.

3. Operative Habits

Since ethics has to do with human actions or conduct, we are here interested in operative habits only, i.e., habits that are related to the powers of the soul by which man places moral actions. From various articles of St. Thomas' *Summa* (S.T. I-II,49,50) we may define an operative habit in a somewhat lengthy but complete manner: *a quality difficult to change, whereby a power whose nature it was to act one way or another indeterminately is disposed easily and readily at will to follow this or that particular line of action.*

In its strictest sense, therefore, an operative habit expresses the readiness, promptness, together with the constant inclination which any given power may possess of performing a given act. It is not the same as power; rather it is something superimposed on a power and disposing that power to act in a constant manner when naturally it is not so disposed. A power that has only one way of working, set and fixed, is not susceptible of habit. A body does not fall with any greater ease after five times than it did the first time. But an operative habit is a thing of rational life, an adjunct of the will, not of course independent of material conditions and bodily alterations, in so far as a rational soul is also a principle of action in a material agent, but essentially acquired, fostered and usable by the will, and brought into play and controlled in its operations by free choice.

The sensitive powers can be considered in two ways: first in so far as they act from natural instinct; secondly, in so far as they act at the command of reason. In so far as they act from natural instinct, they are ordained to one thing, even as nature is. Therefore, just as there are no habits in the natural powers, so likewise there are none in the sensitive powers in so far as they act from natural instinct. But in so far as they act at the command of reason, they can be ordered to various things. And thus there can be habits in them, by which they are well or ill disposed in regard to something. (S.T. I-II,50,3c)

Because some of the powers of the soul, even the will itself, are subject to the will, because these powers are not potentialities in relation to a determined act, habits can be acquired by all of these powers. Such acquisition, with a few exceptions such as the habit of understanding first principles which is acquired almost immediately by the intellect or with one or few acts, is through the frequent repetition of the same act. A habit is a living thing, it is acquired by acts, grows by act, under the command of the will, and it must be fed by acts of free choice. Unexercised, a habit diminishes, corruption sets in, and disintegration follows. A man, we will say, has a habit of reading a language, of using a language, that he has learnt. He gives up using the language. That means that he either takes to using his mind and memory in another way, or he takes up a line of intellectual activity to the exclusion of the language. Either way, before long there is a new formation to the gradual ruin of the old habit.

Because operative habits are dispositions of the powers of the soul, they may be distinguished in several ways as the powers themselves are distinguished: (1) By reason of the active principles in which they are; thus there are habits of intellect, of will, of the sensitive powers. (2) By reason of the object of the act of the powers; thus we have habits of science, understanding, prudence, temperance. (3) By reason of the nature in which the habits exist; thus we have good and bad habits.

A habit is both a form and a habit. Hence the specific distinction of habits may be taken in the ordinary way in which forms differ specifically, or according to that mode of distinction which is proper to habits. Now forms are distinguished from one another in reference to the diversity of their active principles, since every agent produces its like in species. Habits, however, imply order to something, and all things that imply order to something are distinguished according to the distinction of the things to which they are ordained. Now a habit is a disposition implying a twofold order: viz., to nature, and to an operation consequent to nature. Accordingly habits are specifically distinct in respect of three things. First, in respect of the active principles of such dispositions; secondly, in respect of nature; thirdly, in respect of specifically different objects, as will appear from what follows. (S.T. I-II,54,2c)

Just as we have shown in Chapter V in which we spoke of the good and evil of human acts, that human acts are specifically determined good or bad by their conformity or difformity with the nature which places them, so operative habits are specifically determined good or bad by their conformity or difformity with the nature of man.

Habits are specifically distinct not only in respect of their objects and active principles, but also in their relation to nature. Now this happens in two ways. First, by reason of their suitableness or unsuitableness to nature. In this way a good habit is specifically distinct from a bad habit. A good habit is one which disposes to an act suitable to the agent's nature, while a bad habit is one which disposes to an act unsuitable to nature. Thus, acts of virtue are suitable to human nature, since they are according to reason, whereas acts of vice are opposed to human nature, since they are against reason. Hence it is clear that habits are distinguished specifically by the difference of good and bad. (S.T. I-II,54,3c)

Now a good habit is called a virtue, and if the object of the virtue is the truth in knowledge, we have intellectual virtues; if the object of the virtue is the good in action, we have the moral virtues. Moral virtues are required that man may be simply good. Certainly, it is not enough that man perform good actions occasionally and at irregular intervals: he must persistently tend to and aim at that which is good; to do what is good at all times and under all circumstances must be as it were his second nature. Now the permanent and constant direction and inclination to good acts is moral virtue. It is virtue that must give to the moral conduct of man that moderation, evenness, proportion, and consistency which befits him as a rational being, makes him always prompt and ready to act aright, and confers upon him facility and ease in acting aright.

As we know, the intellect does not ordinarily necessitate the will nor the human passions. Rather the will and passions often fight against and resist reason. When they do, unless a man has acquired a habit of obeying reason in the conduct of his will and passions he will at times act inconsiderately and do wrong. Man must possess habits not only in the will so that this power may readily choose that which reason points out as good, but also in the sensitive appetites, in both the concupiscible and irascible parts, so far as they are under the control of the will, so that they may be subject to the guidance of reason. These habits of the will and sensitive appetites are called moral virtues, and to them the name of virtues is usually confined.

4. The Definition of Virtue

A virtue, consequently, is an immediate perfection of a power, not of the being, of the soul, because virtue is that which disposes man to act in a definite way. Because of its human quality, therefore, virtue cannot be related to the body and to the powers of the body which man possesses in common with the animals. This can be gathered from the nature of an operative habit, which by definition is related to the will and to those powers over which the will has dominion.

Virtue, from the very nature of the name, implies some perfection of power, as we have said above. Therefore, since potency is of two kinds, namely, potency in reference to being, and potency in reference to act, the perfection of both these is called virtue. But potency in reference to being is on the part of matter, which is potential being, whereas potency in reference to act is on the part of the form, which is the principle of action, since everything acts in so far as it is in act.

Now man is so constituted that the body holds the place of matter, the soul that of form. The body, indeed, man has in common with other animals; and the same is to be said of the powers which are common to the soul and body; and only those powers which are proper to the soul, namely, the rational powers, belong to man alone. Therefore, human virtue, of which we are speaking now, cannot belong to the body, but belongs only to that which is proper to the soul. Hence human virtue does not imply reference to being, but rather to act. Consequently it is essential to human virtue to be an operative habit. (S.T. I-II,55,2c)

Not only should virtue dispose man to a certain kind of action; it must also dispose him to act in a way that is good and perfecting so that a virtue is in reality for the good of the soul. With this we can explain and justify the celebrated definition of virtue taken from St. Augustine: *Virtue is a good quality of the mind, by which we live righteously, of which no man can make bad use, which God works in us without us.* (*Lib. Arb.* II,19) If we except for the present the last part of the definition, i.e., "which God works in us without us," which is applicable to the infused virtues, we may say:

This definition comprises perfectly the whole essential notion of virtue. For the perfect nature of anything is gathered from all its causes. Now the above definition comprises all the causes of virtue. For the formal cause of virtue, as of everything, is obtained from its genus and difference, when it is defined as a good quality: for quality is the genus of virtue, and the difference, good. To be sure, the definition would be more suitable if for quality we substitute habit, which is the proximate genus.

Now virtue has no matter out of which it is formed, as neither has any other accident; but it has matter about which it is concerned, and the matter in which it exists, namely, the subject. The matter about which virtue is concerned is its object, and this could not be included in the above definition because the object fixes the virtue to a certain species, and here we are giving the definition of virtue in general. And so for the material cause we have the subject, which is mentioned when it is said that virtue is a good quality of the mind.

The end of virtue, since it is an operative habit, is operation itself. But it must be observed that some operative habits are always referred to evil, as are vicious habits. Others are sometimes referred to good, sometimes to evil. For instance, opinion is referred both to the true and to the untrue. But virtue is a habit which is always referred to good. Hence the distinction of virtue from those habits which are always referred to evil is expressed in the words by which we live righteously; and its distinction from those habits which are sometimes directed to good, and sometimes to evil, is expressed in the words, of which no one makes bad use.

Lastly, God is the efficient cause of infused virtue, to which this *definition applies; and this is expressed in the words which God works in us without us. If we omit this phrase, the remainder of the definition will apply to all virtues in general, whether acquired or infused. (S.T. I-II, 55,4c)*

5. Difference between Intellectual and Moral Virtues

We have now to inquire in what powers of the soul the operative habits which dispose our actions reside. Since we are concerned with virtue in the strict sense of the word, and since virtue is always a principle of actions suitable to human nature, virtue properly speaking can reside only in the will since the will is always the immediate principle of action. If virtue is in other powers it is in them only in so far as they are moved by the will.

If we remember that a virtue is a disposition of a power for good actions under the command of the will, we will have to say that virtue consists not only in an aptness or disposition for good actions but also in the actual performance of good actions. Because of this double element in virtue we can distinguish two kinds of virtue: intellectual and moral. To understand the intellectual virtues we must distinguish between the speculative and practical intellect, two functions of the same power.

If we take its speculative function first, it will seem to be, by definition, unconcerned with anything practical and active; as such it cannot be the seat of genuine virtue, since the virtues, strictly speaking, are dispositions for action. There are several reasons why the speculative intellect cannot be the subject of virtues in the full sense of the word. Since these reasons will become clearer as we advance in our study of virtue, we will only enumerate them now. (1) The object of the speculative intellect is truth, which necessitates; hence the operation of the speculative intellect is not under the control of free choice. (2) The acquisition of truth in the speculative intellect does not confer a facility for using it well in practical matters; hence one may have the speculative habit of physics but be unable to use it well as an engineer. (3) The speculative habits do not make a man simply good, but good only in a restricted sense. Consequently, the intellectual virtues of *understanding*, whereby the intellect has a facility of acquiring the first and immediately evident principles of knowledge—such as the principle of contradiction and its derivatives: that of *science* whereby the intellect knows the conclusions of particular branches of study, the knowledge of which is not immediately evident; that of *wisdom* whereby the intellect knows the most universal principles and first causes—are not virtues in the strict sense of the word, but virtues relatively speaking either in so far as they confer aptness upon the intellect for acquiring truth and therefore perfecting its own being, or in so far as they give to the possessor knowledge which he could use to perform good actions. Hence, in a roundabout way, these habits are called virtues. In one respect, however, the speculative intellect is subject to virtue in the full sense of the word. The intellect in its habit or act of faith is subject to the will, which commands it to accept an object the truth of which is not compelling like the truth of the other objects of the acts of the speculative intellect.

With the exception of faith, then, the speculative intellect cannot be the subject of virtue in the complete sense of the word. It is quite different with the practical intellect, which can possess habits which wholly realizes the meaning of virtue. One such virtue is prudence. But, again, as we did in the first chapter, we must clearly distinguish between prudence and art. *Art* is a habit of the practical intellect, for it is a habit of reasoning properly about things to be made. To possess an art the agent must have the knowledge whereby he plans and directs the making of an object. Wherefore, a work of art is produced according to reason, and the perfection of a work of art is determined by how much it agrees with reason. Consequently, the perfection of a work of art of a sculptor is different from the perfection of a work of art of a medical doctor. Because art perfects the practical intellect by giving it a facility for making things, there are many arts: carpentry, masonry, cooking, etc. Art, then, does confer a facility for making things, and in this sense it may be called a virtue, but it falls short of the meaning of virtue in that it does not make a man simply good. It is obvious that a man may be a very good artist and still be a bad man. Since this is true, art cannot be classified with virtues, but must be numbered among the intellectual habits.

But when the act of the intellect receives from the will at least the specification of its end, which is the good willed by a good will, it has the virtue of *prudence*. And more than this, there are two other virtues of the practical intellect which are supposed by prudence: *good counsel*, which is the power to deliberate well, and *good judgment*, which is the power to judge well in accord with natural or common law. Although these two powers are rightly speaking acts of the speculative intellect, nevertheless they are for the purpose of immediate practical use and can under the command of the will become better and better.

As we have said before, virtue is a habit by which we act well. Now a habit may be directed to a good act in two ways. First, it may be so directed in so far as by the habit a man acquires an aptness for a good act. For example, by the habit of music man has an aptness to play the piano well. But this habit does not make a man always to play well, for a pianist may be guilty of mistakes; and the same is true of other sciences and arts. Secondly, a habit may confer not only an aptness to act, but also the right use of that aptness. For example, justice not only gives man the prompt will to do just actions, but also makes him act justly.

Since both good and being are said of things not in so far as they are potentially, but in so far as they are actually, it follows that if a man has habits of the latter sort he is said to do and to be good absolutely; for example, he is just or temperate. And the same is true of other such virtues. And since virtue is that which makes its possessor good and his work good, these latter habits are called virtues in the complete sense of the word, because they make the work actually good and the subject absolutely good. But the former habits are not called virtues in the strict or full sense of the word, because they do not make the work good except in regard to a certain aptness; neither do they make their possessor absolute good. For even though a man is gifted in science or art, he is not said to be good absolutely, but relatively; for example, a good grammarian or a good smith. Wherefore, science and art are often distinguished from virtue, and at other times they are called virtues.

Hence the subject of a habit which is called virtue in a qualified sense can be the intellect, and not only the practical intellect, but also the speculative, without any connection with the will. In this sense the Philosopher (Nic. Ethics VI,2,1139a,14-17) holds that science, wisdom and understanding, and art too, are intellectual virtues. But the subject of a habit which is called virtue in the complete sense of the word, can only be the will, or some power which is moved by the will. The reason for this is, that the will moves to their acts all those other powers which are in some way rational, as we have said above. If, therefore, a man actually does well it is because he has good will. Therefore, the virtue which makes a man to do well actually, and not merely to have the aptness to do well, must be either in the will itself, or in some power which is moved by the will.

Now the intellect is moved by the will just as the other powers are; because a man considers actually because he wills to do so. Hence the intellect, in so far as it is subject to the will, can be the subject of virtue in the full sense of the word. In this way the speculative intellect, or reason, is the subject of faith, for the intellect is moved by the command of the will to assent to the things that are of faith: for no man believes, unless he wills. The practical intellect, however, is the subject of prudence. Since prudence is right reason about things to be done, one of its conditions is that man be rightly ordered in regard to the principles of this reason of things to be done, that is, in regard to their ends. Now man is rightly ordered by the rectitude of the will, just as in the principles of speculative truth he is rightly ordered by the natural light of the agent intellect. Consequently, just as the subject of science, which is the right reason of speculative truth, is the speculative intellect in relation to the agent intellect, so the subject of prudence is the practical intellect in relation to a right or good will (S.T. I-II,56,3c)

To sum up what we have said about the difference between intellectual and moral virtues. An intellectual virtue gives one a facility in knowing the truth; a moral virtue not only gives facility, but also makes one put the facility in use. Thus a habit of science enables one to arrive at conclusions in a particular science, but does not insure that one will always do so, for a scientist can make mistakes; whereas a habit of prudence not only makes a man prompt and ready to do good deeds, but makes him really do so. Not that habits necessitate the will, but they do facilitate the act of the will. Another distinction may be expressed. The intellectual virtues perfect the faculty of knowledge, but do not necessarily perfect man himself. Thus the habit of understanding, in so far as it gives man a facility of apprehending first principles, perfects the intellect in its operations, but such understanding does not make man a good man. The intellectual habit called art, for example, disposes a man to act correctly towards some particular end, but a moral habit disposes towards the common end and purpose of all human life. Thus medical skill ministers to the particular end of healing; while the moral habit of temperance serves the general end, which is final happiness and perfection. So to give a wrong prescription through sheer antecedent ignorance is to fail as a doctor; but to get drunk knowingly and willingly is to fail as a man.

Thus we cannot say that virtue properly so called is knowledge. As we saw before, it was the teaching of Socrates, largely shared by Plato, to make all virtue intellectual, so that to know was to perform good acts, and to be ignorant was to sin. But such a teaching is based on a false supposition: that the will and the sense appetites always follow reason. For a man to do a good act, more than theoretical knowledge is required. The right disposition of the will and appetitive powers is necessary and this is had only through the moral virtues, in which the will commands itself and the sensitive appetites to act in accord with reason.

Yet we must say that to have the moral virtues we must have at least some of the intellectual virtues. To act in a manner suitable for human nature, which is the end of the moral virtues, requires that we have knowledge and, consequently, that we follow reason. If virtue of the moral order consists in the habit of choosing well, we must first of all know what the good is and then command that the appetites be in accord with the known good, and this we do by the virtue of prudence, which is a habit both of the intellect whereby the good is known and of the will whereby the intellect is determined to judge of the good. But such judgment of the good requires that understanding of the first principles of knowledge be present. Although, therefore, the moral virtues can be had without wisdom or science or art, they cannot be present without prudence and understanding.

Moral virtue can be possessed without some of the intellectual virtues, viz., wisdom, science and art; but not without understanding and prudence. No moral virtue can be had without prudence, because moral virtue is a habit of choosing, i.e., making us choose well. Now in order that a choice be good, two things are required. First, that the intention be directed to a proper end; and this is done by moral virtue, which inclines the appetitive power to the good that is in accord with reason, which is a proper end. Secondly, that man choose rightly those things which are means to the end; now this he cannot do unless his reason counsels, judges and commands rightly, which is the function of prudence and the virtues annexed to it. . . . Wherefore, there can be no moral virtue without prudence, and consequently, neither can there be without understanding. For it is by virtue of understanding that we know naturally known principles both in speculative matters and in practical matters. Consequently, just as right reason in speculative matters, in so far as it proceeds from naturally known principles, presupposes the understanding of principles, so also does prudence, which is the right reason about things to be done. (S.T. I-II,58,4c)

Just as we cannot possess the moral virtues without prudence by which man judges correctly what is to be done in each particular instance, and the virtue of understanding by which man has a knowledge of principles, so we cannot possess the virtue of prudence unless we have the other moral virtues.

Since man must live well, prudence is a most important virtue; yet it is not by prudence alone that man lives well. For although prudence is a good disposition by which the intellect has a knowledge of the right means to an end, nevertheless it is the will and the passions which are inclined to the end; if these are not properly inclined to the real good, the intellect judging according to the good proposed by the will and passion will, as a result, choose means which are not really good because of the good proposed by the will and the passion. Prudence is possible only if the will and the passion are so properly disposed to the rational good of man that they do not interfere with nor deter the practical intellect in its judgment of the true means to a real good.

The other intellect virtues can exist without the moral virtues, but not prudence. This is true because prudence is right reason about things to be done, and this not merely in the sphere of the general, but in the sphere of the particular in which actions are done. Right reason, indeed, demands principles from which reason proceeds. Now when reason is occupied with particular actions, it needs not only universal principles, but more especially particular principles. For a man is rightly disposed to universal principles of action by the natural understanding of principles by which he knows that he should not do evil; or, again, he might be rightly disposed by some particular science. But all of these are not sufficient in order that man might reason rightly about particular actions. For it happens at times that these particular principles which are known by the understanding or by science, are destroyed in a particular case by passion. For example, when one is swayed and overcome by concupiscence, the object of his desire seems good to him, but actually it is opposed to the universal judgment of his reason. Consequently, just as a man is rightly disposed in regard to the universal principles by the habit of natural understanding or of science, so in order that he might be rightly disposed to the principles of action, viz., the ends, he must be perfected by certain habits by which it becomes connatural to him, as it were, to judge rightly about the end. This is done by the moral virtues, for the virtuous man judges rightly of the end of virtue, because such as a man is, so does the end seem to him. Consequently, the right reason about things to be done, viz., prudence, requires man to have moral virtue. (S.T. I-II, 58,5c)

6. The Moral Virtues in General

Because a moral virtue is that whereby man has a facility for acting under the control of the will, man can possess as many moral virtues as he has powers of acting which can be subject to the control of the will. It is obvious, then, that man can have virtues in the will, intellect, and sensitive powers.

Without going into a detailed proof why this is so, let us briefly state the reasons why moral virtues can reside in these powers alone. That virtue cannot reside in the vegetative powers of the soul follows from the very definition of moral virtue, viz., that it must reside in a power that can be subject to the will. Since, however, the vegetative power acts necessarily and is a principle of what we have called acts of man, no virtue is possible in it.

The same is not true, however, of the sensitive powers. Although they are, under one aspect, principles of acts of man and as such necessarily produce their acts, nevertheless, under another aspect they are subject to reason and consequently to the will and as such can be subjects of virtue. The sensitive appetites are common to man and to brutes; they are moved to action at the presence of the proper stimulus or good, but they are, in man, subject to reason and will in so far as man can control and regulate their activity. The food appetite in animals, for example, necessarily operates at the presence of food, but in man the appetite can be controlled and regulated for the reasoned good of man.

Now since the sensitive appetites are divided into a twofold appetite, the irascible and the concupiscible, as we have seen in the chapter on the passions, two virtues can be present in the sensitive appetite: *fortitude* in the irascible power; *temperance* in the concupiscible power.

The irascible and concupiscible powers can be considered in two ways. First, in themselves, in so far as they are parts of the sensitive appetite; and in this way they are not competent to be the subject of virtue. Secondly, they can be considered as participating in the reason, because it belongs to their nature to obey the reason. And thus the irascible or the concupiscible power can be the subject of human virtue; for, in so far as it participates in the reason, it is the principle of a human act. And to these powers we must assign virtues.

For it is clear that there are some virtues in the irascible and concupiscible powers. Because an act which proceeds from one power, according as it is moved by another power, cannot be perfect unless both powers be well disposed to the act; for instance, the act of a craftsman cannot be successful unless both the craftsman and his instrument be well disposed to act. Therefore, in the case of the objects of the operations of the irascible and concupiscible powers, according as they are moved by reason, there must needs be, not only in the reason, but also in the irascible and concupiscible powers, some habit aiding for the work of acting well. And since the good disposition of the power which moves through being moved depends on its conformity with the power that moves it, therefore, the virtue which is in the irascible and concupiscible powers is nothing else but a certain habitual conformity of these powers to reason. (S.T. *I-II,56,4c*)

The practical intellect, too, as we have seen, is subject to the moral virtue of *prudence*. Although prudence is in one sense, and essentially, a virtue of the practical intellect in so far as it is concerned with the knowledge of means to an end, yet in another sense prudence is a moral virtue in so far as the practical intellect must be rightly disposed to the good of man before it can choose rational means to the end. This disposition to the good depends upon the rectitude of the will. Because, then, prudence is the right reason about things to be done, it depends upon the will for its principles of judgment, that is, upon the good or end proposed by the will. The habitual judgment about means to an end proposed by the good will is prudence.

The will, also, is subject to virtue. Although the will, as we have said before, naturally tends towards good, yet it does not necessarily tend towards any particular good. Moreover, in order that it may tend towards a particular good it depends upon reason proposing a good. That it should constantly and easily choose the good so proposed by reason requires a virtue in the will. In this sense, all the moral virtues depend upon the virtue of the will commanding the other powers to good action in the light of reason. In this sense all the other virtues participate in the virtue of justice, since all receive their due by the will issuing its commands under the guidance of reason. But in another sense, when the good proposed by reason exceeds the will's capacity, when the reasoned good is not for the good of the individual immediately but for the good of others, whether of God or of one's fellow men, the virtue inclining the will constantly and easily to choose the good of others is *justice* in the strict sense of the word.

These four virtues—fortitude, temperance, prudence, and justice—have been called the *Cardinal Virtues,* from the Latin word *cardo* meaning a hinge, because they are the guiding virtues under which all the other moral virtues can be classified, and if human conduct is pivoted upon them and held up by them, it will move upright as a door upon its hinges. St. Thomas gives three reasons why there should be only four principal moral virtues. First, because there are four principles or potencies for moral action. Of these, three are the three appetites that man possesses: rational, concupiscible, and irascible. The fourth potency is the practical intellect. Although this intellect does not immediately tend to action, its cardinal virtue, prudence, is concerned with moral actions, which are practical. As we have seen, prudence is essentially an intellectual virtue, but in the matter to which it applies, it is a moral virtue.

Human virtue is a habit perfecting man in view of his doing good deeds. Now, in man there are but two principles of human action, viz., the intellect or reason and the appetite: for these are the two principles of movement in man as stated in De Anima (3,9,433a 4). Consequently every human virtue must needs be a perfection of one of these principles. . . . Prudence is essentially an intellectual virtue. But considered on the part of its matter, it has something in common with the moral virtues: for it is right reason about things to be done. It is in this sense that it is reckoned with the moral virtues. (S.T. I-II,58,3c).

The second reason why there are only four principal moral virtues is found in the formal principles, or in that which makes a virtue a virtue in its most essential sense. Because a virtue in its most definitive essence is a habit which gives a man readiness in acting according to the reason that is in him, we must necessarily conclude that all virtues can ultimately be classified under the principal virtues by which the order of reason is introduced into the various powers which are under the control of reason and will. Consequently, every virtue that effects good in the reason itself is related to prudence; every virtue that directs our activity towards the good of others is related to justice; every virtue that tempers the passions is in the field of temperance; and every virtue that makes the soul strong against the passions is found in fortitude.

For the formal principle of the virtue of which we speak now is good as defined by reason; which good can be considered in two ways. First, as existing in the very act of reason: and thus we have one principal virtue, called Prudence. Secondly, according as the reason puts its order into something else; either into operations, and then we have Justice; or into passions, and then we need two virtues. For the need of putting the order

of reason into the passions is due to their thwarting reason: and this occurs in two ways. First, by the passions inciting to something against
reason; and then the passions need a curb, which we call Temperance.
Secondly, by the passions withdrawing us from following the dictate of
reason, e.g., through fear of danger or toil: and then man needs to be
strengthened for that which reason dictates, lest he turn back; and to
this end there is Fortitude. (S.T. I-II,61,2c)

The third reason why there are four principal moral virtues
is found in the subject matter of morality with which they deal.
Moral problems are necessarily of four kinds only. Some lie in the
area of thought. Before a man can act morally he must not only be
inclined by a reasonable motive but must also deliberate and judge
of his action. Otherwise the element of reason and will is absent.
Hence man must know the direction and consequences of his inclinations. And this is the subject matter of prudence. Besides the
problem of knowledge, the rest of man's moral problems are in the
area of the appetites. It is true that man has no trouble in desiring
what is personally good for him, but he does have trouble in desiring
to give the good that belongs to others. This then is another subject
matter for virtue. Man needs to strengthen his will by justice, so that
he may easily and constantly give to others what he himself desires
for himself, namely, his rights.

And more: man has difficulties in the area of his concupiscible
and irascible appetites. Man is often beset by the problem of con-
straining his inordinate passions for food and drink and for the
pleasure of sex. To regulate these appetites and keep them within
the bounds of reason is most difficult at times. It is often no less a
problem to overcome one's fear of sensible evils which lie in the path
of one who is pursuing the moral good. Everyone is naturally
afraid of and is inclined to flee from suffering and death. But sometimes reason demands that man not only submit to but actually
accept such pain or suffering because such acceptation is a means
to a moral good. Sometimes, on the other hand, reason demands
that a man oppose such sensible evils for the sake of obtaining a
moral good. In the face of these evils man's irascible appetite needs
to be strengthened so that he pursue the moral good reasonably
well. The virtue which makes the concupiscible appetite submissive

to reason is temperance; the virtue which does the same for the irascible appetite is fortitude.

Secondly, they may be considered in point of their being denominated, each one from that which is foremost in its respective matter, and thus they are specific virtues, co-divided with the others. Yet they are called principal in comparison with the other virtues, on account of the importance of their matter: so that prudence is the virtue that commands; justice, the virtue which is about due actions between equals; temperance, the virtue which suppresses desires for the pleasures of touch; and fortitude, the virtue which strengthens against dangers of death. (S.T. I-II, 61,3)

7. The Theological Virtues

These four cardinal virtues are the basic moral virtues, but they are not the highest virtues, for the theological virtues in turn perfect and crown them. The cardinal virtues perfect human nature in its natural powers by giving the intellect and will and sensitive appetites a facility to attain the end that is befitting man as a human being, the end which perfectly human good could satisfy; for every virtue that effects good in the name of human reason is related to prudence; every virtue that directs man's activity towards the good of others relates to justice; every virtue that tempers the passions pertains to temperance; and every virtue that makes the soul firmer against the passions is a part of fortitude. The formal object of all these virtues is the rectitude of the human powers relative to a perfectly natural good.

But, when we were considering the end of man, the end to which man is actually ordered, we saw that man's nature, because it is in an elevated state, is actually demanding a participation in God's life, the Beatific Vision, which no purely human good can satisfy. Now, it is clear that if man in the present order of things is meant for an end beyond that which his natural activities can attain, it is necessary that fit means be given to him so that he may advance towards and actually attain this end. What man needs to

attain this supernatural end is not a new nature, not new operational potencies; for, if man received a new nature or potencies
specifically different from his intellect and will, he would become a
member of a new species of being and would attain the end towards which these new potencies are directed not as a human being
but as some other kind of being. What man needs is that God elevate the nature, the intellect, and will of man to a higher level of
being, and infuse into the potencies certain habits by which man
may direct himself to this supernatural end. Consequently, whereas
the natural virtues give man a facility of knowing and choosing the
right means to a good natural human life, the theological virtues
confer upon man an ability to know and be inclined towards his
ultimate end, which is God in the Beatific Vision.

   We may, then, define the theological virtues as principles of
action which God infuses into the rational potencies of man that
they may direct human actions immediately to God, man's ultimate and supernatural end.

Man is perfected by virtue for those actions by which he is directed to
happiness. Now man's happiness is twofold. One is proportioned to human nature, i.e., a happiness which man can obtain by means of the principles of his nature. The other is a happiness surpassing man's nature, and
which man can obtain by the power of God alone, by a kind of participation in the divine nature; and thus it is written (II Pet. 1,4) that by
Christ we are made partakers of the divine nature. Now because such happiness surpasses the power of human nature, man's natural principles, by
which he can act well according to his power, are not sufficient to direct
man to this same happiness. Hence it is necessary for man to receive from
God some additional principles, by which he may be directed to supernatural happiness, even as he is directed to his natural end by means of
his natural principles, although not without the divine assistance. Such
principles are called theological virtues. They are so called, first, because
their object is God, inasmuch as they direct us rightly to God; secondly,
because they are infused in us by God alone; thirdly, because these virtues
are not made known to us, save by divine revelation, contained in Holy
Scripture. (S.T. I-II,62,1c)

   We can conclude from this quotation that the theological virtues are principles of actions, that is, they are beginnings or sources

of actions which lead not to the natural end of man but rather to man's supernatural end. In other words, there is a likeness between the supernatural or theological virtues and the natural virtues which man can acquire.

Let us look at the similarity in the following manner: Man may and does obtain a facility in knowing the first principles of judgment about practical actions by the power of his intellect and the easily acquired habit of understanding. Following upon these first principles man may acquire the moral virtues which give him a facility to perfect his potencies for performing morally good acts. In a like manner, in the supernatural order, the theological virtues, which elevate the natural powers of man so that he might know and love his supernatural end, give him the principles by which he may act on a level higher than his natural potencies permit. Following upon the reception of these theological virtues man receives infused moral virtues which complete the supernatural organization. The infused moral virtues have the same names as those of the natural moral virtues. Thus, there are infused prudence, justice, fortitude, and temperance. But we should notice that while the infused moral virtues have the same names as the acquired natural virtues, they are not the same virtues; rather they are entitatively different because they bestow upon man a different capacity. For example, the natural virtue of fortitude gives man an ability to remain firm against the evils that might deter him from moving towards his natural end, which he knows from human reason; infused supernatural fortitude, on the other hand, bestows upon man an ability to moderate his irascible passions by means of truths which are known by divine revelation. To give a concrete example; the acquired natural virtue of fortitude would lead a man to undergo pain and suffering for the sake of his body's health so that he might live a longer life on earth. But infused supernatural fortitude moves a man to give up his life rather than commit a moral evil, as St. Thomas More did in accepting martyrdom rather than consent to Henry VIII's acting as the head of the Church which Christ founded. The theological virtues and their accompanying infused moral virtues order man's actions directly to God; the natural moral virtues order man's actions to man's own good.

But the theological virtues are distinguished from the moral virtues not only by reason of their direct objects but for two other reasons. The moral virtues are acquired by the repetition of the same action of a power which is under the control of the will; the theological virtues are infused by God alone and are not the result of human effort. Finally, the moral virtues are known through the natural light of human reason, whereas the theological virtues are the matter of divine revelation.

Because human acts are those that proceed from the intellect and will, so moral virtues must be principles which give the intellect and will of man the ability to move towards natural ends which are known and loved. Similarly, supernatural motivation of human action requires principles in the intellect and will. These principles are the three theological virtues of *faith, hope,* and *charity*.

If man is to move towards God as his supernatural, ultimate end, he must know this end and the means to obtain it. He cannot know these by the light of human reason; hence he must obtain them from God. This is *faith*. Faith is an intellectual virtue, perfecting the mind by giving it truth, but it is not truth that is clearly or comprehensively understood; hence it is the will that moves the intellect to assent to it. Consequently, St. Thomas defines faith as *"a habit of the mind, whereby eternal life is begun in us, making the intellect assent to what is non-apparent."* (S.T. II-II,4,1c) Or faith may be defined as *a theological virtue that inclines the intellect, under the influence of the will, to give a firm assent to revealed truths, because of the authority of God.* Faith, then, gives to man a knowledge that he could not have of himself, whereby he knows what his ultimate end is and the means to obtain it; it directs the intellect of man to his real ultimate end. This knowledge is of things revealed by God to help man towards his goal. It is a source of light to the mind whereby the scope of man's knowledge of God and the things of God is widened, or insight into moral truths deepened. Faith, in other words, perfects the intellect of man by helping it to apprehend not only the supernatural end of man, but also the means towards that end, by uniting man's intellect to the divine wisdom. Far from being a curb to man's inquiry into truth, it is an invitation to search and a direction to truth.

Hope, on the other hand, directs the will by pointing it to its supernatural end as something accessible to man. It is defined as *a theological virtue that makes us desire God as our highest good, and expect with a firm confidence perfect happiness and the means of attaining it, because of God's goodness and power.* (S.T. II-II, 17-20) Just as faith gives us a knowledge of the supernatural end, so hope moves our will to direct our actions to it by making us trust that this end, though difficult of attaining, will be ours by the assistance of divine omnipotence which elevates us and helps us to overcome the difficulties in a good moral life.

Charity, finally, perfects the will and by so doing attaches it to the supernatural good of man, which is God. It is defined as *a theological virtue that causes us to love God above all things, and, therefore, as the object of our perfect happiness.* (S.T. II-II,65,5 ad 1) Charity, then, is the most perfect love that man can have, the love of God which puts in order all other loves, desires, and acts. By reason of the virtue of charity, man is directed to his last end, God himself. Through charity man loves God himself, and, consequently, with this virtue man is directed to the ultimate and supreme end which instigates and directs all the moral actions of man, giving the moral acts and virtues an excellence and value which they could not possess of themselves.

We must conclude, then, that on the supernatural level there are seven principal infused virtues which are habitual principles of good human action. They are: faith, hope, and charity, which are called theological virtues because their acts are ordered immediately to God; and the four infused moral virtues which parallel in name and in object the four natural or cardinal virtues of prudence, justice, temperance, and fortitude. How these infused moral virtues differ from the cardinal virtues has been indicated. But why there should be a need for the infused moral virtues and all their cognate virtues is discovered in the fact that the supernatural life does not suppress nor destroy human nature but it supposes and builds upon it. If we were to understand how this is true we would have a knowledge of grace. But since a knowledge of grace is one of the objects of theology, let us leave the subject by indicating the line of reasoning which theology uses to demonstrate the meaning and need of the supernatural life. If man is to perform morally good acts which lead him to his ultimate end he needs not only a principle of existence or human soul and its operational powers of intellect and will but he also needs the moral virtues; if he is to perform acts which are suitable for his supernatural vision of God, he must possess a principle of existence or sanctifying grace, which elevates the soul to the divine level of existence, and in addition the theological virtues which elevate the intellect and will so that they in their acts may be ordered to this supernatural end, as well as the infused moral virtues by which man may habitually perform actions which lead directly to this supernatural end.

8. *The Mean of Virtue*

Before concluding the consideration of virtue, we should say something about the *mean* of virtue. In defining virtue we have always insisted that it is a power to perform actions which are in accord with right reason. Doing right is doing what is conformed to rational nature and avoiding what is unsuitable either by excess or by defect: the rational choice is in the mean between these two. The moral order may be illustrated by the physical. Too much exercise and too little impair the strength; so too with meat and drink in regard to health; but diet and exercise in moderation and in proportion to the subject create, increase, and preserve both health and strength. To acquire a good, which is the purpose of virtue, is to use the right means; the using of means to an end implies the using of them in moderation, not in excess for then we shall overshoot the mark, nor again so feebly and inadequately as to fall short of it. Since virtue, then, is a means that reason uses to attain the rational good of man, virtue must be used by reason so that the end in view will be attained. We must, then, conclude that the mean of virtue is reason itself.

The mean of virtue, however, cannot be settled by an abstract rule that gives a definite measure which will apply in every case. Reason, it is true, is the mean, but reason does not prescribe the same course of conduct for every variety of circumstances and character; rather, reason varies in its requirements according to individual opportunities, character, and circumstances; and, therefore, the mean will have to be judged not with reference to the thing or action but with reference to the relation of the thing or action to the person. St. Thomas says that the mean of moral virtue is determined in relation to ourselves, and that it is a mean not of the thing but of reason.

However, the mean of reason coincides with the mean of the thing in the case of one virtue, namely, the virtue of justice. For justice is concerned with action and not with passions. Now it is in relation to our passions and other subjective needs that the requirements of individuals differ from one another. The mean, therefore, of the virtue of justice is the mean of the thing, which is the same for all men. But in the case of the other moral virtues the mean is a mean of reason, not of things. Consequently, the mean of the other moral virtues is not the same for all men. What would be a sin in one man might be a morally good act in another. Prudence, temperance, and fortitude, for example, will always make allowance for needs and character. But the law of justice is that we give to each other his due.

The mean of virtue can be understood in two ways. First, according as the mean is found in the act itself of reason, as though the very act of reason were reduced to a mean. In this sense, since moral virtue perfects, not the act of reason, but the act of the appetitive power, the mean of moral virtue is not the mean of reason. Secondly, the mean of reason may be considered as that which the reason establishes in some particular matter. In this sense, every mean of moral virtue is a mean of reason; for, as was stated above, moral virtue is said to consist in a mean through conformity with right reason.

But it happens sometimes that the mean of reason is also a real mean, and in that case the mean of moral virtue is the real mean (for instance, in justice). On the other hand, sometimes the mean of reason is not the real mean, but is established in relation to us. Such is the mean in all the other moral virtues. The reason for this is that justice is about operations, which deal with external things, wherein the right has to be established absolutely and in itself, as was stated above. Hence the mean of reason in justice is the same as the real mean, in so far, namely, as justice gives to each one his due, neither more nor less. But the other moral virtues deal with interior passions, wherein the right cannot be established in the same way, since men vary in their relations to their passions. Hence the rectitude of reason has to be established in the passion with reference to us, who are influenced through the passions. (S.T. I-II,64,2c)

The moral virtues, then, have a mean, but have the intellectual virtues? To answer this question, we must distinguish between the virtues which belong to the speculative intellect and the virtue of prudence which belongs to the practical intellect. Now, the virtues of the speculative intellect, like the moral, are ordered to the good. But the good of the speculative intellect is truth, according to which the mind affirms that a thing is that which it is, or is not that which it is not. Consequently, the measure of truth of the virtues of the speculative intellect is reality itself. If the intellect is not conformed to it either because it attributes more to reality than is really there, or because it does not predicate enough of reality, it misses the mean of these virtues, which is conformity between intellect and object. But in the practical intellect, the virtue of which is prudence, the mean is somewhat different. The proper object of the practical intellect is that which the will ought to truly desire. In other words, the mean of the practical intellect is that which a man ought to do to attain the end which is perfect good. Hence, we may say that while the reality of things is the measure of truth in the speculative as well as in the practical intellect, the reality as it is in itself is the measure for the speculative intellect, the reality of things as it is apprehended by the intellect is the measure of truth in the practical intellect. Consequently, we may say that the mean of prudence is that which a prudent man ought to desire: the subject is the measure of the mean of the virtue of prudence.

We may add, since we have been treating of the moral virtues alone, that there is both a mean and no mean in the theological virtues. This peculiarity arises from the fact that these virtues are concerned immediately with God himself. Since God is the object of these virtues, it is impossible for man to believe, hope, and love God enough, for he is infinite Truth, Omnipotence and Goodness.

But in relation to man who has these virtues there is a mean which is to be determined by the individual capacity of the individual man himself. What is the individual capable of believing, hoping for, and loving? This is the mean of the theological virtues.

As was stated above, the mean of virtue depends on conformity with its rule or measure, in so far as one may exceed or fall short of that rule. Now the measure of theological virtue may be twofold. One is taken from the very nature of virtue, and thus the measure and rule of theological virtue is God Himself. For our faith is ruled according to divine truth; charity, according to His goodness; hope, according to the immensity of His omnipotence and loving kindness. This measure surpasses all human power, so that never can we love God as much as He ought to be loved, nor believe and hope in Him as much as we should. Much less, therefore, can there be excess in such things. Accordingly the good of such virtues does not consist in a mean, but increases the more we approach to the summit.

The other rule or measure of theological virtue is by comparison with us: for although we cannot be borne towards God as much as we ought, yet we should approach Him by believing, hoping and loving, according to the measure of our condition. Consequently, it is possible to find a mean and extreme in theological virtue, accidently and in reference to us. (S.T. I-II,64,4c)

9. Sin and Malice

Virtue, as we have defined it, is essentially ordered towards the doing of good acts. The acts that produce virtues, or that follow after virtue, are ordered acts, that is, they are acts which lead to man's ultimate end. Disordered acts and those that are not related to their end as they should be are given the name of *sins*. Moreover, virtue is a good disposition. The evil quality opposed to it goes by the name of *malice*. Lastly virtue is also a habit, an acquired and set or permanent disposition, and what is directly opposed to it as a habit is called *vice*. Sin then is an act contrary to the act that produces virtue; malice is the quality contrary to the quality of virtue; vice is the habit contrary to the habit which is virtue. Now if we ask in what powers of the soul sin and vice can be, it will appear that they can be in any power in which virtues can be. Moral evil, sin, malice, or vice can be in those powers of the soul which are under the control of the will.

In general, there is but one immediate or efficient cause of sin, malice, and vice, as there is but one efficient cause of good moral acts and virtues, and that is the will. The will alone is the ultimate source of sin, for it alone can never be forced to sin. This we have seen in Chapter III on The Moral Act. We have also seen that the will chooses to commit sin when it chooses to act contrary to reason. When it so chooses, it is not because it desires evil for evil's sake, but because it tends towards an apparent good when it should tend towards the rational or real good.

But there can be other things which are the indirect causes of sin. These sources of sin which are internal to man are three: ignorance, passion, and malice. In a previous chapter we have considered the influence that the passions and ignorance may have upon the will. Consequent ignorance affects the moral act, but antecedent ignorance does not.

If we suppose that ignorance is vincible, but that it really exists, that it deals with something we are not bound to know, and that it keeps from us such a circumstance of the act that we would not do the act if we knew the circumstance, the effect of such ignorance is to make the act really involuntary. If we are in such ignorance we then do one thing, though we think we do another. In such teaching as that of St. Thomas, in which the willed act is based on the rational knowledge of the end desired, the voluntary quality of acts that are done is in proportion to their rationality. As for measuring in each particular case the degree of ignorance which is mixed with the act, and the resulting degree of freedom, this is plainly a complex task, and we cannot formulate *a priori* any but general directions for it.

Just because every sin is willed, ignorance can cut down the sin just as far as it cuts down the freedom of the act; but if ignorance does not re-

strict freedom, it in no way lightens the sin. And certainly the ignorance which excuses outright from sin because it takes away freedom, does not merely make the sin less, but does away with it. On the other hand, an ignorance that does not cause, but simply accompanies sin neither decreases nor increases the sin. The only ignorance that can lessen sin is that which is the occasion of sin, yet this is not a blanket excuse from sin. It may be, first, that the ignorance, directly and in itself, is willed, as when one of his own will remains ignorant of something so that he can the more freely sin; such an ignorance seems to increase the voluntariness and the sin, for it is the attachment of the will to the sin that makes one willing to bear the evil of ignorance so as to have the liberty to sin. But sometimes the ignorance which causes sin is willed not directly, but indirectly and by accident; for instance, when a man is not willing to trouble himself with studies, and the result is that he is ignorant, or when he wills to take an immoderate sip of wine, and the result is that he gets drunk and lacks discretion. Such ignorance does lessen freedom and, therefore, the sin; for when a man does not know that a thing is a sin, we may not say that his will directly and of itself commits the sin, but only as a by-product, and there is then less contempt and, as a consequence, less sin. (S.T. I-II,76,4c)

The same is true of the passions. Some passions may be so violent and sudden that they wholly prevent the use of reason. Such passions make deliberation impossible and the act performed under their influence is neither voluntary nor free. In all but these extreme cases, however, a man remains master of his acts because he is able to deliberate and to choose freely. Consequently, most often passions are consequent, that is, they are either deliberately caused or they are not reasonably controlled; in either case the actions which are done under the influence of passion are morally imputable to the agent. Such passions can be the indirect cause of evil actions because they influence the reason by exaggerating the sensible good or evil of an object contrary to what the reason knows to be the rational good, or they influence the will by distracting it from its proper function of following reason, i.e., the passion may be of such intensity that the agent's attention is so wholly occupied with the passion that the will does not follow reason. Thus passion may prevent the will from choosing its proper good, namely, the rational good.

As the Philosopher states (Ethic. vii.2,1145b23), the opinion of Socrates was that knowledge can never be overcome by passion; wherefore he held every virtue to be a kind of knowledge, and sin a kind of ignorance. In this he was somewhat right, because, since the object of the will is a good or an apparent good, it is never moved to an evil, unless that which is not good appear good in some respect to the reason; so that the will would never tend to evil, unless there were ignorance or error in the reason. Hence it is written (Prov. 14,22): They err that work evil.

Experience, however, shows that many act contrary to the knowledge that they have, and this is confirmed by Divine authority, according to the words of Luke 12,47: The servant who knew the will of his lord . . . and did not . . . shall be beaten with many stripes, and James 4,17: To him . . . who knoweth to do good, and doth it not, to him it is a sin. Consequently he was not altogether right, and it is necessary, with the Philosopher (Ethic. vii.3,1146b31) to make a distinction. Because, since man is directed to right action by a twofold knowledge, viz., universal and particular, a defect in either of them suffices to hinder the rectitude of the will and of the deed, as stated above (q.76,a.1). It may happen, then, that a man has some knowledge in general, e.g., that no fornication is lawful, and yet he does not know in particular that this act, which is fornication, must not be done; and this suffices for the will to follow the universal knowledge of the reason. Again, it must be observed that nothing prevents a thing which is known habitually from not being considered actually: so that it is possible for man to have correct knowledge not only in general but also in particular, and yet not to consider his knowledge actually: and in such a case it does not seem difficult for a man to act counter to what he does not actually consider. Now, that a man sometimes fails to consider in particular what he knows habitually, may happen through mere lack of attention: for instance, a man who knows geometry, may not attend to the consideration of geometrical conclusions, which he is ready to consider at any moment. Sometimes man fails to consider actually what he knows habitually, on account of some hindrance supervening, e.g., some external occupation, or some bodily infirmity; and, in this way, a man who is in a state of passion, fails to consider in particular what he knows in general, in so far as the passions hinder him from considering it. Now it hinders him in three ways. First, by way of distraction, as explained above (q.77,a.1). Secondly, by way of opposition, because a passion often inclines to something contrary to what man knows in general. Thirdly, by way of bodily transmutation, the result of which is that the reason is somehow fettered so as not to exercise its act freely, even as sleep or drunkenness, on account of some change wrought on the body, fetters the use of reason. That this takes place in the passions is evident from the fact that sometimes, when the passions are very intense, man loses the use of reason altogether: for many have gone out of their minds through excess of love or anger. It is in this way that passion draws the reason to judge in particular, against the knowledge which it has in general. (S.T. I-II,77,2c)

The third and last interior cause of sin is in the will. Just as the intellectual cause of sin is *ignorance,* and its sense cause is *passion,* so its voluntary cause is *malice,* or, to use the expression of St. Thomas, *certain malice.* Malice means a disorder in the will itself. The meaning of this is as follows: to sin by malice is not to commit moral evil through ignorance nor under the urge of passion, but by the deliberate will to choose a lesser good when it ought to choose the greater.

Man like any other being has naturally an appetite for the good; and so if his appetite incline away to evil, this is due to corruption or disorder in some one of the principles of man: for it is thus that sin occurs in the actions of natural things. Now the principles of human acts are the intellect, and the appetite, both rational (i.e., the will) and sensitive. Therefore even as sin occurs in human acts, sometimes through a defect of the intellect, as when anyone sins through ignorance, and sometimes through a defect in the sensitive appetite, as when anyone sins through passions, so too does it occur through a defect consisting in a disorder of the will. Now the will is out of order when it loves more the lesser good. Again, the consequence of loving a thing less is that one chooses to suffer some hurt in its regard, in order to obtain a good that one loves more: as when a man, even knowingly, suffers the loss of a limb, that he may save his life which he loves more. Accordingly, when an inordinate will loves some temporal good, e.g., riches or pleasures, more than the order of reason of Divine law, or Divine charity, or some such thing, it follows that it is willing to suffer the loss of some spiritual good, so that it may obtain possession of some temporal good. Now evil is merely the privation of some good; and so a man wishes knowingly a spiritual evil, which is evil simply, whereby he is deprived of a spiritual good, in order to possess a temporal good; wherefore he is said to sin through certain malice or on purpose, because he chooses evil knowingly. (S.T. I-II, 78,1c)

Malice may be either actual or habitual. A man may choose evil deliberately in a particular act; thus, a man may knowingly and willingly choose to perjure himself rather than to go to prison. This would be actual malice. Habitual malice is a quality of the will acquired by repeated acts which inclines the will to repeated evil acts.

The malice through which anyone sins, may be taken to denote habitual malice, in the sense in which the Philosopher (Ethic. II,5,1105b19) calls an evil habit by the name of malice, just as a good habit is called virtue: and in this way anyone is said to sin through malice when he sins through the inclination of a habit. It may also denote actual malice, whether by malice we mean the choice itself of evil (and thus anyone is said to sin through malice, in so far as he sins through making a choice of evil. (S.T. I-II,78, ad 3)

That the habitual disorder of malice occur, it is necessary that a permanent vicious disposition, otherwise called a habit, incline the will towards the evil act, as the habits which are virtues incline it towards well-doing. Each time, then, that a habit, or a permanent and acquired disposition is the cause of the evil act which the will chooses, we say that the sin is committed with malice certain of its deed and fully responsible for its choice. Yet the reverse is not true. While every evil act chosen by a vicious disposition is of certain malice, there are some acts of certain malice that are not born of a vice. We can do some acts conformed to virtue without being virtuous, and we can equally commit some evil acts without falling into the vice to which they correspond, for virtues and vices are habits, whereas an isolated act is not a habit.

As St. Thomas indicates, it is obvious that sin committed with malice is the most grievous of sins. Because, first of all, sin is ultimately caused by the will, and never does the will more completely cause sin than when it commits the sin of itself as it does when it acts from malice, and not from ignorance or passion. Secondly, passion and ignorance need not be permanent, for the former comes and goes and the latter can be corrected, but malice is a permanent quality so that he who sins through malice remains longer in his sin. Finally, the malicious or vicious man is ill-disposed with regard to his end, but the man who suffers a passion is turned from his end only for a while, until the passion passes. The malicious man overthrows the very principle of morality, for he hates his rational good; the man who is influenced by passion does not deny the principle of morality, but refuses to be guided by it for the moment.

Let us conclude this consideration of virtue and vice by contrasting the two. To the good moral habit, which is called virtue, there is opposed the contrary evil moral habit, which is vice. To the virtuous act, there is opposed the evil act, which is sin. To the inclination of the will to good, which is the result of virtue, there is opposed the inclination of the will to moral evil, which is the result of vice. (S.T. I-II,78,4c)

10. *The External Causes of Sin*

To round out our consideration of the causes of sin, we must mention two external causes of sin. These are the devil and original sin.

The devil is not a direct nor a sufficient cause of sin, but he can incite men to sin by suggesting objects to the senses or by persuading the reason. Original sin, too, is an external cause of sin in so far as a result of this sin, which was committed by another man, Adam, has been to so weaken man's nature that he is more inclined to evil now than he would have been if this sin had not been committed. It is true that we know of these two external sources of sin only from faith, nevertheless we must take them into consideration when we are attempting to give a complete explanation of the moral life of man as he is in this present existential order.

Readings

Adler, M., A *Dialectic of Morals*, c. 6, pp. 74-107.
Aristotle, *Nicomachean Ethics*, bk. I, c. 13; bk. II, cc. 1-9; bk. III, cc. 6-12; bk. IV, complete.

Bourke, V. J., "Habitus in the Thomistic Metaphysics of Potency and Act," *Essays in Thomism*, ed. R. E. Brennan, pp. 101-109.

Brennan, Sr. Rose Emmanuella, *The Intellectual Virtues According to the Philosophy of St. Thomas*, pp. 77-110.

Butler, J., *A Dissertation upon the Nature of Virtue, Ethical Theories*, ed. Melden, pp. 241-246.

Cronin, Michael, *The Science of Ethics*, vol. I, c. 18.

Farrell, W., *A Companion to the Summa*, vol. II, cc. 8-11.

Gilson, E., *The Philosophy of St. Thomas Aquinas*, pp. 311-324.

—— *Moral Values and Moral Life*, c. 5.

James, W., *Psychology*, c. 10.

Klubertanz, George, "The Unity of Human Activity," *The Modern Schoolman*, XXVII (1950), pp. 75-85.

Leibell, J. F., *Readings in Ethics*. The following articles on virtue are suggested:

"Virtue," Augustine Waldron, pp. 213-221.
"The cardinal virtues," Joseph Rickaby, pp. 236-240.
"Perfect virtues are never one without the other," St. Francis de Sales, pp. 241-245.

Pieper, Josef, "On the Christian Idea of Man," *The Review of Politics*, XI, 1 (Jan., 1949), pp. 3-16.

Plato, *Meno, Protagoras, Phaedo*, and bk. IV of the *Republic*.

St. Thomas, *Summa Theologica*, I-II, pp. 49-67.

CHAPTER XIII

SUMMARY

1. Grace Is an Extrinsic Principle of Human Acts

In Chapter VI on "Law in General," it was said that the ethicians know of an external source of good actions, a principle which regulates man from the outside to a definite course of action. This principle is law and it has its source in God himself. But another help of God is also required if man is to lead the good life. This external help is grace.

While admitting that grace is not an object of philosophical study, yet it seems necessary that we must go outside the limits of philosophy to the field of theology if we are to have a complete ethics. This need, we remember, was shown in the discussion about man's perfect happiness. But theology is also necessary in other matters of ethics as well, particularly when it is a question of knowing how man can act so as to attain perfect happiness. This knowledge which theology offers is the fact of grace, which God offers to man so that he may lead a morally good life and ultimately enjoy perfect happiness.

However, we must clearly distinguish the help which God gives man by grace from the help which he gives by his general concursus. Let us recall from the study of natural theology that this world and all within it is not self-sufficient. Not only is God's creative act required if the world is to be, but he must continue this same creative act if things are to continue to exist and to act. The same is true of man and his human actions. If man is to exist God must create him; if man is to act in a human way God must help him; God must concur with man when he freely acts. Such a concursus does not mean that man does not possess the natural capacity for knowledge and free choice by which he can freely choose those acts which he knows are conducive to perfect happiness. It does mean, however, that man, like any creature, is dependent upon the power of God to act and reach his perfection. As the earth is dependent upon its own natural capacities together with the divine concursus to initiate and complete its revolutions about the sun, so man is dependent on his own natural powers together with the concursus of God to initiate and complete his moral actions.

This power which God gives in order that his creatures may exercise their natural powers must be clearly distinguished from grace, which is not only a help to exercise man's natural powers in a natural way but also in a supernatural manner. In a summary way, for the profound nature of grace belongs to theology, let us explain the need that man has for grace in a natural as well as in a supernatural way.

2. Reasons for the Need of Grace

St. Thomas has written the summary which is useful for our purposes. He writes:

Man's nature may be looked at in two ways: first, in its integrity, as it was in our first parents before sin; secondly, as it is corrupted in us after the sin of our first parents. Now in both states human nature needs the help of God, as First Mover, to do or will any good whatever, as was stated above. But in the state of integrity of nature, as regards the sufficiency of operative powers, man by his natural endowments could will and do the good proportioned to his nature, which is the good of acquired virtue;

but he could not do the good that exceeded his nature, which is the good of infused virtue. But in the state of corrupted nature, man falls short even of what he can do by his nature, so that he is unable to fulfill all of it by his own natural powers. Yet because human nature is not altogether corrupted by sin, namely, so as to be shorn of every good of nature, even in the state of corrupted nature it can, by virtue of its natural endowment, perform some particular good, such as to build dwellings, plant vineyards and the like; yet it cannot do all the good natural to it, so as to fall short in nothing. In the same way, a sick man can of himself make some movements, yet he cannot be perfectly moved with the movement of one in health, unless by the help of medicine he be cured.

Hence in the state of the integrity of nature, man needs a gratuitous strength superadded to natural strength for one reason, viz., in order to do and will supernatural good; but in the state of corrupted nature he needs it for two reasons, viz., in order to be healed and, furthermore, in order to carry out works of supernatural virtue, which are meritorious. Beyond this, in both states man needs the divine help that he may be moved to act well. (S.T. I-II,109,2c)

The first reason why man needs grace is the present state of his nature. Theologians tell us that man is not now living in the same condition as Adam was before the fall, before Original Sin. Before his sin Adam's nature needed no other help of God to perform naturally good acts except the help which we have described as the general concursus of God, as the First Mover. The reason was that the nature of Adam was integral, that is, not only was man himself favorably situated in his relation to irrational creatures about him, but within himself there was a most perfect harmony between his powers of sense and rational appetites. In addition to this, man's will was subject to God. Because of this condition of harmony and peace between man and God and man and all other things man could habitually act in a manner befitting his nature. He could, for example, do those acts prescribed by the Ten Commandments, without any special help of God. This is not to say, however, that he could perform acts which exceeded his nature without a special divine help which we call grace.

Though Adam and nature in this original state of integrity were so admirably situated for the performance of natural actions, Adam was still free; his nature was still a free nature. Being free, there was always the possibility of sin. In fact, Adam did sin and as a result many effects followed. Because Adam in his sin refused to subject his will to God, the human will is not now so perfectly adjusted to God, as the Supreme Good and Ultimate End; neither are the powers within man himself harmoniously ordered among themselves, but the rational powers have lost their original ease in controlling the lower sense powers. Finally, man is not as favorably related to irrational nature as he was in the state of integrity. All of these effects of Adam's sin theologians have called Original Sin.

Because human nature is now lacking its original condition of being well ordered towards God and within itself, man now needs a special help of God not only to perform good acts which exceed his nature, but also to habitually act in a naturally good manner. This does not mean that man has lost his nature or that his nature has been intrinsically corrupted, for man can now perform many naturally good acts such as building houses, planting seed, making clothes, eating and drinking and other usual actions necessary for the physical well-being of his body; but it does mean that man cannot now perform all naturally morally good acts without the help of grace.

We should be clear about this. In the state of integrity man, as we have said, could have observed what is prescribed in the Decalogue (S.T. I-II,109,4) without any special help of God. In the state of fallen nature man cannot observe the commandments without a special help of God; not because man's nature is essentially different, but because the original disposition of his nature which made it easier for him to act has been lost. But in both the state of integrity and his present state man needs the special help of God to perform actions which are supernaturally good and meritorious for his supernatural end.

The second reason why man needs grace is his supernatural end. This problem has been discussed in Chapter II, The End of Man. There it was shown that the philosopher can demonstrate that nothing short of God can be man's perfect happiness, but the philosopher knows nothing about the character of this possession of God. To complement the inadequacy of ethics as a philosophical science, the philosopher must permit the theologian to help him understand the meaning of man's ultimate happiness. Although the theologian does not have an exhaustive knowledge of the nature of the Beatific Vision, still his knowledge of man's perfect happiness is fuller than the philosopher's. The theologian tells us that man's ultimate end, which is the knowledge and love of God, is not a natural but a supernatural end. To achieve this end, to perform actions which will merit this end, man must be raised to a supernatural level wherein he may act in a supernatural manner. The means by which God elevates man is called grace.

St. Thomas, following the belief of all Catholics, tells us that grace is a gift freely bestowed on man by God in order that man may act in a supernatural manner. The nature of grace is "a supernatural quality superadded to the soul, whereby man may be moved by Him sweetly and promptly to acquire eternal good." (S.T. I-II,-110,1 and 2)

3. Ethics a Philosophical Science

With St. Thomas, then, we conclude that fallen nature or man needs grace because of the weakened state of fallen nature and because of the supernatural character of man's perfect happiness. However, we must not miss the point that although man's present nature is a fallen nature it is still a human nature and so possesses all that is essential for human nature. We can, therefore, acquire knowledge of many things about existing man, and what we do acquire is certainly true, even though it may be incomplete.

Consequently, having accepted the facts about man which metaphysics and the philosophy of man give, we have gone on to build the philosophical science of ethics. Like all sciences, ethics must begin with, and be held accountable to, data or given facts. The data of physics are observed motions; with these it starts, and to these, no matter how elaborate its intermediate constructions, it must be kept responsible. What, then, are the data of ethics? There are two: *good* and *ought*. These two are facts of man's consciousness, namely, when man acts deliberately he must seek the good.

Good then is the end of all voluntary actions. It is here that the word *end* shows its importance, for if a science is a certain knowledge of things in their ultimate causes, then ethics must explain the end, for it is the reason why men act deliberately; ethics must inquire what is meant by end and what this end is and how it may be the same as good. This explains the most fundamental meaning of the science of ethics. It belongs to ethics to consider human acts as ordered to man's ultimate end. Ethics, then, is the science of the ultimate end as such and in this it differs formally from all other sciences.

But the science of the ultimate end or good is only part of the science, because ethics is also concerned with the realization of happiness; hence, the human act must be understood in order to have a complete understanding of happiness. The human act is a most complex entity and ethics treats of its many components separately but does not deny that there is a unity of being in the very complexity. The ethician particularly recognizes that the human act is not merely the result of man's rational powers, but that it is inseparably bound up with the passions or the emotions and how man experiences them.

It is comparatively easy to distinguish and explain the three rational operations of knowledge, voluntariness, and free choice which are necessary elements of the human act. It is also comparatively easy to explain the role which the passions may play in the human act. For all of these explanations the science of ethics has recourse to the conclusions of the philosophy of man and experimental psychology. Thus ethics is a wholly rational science in its treatment of the human act.

4. The Problem of the Passions

The human act is always a unit action composed of these rational and nonrational elements. This duality presents a problem. As far back in the history of thought as it is now possible to go we find men who have observed that there is a conflict between the rational and nonrational elements, between the human spirit and the human body, between, as St. Paul writes, a "law in my members fighting against the law of my mind." (*Romans* 7,23) Everyone at times is conscious of this conflict within himself. Medical men, religious counselors, psychologists see this conflict in its more extreme forms many times. But it is difficult, if not impossible, to give a satisfactory explanation of it on purely rational grounds.

The philosophy of man tells us that man has passions because of his animal nature. This is why the Stoics in Greek thought, and Kant in modern thought, looked upon the passions as foreign to man's rational nature, and because of the passions' antirational tendencies these philosophers thought that man should put down or root out his passions as far as possible. That the passions are, at times, the source or cause of unreasonable actions, is a fact known to all. If man is a rational being, then, these philosophers argue, man must destroy his passions.

St. Thomas takes another view of man's animal nature. Because man is by definition a rational animal, his animal nature and his passions are good in themselves and can act in a morally good way if they are under the control of reason. To keep them under the control of reason, however, is not always easy. There is many a conflict waged within man himself between reason and passion. But if man is a living unity how shall we account for this apparent duality? There is no acceptable answer to be found in philosophy. There is an answer in theology and it is to be found in *Original Sin*. We may recall that we have said that nature, in its state of integrity, was not only harmoniously ordered to God as its Highest Good, but its powers were also harmoniously ordered among themselves. Because of Original Sin, however, such order is not found in the present state of man's nature. It is this disorder which we now experience in the conflict between reason and passions. As St. Thomas writes:

As a result of original justice, the reason had perfect hold over the lower parts of the soul, while reason itself was perfected by God and was subject to Him. Now this same original justice was forfeited through the sin of our first parent; so that all the powers of the soul are left, at it were, destitute of their proper order, whereby they are naturally directed to virtue; which destitution is called a wounding of nature.

Again, there are four of the soul's powers that can be the subject of virtue, viz., the reason, where prudence resides, the will, where justice is, the irascible, the subject of fortitude, and the concupiscible, the subject of temperance. Therefore in so far as the reason is deprived of its order to the true, there is the wound of ignorance; in so far as the will is deprived of its order to the good, there is the wound of malice; in so far as the irascible is deprived of its order to the arduous, there is the wound of weakness; and in so far as the concupiscible is deprived of its order to the delectable, moderated by reason, there is the wound of concupiscence.

Accordingly these are the four wounds inflicted on the whole of human nature as a result of our first parent's sin. (S.T. I-II, 85,3)

Not only, then, does theology give the reason why man sometimes experiences difficulty with his passion in his attempts to act reasonably, it also tells us how man is to surmount such difficulties: if the loss of the ease of performing morally good actions is due to the wound inflicted by the loss of grace it can be repaired only by the help of grace.

5. The Norm of Goodness

If ethics demonstrates that only morally good acts can lead man to his ultimate good, it also shows how man is to know whether he is acting in a good manner. If ethics is to be a science of the good of human acts, it must not only prove what this ultimate good is, but it must also establish the measure or norm by which man can know good and evil actions so that he can arrive at this ultimate good. To demonstrate such a norm or measure ethics once more accepts the principle from the philosophy of man that, unlike other living things, it is proper to man to live according to what he knows to be true. This is not denying that human acts must be voluntary, but a man wills only according to what he knows. For an act to be human or moral it must be subject to reason.

This subjection of an act to reason is not to merely any reason, but to *right* reason. It is in this sense that St. Thomas thinks that the measure of good and bad in morality is right reason. But we must be clear about the meaning of *right* as a word qualifying *reason*. There can be reason in both the speculative and practical orders of reasoning. Since human acts are in the practical order, right reason in this order does not mean logical thinking as much as it means thinking rightly about the end with the intention of willing in accord with this reason. This meaning of *right* follows from the nature of the practical order wherein end is primary and the reason is concerned with action only as ordered to an end.

But even though right reason is the norm of morality, we must remember that reason does not operate in a vacuum nor does right reason about one's moral actions determine its own right and wrong spontaneously without relation to being. Like all reasoning, moral reasoning depends upon the content which reality or being itself gives to it. Now in moral reasoning the object or content that is given is that man's ultimate end is God himself, and if right reason is the measure of morality it is only such on the condition that it is thinking rightly about this as this end is known to it.

But more than this. Because Thomistic ethics is dependent on its metaphysics, ethics accepts the fact that there are natures and that ends or purposes are proportioned to natures. From this we may conclude that if natures are known ends are also known, and if ends are known natures are also known. Wherefore, if right reasoning about the end of man with the intention of willing in accordance with reason is the measure of morality, we can conclude that right reason about the nature of man with the intention of willing in accordance with reason is the measure of morality. In both actions of reasoning, reason does not arbitrarily make its own object, but it begins with an object that being itself gives it: the end of human nature.

It should not be a matter of surprise that right reason as a measure of morality can develop, for we know that right reason about any other matter of scientific knowledge can develop. Right reason in moral matters develops by gaining a greater knowledge of the ultimate end of man and man's existential nature. As a matter of fact we begin developing right reason when we are young with our parents helping us. Growing older, we learn more about the meaning of human nature and perfect happiness from our teachers, secular as well as religious, from our friends and our own personal experience. Our civil and religious authorities who promulgate their many laws are aids in this development of right reason about our moral acts. Right reason, then, about moral actions is formed not only by our own insights into the meaning of man's human nature and his ultimate end, but it is also helped by those who are well acquainted with these matters.

6. *Law and Obligation*

Just as ethics demonstrates the different aspects of the good necessary for man to live the good life, the moral life, so it is concerned with proving the origin of obligation, which is an evident fact in man's moral activity. St. Thomas' opinion is that the source or reason of this self-evident experience is not to be found within the will of man, but rather in something external to the will, namely, in the ultimate end of man. Such is a necessary conclusion of Thomistic metaphysics, where it is proven that all things must act for ends or goods to be attained by their different activities. If ethics, as a teleological science, proves that the end for which man must act is ultimate happiness, it must conclude that the end is the ultimate source of obligation, which is a conscious recognition of what man must do in view of his end, which is absolutely necessary. Or to put it in a more descriptive manner. If an orange tree were intellectually conscious of its activity, it would not only recognize that the actions which progressively lead to the production of oranges are good but it would also recognize that they must be done; the reason being that these actions lead to an end or a good that must be attained because it is of the nature of an orange tree to produce oranges. The same is true of man, not in a metaphorical sense but in a true sense. Because his will is necessitated to seek the ultimate good, man not only recognizes that actions which lead to it are good but is also obligated to perform them.

The source of obligation can also be found in a more proximate principle, the natural law, for this law, like all laws, obliges man. But natural law is meaningless in Thomistic ethics unless there be an end, a common good to which it is ordered. Just as the common good is the rational ground of the necessity of all law, so the ultimate good of man is the source of the obligating force of the natural law as well as in the ultimate end; but neither of these as the source of obligation is meaningful without the other. Let us recall why this is true.

God being a person acts for the sake of ends; hence he wills created natures proportionate to their ends. In the case of man, then, God wills that man by acting according to his nature will attain to his end. Both the end of man and his nature are determinants of the naturalness of his acts. Now because man's proper action is a reasonable action, he must know not only his end but also his nature in order that he may know why he is acting and how to act to attain the end intended. Clearly, then, man can know how to act for his end if he knows his nature which is proportionate to his end.

But more is required than man's knowledge of end and nature if God's efficacious will is to be realized. Man must be necessitated to reach his end. However, this necessity must be proportionate to or determined by man's ultimate purpose as well as by his nature, for it would argue a contradiction in God if he were to oblige man to actions which were proportionate neither to man's purpose nor to man's nature. The obligation, then, which man has of performing acts is determined both by man's last end and by his nature, because natures and ends are exactly proportionate to each other, but ultimately by man's end because natures are what they are in view of ends. Obviously, then, the greater the knowledge that one possesses either of his nature or of his ultimate end, the more determined and sure will be his obligation of performing or omitting acts.

With this conclusion we have returned to what was said about right reason being the measure of morality: the more man knows about his end and his nature, the greater his knowledge of good and bad acts. So, too, the clearer his knowledge about his end and nature, the more precise his obligations to perform or omit acts; the more exact, in other words, his knowledge of the natural law. And just as right reason can be developed, so can man's knowledge of the natural law.

Primarily the ignorance of many of the dictates of the natural law is a deficiency in man's knowledge of metaphysics. It is a fact discoverable in the history of philosophy that the condition of the human understanding is such that man's knowledge of natural truth, with regard to subjects which concern man's destiny in the most direct fashion, is badly deficient and precarious wherever the power of natural reason is not strengthened by revelation or supernatural help. Natural reason can attain to many truths concerning God and man, but this rational ability is so subject to accident that the metaphysics of God and man seem bound to quick decadence as soon as revelation is no longer there to direct the work of reason.

What holds for the best and most difficult parts of metaphysics holds also for ethics. The theory of natural law is by definition something entirely natural and entirely rational. If our reason were in a perfect state of health we should be able not only to perceive as absolutely obvious the general principles of natural law but also to establish with full clarity and certainty any particular proposition, even the most remote, deductively connected with these principles. But experience reveals a discrepancy between a *de jure* possibility and what is possible *de facto*. The circumstances of past history and of our time make it clear that the knowledge of natural law is firmest and clearest when it is associated with revelation, with grace which heals the wound of ignorance inflicted by Original Sin. It is supernatural help, then, that offers man the greatest and most necessary truths for a clearer and surer knowledge of his nature and ultimate end and of the obligations of the natural law.

Right reason, let us conclude then, is a measure of morality and it also makes the demands of the natural law known to man, but it itself has a measure; it itself is subordinated to a higher measure and a higher knowledge. This more ultimate reason is divine reason. True, we can come by natural reason to some knowledge of what divine reason measures and demands, but human reason is limited and defective in such knowledge. For a more exact and surer knowledge of divine reason, divine revelation and grace are required.

7. The Help of Virtue

Enlightened by such knowledge of the good and of obligation, man is able to make his judgments of conscience about what he should or should not do in the concrete circumstances of place and time. But does it follow that a man will do here and now what he judges he should do? One's experience shows that a man does not always "follow" his conscience. The reason for this is to be found in the judgment of choice and the will's act of choice, both of which accompany the judgment of conscience.

We have treated of these two judgments in Chapter XI on Conscience. Needless to say conscience, since it is an act of the intellect, is absolutely necessary if man is to know what individual moral acts he should perform. In a like manner the judgment of choice, which is an act of the practical intellect in which both intellect and will take part, is absolutely necessary if man is to perform these same acts. Clearly, the will does not always choose in accord with knowledge. But if the good life is to be fostered and developed in any permanent way the will must accustom itself to choose the known good. This can be accomplished by developing virtue, which means that not only the will but all the powers which are subject to the will shall be guided by right reason.

If man were actually ordained to a natural end, and if his natural powers had not suffered their several wounds by Original Sin, the cardinal virtues and all of their related natural virtues would be adequate for living the good life. But as we have seen, man is ordained to a supernatural end and the order of his powers has been disturbed, so that now he has need of supernatural help. This help of which he stands in need is not, however, a substitute for his natural powers, for these natural powers must remain if man is to remain human; but it is a help by which his rational powers of intellect and will are raised to operate on a supernatural level, so that man may know his supernatural end, God, and may will to act according to this knowledge. This help which is needed and which God bestows is the theological or infused virtues. With these virtues and their associated virtues man is completely equipped to lead the good moral life, to make his judgments of choice, and to choose in the light of the good known by right reason.

8. *Ethics as an Open Science*

Let us end where we began. We have said that ethics is different from other sciences because it is a teleological science, a science concerned with the ultimate end of man—happiness as the possession of God in knowledge and love—and with the means of acquiring such happiness. Immediately a difficulty arises about the adequacy of ethics as a philosophic moral science. The difficulty arises from the fact that man's life is lived in the order of grace and not in the state which has been called pure nature divorced from grace. Therefore, it would seem that ethics as a philosophic science is impossible, because such a science would be concerned not with man living in a supernatural order wherein man's end and the means ordained to it are above nature, but with man in a natural order in which he actually does not exist and never has existed. A science of such a kind would be completely speculative or abstract in an illusory sense and not a practical science which ethics is supposed to be.

We have attempted to offer at least a tentative answer to the difficulty by saying that ethics as a philosophic science is true but is not complete. It is true because the supernatural does not destroy the natural but builds upon it, aids it, and elevates it; hence what natural reason knows and can know about man's ultimate end and the means ordered to it is a true knowledge even though it is not a complete knowledge. Its completion is to be found in moral theology, which contains no knowledge opposed to what is found by natural reason but which augments, clarifies, and strengthens the knowledge which natural reason has acquired about man's moral actions.

This is not to identify ethics and moral theology, for the principles with which they begin and upon which they establish their conclusions are formally different. Even though moral theology gives us revealed truths about man's end and the means which are necessary for the attaining of this end, it does not eliminate the need that the human intellect has for the truths demonstrated in ethics. Unless moral theology presupposes the natural knowledge of philosophy it is unintelligible. And by the same token the importance and self-sufficiency of ethics should not be overemphasized, for unless we allow ethics to remain open to the truths of theology we will not have a complete science.

BIBLIOGRAPHY

Adler, M., A *Dialectic of Morals*. Notre Dame, Indiana: *The Review of Politics*, 1941.
—— "A Question about Law," in *Essays in Thomism*, ed. R. E. Brennan. New York: Sheed and Ward, 1942, pp. 205-236.
Aristotle, *Nicomachean Ethics*, trans. by W. D. Ross, in *The Basic Works of Aristotle*, ed. McKeon. New York: Random House, 1941; pp. 935-1112.
—— *The Works of Aristotle Translated into English*, edited by W. D. Ross, 12 vols. Oxford: Clarendon Press, 1921-1952.
Blackstone, William, *Commentaries on the Laws of England*, 4 volumes. New York: Banks and Brothers, 1884.
Bourke, Vernon J., *Ethics*. New York: Macmillan, 1951.
—— "Habitus in the Thomistic Metaphysics of Potency and Act," in *Essays in Thomism*, ed. Brennan, pp. 101-109.
—— *St. Thomas and the Greek Moralists*, Aquinas Lecture. Milwaukee: Marquette University Press, 1947.
Brennan, Robert E. (editor), *Essays in Thomism*. New York: Sheed and Ward, 1942.
Brennan, Sr. Rose Emmanuella, *The Intellectual Virtues According to the Philosophy of St. Thomas*. Washington: Catholic University Dissertation, 1941.
Brosnahan, T. J., *Prolegomena to Ethics*. New York: Fordham University Press, 1941.
Butler, J., "A Dissertation upon the Nature of Virtue," in *Ethical Theories*, ed. Melden. Englewood Cliffs: Prentice-Hall, 1953; pp. 241-246.
Corwin, Edw. S., "The Natural Law and Constitutional Law," *University of Notre Dame Natural Law Institute Proceedings*, 1950, pp. 47-84.

Cronin, Michael, *The Science of Ethics*, rev. ed. Dublin: Gill and Son, 1939, 2 vols.

D'Arcy, M., *Christian Morality*. New York: Longmans, 1937.

Davitt, T., *The Nature of Law*. St. Louis: Herder, 1951.

Deploige, S., *The Conflict Between Ethics and Sociology*, trans. by C. C. Miltner. St. Louis and London: Herder, 1938.

Doheny, Wm., C.S.C., "The Eternal Law Background of Natural Law," *University of Notre Dame Natural Law Institute Proceedings*, 1947, pp. 104-142.

Doolan, Aegidius, *Order and Law*. Westminster: The Newman Press, 1954.

Farrell, W., *A Companion to the Summa*. New York: Sheed and Ward, 1939-1942, 4 vols.

Ford, John C., S.J., "The Fundamentals of Holmes' Juristic Philosophy," *Fordham Law Review*, Nov. 1942, pp. 2-28.

Gilson, E., *Moral Values and the Moral Life*, translated by Leo Ward. St. Louis: Herder, 1931.

——— *The Philosophy of St. Thomas Aquinas*. St. Louis: Herder, 1929.

——— *The Spirit of Mediaeval Philosophy*. New York: Scribners, 1936.

Hart, Chas., "The Natural Law and International Relations," *Proceedings of the American Catholic Philosophical Association*, XXIV (1950). Papers by various authors.

Higgins, Thomas, *Man as Man*. Milwaukee: Bruce, 1949.

Hill, Owen, *Ethics, General and Special*. New York: Macmillan, 1920.

Howe, Mark, "The Positivism of Mr. Justice Holmes," *Harvard Law Review*, 64 (Feb. 1951), pp. 529-546.

Humphrey, G., *Conscience and Law*. Oxford: Clarendon, 1949.

James, William, *Psychology*. New York: Holt, 1905, c. 10.

Kendzierski, Lottie H., "Object and Intention in the Moral Act," *Proceedings of the American Catholic Philosophical Association*, XXIV (1950), 102-110.

——— "Wisdom, Synderesis, and Practical Principles," *Proceedings of the American Catholic Philosophical Association*, XXVI (1952), pp. 168-179.

Klubertanz, George, "Ethics and Theology," *The Modern Schoolman*, XXVII (1949), 29-39.

——— *The Philosophy of Human Nature*. New York: Appleton, Century, Crofts, 1953.

——— "The Unity of Human Activity," *The Modern Schoolman*, XXVII (1950), pp. 15-85.

LeBuffe, F. P. and Hayes, J. V., *The American Philosophy of Law*. New York: Jesuit Educational Association, 1953.

Lehu, L., "À propos de la régle de la moralité," *Revue des sciences philosophiques et théologiques*, XVII (1929), pp. 449-466.

——— "À quel point précis de la Somme Théologique commence le trait de la moralité," *Revue Thomiste*, XXXIII (1928), pp. 521-532.

——— "La Raison, Règle de la Moralité d'après Saint Thomas," *Revue Thomiste*, XXXII (1927), pp. 437-482.

——— "La recta ratio de s. Thomas signifie-t-elle la conscience?" *Revue Thomiste*, n.s., VIII (1925), pp. 159-166.

Leibell, J. F., *Readings in Ethics*. Chicago: Loyola University Press, 1926.

Lottin, Odon, *Le Droit Naturel chez Saint Thomas d'Aquin et ses predecesseurs*. Bruges: Beyaert, 1931.

——— "La loi en géneral. La definition thomiste et se antecedents," *Psychologie et Morale aux XIIe et XIIIe siècles*, 3 vols. Louvain-Gembloux: Duculot, 1942-1949, vol. 2, pp. 11-47.

——— *Principes de morale*. Louvain: Éditions de l'Abbaye du Mont-César, 1947, 2 vols.

McDougall, William, *Body and Mind*, 5th ed. London: Methuen, 1920.

McKeon, R., *Basic Works of Aristotle*. New York: Random House, 1941.

McKinnon, Harold J., *The Higher Law*. Berkeley: Gullick, 1946.

——— "Natural Law and Positive Law," *University of Notre Dame Natural Law Institute Proceedings*, 1947, pp. 85-103.

Manion, C., "The Natural Law Philosophy of the Founding Fathers," *University of Notre Dame Natural Law Institute Proceedings*, 1947, pp. 30-65.

Maritain, J., *Existence and the Existent*. New York: Pantheon, 1948.

——— *Freedom in the Modern World*. New York: Scribner's, 1936.

——— *Man and the State*. Chicago: University of Chicago Press, 1951.

——— "Natural Law and Moral Law," *Moral Principles of Action*, ed. Ruth Nanda Anshen. 1956, pp. 62-76.

——— "On the Philosophy of Human Rights," *Human Rights*, A symposium, ed. UNESCO. London: Wingate, 1955, pp. 72-77.

——— *The Person and the Common Good*. New York: Scribner's, 1947.

——— *The Rights of Man and the Natural Law*. New York: Scribner's, 1943.

——— *Science and Wisdom*. New York: Scribner's, 1940.

——— *St. Thomas and the Problem of Evil*, Aquinas Lecture. Milwaukee: Marquette University Press, 1942.

Meehan, Francis X., "Absolute and Relative in the Moral Order, *Pro-*

ceedings of the American Catholic Philosophical Association, XXII (1947), pp. 53-79.

Melden, A., Ethical Theories. Englewood Cliffs, N.J.: Prentice-Hall, 1955.

Messner, J., Social Ethics. St. Louis: Herder, 1949.

Miltner, Charles, The Elements of Ethics. New York: Macmillan, 1925.

Moore, Thomas Verner, The Driving Forces of Human Nature and Their Adjustment. New York: Grune, 1948.

———— Principles of Ethics. New York: Lippincott, 1935.

Morgan, Clifford T., and Stellar, Eliot, Physiological Psychology. New York: McGraw, 1950.

Mullahy, B. I., "Practical Knowledge and Relativity," Proceedings of the American Catholic Philosophical Association, XXII (1947), pp. 151-166.

Murray, John C., "Freedom of Religion," Theological Studies, VI (Jan. 1945), pp. 229-286.

Murray, T. B., "Reason and Morality according to St. Thomas," The Month, CLI (1928), pp. 417-423.

Newman, John Henry, Grammar of Assent. New York: Doubleday, 1955.

Noonan, John, General and Special Ethics. Chicago: Loyola University Press, 1947.

Noble, H. D., Les Passions dans la vie morale. Paris: Lethielleux, 1932.

O'Brien, Sr. M. Consilia, "Recta Ratio in Relation to Moral Truth," Proceedings of the American Catholic Philosophical Association, XVII (1942), pp. 120-126.

O'Connor, W. R., The Eternal Quest. New York: Longmans Green, 1947.

———— The Natural Desire for God. Milwaukee: Marquette University Press, 1948.

———— "The Natural Desire for God in St. Thomas," New Scholasticism, XIV (1940), pp. 213-265.

Oesterle, John A., Ethics. Englewood Cliffs, N.J.: Prentice-Hall, 1957.

O'Neil, C. J., "Practical Knowledge and Liberty," Proceedings of the American Catholic Philosophical Association, XXIX (1955), pp. 1-13.

———— "Prudence, the Incommunicable Wisdom," Essays in Thomism, ed. R. E. Brennan, New York: Sheed and Ward, 1942.

O'Rahilly, Alfred, "The Law of Nations," Readings in Ethics, ed. J. F. Leibell. Chicago: Loyola University Press, 1926, pp. 1016-1032.

O'Sullivan, Richard, "The Natural Law and Common Law," University of Notre Dame Natural Law Institute Proceedings, 1950, pp. 9-46.

Palmer, Ben. W., "The Natural Law and Pragmatism," *University of Notre Dame Natural Law Institute Proceedings*, 1947, pp. 30-65.

Paton, H. J., *The Moral Law*. London: Hutchinson House, 1948.

Pegis, A. C., *Basic Writings of St. Thomas Aquinas*, 2 vols. New York: Random House, 1945.

—— "Matter, Beatitude and Liberty," *Maritain Volume of the Thomist*. New York: Sheed and Ward, 1943, pp. 265-280.

—— "Nature and Spirit: Some Reflections on the Problem of the End of Man," *Proceedings of the American Catholic Philosophical Association*, XXIII (1949), pp. 62-79.

—— "Necessity and Liberty," *New Scholasticism*, XV (1941), pp. 18-45.

Phelan, G. B., "Person and Liberty," *New Scholasticism*, XV (1941), pp. 53-68.

—— "Theology in the Curriculum of Catholic Colleges and Universities," *Man and Secularism*. New York: National Catholic Alumni Association, 1940, pp. 128-140.

Pieper, Josef, "On the Christian Idea of Man," *The Review of Politics*, XI, 1, (1949), pp. 3-16.

Plato, *The Dialogues of Plato*, translated by B. Jowett, 5 vols. Oxford: Oxford University Press, 1892.

Ramirez J.-M., "De philosophia morali Christiana," *Divus Thomas*, vol. 14 (1936), pp. 87-112; 181-204.

Renard, H., *The Philosophy of Man*. Milwaukee: Bruce, 1948.

—— *The Philosophy of Morality*. Milwaukee: Bruce, 1953.

Rickaby, Joseph, *Aquinas Ethicus*. London: Burns, Oates, 1892.

—— *Moral Philosophy*. Stonyhurst Series, London: Longmans Green, 1910.

Rommen, H., *The Natural Law*. St. Louis: Herder, 1946.

—— *The State in Catholic Thought*. St. Louis: Herder, 1945.

Ryan, John A., and Boland, Francis J., *Catholic Principles of Politics*. New York: Macmillan, 1936, c. 14.

Salmon, E., *The Good in Existential Metaphysics*. Milwaukee: Marquette University Press, 1953.

Sertillanges, A. D., *La philosophie morale de saint Thomas d'Aquin*, nouvelle edition. Paris: Aubier, 1946.

Sidgwick, H., *History of Ethics*. London: Macmillan, 1931.

—— *The Methods of Ethics*. London: Macmillan, 1901.

—— *Outlines of the History of Ethics for English Readers*. London: Macmillan, 1886.

Simon, Yves, *The Nature and Functions of Authority*. Milwaukee: Marquette University Press, 1940.

Smith, G., "Intelligence and Liberty," *New Scholasticism*, XV (1941), 1-17.

―――― "The Natural End of Man," *Proceedings of the American Catholic Philosophical Association*, XXIII (1949), 47-61.

―――― *The Truth that Frees*. Milwaukee: Marquette University Press, 1956.

Suarez, Francisco, *De Legibus ac de Deo Legislatore (On Laws and God the Lawgiver)*, Paris: Vives, 1872. Translation of the important sections in J. B. Scott, *The Classics of International Law*. Oxford: Clarendon Press, 1944.

Sullivan, Joseph F., *General Ethics*. Worcester: Holy Cross College Press, 1931.

Thomae Aquinatis, S., *Opera Omnia jussu impensaque Leonis XIII, P.M., edita*. Rome: Typis R. Garroni, 1882-1948, 16 vols.

―――― *Opera Omnia*. Parma: 1852-1873; reprinted New York, Musurgia, 1949-1950, 25 vols.

―――― *In X Libros Ethicorum Aristotelis ad Nicomachum*, ed. A. Pirotta. Turin: Marietta, 1934.

―――― *Basic Writings*, ed. A. C. Pegis. New York: Random House, 1945, 2 vols.

―――― *The Summa Theologica*, trans. by the Fathers of the English Dominican Province, 2d rev. ed. London: Burns, Oates, 1912-1936, 22 vols.—American Edition. New York: Benziger Brothers, 1947.

―――― *Summa Contra Gentiles*, trans. as: *On the Truth of the Catholic Faith*, by A. C. Pegis, J. F. Anderson, V. Bourke, C. J. O'Neil. Garden City: Hanover House, 1955-1957.

―――― *The Trinity*, translated Sr. Rose Emmanuella Brennan. St. Louis: Herder, 1946.

Tsanoff, R., *Ethics*. New York: Harper, 1947.

Vitoria, Francisco, *De Jure et Naturali (The Law of Nations)* translated by J. B. Scott, *The Spanish Origin of International Law; Francisco de Vitoria and His Law of Nations*. Oxford: Clarendon Press, 1934.

Wild, John, *Introduction to a Realistic Philosophy*. New York: Harper, 1948.

Woodworth, Robert S., *Experimental Psychology*. New York: Holt, 1938.

INDEX